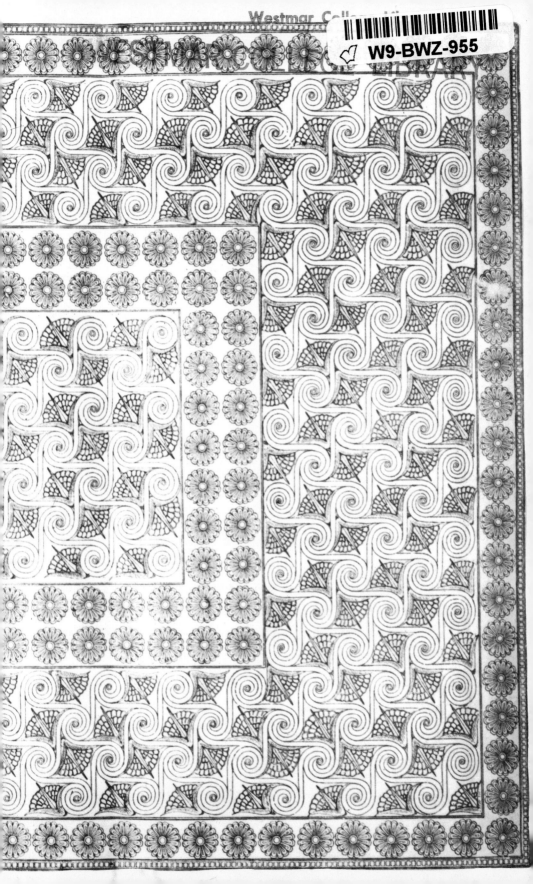

MEMOIRS
OF HEINRICH
SCHLIEMANN

Other books by Leo Deuel

THE TREASURES OF TIME

TESTAMENTS OF TIME

CONQUISTADORS WITHOUT SWORDS

FLIGHTS INTO YESTERDAY

MEMOIRS
OF HEINRICH
SCHLIEMANN

A Documentary Portrait Drawn

from His Autobiographical Writings,

Letters, and Excavation Reports

by LEO DEUEL

HARPER & ROW, PUBLISHERS

New York, Hagerstown, San Francisco, London

Grateful acknowledgment is made for permission to reprint the following:

Excerpts from *By Nile and Tigris*, by E. A. Wallis Budge. Reprinted by permission of John Murray (Publishers) Ltd.

Lines from "In Memory of Sigmund Freud" from *Selected Poetry of W. H. Auden* by W. H. Auden. Copyright 1940, renewed 1968, by W. H. Auden. Reprinted by permission of Random House, Inc.

Excerpt from "The Most Unforgettable Character I've Met" by Andromache Schliemann Mélas, *The Reader's Digest*, June 1950. Copyright 1950 by The Reader's Digest Assn., Inc. Reprinted by permission.

Excerpts from *Reminiscences* by A. H. Sayce. Reprinted by permission of Macmillan, London and Basingstoke.

Excerpts from *Schliemann's First Visit to America, 1850–1851*, edited by Shirley H. Weber. Reprinted by permission of the American School of Classical Studies of Athens.

Excerpt from *Schliemann: The Story of a Goldseeker*, by Emil Ludwig, translated by D. F. Tate. Published by Little, Brown & Company.

Excerpts from *Schliemann in Indianapolis*, edited by Eli Lily. Reprinted by permission of the Indiana Historical Society.

FIRST EDITION

Designed by Dorothy Schmiderer

Page layout: Janice Stern

Picture research: Leo Deuel, Olivia Buehl

Copy photography (partial): Jim Kalett

Library of Congress Cataloging in Publication Data
Deuel, Leo.
    Memoirs of Heinrich Schliemann.
    Bibliography: p.
    Includes index.
    1. Schliemann, Heinrich, 1822–1890. I. Schliemann,
Heinrich, 1822–1890. II. Title.
DF212.S4D48   1976   930'.1'0924 [B]   74–15820
ISBN 0–06–011106–2

77 78 79 80 10 9 8 7 6 5 4 3 2 1

CONTENTS

"Talent means energy and perseverance and nothing more."[1]

"I was always in good spirits and my biggest fault, being a braggart and bluffer yielded me . . . countless advantages."[2]

"I flatter myself that I have discovered a new world for archaeology."[3]

—Heinrich Schliemann

MEMOIRS
OF HEINRICH
SCHLIEMANN

INTRODUCTION

THE LIFE OF HEINRICH SCHLIEMANN (1822–1890) is a nineteenth century adventure and success story in two worlds. His fame and claim to our attention lie in the antiquarian explorations that, somewhat inauspiciously, he took up in middle age, but his career as a young man of commerce was no less colorful. In fact, his achievements in both worlds are easily matched by the drama of his life. No one was more aware of that than Schliemann himself—so much so that in later years he self-consciously saw all phases of his life in one piece: his naïve childhood fantasies of buried treasures and mysterious ruins inevitably put him, no matter how tortuous the detours, on the road to Troy and Mycenae. It all began in an idyllic backwater North German parsonage. Everything fell snugly into place. His misfortunes as well as his stunning rise in international commerce became necessary milestones toward the triumphant discoveries that made him a giant in the recovery of prehistoric Mediterranean civilizations. According to that gospel, he assumed in his early years the greedy guise of a trader only in order to realize the great self-denying ideal of his later life.

Most of Schliemann's biographers, and there is an ever-growing rash of them (in addition to as many novelists), have tended to adopt that retouched self-image as a guideline. It is the standard version in outlines of archaeology.[1]* Invariably we are told by narrator after narrator how as a youth Schliemann decided to become a businessman and accumulate a fortune for no other reason than to devote himself to the excavation of ancient Troy, in whose existence he believed with an unshakable faith. To resurrect the Homeric world of the *Iliad* and *Odyssey* was the ultimate goal, which, during his weary years as office clerk and later as rising commodity merchant and millionaire magnate, was never far from his mind. Money-making, basically distasteful to the high-minded idealist, was just part of a shrewdly laid plan. This pious tale has by now become so enshrined in the annals of archaeology

* Notes and References begin on p. 363.

1

that it is reverently invoked not just by popularizers but by latter-day archaeologists who have come to look up to Schliemann as one of the masters—
and patron saints—of their discipline.

On a somewhat different and more critical plane, Schliemann is also
viewed as a treasure seeker at heart. This is the underlying thesis adopted
in the excellent pioneering biography by Emil Ludwig, which used for the
first time original materials from the Schliemann papers deposited in Athens.[2]
Such a thesis admittedly, gains considerable weight from many of Schliemann's
own actions and utterances.[3] But the common denominator gold has haunted
Schliemann biographers for years, both those who have attempted to show
that Schliemann the merchant prince and Schliemann the excavator were
motivated solely by the search for gold, and those who have attempted to
deny a "materialistic" interpretation.

Here then are the two basic and ineradicable preconceptions about the
man—the preordained single-minded awakener of the Homeric past and the
treasure seeker. Both give a simplistic and distorted view of the stormy life of
a very complex, if not paradoxical, man—a slave of Mammon and a vision-
ary—whose motivations as well as aspirations were almost always confused
and usually at cross-purposes.

It is time that Schliemann spoke for himself. In addition to the works
he published, Schliemann was an obsessive correspondent and diarist.[4] Thus,
it has been my intention, without any preconceptions, to assemble his own
accounts of himself and his career—several of them previously not available
in English or otherwise difficult of access—and thereby chart the principal
way stations of his life as he himself saw them.

During his lifetime Schliemann published some eleven books, the first
two on travel and the rest dealing with his archaeological campaigns. These
volumes, rarely read nowadays, are generally considered badly dated and
valuable only for their descriptions and copious illustrations of artifacts. However, they are, at least in part, entertainingly written, and testify to their
author's literary flair as well as to his irrepressible urge to talk about himself,
his adventures, his struggles, his disappointments, and his moments of elation.
Selections from these volumes, supplemented by excerpts from his journals
and correspondence, have been gathered together to form Schliemann's
"memoirs," not, to be sure, as he might have composed them had he completed the autobiographical essay introducing the comprehensive *Ilios: The
city and country of the Trojans* (1880). Yet taken all together they form a
revealing, zestful, and multilayered portrait of considerable spontaneity and
range. Naturally I have had to choose, but in the selections, and in my
biographical commentaries, I have tried to cover as much of Schliemann's life

as possible, along with the highlights of his two careers and the many facets of his remarkable personality.

Schliemann was a true representative of his century, and his rags-to-riches tale matches any Victorian romance with its Dickensian touches of impoverished youth, a tenacious climb through hard work in the business world, travel around the globe, growing fame and success, marital tragedy, and eventual bliss in the arms of a remarkable Greek beauty, thirty years his junior, who shared his love for Homer and Hellenic antiquity.

Not only is Schliemann a prime example of those great nineteenth century dilettantes who helped revolutionize scholarship—without necessarily being scholars themselves—he covers the gamut of bourgeois attitudes: capitalist enterprise, speculative schemes, building fever, intoxication with technology (he was fascinated by railroads and bridges and steamboats, not to speak of the telegraph), self-advertisement and self-promotion, moral latitude for the sake of success, and supreme confidence in his own abilities. The world was his oyster. The pride in his own accomplishments he once summed up well, with his customary overtones of boastful smugness and exaggeration, in a letter to his son Sergei written in June 1870:

> . . . In every situation of my life I always proved how much a person can accomplish with iron energy. I performed miracles during my four-year stay in Amsterdam from 1842 to 1846. I did what nobody else has ever done and ever could do. When I became a merchant in St. Petersburg, I was the most able and prudent businessman of the entire exchange. Later as a traveler, I was a traveler *par excellence*. Never has any St. Petersburg merchant been able to write a scientific book. But I wrote one that has been translated into four languages and which has been the object of universal admiration. At present I am putting all Europe and all America into ecstasy over my discovery of the ancient city of Troy, the Troy which archaeologists from all countries have searched for in vain for 2,000 years. . . .[5]

He furiously traveled across oceans and continents as often as any tycoon or ambassador-at-large of the jet age. In his "first life" quite naturally he was attracted by the enormous commercial potential of both the vast Russian colossus and the expanding frontiers of the United States. But it was America, in the end, that claimed greater loyalty. In many ways Schliemann *was* the new *Homo americanus*, courtesy of Horatio Alger, who rose from dismal poverty, and made several fortunes (none of which he lost), yet cultivated sobriety, parsimony, clean living, long working hours, self-discipline, determination, and fellowship. Not a gentleman in the British sense, he was an avanceur who played his own game—softhearted and ruthless, loyal almost to excess and tricky to the verge of delinquency, enamored with culture, but essentially lacking in taste. His sensitivity to art, be it "modern" or ancient, was minimal. The Homeric poems, which never ceased to enrapture him, he appreciated not so much as exquisite poetry but as incomparable tales of moral grandeur. When he lamented the materialism of other merchant-adventurers in California and elsewhere, he meant it, but his outrage smacked of the sanctimoniousness of Puritanic robber barons.

Throughout most of his mature life, Schliemann considered himself a citizen of the United States and broadcast his *civis Americanus sum* to the world long before he ever assumed legal title to it. American to a fault, he could also be a cosmopolite, and until his later years when he made peace with his native Germany, he was on the whole free of national preferences and chauvinist prejudices. However, his bigotries toward non-European races were staggering ("The laziness of Negroes is beyond description." "The physiognomy of the Californian Indian is the most stupid and ugly I have seen in my life"),[6] though not without occasional changes of mind.

A tormented youth, with a father whom he seems to have both despised and adored, a catastrophic marriage to a frigid, predatory woman, he yet kept, wherever he was, the closest ties to his family, his brothers, half-brothers, sisters, and aged father, and, though often grudgingly and tyrannically, he supported, advised, and admonished them with the Napoleonic zeal of a Corsican clan chief. Once, when transmitting a liberal donation to his father, he attached the following note:

> By today's mail I have forwarded instructions for 500 Prussian thalers to be credited to your account, which sum I expect you to use in establishing yourself . . . in a manner befitting the father of Heinrich Schliemann [this was in 1855, before the son became famous as an archaeologist]. In placing this sum at your disposal I must, however, stipulate that in future you keep a respectable manservant and a respectable maid, and above all preserve a decent standard of cleanliness in your house, that your plates, dishes, cups, knives, and forks always shine with cleanliness, that you have all boards and floors scrubbed three times a week and have at your table food that befits your station in life.[7]

Victorian in his outlook, cant, bias, and virtues, he believed strongly in the value of education and man's (particularly Western man's) perfectibility and had the greatest respect for learning. That impulse was undoubtedly stronger in the parson's son than in many of his contemporary capitalistic peers and was a wellspring of his second career. To Sergei he wrote in 1868: "When I was younger than you someone wrote into my scrapbook [in Latin]: 'Take joy in learning. There is nothing more beautiful than to study a great deal./ Knowledge rewards the learner with wealth and respect.' I have adopted this as the maxim of my life, and everything I accomplished I owe to that wise doctrine."[8]

Though Schliemann made a splash in two widely different fields, there was never the clean break that has become part of the legend. The man's character and idiosyncrasies certainly remained the same. His passions may have shifted (though the one for languages remained), but not the frenzied single-minded pursuit of his goals. In either career, what largely compelled him was recognition, fame, and success. Then and now, it was not just gold as an end in itself, though the shining metal fittingly reflected his achievement. Even when he traveled backward in time, he continued restlessly to travel through space.

During his archaeological phase he never ceased to look after his investments, and he remained active in real estate and securities transactions. Until his last days he busied himself with building schemes in Athens. His excavating, at least in the beginning, was haphazard and reckless—reminiscent of speculations that rested on shrewd intuitions like trading in commodities. The organization of his campaigns and the hiring and exploitation of labor were those of a rigid, reactionary captain of industry. He kept detailed records of his operations, including expenses, like business ledgers. He was combative, self-righteous, and arrogant when dealing with opponents and bureaucrats, though he occasionally manifested a surprising humility toward recognized academic authorities and stood in awe of royalty and Bismarckian strongmen. In short, there remained with him the syndrome of the cocky self-assurance of a successful parvenu and dilettante, who, vainglorious and haughty, is often stricken by feelings of insecurity and inadequacy.

Schliemann took from others liberally but in essentials claimed credit for himself. In the end, it was always *he* who had discovered the site of Troy, the *megara* (longhouses) of the second city, or the relief ceiling of Orchomenos. In order to magnify his accomplishments, he would play down the contributions of others and enlarge on what he considered their errors. The decisive role of Frank Calvert, who had not only dug at Hissarlik-Troy but owned half the tell, in leading Schliemann to the site in the first place was never clearly acknowledged. Even his wife Sophia's active part in excavation and discovery he tended to sweep aside or leave entirely unmentioned. Though patting his "excellent architect" on the back, to the world he would announce with fanfare *his* latest discovery at Tiryns. One can watch him following a typical pattern with reference to Knossos, which prior to him had been partly excavated and identified by a local antiquarian. After two brief visits and no digging at the site, he was already dropping hints that he had discovered Minos' palace, and began to build up his case by summoning only those "authorities" who had expressed the opinion that the island had no rewards to offer to the archaeologist's spade.

Like any executive worth his shot, Schliemann knew how to enlist competent helpers, often finer minds and better scholars than himself, who did his bidding. Rudolf Virchow, one of the age's outstanding scientists, catered to his every whim. Schliemann remunerated several renowned professors for helping him with his publications, while telling them bluntly that their assistance would not be publicly acknowledged. From his dealings with his publisher Brockhaus it becomes clear that he took an active part in promoting his books, paying for reviews, and, with a mixture of flattery and threats, putting pressure on the press. Though he bitterly complained about any adverse criticism, he had his allies and partisans everywhere—in time a kind of claque—who, be it as a pledge of friendship or for more worldly compensation, were called upon to come to his defense and blow his horn. Some just had to lend their names; he would provide the copy to be released to the newspapers.

His relations with even his closest friends and associates remained stormy. At one time or another he fell out with all of them. Touchy to the verge of paranoia, he took offense on the slightest provocation. The mildest criticism of his books and excavation results incensed him. Any disagreement he would take as a personal affront.

As an amateur and outsider with some highly unorthodox, not to say spurious, views on antiquity and Homeric scholarship, Schliemann was naturally not immune to attacks from the academic establishment. But instead of taking it in stride, he turned it into martyrdom. Each and every one was credited with base jealousy. The venerable British classicist R. C. Jebb was supposed to be green with envy because Schliemann had not given his collection to England, and out of resentment turned into a "vicious slanderer." When Schliemann was refused permission to excavate Olympia, mainly because he posed conditions that violated the Greek constitution, he asserted that "the envy of the Greek savants for me has no limits so that they would be willing to crucify, burn, and stab me."[9] Professor Alexander Conze, whose help and recognition he craved, was accused of "poisonous jealousy" when he dared to suggest that Schliemann's proof for the identity of Troy was inconclusive. As to the German philologists, members as they were of a school that refused to accept a strictly literal and historical interpretation of Homer, they stooped to "beastly spite." However, when considering the wide acclaim he encountered quite early from luminaries in England, and increasingly so in Germany from academicians, museum directors, learned societies, and royalty, one comes to suspect that the hostility Schliemann met and never tired of wailing about was exaggerated.

In a way it suited the heroic, crusading role he cast himself in as an isolated, embattled, and derided genius who had solved "the greatest riddle in history."

Of course, Schliemann had to face up to a great deal of real animosity from some quarters. But scholars who were apprehensive of his apodictic claims, being themselves used to low-keyed, analytical, and sober discourse, cannot really be blamed for questioning his soundness. Neither should one be surprised that their view of the man and his creditability was likely to be jaundiced by his self-serving publicity. (That both the Greek and the Turkish governments had good reason to distrust him we shall soon learn.) This is not to say that members of academia could not be wrong or that, indeed, their reasoned judgment might not have turned out to be at least as farfetched as Schliemann's intuitive—and wishful—grasp. Thus, a few professors of the great Continental universities ventured to identify prehistoric Trojan remains as Gothic or Celtic or even Greek. The great German classicist, philologist, and archaeologist Ernst Curtius at one time thought that the Mycenaean treasures were Byzantine. "Agamemnon's mask," he proposed, was an image of Christ.

Despite Schliemann's endless feuds and the alleged slights from the learned profession, he had no reason to complain about lack of fame. After the discovery of "Priam's Treasure" he found himself an instant celebrity. All of a sudden Troy and its ingenious discoverer were a conversation topic in all the civilized centers of the world. The millionaire-amateur, his adventurous life, and his young Greek wife caught the fancy of journalists. A contemporary German museum director reported (1876) that at the time Schliemann's reports on Troy appeared in the *Augsburger Allgemeine Zeitung* "scholars as well as the public at large were filled with such great excitement that sooner or later there had to be a cooling down. All over, in houses and on the streets, in mail coaches and on railroads, Troy was being discussed."[10] When Schliemann opened the gold-laden tombs of Mycenaean princes, containing precious articles of unique artistic style and enormous material wealth, the rapture rose to a fever pitch.

It is with Schliemann, above all, that archaeology became a popular science. Little wonder that in some ways Schliemann, who wanted to achieve immortality by having his name forever linked with Homer, came to personify to some archaeology itself. In two short decades, from 1870 to 1890, the names of Troy, Mycenae, Orchomenos, Tiryns—one after the other—lit up like torches against a dark winter sky. Bulletins from the ancient citadels captured the imagination in the manner of broadcasts of transatlantic monoplane crossings and ventures into space at a later date. From news of the day, the sensational scoops filtered into the consciousness of the age and became a cultural phenomenon. Hence, an American literary critic, Hugh Kenner, in a recent study on Ezra Pound (1971), could credit Schliemann with a seminal influence on the whole spectrum of modern thought. Implausible as it may seem, Schliemann must be counted as a European intellectual event. What W. H. Auden once wrote of Sigmund Freud may well apply to the former grocery assistant of Mecklenburg: "To us he is no more a person/ Now but a whole climate of opinion."

Anything but a modest man, Schliemann knew his worth and was a firm believer in his lucky star. Convinced that Lady Luck watched over him, he never quite ceased to wonder about his good fortune. "I have had more luck than foresight in my life," he told a friend in 1856. "From some of my most stupid mistakes resulted my greatest successes."[11] Throughout his commercial career, he always appeared to be in the right place at exactly the right time, his wealth increased rather than diminished with war and recession. As far as prehistoric Aegean studies went, he also appeared at just the crucial moment. By dint of sheer luck he found the great Trojan treasure, gaining for his Homeric quest attention and respectability, apart from buoying his own spirits. When excavating the Mycenaean graves, he confessed, "I owed my luck alone to the fact that my reading of the passage in Pausanias regarding the site of the five heroic tombs was entirely at variance with any interpretation ever given by scholars."[12] What did it matter that the Mycenaean bonanza was indebted to an arbitrary and probably wrong reading of the Pausanias text? But perhaps Schliemann's outstanding piece of luck was that at every point of both his business life and his archaeological activities he found selfless friends and knowledgeable helpers who were willing to lend their services to the glory of Heinrich Schliemann.

For the longest time of his charmed life, Schliemann was least lucky with women. Unlike his philandering father, who begot a child in old age, he was hardly a favorite with the ladies, or particularly at ease with them. His sparse physical frame, shrill high-pitched voice, stinginess, petulance, and egomania did not mark even the young man for easy conquests. Besides, he was too disciplined and jealous of his time and energy to lose himself in frivolous pursuits. He explained his lack of success with women in another way. "I myself am blind," he wrote a sister. "Passion clouds my vision. I see only the virtues and never the failings of the fair sex."[13] Yet once again luck struck him, and under the most unlikely circumstances. It appeared to him in middle age in the shape of a ravishing Greek mail-order bride, little more than a schoolgirl, who undoubtedly gave the lonely man the greatest human happiness of his life.

It is an extraordinarily lucky, strong-willed, self-centered, ambitious, fiercely independent, intolerant, and yet sentimental and tender man who emerges from the pages of his own writings. He was both a ruthless realist and a gushy romanticist, a man full of curiosity, dogmatism, doubt, and naïveté. All of these qualities are reflected in Schliemann's prose, but for all its ebullience, it suffers from serious limitations. It mirrors the man, who was addicted to hyperbole, braggadocio, clichés—and glib generalizations. His notes and letters are saturated with repetitious "formulaic phrases" in the manner of Homer and the bards, though lacking their sublimeness. Unless he voices sarcasms over his opponents' "heresies," his writing is sadly devoid of gentle irony, reflective pauses, or suggestive silences of a more subtle mind. Everything had to be explicit, either black or white. As an author he ranks below contemporary explorer-archaeologists like Austen Henry Layard of Nimrud-Nineveh fame, John Lloyd Stephens, the Yankee Mayaist, or Richard Burton.[14]

Schliemann was, however, primarily a man of action, not a man of letters and a thinker. A point could be made that Schliemann, the compulsive Homer enthusiast, early in his youth identified with Odysseus, another man of action. His whole life became a peripatetic quest and long-frustrated home-coming. He lived, experienced, wrote, rewrote, and dramatized it as his modern *Odyssey*. Wily and restless, Odysseus was to be his shipmate and alter ego. Yet, it may also be argued, with his sickly physique and far from attractive character, he was hardly cast in the mold of his Homeric paragons. As Matthew Arnold was quick to observe: "Homer was eminently rapid, eminently plain and direct, and eminently noble, and Schliemann was the contrary of all these—a slow, cautious, complex, devious man, often pompous and ill-tempered, with no natural nobility in him."[15]

Nevertheless, Schliemann's long-lasting fixation on Homer is a basic theme of his life. To him the ancient bard and his epics were indisputably and historically true. Since he started out with a total, quasi-religious faith in Homer, Schliemann never really questioned the factual truth of the poems, nor did he come to grips with the tangled arguments tied up with the so-called Homeric Question. Indeed, during his first years at Troy, Schliemann was hopelessly confused about the relation in time between Homer and the Trojan War and tended to place them both in the "Homeric Age" (c. twelfth century B.C.) until he came to realize that Homer could not possibly have been an eyewitness to the war, having lived at least three hundred years later. Chances are that by the time Schliemann became fully aware of the succinct problems raised by classicists and philologists as to the epics' origin, Greek dialect, authorship, time and place of composition, veracity of the incidents described, and so on, his mind was already closed to "destructive criticism," even though he would on occasion make grudging concessions to the "critics," without, however, yielding his fundamental position.

It is well known that nineteenth century scholars (who had precursors going back to antiquity) seriously doubted that there ever was such a person as Homer who wrote both the *Iliad* and the *Odyssey*. If indeed he existed, he may have been a bard—or rather one in a succession of bards—who not so much created but re-created, collected, selected, and edited the lays passed on to him from his predecessors. However, even then he was unlikely to have had a hand in both poems, since the *Odyssey*, at least in its present form, was more recent (Both poems were first written down under orders of the Athenian tyrant Pisistratus in the sixth century B.C.).

Nineteenth century scholars also had disparate views on the Trojan War and its protagonists. Those in the extreme position held that they were part of the Indo-European mythological heritage, at one with the *Mahabharata* of India or the Teutonic *Nibelungenlied*. Even if they contained a remote nucleus of facts, which by no means was ruled out, the Homeric epics were, above all, a work of exalted folk poetry, alien to the spirit of history and pretty worthless as testimony for actual events. With regard to the main setting of the famous war, the Troy or Ilion of King Priam, few people denied outright that there had been such a site—after all no one in his right mind argued against the existence of Mycenae or Tiryns or Pylos either—though its connections with the Trojan War were considered in doubt. In actuality, men who were skeptical about the incidents of the *Iliad*, such as the English historian of Greece, George Grote, or Ernst Curtius, his German peer, the Berlin scholar and excavator of Olympia, agreed that there had been a city or royal citadel of Troy in prehistoric times, but its identity remained a matter of dispute. Even the Indologist Max Müller, who belonged to the extremist wing of the mythological school, conceded that Troy may well have existed.[16] Grote, by the way, long before Schliemann, had placed Troy at Hissarlik.

By now it is a truism that Schliemann slew the skeptics and single-handedly rediscovered Troy, thereby convincing the world that Homer was right after all. It followed that he also demonstrated that the Trojan War, Priam, and Achilles were history. Yet this is simply not the case. Schliemann, of course, came up with a number of corpora delicti he declared to be unmistakably Homeric, but none has stood the test. Hence the frequently mouthed claim that he proved by his excavation at Hissarlik that Homer's poems were essentially historical is at least debatable.

It so happens that the Homeric controversy is as alive today as ever, and important progress has been made along the very lines suggested by the textual critics. Whether there ever was a Trojan War or, rather, several wars, no one has yet been able to establish. The city with its nine superimposed settlements which Schliemann and his associates and successors uncovered at Hissarlik may well have been called Troy, but that has not been

verified either, since no written evidence has so far come to light and contemporary records from elsewhere, such as the Linear B tablets from Greece
and Crete and the Hittite archive of Bogazköy (central Anatolia) fail to
throw any real light on the question. One cannot even rule out the possibility
that "Troy" and "Ilion" or "Ilios" were two different sites, just as the *Iliad*
for all its unique poetic power appears to fuse (by "conflation") various
episodes that neither in place nor time nor personages originally can have
belonged together.[17]

As a matter of fact, the name "Troy" (or, rather, Troia) seems to have
been fairly common in the Aegean area for an intricately walled citadel
(which also approximates the meaning of "Hissarlik") and may have been
carried by several Anatolian-Aegean places, as is the case with the Alcazars of
Spain. If there ever was a war or siege of Troy (even Homer hints at another
previous sack by Hercules), the actual hostilities can have had very little
resemblance to the events in the *Iliad*, considering how much more recent
epics like the *Chanson de Roland* or the *Nibelungenlied*, though relating to
actual incidents, almost totally distort them and are demonstrably worthless
as historical testimony.

As to the Hissarlik site, one can say with certainty only that it fits some
(not all) of the geographic descriptions given for Troy in the *Iliad* and that
hence Homer or some other bard(s) knew the region fairly well and, perhaps
deliberately, chose the location for the setting of the epic, just as a modern
adapter of the Romeo and Juliet story may place it in the slums of Man-
hattan's West Side. Nothing more can as yet be proved. In sum, archaeology
fails to demonstrate that Hissarlik is identical with Troy, though its later
Greek and Roman settlers firmly believed so.

Hissarlik may have occupied an important position in prehistoric
northwestern Anatolia as a strategic stronghold. During the Bronze Age, it
waxed wealthy from trade, the breeding of horses, and the manufacture of
textiles. Like other places in Anatolia, the islands, Greece, and beyond,
Hissarlik undeniably contains among its several strata settlements that were
of the Mycenaean Age. These one may tentatively associate with a Trojan
war, in particular levels Troy VI and Troy VIIa (and perhaps Troy VIIb),
the first identified by Wilhelm Dörpfeld and the second by Carl W. Blegen
of the University of Cincinnati. But either settlement is a far cry from
Homer's many-splendored royal citadel. In addition, Troy VI, which comes a
bit closer to the Homeric image, was apparently destroyed by an earthquake,
while Troy VIIa, though ransacked by human hands and put to the torch,
was a pitiful compound of hovels—in no way whatever resembling the *Iliad*
description—which seems to have been stormed by attackers around 1260 B.C.
(according to Blegen). Thus its fall was removed by two generations from the

traditional date of the Trojan War. Since Blegen other scholars—mainly on ceramic evidence—prefer to put the fall of Troy VIIa at a later date, around 1190 B.C. Though close to the alleged date of the Trojan War, this was a time when most Mycenaean centers were victims to similar assaults by invading hordes ("Sea People"?) and hence were unlikely to have launched any aggressive military ventures of their own, certainly not a major expedition across the Aegean and a ten-year siege.

Thus, while there may be a likelihood that Hissarlik was called Troy and a bare possibility that the site was destroyed during a raid that may be vaguely linked with the Trojan War of the *Iliad*, the Homeric epics as such do not represent a historical account but first and above all a supreme work of poetic imagination. Just as it cannot be archaeology's task to verify the Bible in order to defeat skeptics and restore faith, it is a futile undertaking to enlist the spade in the cause of Homeric fundamentalism.[18] Of course, much of the poems' content dealing with Olympian gods, supernatural incidents, or divine interventions, even a Schliemann—though he does not dwell on the subject—would have considered outside the realm of history.

Science then finds little validity in any of Schliemann's Homeric beliefs and ascriptions. Yet it must at once be conceded that virtually all specialists in Homeric and Mycenaean studies will generously pay tribute to the remarkable plodding amateur of genius, "the father of Aegean prehistory," who laid the foundation of their work. As a pioneer, it is said with some justice, he could hardly be expected to solve questions whose definitive answers elude students today. But if Schliemann's proud boasts cannot be verified it was due to his Homeric faith and unsophisticated conviction that Greek myths should be taken literally that he picked up his spade in the first place. He missed both the Troy of Priam and the tomb of Agamemnon by a long shot, but he hit upon two then virtually unknown epochs of prehistory, the early Bronze Age Aegean culture of northwestern Anatolia and the Mycenaean Age of the Greek mainland. In a profounder sense than he realized, he was right when hammering out—and repeating ad nauseam—his declaration that he had opened up new chapters for archaeology. His researches, reaching beyond anything he himself envisaged and, in truth, eluding his understanding, wrought a revolution in all Mediterranean and Hellenic studies. Once again he was the luckiest of all archaeologists. Like another Saul, who set out to look for a stray animal, he found a kingdom instead. He was a prince of Serendip whose discoveries, if not entirely accidental, were of unanticipated scope and meaning.

Where the expert would have contented himself, at least at the start, with smaller classical ruins. Schliemann immediately aimed at the highest target. Apart from Troy, he was interested only in sites that either had

Homeric credentials or promised to yield capital returns in objects and historical information. (Places like the Phoenician Motye [Motya] off Sicily, where other archaeologists in later years met with rewarding results, he abandoned as unpromising after a few days.)

A man of greater subtlety and profounder knowledge would have hardly embarked on these grand projects. The way to discovery on occasion is paved, if not with ignorance, with childlike faith, intuition, and blind self-confidence. Schliemann possessed these qualities in abundance. Schopenhauer once remarked that the greatest deeds have always been wrought by dilettantes and not by employed professionals. Emil Ludwig seconded that opinion when he wrote that his hero Schliemann was "an outstanding example of my repeated contention that the enlightened amateur beats the solid expert every time."[19]

Much ink has been spilled on Schliemann's record as an excavator. Certainly during his lifetime, opinion was fiercely divided. Then and for some years after his death, quite a few held that he was an archaeologist in name only, but in fact an impatient, irresponsible treasure seeker who, in order to get to the objects he was after, ruined rather than recovered ancient sites. Others, perhaps blinded by his results or confusing Schliemann with Dörpfeld, turned him into an inspired expert and insisted they saw wise planning where the dissidents perceived little but blundering and plundering.

Since then tempers have cooled. The consensus today seems to be that the debate on the issue has been closed. The almost unanimous verdict: though Schliemann undoubtedly proceeded brutally in his initial seasons at Troy and destroyed valuable evidence, his were the faults of his age. He was no better or worse than any of his accredited colleagues. On the contrary, he quickly learned, improved his practices, and in the course became, if not the founder, one of the pacesetters, of scientific archaeology. To hold against him his failure to plan and organize his digs properly and to preserve or document all the finds, in the manner of twentieth century professionals, is as absurd as accusing the captain of the *Titanic* of neglecting to carry radar instruments on its maiden voyage. When Schliemann appeared on the scene, according to Ludwig and virtually all Schliemann biographers after him, the science of archaeology was not yet born.

Granted, it would be unfair and unsound to reproach Schliemann for methods and interpretations which were not up to our standards. But on closer examination it turns out that archaeology in the age of Schliemann was by no means as primitive as we are made to believe, and Ludwig himself admits that among Schliemann's contemporaries opinion on his excavations was highly critical and in some cases devastating. But echoing Schliemann, we are left with the impression that such condemnation was inspired by little but the jealousy of academic dry-as-dusts against a talented, trailblazing outsider and was devoid of any objective foundation.

The man most frequently quoted for such an "unfair" judgment was Adolf Michaelis, a professor of Strasbourg University and himself an archaeologist who had dug in Greece with Alexander Conze. He wrote the still valuable A Century of Archaeological Discovery, which appeared in English translation in 1908 (first German edition, Leipzig, 1905). In it he devoted quite some space to Schliemann, reciting sympathetically his career and distributing both praise (for effort and enthusiasm) and censure. With regard to the latter he stated that Schliemann was "a complete stranger to every scientific treatment of his subject and had no idea that a method and a well-defined technique existed."[20] Such a remark is in flagrant contrast to the latter-day plaudits which could be quoted ad infinitum.

It would be facile to say that the truth can be found somewhere between these two extremes. Yet, Schliemann himself was a man of extremes rather than of the middle. Michaelis, unlike latter-day Schliemann worshipers, was closer to him in time; in fact he knew him, had seen for himself the excavation sites, and had firsthand experience with actual digging. His book bespeaks of a fair-minded and sound historical approach to the development of archaeology over the span of a century, and hence there seems little justification in charging his comment to any personal bias. Besides, even Schliemann friends and loyalists, such as Virchow, Dörpfeld, and Carl Schuchhardt, freely conceded that at least his early excavations were erratic and recklessly destructive.

What then is the historical evidence? Was Michaelis' blaming Schliemann for his neglect of scientific technique just an anachronism? Ludwig and other German authors rightly made the point that the first thoroughly scientific campaign ever launched was the one by the German Archaeological Institute at Olympia under Curtius in 1875—that is, two years after Schliemann had closed his own first campaign at Hissarlik and a year prior to his season at Mycenae. However, the fact that Olympia could be tackled with firmly established and neatly defined principles—foremost in regard to stratification and the complete recording and preservation of all the material evidence no matter of what period—allows us to conclude that they had not just sprung from the brow of a German professor of classics but had been tried, formulated, and previously elaborated. And this is indeed what the record shows. Before Olympia, Alexander Conze had been guided by similar principles when directing excavations for the Austrian government from 1873 on Samothrace. And he in turn had a long line of predecessors. One of the most resourceful was Schliemann's later friend Charles T. Newton of the British Museum who, as early as 1846, tracked down a lost ancient site in Asia Minor, Halikarnassos, with its famous Mausoleum, and afterward (1858–1859) recovered the plan of a city, Cnidos (in southwestern Asia Minor), thereby invalidating the claim that Schliemann was the first to search not just for individual objects of art or buildings, but a whole settlement. Of even greater significance were the Italian excavations of the buried cities at the foot of Mount Vesuvius which aimed at freeing an urban environment in all its aspects and with all its vibrant minutiae. Particularly under Giuseppe Fiorelli—another acquaintance of Schliemann's—who directed excavation at Pompeii beginning in 1860 and whom Michaelis referred to as "a thoroughly scientific man," were mature concepts of the aims and procedures of archaeology evolved in advance of almost everything Schliemann either voiced or practiced. Glyn E. Daniel in his A Hundred Years of Archaeology (1950) affirms that Fiorelli "was certainly one of the pioneers of stratigraphical analysis."[21] Finally, it should be mentioned that an understanding of successive strata joined with meticulous standards of excavation and preservation was still earlier perfected by prehistorians working at the bogs of Denmark and the lake dwellings of Switzerland.

Though no textbook code of archaeological principles may have been available when Schliemann appeared on the scene, there is no reason why a relatively new field of knowledge could not be approached in the spirit of careful, step-by-step, methodical responsibility rather than with the gusto of reckless adventurism. In an age of science, all inquiry, even in realms not yet fully charted, can proceed along general scientific lines. The fact that such a study has not yet grown into a science itself hardly serves as an alibi for a recourse to alchemy or battering rams. Archaeology had only to borrow from geologists, paleontologists, and evolutionists to improvise solid rules. But impulsive and impatient Schliemann, let us agree with Michaelis, did not give science any thought when he set out to ravish the hill of Hissarlik in order to get to Priam's citadel. As Ludwig once perceptively observed, he approached the hill like a child trying to find out what makes a clock work and in the process dismantles and ruins its mechanism.

In the years after his retirement from business when, according to his chroniclers, Schliemann prepared himself in Paris for a career in archaeology, he apparently made no serious attempt to acquire practical training in excavation. Nor did it seem to have occurred to him to learn from watching other archaeologists in the field before embarking on his own excavations. As late as 1879 he insisted that "an explorer must be a self-taught man, excavation being an art by itself which cannot be learned in colleges.[22]

If anything, it is puzzling that it took Schliemann so long to acquire the fundamentals of stratigraphy at Hissarlik and to dig himself out of the self-created confusion, which placed the Homeric city first at the bottom, then in turn at the second, the third, and back at the second levels. When he visited the Olympia excavations in 1876 and gained the impression that the work was progressing too slowly, he is reported to have volunteered his advice with the words: "You gentlemen do everything wrong. You remove one stratum after another. In this manner you waste a lot of time and money. One has to dig immediately into the depth, only then will one find things."[23] Apologists for Schliemann's bold cut through the Hissarlik hill, which obliterated a good part of it including what he later came to regard as Homeric Troy (not to mention Mycenaean remains), accepted Virchow's excuse that had it not been for this daring enterprise, Schliemann would have never reached the "real" Troy and made the great discoveries he had. But the very fact that, as it turned out, he thereby missed what he was searching for deprives that glib thesis of any sense. It also runs counter to what is sometimes hailed as Schliemann's outstanding accomplishment: to have been the first to dig systematically a multilayered Near Eastern tell and to recapture its evolving history and life through millennia. To claim that Schliemann, the fanatical Homerist, was after such a historical totality amounts to a misapprehension of his goals and procedures.

In truth, Schliemann's work only began to approximate scientific standards after he had learned to depend on men like Virchow and above all the gifted young architect-archaeologist Dörpfeld, who had won his spurs at Olympia. Without these "assistants" Schliemann by himself would have been unable to approach the detached analytic attitude of the scholar. It is equally doubtful whether without Dörpfeld Schliemann would have made any further progress at Troy. The royal palace of Tiryns, just because it was near the surface, would have most likely escaped him altogether, as in fact it had on his preliminary dig there in 1876.[24]

But if Schliemann's scholarship and technique were questionable, his successes are the more astonishing. And who will argue against success? The cliché must stand: his faults were also his virtues. He had the courage of his fantasies. Over his whole archaeological career may stand as motto the oft-quoted saying by George Bernard Shaw: "Some people see things as they are and ask why? I dream dreams that never were and ask why not?" What is more, dreamer though he may have been, haunted by an idée fixe, Schliemann was at the same time realist and activist enough to test his views. With all his dogmatism, his bizarre theories, the wrongheaded attributions, and his ever-readiness to read Homeric connotations into any object found, he had a capacity to grow and, if reluctantly, change or modify some of his views. In the end he came to widen his horizon beyond Homer into Mediterranean and European prehistory.

A loner of phenomenal will power, fierce independence, and vast ambition, he braved the guild of experts and doggedly upheld his heterodox ideas until he saw them triumph spectacularly. A cunning operator in materializing his schemes and as indefatigable a self-promoter as his fellow dreamer George Bernard Shaw, he yet served a great ideal. His dedication and zeal may, on occasion, have reached a compulsive stage. But this is what gave them depth, conviction, and a kind of monolithic grandeur. Matthew Arnold notwithstanding, the pale, almost comical, little man with a drooping mustache and domed forehead, unimpressive though he seemed, was possessed by a demon that raised him to kinship with his beloved Homeric race of warriors. Has it not been said that love bestows equality on the lover? Everything we associate with a skeptical, objective mind of quiet unobtrusive scholarship was anathema to this fiery, mercurial subjectivist who may have looked in his later years like a provincial German professor but had the élan and energy—not to say ruthlessness—of a condottiere.

A man of such enthusiasm does not stake his reputation on scientific skill. Nor should he be judged on such terms. The Mycenaean civilization was about to be discovered even without his brilliant strike at the Mycenae grave circle, and Troy may have been better off waiting for another man's spade. It is an exaggeration to maintain that before him no one had an inkling that classical Greece had been preceded by an impressive prehistoric culture. The Lion Gate, the magnificent *tholos* tombs, and occasional finds of ceramics and treasures offered ample evidence to the contrary. Yet, driven by his Philhellene frenzy, he was the one to appear by dint of luck and perseverance at the opportune moment to conjure up—without fully realizing so himself—the lost millennia of the Aegean past. To be sure, what he set out to find, he essentially failed to do, but he found something far more substantial. Whether a wayward prince of Ceylon or the Columbus of Mediterranean archaeology, he wrought a revolution in knowledge. His discoveries and the legends he created about himself electrified a global audience. He became a culture hero.

Schliemann's pedantries, dishonesties, and vanities have receded over the years. German academe, once his severest critic, has canonized him "the father of archaeology.[25] The stately tomb he built himself by the Ilissos in view of the Acropolis fittingly bears the inscription "To the *Heros* Schliemann."

Certainly, the legend cannot be ignored. As an object lesson in the vitality of the Schliemann myth, I recall an experience in Greece in 1973 when, on revisiting Mycenae's Grave Circle A, I was unable to convince a Greek guide that not the German Schliemann but his own countryman Panagiotes Stamatakes (Stamatakis) was the discoverer of the sixth shaft grave. Some days later I overheard a lecturer at the National Museum in Athens tell a group of ecstatic foreign tourists that it was none other than the great Schliemann who had dug up the unique Vaphios (Vapheio) gold cups, which, of course, another Greek archaeologist—and one of the most illustrious —Chrestos Tsountas, had found near Sparta. Both incidents reminded me of the humble German servant girl who refused to believe that there were poems in her language that had not been written by Goethe. It then occurred to me that it was not the least of Schliemann's triumphs that he persuaded the world to accept his own myth.

In the nature of myths, it is still growing. And if a nineteenth century figure in so short a time could be transposed from the sober prose of history to the rhapsodical idiom of legend, does this not also cast doubt on the plausibility of Schliemann's manic belief in the historical essence of the Homeric epics? The irony did not escape me. Granted, Schliemann's eventful life, as mirrored in his own writings, has the trimmings of a romantic epic. But he was—whatever the legends that surround him, whatever the legends he created himself—not a myth but a man.

Aeneas fleeing the destruction of Troy, the picture
that inspired Schliemann's determination to discover
the site of the ancient city.

Heinrich Schliemann was nearly sixty years old when he wrote, in English, his so-called autobiography, a personal introductory chapter to *Ilios: The city and country of the Trojans* (London, 1880; New York, 1881).[1] He was then at the zenith of his fame. The treasures of Troy and Mycenae had been dug up to the gasps of a worldwide audience. A slew of articles on him and his work had appeared in the popular magazines. His name was becoming a household word. *Ilios*, a tome of nearly nine hundred pages, was conceived as a definitive compendium of his researches at Troy (Hissarlik). At the time Schliemann was certain that the riddles of the Homeric site had been solved and, upon his own declaration, excavations there had been closed "forever."

Unlike Schliemann's previous archaeological publications *Ilios* was arranged systematically by topics rather than as a series of dated first-person accounts of campaigns in progress, in which his opinions were likely to change in alarming succession. Therefore, Schliemann, who always found it difficult to exclude himself from his writings, felt the need to add a personal touch to *Ilios* through a lengthy introduction. This autobiographical essay was to supply, apart from a historical sketch of his excavations until then, a review of his eventful life, particularly prior to his switch to archaeology. If it was meant to be a stocktaking, it also reflected the wonder and pride over his fortunes and how, despite vicissitudes, he had made his fondest dreams come true. Not unjustifiably, he must have been convinced that the many people who had followed his discoveries wanted to know first hand by what road he had traveled from humble beginnings to become the awakener of ancient heroes. Though several friends advised against publishing his rather romantic tale in a serious academic work, Schliemann went ahead. However, he agreed to cut or tone down passages of too sensitive a nature, such as a discussion of his divorce, which was considered unsuitable for his English readers.[2]

The purpose of the autobiographical sketch was clearly stated in the opening paragraph. He had not undertaken it, he wrote, "from any feeling of vanity, but from a desire to show how the work of my later life has been the natural consequence of the impressions I received in my earliest childhood. . . . The pickaxe and spade for the excavation of Troy and the royal tombs of Mycenae were both forged and sharpened in the little German village in which I passed eight years of my earliest childhood."[3] Besides, he expressed the pious wish that he might arouse in others with his own exemplary tale "a taste for those high and noble studies which have sustained my courage during the hard trials of my life and which will sweeten the days yet left to me to live."[4]

Not surprisingly that moral is rarely lost sight of. Even so, the result is an extraordinarily charming story which remains a principal source for Schliemann's early life. Moreover, as Schliemann himself decreed, it has become the "official" version according to which later generations have chosen to view his career. To comply with the wishes of the Brockhaus publishing house, shortly after Schliemann's death, his widow commissioned an associate to complete the narrative.[5] The resulting volume was issued under the misleading title *Heinrich Schliemanns Selbstbiographie, bis zu seinem Tode vervollständigt, herausgegeben von Sophie Schliemann* (*H.S.'s Autobiography, completed to his death,* issued by Sophie S.). For some odd reason it used only part of the *Ilios* autobiographical material and, after Schliemann's own narrative, covered little but the archaeological exploits, and those in summary fashion. But enjoying unabated popularity in Germany, it has gone through numerous editions.[6]

Actually, Schliemann's account of his life in *Ilios* is only the last of several such outlines which differ considerably not only in length and style but in emphasis and factual details. The travel diary of Schliemann's first American journey (1850–1852) was prefaced by a shorter sketch stressing his rise to commercial success. But no mention was made of the ghost stories that enchanted his childhood or of his father's tales of burning Troy and lava-buried Pompeii. Some fifteen years later, Schliemann wrote an introduction to his book *Ithâque, le Péloponnèse, et Troie* (1869) which incorporated some of the data of the previous version, though now his fascination with buried secrets and Greek antiquity and, in particular, with Homer had become leitmotifs. In virtually the same form it was used again to introduce *Troy and Its Remains* (1874).

In *Ilios,* as in several contemporary letters furnishing biographical data, the transformation is virtually complete. Schliemann says relatively little of his early struggles in the commercial world. Also, his first long sojourn in America is just skimmed. By the same token, the downfall of his father is glossed over, though it was responsible for young Heinrich's estrangement from his childhood sweetheart and changed the course of his life.

Nevertheless, there is little doubt about the credibility of the main events depicted. But "poetic" touches have been added, as Schliemann himself admits in his correspondence. To enhance his story, he read up on the folk tales centering on Ankershagen, the Mecklenburg village where he spent his youth, and inquired about the background of the area's ruins. Upon the publication of *Ilios*, he found it necessary to apologize to his early love Minna for embellishing their romance.[7] Further on in his autobiographical notes, he appears to have taken even greater liberties (some of his embarrassed biographers, quite implausibly, credit him with "lapses of memory"). The same cavalier attitude toward truth is likewise evidenced by the underplaying of his education in order to make himself appear entirely self-taught. As a matter of fact, he learned French, English, and Latin in school and took private lessons in English before he left home.[8]

In this document, however, even when juggling or coloring facts, Schliemann uniquely revealed himself: the merchant-adventurer-explorer who, on the threshold of old age, saw his own hard, thorny, and ultimately triumphant life fusing into a tale of unity and meaning. This may not be everybody's view of what "autobiography" is all about—though it compares with Goethe's *Dichtung und Wahrheit*—or what it ought to be, but it partakes of history and truth. It is an inner as well as external testimony.

CHILDHOOD IN MECKLENBURG

from *Ilios* and *Schliemann's* *First Visit to America*

. . . I was born on the 6th of January, 1822, in the little town of Neu Buckow, in Mecklenburg-Schwerin, where my father, Ernest Schliemann, was Protestant clergyman, and whence, in 1823, he was elected in that capacity to the parish of the village of Ankershagen between Waren and Penzlin, in the same duchy.[1] In that village I spent the eight following years of my life; and my natural disposition for the mysterious and the marvellous was stimulated to a passion by the wonders of the locality in which I lived. Our garden-house was said to be haunted by the ghost of my father's predecessor, Pastor von Russdorf; and just behind our garden was a pond called "das Silberschälchen," out of which a maiden was believed to rise each midnight, holding a silver bowl. There was also in the village a small hill surrounded by a ditch, probably a pre-historic burial-place (or so-called *Hünengrab* [dolmen]), in which, as the legend ran, a robber knight in times of old had buried his beloved child in a golden cradle. Vast treasures were also said to be buried close to the ruins of a round tower in the garden of the proprietor of the village. My faith in the existence of these treasures was so great that, whenever I heard my father complain of his poverty, I always expressed my astonishment that he did not dig up the silver bowl or the golden cradle, and so become rich.

There was likewise in Ankershagen a medieval castle, with secret passages in its walls, which were six feet thick, and an underground road, which was supposed to be five miles long, and to pass beneath the deep lake of Speck; it was said to be haunted by fearful spectres, and no villager spoke of it without terror.[2] There was a legend, that the castle had once been inhabited by a robber knight of the name of Henning von Holstein, popularly called "Henning Bradenkirl," who was dreaded over the whole country, for he plundered and sacked wherever he could.[3] But, to his vexation, the Duke of Mecklenburg gave safe-conducts to many of the merchants who had to pass by his castle. Wishing to wreak vengeance upon the duke, Henning begged him to do him the honour of a visit. The duke accepted the invitation, and came on the appointed day with a large retinue. But a cowherd, who was cognizant of Henning's design to murder his guest, hid himself in the under-wood on the roadside, behind a hill a mile distant from our house, and lay in wait for the duke, to whom he disclosed his master's murderous intention, and the duke accordingly returned instantly. The hill was said to have derived its present name, "Wartensberg" or "Watch-mount," from the event. Henning, having found out that his design had been frustrated by the cowherd, in revenge fried the man alive in a large iron pan, and gave him, when he was dying, a last kick with his left foot. Soon after this the duke came with a regiment of soldiers, laid siege to the castle, and captured it. When Henning saw that there was no escape for him, he packed all his treasures in a box and buried it close to the round tower in his garden, the ruins of which are still standing, and he then committed suicide. A long line of flat stones in our churchyard was said to mark the malefactor's grave, from which for centuries his left leg used to grow out, covered with a black silk stocking.[4] Nay, both the sexton Prange and the sacristan Wöllert swore that, when boys, they had themselves cut off the leg and used its bone to knock down pears from the trees, but that, in the beginning of the present century, the leg had suddenly stopped growing out. In my childish simplicity I of course believed all this;

nay, I often begged my father to excavate the tomb or to allow me to excavate it, in order to see why the foot no longer grew out.

A very deep impression was also made upon my mind by the terra-cotta relief of a man on the back wall of the castle, which was said to be the portrait of Henning Bradenkirl himself. As no paint would stick to it, popular belief averred that it was covered with the blood of the cowherd, which could not be effaced. A walled-up fireplace in the saloon was indicated as the place where the cowherd had been fried on the iron pan. Though all pains were said to have been taken to obliterate the joints of that terrible chimney, nevertheless they always remained visible; and this too was regarded as a sign from heaven, that the diabolic deed should never be forgotten.

I also believed in a story that Mr. von Gundlach, the proprietor of the neighbouring village, Rumshagen, had excavated a mound near the church, and had discovered in it large wooden barrels containing Roman beer.

Though my father was neither a scholar nor an archaeologist, he had a passion for ancient history. He often told me with warm enthusiasm of the tragic fate of Herculaneum and Pompeii, and seemed to consider him the luckiest of men who had the means and the time to visit the excavations which were going on there. He also related to me with admiration the great deeds of the Homeric heroes and the events of the Trojan War, always finding in me a warm defender of the Trojan cause. With great grief I heard from him that Troy had been so completely destroyed, that it had disappeared without leaving any traces of its existence. My joy may be imagined, therefore, when, being nearly eight years old, I received from him, in 1829, as a Christmas gift, Dr. Georg Ludwig Jerrer's *Universal History* [*for Children*, Nürnberg, 1828], with an engraving representing Troy in flames, with its huge walls and the Scaean Gate, from which Aeneas is escaping, carrying his father Anchises on his back and holding his son Ascanius by the hand; and I cried out, "Father, you were mistaken: Jerrer must have seen Troy, otherwise he could not have represented it here." "My son," he replied, "that is merely a fanciful picture." But to my question, whether ancient Troy had such huge walls as those depicted in the book, he answered in the affirmative. "Father," retorted I, "if such walls once existed, they cannot possibly have been completely destroyed: vast ruins of them must still remain, but they are hidden away beneath the dust of ages." He maintained the contrary, whilst I remained firm in my opinion, and at last we both agreed that I should one day excavate Troy.

What weighs on our heart, be it joy or sorrow, always finds utterance from our lips, especially in childhood; and so it happened that I talked of nothing else to my playfellows, but of Troy and of the mysterious and wonderful things in which our village abounded. I was continually laughed at by every one except two young girls, Louise and Minna Meincke, the daughters

Mount Vesuvius

of a farmer in Zahren, a village only a mile distant from Ankershagen; the former of whom was my senior by six years, the latter of my own age. Not only did they not laugh at me, but, on the contrary, they always listened to me with profound attention, especially Minna, who showed me the greatest sympathy and entered into all my vast plans for the future. Thus a warm attachment sprang up between us, and in our childish simplicity we exchanged vows of eternal love. In the winter of 1829–30 we took lessons in dancing together, alternately at my little bride's house, at ours, and in the old haunted castle, then occupied by the farmer Mr. Heldt, where, with the same profound interest, we contemplated Henning's bloody bust, the ominous joints of the awful fireplace, the secret passages in the walls, and the entrance to the underground road. Whenever the dancing-lesson was at our house, we would either go to the cemetery before our door, to see whether Henning's foot did not grow out again, or sit down in admiration before the church-registers, written by the hand of Johann Chr. von Schröder, and Gottfriederich Heinrich von Schröder, father and son, who had occupied my father's place from 1709 to 1799; the oldest records of births, marriages, and deaths inscribed in those registers having a particular charm for us. Or we would visit together the younger Pastor von Schröder's daughter, then eighty-four years of age, who was living close to us, to question her about the past history of the village, or to look at the portraits of her ancestors, of which that of her mother, Olgartha Christine von Schröder, deceased in 1795, was our special delight, partly because we thought it a masterpiece of workmanship, partly because it resembled Minna. . . .

From our dancing-lessons neither Minna nor I derived any profit at all, whether it was that we had no natural talent for the art, or that our minds were too much absorbed by our important archaeological investigations and our plans for the future.

It was agreed between us that as soon as we were grown up we would marry, and then at once set to work to explore all the mysteries of Ankershagen; excavating the golden cradle, the silver basin, the vast treasures hidden by Henning, then Henning's sepulchre, and lastly Troy; nay, we could imagine nothing pleasanter than to spend all our lives in digging for the relics of the past.

Thanks to God, my firm belief in the existence of that Troy has never forsaken me amid all the vicissitudes of my eventful career; but it was not destined for me to realize till in the autumn of my life, and then without Minna—nay, far from her—our sweet dreams of fifty years ago.

My father did not know Greek, but he knew Latin, and availed himself of every spare moment to teach it me.[5] When I was hardly nine years old, my dear mother died [1831]: this was an irreparable misfortune, perhaps the greatest which could have befallen me and my six brothers and sisters. But my mother's death coincided with another misfortune, which resulted in all our acquaintances suddenly turning their backs upon us and refusing to have any further intercourse with us. I did not care much about the others; but to see the family of Meincke no more, to separate altogether from Minna—never to behold her again—this was a thousand times more painful to me than my mother's death, which I soon forgot under my overwhelming grief for Minna's loss. In later life I have undergone many great troubles in different parts of the world, but none of them ever caused me a thousandth part of the grief I felt at the tender age of nine years for my separation from my little bride. Bathed in tears and alone, I used to stand for hours each day before Olgartha von Schröder's portrait, remembering in my misery the happy days I had passed in Minna's company.

The future appeared dark to me; all the mysterious wonders of Ankershagen, and even Troy itself, lost their interest for a time. Seeing my despondency, my father sent me for two years to his brother, the Reverend Friedrich Schliemann,[6] who was the pastor of the village of Kalkhorst in Mecklenburg, where for one year I had the good fortune of having the candidate Carl Andres from Neu Strelitz as a teacher; and the progress I made under this excellent philologist was so great that, at Christmas 1832, I was able to present my father with a badly-written Latin essay upon the principal events of the Trojan War and the adventures of Ulysses and Agamemnon. At the age of eleven [1883] I went to the Gymnasium at Neu Strelitz, where I was placed in the third class. But just at that time a great disaster befell our family, and, being afraid that my father would no longer have the means of supporting me for a number of years, I left the gymnasium after being in it only three months, and entered the *Realschule* of the same city, where I was placed in the second class.[7] In the spring of 1835 I advanced to the first class, which I left in April 1836, at the age of fourteen, to become apprentice in the little grocer's shop of Ernest Ludwig Holtz in the small town of Fürstenberg in Mecklenburg-Strelitz.

A few days before my departure from Neu Strelitz, on Good Friday 1836, I accidentally met Minna Meincke, whom I had not seen for more than five years, at the house of Mr. C. E. Laue. I shall never forget that interview, the last I ever had with her. She had grown much, and was now fourteen years old. Being dressed in plain black, the simplicity of her attire seemed to enhance her fascinating beauty. When we looked at each other, we both burst into a flood of tears and fell speechless into each other's arms. Several times we attempted to speak, but our emotion was too great; neither of us could articulate a word. But soon Minna's parents entered the room, and we had to separate. It took me a long time to recover from my emotion. I was now sure that Minna still loved me, and this thought stimulated my ambition. Nay, from that moment I felt within me a boundless energy, and was sure that with unremitting zeal I could raise myself in the world and show that I was worthy of her. I only implored God to grant that she might not marry before I had attained an independent position.

I was employed in the little grocer's shop at Fürstenberg for five years and a half; for the first year by Mr. Holtz, and afterwards by his successor, the excellent Mr. Theodor Hückstaedt.[8] My occupation consisted in retailing herrings, butter, potato-whiskey, milk, salt, coffee, sugar, oil, and candles; in grinding potatoes for the still, sweeping the shop, and the like employments. Our transactions were on such a small scale that our aggregate sales hardly amounted to 3,000 thalers, or £450 annually; nay, we thought we had extraordinary luck when we sold two pounds' worth of groceries in a day. There I of course came in contact only with the lowest classes of society. I was engaged from five in the morning till eleven at night, and had not a moment's leisure for study. Moreover I rapidly forgot the little that I had learnt in childhood; but I did not lose the love of learning; indeed I never lost it, and, as long as I live, I shall never forget the evening when a drunken miller came into the shop. His name was Hermann Niederhöffer.[9] He was the son of a Protestant clergyman in Roebel (Mecklenburg), and had almost completed his studies at the Gymnasium of Neu Ruppin, when he was expelled on account of his bad conduct. Not knowing what to do with him, his father apprenticed him to the farmer Langermann in the village of Dambeck; and, as even there his conduct was not exemplary, he again apprenticed him for two years to the miller Dettmann at Güstrow. Dissatisfied with his lot, the young man gave himself up to drink, which, however, had not made him forget his Homer; for on the evening that he entered the shop he recited to us about a hundred lines of the poet, observing the rhythmic cadence of the verses.[10] Although I did not understand a syllable, the melodious sound of the words made a deep impression upon me, and I wept bitter tears over my unhappy fate. Three times over did I get him to repeat to me those divine verses, rewarding his trouble with three glasses of whiskey, which I bought with the few pence that made up my whole fortune. From that moment I never ceased to pray God that by His grace I might yet have the happiness of learning Greek.

There seemed, however, no hope of my escaping from the hapless and humble position in which I found myself. And yet I was relieved from it, as if by a miracle. By lifting too heavy a cask of chicory, a blood-vessel sprung in my lungs and I got a heavy blood-spitting, which rendered me in-

II
SELF-MADE MAN
1841–1850

View of the great North German port city of Hamburg,
the scene of Schliemann's first ventures in commerce.

THE DEATH OF Schliemann's mother in 1831 was indeed a misfortune for her large family. Schliemann refers, however, only obliquely to "another misfortune" that occurred at about the same time. It was his father's scandalous liaison with a maid, on whom he lavished expensive jewelry. The pastor's affair, which had probably started before his wife's death, became the talk of the village and led to his being publicly censured. In time he was also accused of misappropriating church funds. That, in turn, was followed by his suspension and eventual "voluntary" resignation. He was cleared by a tribunal in 1834 and given monetary compensation. But meanwhile his family was ostracized. The children had to be sent away. Brothers and sisters were separated. Young Heinrich's sheltered childhood came to a harsh end.

His wanderings began when he was barely ten years old, though they seemed to have reached a standstill when he returned to live with his father briefly and served five and a half years of peonage (1836–1841) as a grocery clerk. But what could have been a dismal dead end, a hopeless drudgery to which weaker souls would have resigned themselves, opened a window to a wider world. Whether by accident (probably an attack of incipient tuberculosis) or long-planned design, young Schliemann, by now past eighteen, was determined to seek his luck elsewhere. And determined he was to better himself, to overcome the gaps in his abortive education, and to cast out for lucrative opportunities in commerce and finance. For him his native Mecklenburg was simply too narrow. Emigration to America was first on his mind. The failure of that project did not in the least discourage him. On the contrary, it was now that he showed his true character. The slight, weak-chested, unhealthy-looking adolescent, half-educated, awkward, and without any noticeable skills, became a dynamo, and his life turned into a chain of almost picaresque episodes.

According to his "autobiography," Schliemann, after losing his lowly

job at the Fürstenberg grocery, immediately made his way to the big city—
Hamburg. All that happened between then and his employment at Schröder's, a large Amsterdam import house that guided him to rapid rise in
international business, is skipped over. Luckily we have an extensive letter,
one of the longest he ever wrote, which he sent to two of his sisters, Wilhelmine and Doris (Dorothea), soon after he arrived in Amsterdam
on February 20, 1842.[1] The letter happily fills the gap. Since it was written
some thirty-five years before the "autobiography," when he was just twenty
years old, we have for once the young Schliemann speaking to us directly. As
such, discrepancies with other, later sources are on occasion considerable.
It is reasonable to assume that closeness to the events may, on the whole,
mean greater veracity; however, Schliemann's ever-present itch for self-
dramatization cannot be discounted. Apparently he already was known
to members of his family to be a teller of tales that were likely to strain
credulity, because in the very letter he explicitly assured his sisters that
his lengthy story is given "according to purest truth" and in a postscript
he mentioned a hospital bill and a consular document which he enclosed
"so that you can see for yourself that I have not been lying to you."[2]

The excerpted letter, here reprinted in translation, certainly does credit
to the young man's narrative talent and vivid style. Though among the
earliest of Schliemann's writings, it reflects much of the man and his lifelong preoccupations and peculiarities. There are such recurring themes as
supreme trust in his fate—ever ready to turn disaster into a blessing; his
lust for travel; and his indomitable will to survive. There are also characteristic ruses to further his own ends, his interest in languages, religious skepticism,
belief in cold sea bathing as a panacea for all ills, and mania for trivial
data (names of hotels, room numbers, prices, etc.), together with his
simplistic views of foreign races, people, and places. He is forever prone
to superlatives and exaggeration. Yet his description of the North Sea
hurricane and maritime disaster, in which he nearly lost his life, is quite remarkable considering that it was written by so young and untutored a man
and one who had not been on the high seas before.

Schliemann's first sea voyage succeeded only in transporting him
from Hamburg to Amsterdam. There, after a brief temporary job, he obtained employment as a messenger-mailboy, which offered him few challenges
and was ill-paid to boot, but it gave him ample opportunity to pursue
his private interests. Writing in *Ilios* of his early experiences in Amsterdam,
Schliemann stresses a second major theme that dominated the view of his
own life. Good fortune may have sent him to Amsterdam, but his climb
up the commercial ladder was due to temperance, self-denial, and hard work.
Though captivated by the attractions of lively, international-minded Am-

sterdam and not immune to the charms of the fair sex, he was resolved
to remain little but an onlooker. He had to turn his energies to greater
profit. Bumptiously aware that knowledge is power, he made up his mind
to renew his education. Only thus could he hope for substantial advance-
ment. A calculated pragmatic scheme it may have been. But for a man
of Schliemann's compulsive single-mindedness and ingrained respect for
learning, study—and foremost the study of languages—soon became a passion in itself.

It was in the early stage of his business career in Amsterdam that
Schliemann discovered his love for foreign tongues. As quickly, he realized
his almost unlimited capacity to acquire, if not master them, which he attributed not so much to an innate talent but to a method which he devised
himself. He was to follow it throughout his life, in the course of which he
gained fluency in some eighteen ancient and modern idioms.

Years later, during a stay in the United States, he would dispatch a lengthy
paper, in not exactly faultless English, to the 1869 Convention of American
Philologists at Poughkeepsie, N.Y. Enterprising publishers asked him to
lend his name to a series of language books, loosely based on his method.
However, philologists tend to be of the opinion that his "unique" method
notwithstanding, it was mainly his dedication and enthusiasm—in time, of
course, he had trained his memory—that was responsible for his amazing
command of so many languages. Interestingly enough, his school certificate
shows no scholastic distinction in language studies, just as his German teacher
judged young Schliemann's compositions "industriously executed but lacking
in clear thought."[3]

The passion for languages was to be one of Schliemann's absorbing
pastimes from now on. In his letters and notes it is a recurrent theme.
In all his travels, high points are marked by encounters with fellow
linguists, be it in a remote California settlement or a Chinese provincial
town. During periods of his most hectic commercial transactions, on his
many voyages, on Sundays, at night, and whenever he could steal a few
minutes, he would resume his studies—just as the lowly mail clerk had
done on the way to the Amsterdam post office or when waiting in line.

Eventually his zeal seems to have cost him his job. It had outlived
its usefulness anyway and he soon found another. Joining Messrs. B. H.
Schröder & Co. early in 1844, he began his rapid rise in commerce. Cunningly guessing that his future stood much to profit from a command of
Russian, he added that difficult language to his repertoire.

Schliemann's letter to his sisters, written only two months after his
arrival in Amsterdam, concludes with a prophetic aside that, once he had
been six years in the Netherlands and had gained thorough experience in

Indigo, principal source of Schliemann's fortune

the import business, "I shall go via Batavia [Jakarta] to Japan, to try my luck there; because instinct tells me: 'You must not stay in Europe, your fortunes wait for you far away from there.' "[4] In time he would reach Java and Japan, as he had predicted. But for the main part of his commercial career, Russia was to be his abode, so much so that he became—for a while—a fervent Russian patriot, and a worshiper of Czardom and its mission. He would marry a Russian woman, raise a family there, and, on occasion, dream of acquiring a large estate and leading the leisurely life of the landed gentry.

What drew Schliemann to Russia at first was, however, golden opportunity—or rather opportunity indigo. Amsterdam trade connections made him quickly realize the unlimited market for commodities offered by the vast eastern land. As soon as his Amsterdam employers needed someone to represent them in St. Petersburg, he was already linguistically and otherwise so well prepared that he had to be their "natural" choice. The road to such meteoric success was paved by the work ethic typical of the nineteenth century—and by Schliemann's shrewdly directed industry.

HAMBURG—AMSTERDAM—ST. PETERSBURG

from *Heinrich Schliemann*
Correspondence Vol. I and *Ilios*

At Fürstenberg I had made an agreement with Magistrat Türke of the Türkhof [estate] near Lychen to leave with him and his son, my former school-mate, on July 25 [1841] for New York in North America on the packet boat *Howard*. The voyage came to naught, however, because my father categorically refused to give his consent. On account of this project I had not bothered to look for another position; indeed I had rejected several offers. Thus I found myself around midsummer without employment. I therefore decided to move on to Rostock in order to add to my commercial skills by taking up double-entry bookkeeping and afterward to try my luck in Hamburg.

Unfortunately I was condemned to spend the lovely summer in misery. Since I couldn't stay at home without being driven to despair, I rented a little room in the house of a friend of my former employer so that I would be able to better concentrate and complete my studies as early as possible.[1]

I began now with great fervor the enormous task of mastering the Schwanbeck system of bookkeeping, working from early morning to late at night. To the surprise of instructors and fellow students alike I had already finished the course by September 10—even though I myself drew the rules for all the nine exercise books—while others took one to one and a half years.

The heinous goings-on in my father's house at Gehlsdorf caused me much grief. No sooner did the day dawn than the miserable couple started to insult each other with vulgarities which even the most common rabble would be ashamed to utter. The curses and damnations, reverberating to the depths of Tartarus, continued from early morning to late at night. At one moment they would kiss, and at the next they did not consider each other worthy to spit at. One cannot imagine the dreadful scenes that took place there. A showdown came in spring when Sophie, after spending a long time shut up in the woodshed—to escape being beaten to death, she said—took lodging in Rostock with the innkeeper Krüger. The affair was then taken to court and father had to promise before the full assembly to treat her better, otherwise he would have to pay her 30 reichsthaler annually. . . . Similar incidents happened, however, the next summer.

Under these circumstances it was out of the question for me to live with father. But I swear a most solemn oath that my conduct at Rostock was entirely blameless despite father's insinuations that I led the life of an irresponsible student vagabond.

When I had finished my bookkeeping course on September 10, father handed over to me my maternal inheritance, which amounted to 29 reichsthaler after he deducted 88.32 reichsthaler for expenses I had incurred in Rostock. The same evening I left by postal coach for Neubukow. There I stayed at Zur goldenen Trompete [Golden Trumpet] on the market square and was welcomed by the proprietor with extravagant friendliness and warmth. He conversed with me on matters of state and learning, and we became fast friends when I told him that I was also from Neubukow and that my father was the former parson. All of a sudden, he was sure that he recognized me—only that, as he suspected, I had somewhat grown in the past nineteen years. Despite such agreeable conversation, the creature charged me 6 shillings for a portion of half-done scrambled eggs.

After visiting poor little Heinrich's grave, I continued the journey to Wismar with its three towers, without, however, coming across anything interesting enough to report in my diary.[2] . . . [At Wismar] I also had the pleasure of meeting Cousin Sophie.[3] God Almighty, how nature has reshaped this girl in eight years! Her figure is now slim and graceful; her movements are of an innate spontaneous charm. The sweetness and beauty of her face as much as the way she glanced at me with her ravishing shining eyes nearly bewitched me, and I dare say that a poet's blessed fantasy when creatively inspired by his muse did never gaze upon such an ideal of noble beauty as the one that stood here before me in infinite loveliness. She, too, appeared very touched, for I noticed how her beauteous cheeks first turned red, then pale. I had to tell my whole life history.

Even though it was already two o'clock in the afternoon and the family had eaten earlier, another meal was prepared for the new arrival. Cousin Sophie, in particular, did her best to serve an opulent lunch. The guest employed all his Ciceronian talents to dissuade them by declaring that he had just lunched at the Erbgrossherzog [Hereditary Grandduke]. Yet he was eagerly, and almost impatiently, looking forward to the steaming dishes, because he had not eaten anything since the previous noon except for the miserable scrambled eggs. . . . At the end of the meal I apologized that my time was up, and everybody accompanied me to the coach. I planted a few passionate kisses on little cousin's lips, climbed into the coach, the driver lashed the horses, and we were on our way through the Schwerin Gate. . . .

Toward evening we reached Heydkrug, two miles from Hamburg, where we stayed overnight. When I woke up the next morning, I looked out of the window and saw the five tallest towers of Hamburg. Their great distance from each other gave an idea of the size of the city. At the sight I was overcome by sublime, indescribable emotions. Now, at last, I saw before my eyes the great goal for which I had yearned so long and which has kept me awake so often. Now I beheld the city which ranks above all others in the world of commerce. For more than an hour I stood there in the nude without being aware of it. The view of Hamburg almost had carried me off to seventh heaven. Contemplating Hamburg, I turned into a dreamer. . . .

At last around eleven in the morning we passed the magnificent Steinthor [Stone Gate] and moved into famous Hamburg itself. There we put up at the Weissen Ross [White Horse] in the Breitenstrasse [Broadway] near the horse market.

And what a bustle of people! What masses, what a commotion . . . everybody runs, everybody races, everybody pushes everybody, and the total picture seems an immense chaos. The endless screaming of vendors who broadcast their merchandise while carrying it on their heads and speedily trotting with it through the streets; the continuous clatter of wagons which chase through the streets one after the other; the striking of the clocks and the delightful chimes of the church bells from every belfry—all deafen the stranger's ears so harshly that he is unable to hear his own voice. . . .

After I had a frugal lunch, I started out to present various letters of recommendation. I had been assured that the best place to meet the addressees would be at the Old Exchange, which opens at 1 P.M. Hence I had little time to lose, hurried over there, and arrived just before they closed the doors (precisely at one P.M. the exchange is locked, and any late arrival has to pay 4 shillings to gain admission).

The Old Exchange, supported by one hundred majestic columns and surrounded by enormous iron gates, is an antiquated building that has braved four centuries. Before coming to Hamburg I hardly imagined that the whole city had as many people as those who crowd here under one roof while watching the ups and downs of the market with apprehensively searching glances.

I succeeded in tracking down the businessmen to whom I had letters of recommendation. . . . All of them gave their friendly promise to do everything within their power to help me reach my goal; I should just submit samples of my handwriting on the following day.

After taking leave I continued my sightseeing of Hamburg. Next to the Old Exchange there is the sumptuously decorated Exchange Hall, where more than one hundred newspapers in thirteen different languages are made available to the merchants of the town. Quite close by is the great Hamburg Bank, apart from various other banks and the palatial Town Hall.

Thereupon I inspected the New Exchange at Adolph Square, which by far exceeds in size the old one and whose splendor, magnificence, and interior decor surpass all other buildings in Hamburg. Just completed, it was inaugurated on December 5 with the ringing of all the bells and a big celebration that perhaps will remain unique for millennia to come.

I then turned to the new port, looked over the numerous ships that converge here from all continents, walked up the Stintfang with its fine view of the harbor, and then climbed up the belfry of St. Michael's Church that rises 480 feet into the blue sky, offering an impressive panorama of many miles.

Oh, you can have no idea of the loveliness of Hamburg's and Altona's environs! No paint can capture the beauty of the landscape that one perceives in such richness from this height. I stood for several hours at the top and searched through the telescope of the watchman, who had accompanied me, for everything that escaped the naked eye. . . . Afterward I was shown the splendid interior of St. Michael's with its vast nave of 291 feet.

I returned home tired and asked to be served some food. . . . I rose at five o'clock [the following] morning, composed some fourteen handwritten commercial letters in three languages and, after taking refreshments, betook myself to Altona with the purpose of getting to know that city and of paying my compliments to Köppens.[4]

Altona is reached through the suburb of St. Pauli. I was barely able to pass through the Altona Gate in Hamburg because a multitude of people pushed through it like an avalanche. Since no market is held in Hamburg itself, St. Pauli keeps common market days with Altona. Everything was in a state of agitation. . . .

After I had taken in the sights, I rushed on to Altona. Everything was as lively here as at St. Pauli, and buyers and sellers milled around. Although Altona is a busy place, it is altogether dead compared with Hamburg. The streets may be cleaner and wider, yet the houses are far from being as tall and beautiful. . . .

The following day I returned to the Hamburg exchange. Agents had been busy on my behalf, and one of them, W. Wollmer, had recommended me for a position with the firm of S. H. Lindemann, Jr., in Altona. I went there and was hired without hesitation after showing my references. I started the very same day. . . .

The port of Hamburg

Lindemann's occupies Altona's finest location at the fish market, commanding a wonderful view over the Elbe. Every ship that leaves the Hamburg harbor has to pass its door. However, this mattered little to me; the main thing was the business itself—and that I did not like a bit. The firm traded in groceries, both wholesale and retail. The latter, which had little volume, was directed by an apprentice who alone took care of the office I had hoped to work in. Instead I was relegated to the store room. But such labors were beyond my physical strength. Apart from assisting in loading and unloading, I had to spend the whole day in the warehouse with the workmen. I was therefore afraid that I might suffer a relapse of my former chest ailment. As early as the third morning I asked to be let go by raising this important issue. Mr. Lindemann consented, and I promptly departed.

Once I had resolved not to accept a similar position, but to seek only office work, I rented a small room at the Hoppenmarkt in Hamburg into which I moved the same day. From now on I tried hard to find other employment and visited the exchange daily. Within a few days I succeeded, with the help of an agent, to land a second job. . . . Unfortunately it did not pay any salary, and I accepted it for an indefinite length of time. Actually I liked the firm, a leading trader in groceries, and I did only office work. But I could not reconcile myself to the fact that the tightwad would not pay me any wages.

In the meantime my money resources had melted away to 17 reichsthaler after taking out the agent's fee. It became clear to me that I could not go on much longer: every day, no matter how much I cut down on expenses, I had to spend considerable amounts. Of course, I did my best to find a new post. I asked all my friends to lend me a hand, searched through the newspapers, and submitted name and address with a letter of application if I read of any opening. Nevertheless, Fortuna continued to withhold her favors from me. At length, after the passage of eight weeks . . . all my money had vanished, and I owed my landlord a few reichsthaler, despite making do with as little as possible. Too weak to be able to help myself, I wrote to our uncle at Vipperow, explained to him my needs, and asked him to lend me 10 thaler until Christmas.[5] Though he forwarded the desired sum at once, he made his daughter write such an impertinent and nasty letter that I would have returned his wretched money without second thought had I not been in such great distress. But then and there I swore a solemn oath that, no matter how desperate my situation, I would never again ask a relative for aid; rather would I starve to death than beg such a man for the loan of a bread crumb. . . .

Two days before I was to take a job at Stade, I was as usual at the exchange when an agent came over and asked me whether I had been placed. I answered yes. He said he was sorry for being too late because otherwise he could have helped me to a splendid position in La Guaira in Colombia [Venezuela]. No sooner were these words spoken than all the pipedreams of my childhood returned. At the mention of the word "Colombia," all the old travel and seafaring fantasies, after slumbering for some four years, suddenly sprang up before me. Hence I replied that, even though I had accepted a post, I would immediately give it up if I could secure this one. The agent was quite pleased and told me that I must at once discuss the matter with Messrs. Krogmann and Wachsmuth, who were doing the hiring.

I went directly to them and declared that I had made up my mind to go to La Guaira. In order to test my intentions, these very sensible gentlemen tried to disillusion me. They told me that for some four weeks they had commissioned twenty agents to find a young man for their friends, Messrs. Declisur and Böving in La Guaira. However, of the six hundred youngsters now unemployed in Hamburg none would accept on account of the dreadful climatic conditions. They continued to paint all the dangers and inconveniences of such a long sea voyage of more than two thousand miles and of the constant threat of yellow fever over there. However, I stood even firmer by my decision, and they were prepared to hire me if I had the qualifications. They then gave me a brief test. I had to write several business letters in German, French, and English, and since they were pleased with them, they said that I should get ready, that their ship *Dorothea*, commanded by Captain Siemonsen, was about to sail, and I could go aboard whenever I wanted; I was to have free passage, but as to my salary they could not make any commitments because their friends had written that they would scale the wages according to performance.

I was overjoyed. The following day I received a letter of recommendation from the shippers to my future employers, packed my things, bought a sea grass mattress, two woolen blankets, and my bed was ready. I sent everything aboard, and in the meantime I tried to obtain more letters of recommendation in case I did not hit it off with Declisur & Böving [and had to look elsewhere]. And, indeed, my friend Wendt procured a lot for me, some of them to La Guaira, others to Curaçao. . . .[6]

On November 23, I took leave of all my friends, said good-bye to Köppens and went on board. The crew was already complete; all that was needed was a favorable wind.

The *Dorothea* was a brand-new three-master that had been launched only three weeks before. With her copper bottom she was specially built for fast sailing, and, according to Captain Siemonsen, she excelled all other Hamburg vessels in beauty. She owed her name *Dorothea* to Wachsmuth's sister, the wife of Krogmann. The ship's main quarters formed a circle; walls and floor, as well as the furniture, were of mahogany. The crew consisted of eighteen men, in addition to the three passengers: a Hamburg carpenter named Albrecht, his son, and myself. We passengers had our cabins in the saloon section, as did the captain and his two mates.

We could not get started because of unfavorable wind. But, at last, on the twenty-seventh it turned and the twenty-eighth was marked for our departure. As early as four o'clock in the morning, two pilots came aboard, the ship was untied and thence was guided through a multitude of vessels lying in front of us. Now cannons were fired in the harbor to wish us farewell, our batteries returned the greeting and, with the wind swelling the sails, the brig flew like a seabird over the dark foamy waves of the Elbe, while we lost sight of beautiful Hamburg in the dawn of day.

However, at ten o'clock, when we were outside Glückstadt, the pilot advised throwing anchor because the approaching low tide was barring passage across the sandbanks.

In the evening we once again got contrary wind, which continued throughout the twenty-ninth and only became favorable on the thirtieth. In the morning at eight o'clock we lit anchor, sails were run up, a fine easterly propelled them, and the ship glided along as swift as an arrow. By 10:45 we sailed past Cuxhaven and its handsome tall lighthouse. At 11:30 we passed the island of Neuwerder [probably Neuwerk as below]. The weather was delightful, the sky dazzlingly clear, the sun shone continuously, and everything pointed to a happy voyage. . . .

Now the wind became stronger, the vessel flew faster and faster and covered some eleven miles in four hours.[7] In no time we left behind us Neuwerk and lost sight of land. At twelve o'clock the pilots departed, at 2:45 in the afternoon we first saw Helgoland and did not lose sight of it for two hours. We passed within just two miles and were able to observe it closely: it consists of a single rock on which stand several houses. There is a large passage on one side of the isle.

The wind remained propitious throughout the night. Apart from some giddiness, so far I had not suffered from any symptoms of seasickness. That changed, however, on the second day when the wind turned and violently blew from north-northwest. As a consequence we tacked, and the vessel rolled from one side to the other. Seasickness is an indescribably disagreeable illness that consists of perpetual vomiting. Once the stomach refuses to yield any more, then bile is thrown up.

With each hour the wind increased in vehemence. A heavy gale broke loose by evening, and the waves rose as high as a house. I had always remained on deck but now became sicker and sicker. I therefore took a bucket and went to my cabin. The gale raged for eight days, blowing now from north, now from west, and with it seasickness raged unabated. During eight days I did not eat one bite. The only time I left the cabin was to relieve myself. The other passengers suffered as much; they moaned just like me. Then, at last, a calm set in and the ship became steadier. Even my seasickness seemed to subside. Once more I took some food, and I was able to spend the whole day on the foredeck. It was December 7, the air was icy, though clear, and the sea was getting more tranquil. . . .

By now we were about one hundred miles from Cuxhaven. Toward evening a favorable east wind set in, all sails were unfurled, and accompanied by jubilant cries from the crew, the craft speeded on. Everybody eagerly waited for the moment when we were to pass the English Channel, because we would then be out of danger. Given favorable wind, it can be reached from Hamburg in three days, yet we had taken more time and, nevertheless, remained closer to Hamburg than to the Channel. In the hope that the present wind would last, the captain now charted a southwesterly course. Unfortunately on the following evening we were headed for a northern gale, all sails had to be pulled down, and because we could not turn back, we had to keep steering northwest.

On the ninth the gale grew ever more violent, waves broke constantly over the deck, the vessel leaked, and pumps had to be kept in operation all the time. Our seasickness had subsided. It was replaced by a boundless hunger which we tried to satisfy with hard ship biscuits. All day long I sat in the corner of my cabin, where I had fastened an easy chair, and studied Spanish correspondence. However, I frequently suffered the misfortune of losing my balance and of being mercilessly thrown to the floor. The other passengers, more comfortably, kept to their bunks.

On the tenth the storm continued to rage from the north. We persisted on a northwesterly course. However, as we could hoist only the topgallant sail, we made very little progress and were driven by the storm more and more sideways toward south. This lasted until noon on the eleventh. That day seagulls circled around us in unusual numbers, which everybody considers a bad omen. Many dolphins also appeared frequently. The weather was bad, the air chilly at six degrees below zero, snow fell constantly, and the wind blew with undiminished violence. The pumps were at work night and day, while the sea lashed out with fury.

Toward midday the squall got stronger and stronger and around five o'clock turned into the most frightful hurricane. Waves swelled to mountains—now we were thrown like a shuttlecock hundreds of feet high, now we were sent into the horrible abyss. At six o'clock the main topgallant tore apart. Everybody awaited with anxiety the coming night because the vessel was increasingly thrown off its course. Storm sails were set, but they were in shreds before they could be of any help, and we therefore had to abandon ourselves to our fate. The other passengers and I were lying in our cabins, not knowing what was happening above. I myself did not expect any danger.

The carpenter and his son were, however, extremely jittery. They talked a lot of the dreams they had had the night before, besides turning my attention to the cat below deck and the captain's dog, both of whom had whimpered with fright all day. I did not pay them much attention, though I laughed at father and son, scornfully taking them to task for their excessive worrying. To me it seemed utterly inconceivable that we could suffer shipwreck. The carpenter therefore no longer asked my advice but whispered ever more excitedly with his son.

The crew remained on deck all the time. None had entered the cabins since noon. At seven o'clock the cabin boy brought us as usual tea and biscuits. Crying bitterly, he said that this was the last meal he would be able to serve us. I just roared with laughter.

At about ten o'clock the captain entered with the second mate, took out the charts, and showed the latter where, in his opinion, our position was. His anxious look betrayed considerable alarm. All of a sudden the first mate appeared and told the captain that he had sighted two lights in the distance. The captain ran frightened upstairs and had two anchors dropped. But their chains tore apart like thread in a matter of seconds, and the ship charged ahead like an arrow. Never had I slept so gently and peacefully. I dreamed of the beautiful Colombian plains and had no idea of the impending danger.

It may have been around midnight when the captain abruptly opened the cabin door screaming, "All passengers immediately on deck, we are in great peril!" No sooner had he spoken than a terrible blow bore him out. All cabin portholes were shattered. I jumped as quickly as I could from my bunk, tried to put my clothes on, but water was already entering from all sides. I barely saved my life running almost naked on deck. The first thing awaiting me up there was an enormous wave which broke over me and slung me from starboard to port. Though mercilessly crushed, I managed to hold to the railing. Then I crawled back to the starboard side and tied myself there with a rope.

A similar fate befell the other passengers, who, however, had had sense enough not to undress in the first place. They, too, tied themselves with loose ends of rope next to me. The captain, together with the men, was fully occupied trying to launch the two large midship lifeboats. Everybody was confused and frightened. No one quite knew what to do. The first boat was senselessly lowered on the starboard side facing the gale so that it was filled with water before it reached the surface and had to be cut off. The other, much larger one was lowered at the portside. It was lucky enough to get down, but within a few minutes it, too, was drowned in water.

Now all hope was gone; there was no way we could save ourselves.

For the first time I experienced desperate fear, and I was overcome by sadness. Ah, how often before had I wished to be dead when things did not go my way. But what a fool I was! I had no idea how sweet life is when death is really close. Yes, if anyone had made me the offer in those moments of terror either to die or to spend the rest of my days chained in prison, how gladly would I have chosen the latter. . . . In my thoughts I took leave of all my dear ones, prayed to God, commended my soul to Him for its transition to the somewhat doubtful beyond, and bequeathed my body to the sharks. Thus my last will was made.

I must have spent an hour with such pitiful thoughts in mind, while the waves incessantly broke over my head, when luckily all my confidence returned. Gloomy thoughts vanished. Instead there rose within me a sensation of foolhardiness I had never felt before, and I was resolved to throw myself without any regrets into the arms of death. The carpenter, a Catholic, was much more fainthearted than I. He kept crying and loudly appealed to

St. Mary and all the saints to come to his aid. However, neither the Holy Virgin nor her Son appeared, and the danger grew with every second.

Until now the crew had remained quiet, obeying the captain's orders. But once they saw all hope for rescue gone, they thundered dreadful blasphemies. A few screamed and bemoaned the fate of their families. It was horrible to listen to the battering of the vessel. It was probably this that set the ship's bell in motion and made it ring dolefully without end, as if pulled by an invisible hand.[8]

The night was cold and icy, at least seven to eight degrees below zero. The sky looked like just one black cloud from which snow descended upon us in fine flurries. The ship continued to sink, and with every wave that swept over us I expected death to come. Meanwhile, the crew, thinking they were safer in the rigging, climbed into it, there to await sunrise. I, too, thought I might be better off up there. Hence I untied myself and got ready to struggle up when, with a terrible battering blow, the wreck turned over on its portside and sank. I was plunged with it into the deep. However, I came up to the surface in no time and managed to get hold of a floating empty barrel, whose rim I clasped eagerly and with which I was carried away. Now tossed hundreds of feet into the air, now hurled into the terrible abyss, I must have been thrown around for some four hours in a semiconscious state when I was cast upon a sandbank whose rippling waves and low water level betrayed proximity of land. (As a matter of fact, such sandbanks are a common occurrence along the Dutch coast. Quite dry during low tide, they are underwater only at high tide.)

Numb of body and half-dead from exhaustion, I decided to wait here for death or rescue. Yet neither would come. At long last it was daybreak, and to my great joy I saw land in front of me. I tried to reach it walking but was unable to do so. I wanted to call, but I was too worn-out to raise my voice. Finally someone noticed me. Lots of curious people gathered at the beach, and within a short time several men in a boat appeared. They got as close to me as possible so that one of them could leave the boat and carry me to it.

They questioned me, but I was unable to answer since I did not understand their language. The many floating boards and barrels told them what had happened anyway. They took me to Eislandshuis, took off my shirt and underwear—which was all I wore—and put me to bed. After they gave me a cup of coffee, I fell asleep. I awoke at four o'clock in the afternoon. A little bit refreshed from sleeping, I was nevertheless tormented by the most ghastly pains, which made me burst into loud screams, because two of my front teeth were broken and I had deep gashes on face and body. My whole body seemed paralyzed, and my feet were considerably swollen. When the inn keeper entered, I asked him in English where I was and whether any of my shipmates had been rescued. Fortunately he understood the language, and he told me that we had suffered shipwreck in Eislandsgrund, a reef some three miles away from here. I was now in Eislandshuis on the island of Texel. Both the captain and one seaman had saved themselves on rafters which were driven ashore in the vicinity, and they, too, were at present in his house. Nothing could be salvaged of the ship's cargo, for the wind had changed again toward afternoon and everything was swept into the high sea.[9]

I showed him my wounds and begged him for bandages. He thence brought warm water, washed my wounds, bandaged them, gave me more coffee to drink, and once more I fell into slumber from which I did not awake before next morning. Rest had done me good, but the pains were terrible. Again the innkeeper came to my aid, brought warm rum and soap, washed my swollen feet, and put new bandages on my wounds. He also responded to my wish for a little food, which I devoured greedily, for I had not eaten anything in several days. Meanwhile the captain also entered. But he was no longer the proud, gruff master of his ship. He walked over to me, shook hands with me, was delighted by my wonderful rescue, which I had to narrate to him, and told me how he and a seaman happily saved themselves on a beam.

Thereupon he added that he was going to report the events to the shippers Krogmann & Wachsmuth and that he would gladly write on my behalf if I wanted him to. I gratefully accepted the offer and dictated him a letter to my friend Wendt in Hamburg in which I asked him to discuss with Krogmann & Wachsmuth whether they would be willing to compensate me for my losses with at least two louis d'or and, in case those gentlemen were agreeable, would they then transmit the money to my present address, i.e., H. Schliemann, c/o H. Johannes Branes in Eislandshuis on the Dutch island of Texel.

The innkeeper was much concerned about my early recovery for a number of reasons. Because he considered perspiring beneficial, he loaded me with blankets and filled me with mulled wine so that I broke out into a violent sweat which lasted a whole day. And, lo and behold, this, together with soothing rest, proved a true blessing. The swelling of my feet had drastically decreased, the heaviness in my limbs was more or less gone, and even my toothache and awful other pains took on much milder forms.

I continued the sweat cure with good results the following day. On the fourth day I was already able to walk around my room. It was then that my host hinted that I had outstayed my welcome, since he had instructions to keep me only until I got better, when I should be driven at once to the consulate at Texel Castle. Dispositions about my future would be made there, and I was to move on next morning. Since I had no clothes except a shirt and undergarment, the innkeeper took pity on me and, upon my entreaties, donated me old pants, a torn jacket, and pair of clogs (wooden shoes). Though I would have loved to see these clothes transformed into a fur coat, I nevertheless joyfully accepted them. At seven o'clock the following morning I was put in an open van, and the trip proceeded in company of the rescued sailor. The captain remained behind to await news from Hamburg. I advised the innkeeper, in case I received a letter, to forward it to the consul of Mecklenburg in Amsterdam, where I had made up my mind to go.

We arrived at Texel Castle at noon. Immediately I went to the consulate, administered by Sonderburg and Ramm, who knew all about me.[10] They wanted to send me to Harlingen so that I could be returned from there to Mecklenburg via Hamburg. However, I explained to them that my future was no securer in Mecklenburg than in Amsterdam and I much preferred the latter place.[11] All I wanted was a letter of recommendation to the consul of Mecklenburg in Amsterdam, which would also testify to my misfortunes. Mr. Ramm, an educated man, spoke French fluently, and I got along well with him. I had to take lodging for the night in the castle.

The next morning, December 17, I started out on the voyage across the Zuiderzee to the Dutch capital. Mr. Ramm had paid for my passage.

Unfortunately we hit a southwesterly and the twelve-mile trip, which is usually made in twelve hours, required three full days, so that we only arrived on the twentieth at eight in the morning. I had a miserable time. Despite the horribly cold weather, there was no bed for me aboard. Ill as I was, with my wounds not yet healed, I had to sleep on a bench. But hope that my fortunes would soon improve eased the pains. I patiently bore everything, certain that fate, which had so miraculously saved me and guided me to Holland, would also see to it that I would prosper.

No sooner had we docked at the pier for Texel ferries than I left the boat and wended my way across the bridge. A number of young bootblacks stationed on it got the idea—no doubt because of my comical outfit—that I was a potential colleague and expressed their displeasure over such competition. (There is, by the way, an immense army of bootblacks in this country, who, aside from shoe polishing, perform all kinds of business, just like the "street porters" in Berlin. Like their Berlin counterparts they are also targets of ridicule. Lounging around the many Dutch bridges, they holler at every passerby, "*Mijn heer schoe maken?*")

I then walked to a common hostel in the Ramskoy which had been pointed out to me. There I told the housekeeper my story and asked him for writing material. He gave me paper and pen, and I wrote in French to the consul of Mecklenburg, describing my situation in which I had been abandoned by God and men, asked him for assistance in gaining here an honest livelihood, attached the testimony and letter of recommendation from Sonderburg & Ramm, and presented myself in person.

The consul lived in a palatial building along the Amstel. Nevertheless, I did not hesitate to approach him and to hand him the letters without any further explanation. He read these, commiserated with me, gave me 10 guilders, assigned me a lodging and promised to look out for me in the future. Whenever I needed him, I should come to the exchange, where I would find him at post No. 34.

I now went to a secondhand dealer to fit myself out. I bought an old coat, trousers, waistcoat, shoes, hat, socks—and was completely dressed. Then I betook myself to my new quarters and had refreshments. Alas, I was too much worn-out; a violent fever seized me, accompanied by insufferable toothache. When I was unable to leave my bed even on the second and third day, the landlady was worried that my sickness might be of long duration and declared that she could not keep me any longer; I should go to the hospital (*Gasthuis* or *Siekenhuis*). To be admitted, I needed a certificate from my consul. Upon my entreaties she sent him a message. He responded to my wishes, wrote a few very friendly lines and attached another 10 guilders. I paid the landlady my bill and was taken by sledge to the hospital, where I spent Christmas in agonizing pains. On Christmas Eve they extracted the roots of two broken front teeth. The pains were so dreadful during that operation that I screamed.

On Christmas Day the consul, Mr. Ed. Quack, came to see me himself

Amsterdam

and brought me a letter addressed to me that had been delivered to him. I tore it open. It came from Mr. Wendt, who had received my note from Texel. Because of it he had talked to Messrs. Krogmann & Wachsmuth and had asked them to transfer at his expense a preliminary payment of 30 Dutch guilders to their agents in Texel. The two gentlemen had agreed to this and had also written to their captain about it. Mr. Wendt furthermore had initiated a collection on my behalf and was hopeful that several philanthropists would come to my aid by contributing a few hundred guilders. He also wanted to know of my plans. In his opinion it would be best for me to go to Amsterdam. There was no happier person than I, because now I had tangible reason to hope for a better future. . . .

Was it the good mood into which Mr. Wendt's letter had put me, or was it nature helped along by medication? No matter, I felt a little better the same day. Right after Christmas I was already able to get up and to walk around the sickroom which I shared with 102 patients and which just the same was a model of cleanliness. Not a day passed when they did not carry out three to four corpses.

Two days after Christmas I received still another letter from the consul which had been sent to him by Messrs. L. Hoyack & Co. It was written by the Brothers Kleinwort in Hamburg in answer to a letter which shortly after my arrival in Amsterdam I had mailed to Mr. Wendt. These gentlemen had credited me with 100 florins with which I could do as I pleased, even though they advised me to use the money wisely. This communication gave me another boost, for now I had gained a sure foothold through contact with a firm [the Amsterdam merchants L. Hoyack & Co.] so highly regarded in the mercantile world. The following morning I felt strong enough to leave the hospital where I had spent five days. I paid my debts of 2.50 florins and went to the Hoyack office. My face, disfigured from adhesive tape, I announced who I was, and my benefactors immediately addressed me by my name. I had to tell them my whole story from A to Z. This made them feel sorry for me and they declared that God must have *chosen me for great things*—they, for one, were quite certain that my mishaps would be the root of my future fortune. Kleinwort Brothers had highly recommended me to them, and they would do their utmost to take care of me. [They eventually gave young Schliemann a temporary job.] . . .

Living expenses were extremely high in Amsterdam, no matter how one tried to cut corners. I had to pay 8 guilders rent for a tiny furnished unheated room on the fifth floor. For the small iron stove I borrowed from a smith I had to put out 5 guilders for its use in winter. Coal, the local fuel, was also very costly. . . .

Since all entertainment was weighed in gold, I had no intention to participate in it. Plays were put on every night on magnificent stages in five languages. Concerts, dances, and masked balls took place all over, yet nowhere did a ticket cost less than 3 guilders. Friendships were made in coffee-houses, and since I did not visit any, I had no friend and lived quite isolated. Neither was I on intimate terms with any of my colleagues, because Hepner & Hoyack seemed to frown upon it.

My only pastime consisted in walking around town at night after the office closed and inspecting the splendidly lit streets and houses, for every street lantern and every commercial establishment, including the dairyman's, was beautifully illuminated by gas. I also enjoyed walking outside the Haarlem Gate in order to watch the many steam carriages of the Amsterdam-Haarlem Railway departing. Everything in Amsterdam was truly metropolitan. Every hairdresser had in his window four to six continuously revolving female dolls with the loveliest hairdos. . . .

The misfortune I suffered, fate seemed to have planned for my blessing and advantage. I now enjoyed vigorous health; indeed, I felt reborn. When I remembered how the previous winter I always wore two underdrawers, a cat's fur, and two woolen undershirts and nevertheless continued to spit blood and thought I had become consumptive, I was now a mystery to myself. But of one thing I was certain: the water cure I underwent in Rostock and the cold baths which I continued in Hamburg until November 24 hardened my body. Without them I doubt that I would have been able to withstand such terrible calamities. . . .

In my new [second] situation [with F. C. Quien] my work consisted in stamping bills of exchange and getting them cashed in the town, and carrying letters to and from the post-office. This mechanical occupation suited me, for it left me time to think of my neglected education.

First of all I took pains to learn to write legibly, and this I succeeded in doing after twenty lessons from the famous calligraphist Magnée, of Brussels. Afterwards, in order to improve my position, I applied myself to the study of modern languages. My annual salary amounted only to 800 francs (£32), half of which I spent upon my studies; on the other half I lived—miserably enough, to be sure. My lodging, which cost 8 francs a month, was a wretched garret without a fire, where I shivered with cold in winter and was scorched by the heat in summer. My breakfast consisted of rye-meal porridge, and my dinner never cost more than two-pence. But nothing spurs one on to study more than misery and the certain prospect of being able to release oneself from it by unremitting work. Besides, the desire of showing myself worthy of Minna created and developed in me a boundless courage.

I applied myself with extraordinary diligence to the study of English. Necessity taught me a method which greatly facilitates the study of a language. This method consists in reading a great deal aloud, without making a translation, taking a lesson every day, constantly writing essays upon subjects of interest, correcting these under the supervision of a teacher, learning them by heart, and repeating in the next lesson what was corrected on the previous day. My memory was bad, since from my childhood it had not been exercised upon any object; but I made use of every moment, and even stole time for study. In order to acquire a good pronunciation quickly, I went twice every Sunday to the English church, and repeated to myself in a low voice every word of the clergyman's sermon. I never went on my errands, even in the rain, without having my book in my hand and learning something by heart; and I never waited at the post-office without reading. By such methods I gradually strengthened my memory, and in three months' time found no difficulty in reciting from memory to my teacher, Mr. Taylor, in each day's lesson, word by word, twenty printed pages, after having read them over three times attentively. In this way I committed to memory the whole of Goldsmith's *Vicar of Wakefield* and Sir Walter Scott's *Ivanhoe*. From over-excitement I slept but little, and employed my sleepless hours at night in going over in my mind what I had read on the preceding evening. The memory being always much more concentrated at night than in the day-time, I *found these repetitions at night of paramount use.* Thus I succeeded in acquiring in half a year a thorough knowledge of the English language.

I then applied the same method to the study of French, the difficulties of which I overcame likewise in another six months. Of French authors I learned by heart the whole of Fénelon's *Aventures de Télémaque* and Bernardin de Saint Pierre's *Paul et Virginie*. This unremitting study had in the course of a single year strengthened my memory to such a degree, that the study of Dutch, Spanish, Italian, and Portuguese appeared very easy, and it did not take me more than six weeks to write and speak each of these languages fluently.

Whether from my continual readings in a loud voice, or from the effect of the moist air of Holland, my complaint in the chest gradually disappeared during my first year's residence in Amsterdam, and it has never returned. But my passion for study caused me to neglect my mechanical occupation in the office of Mr. F. C. Quien, especially as I began to consider it beneath me. My principals would give me no promotion; they probably thought that a person who shows his incapacity for the business of a servant in an office proves thereby his unfitness for any higher duties. At last, however, through the intercession of my worthy friends, Louis Stoll of Mannheim and J. H. Ballauf of Bremen, I had on the 1st of March, 1844, the good fortune to obtain a situation as correspondent and book-keeper in the office of Messrs. B. H. Schröder & Co. of Amsterdam, who engaged me at a salary of 1,200 francs (£48); but when they saw my zeal, they added 800 francs a year more by way of encouragement. This gener-osity, for which I shall ever be grateful to them, was in fact the foundation of my prosperity; for, as I thought that I could make myself still more useful by a knowledge of Russian, I set to work to learn that language also. But the only Russian books I could procure were an old grammar, a lexicon, and a bad translation of *Les Aventures de Télémaque*. In spite of all my enquiries, I could not find a teacher of Russian, since, with the exception of the Russian vice-consul, Mr. Tannenberg, who would not consent to give me lessons, there was no one in Amsterdam who understood a word of the language. So I betook myself to the study of it without a master, and, with the help of the grammar, I learned the Russian letters and their pronuncia-tion in a few days. Then, following my old method, I began to write short stories of my own composition, and to learn them by heart. As I had no one to correct my work, it was, no doubt, extremely bad; but I tried at the same time to correct my mistakes by the practical exercise of learning the Russian *Aventures de Télémaque* by heart. It occurred to me that I should make more progress if I had some one to whom I could relate the adven-tures of Telemachus; so I hired a poor Jew for four francs a week, who had to come every evening for two hours to listen to my Russian recitations, of which he did not understand a syllable.

As the ceilings of the rooms of the common houses in Holland consist of single boards, people on the ground-floor can hear what is said in the third storey. My recitations therefore, delivered in a loud voice, annoyed the other tenants, who complained to the landlord, and twice while study-ing the Russian language I was forced to change my lodgings. But these in-conveniences did not diminish my zeal, and in the course of six weeks I wrote my first Russian letter to Mr. Vasili Plotnikoff, the London agent for the great indigo-dealers, Messrs. M. P. N. Malutin Brothers, at Moscow, and I found myself able to converse fluently with him and the Russian merchants Matweieff and Froloff, when they came to Amsterdam for the indigo auctions. After I had completed my study of the Russian language, I began to occupy myself seriously with the literatures of the languages I had learned.

In January, 1846, my worthy principals sent me as their agent to St. Petersburg. Here, as well as in Moscow, my exertions were in the very first two months crowned with the fullest success, which far exceeded the most sanguine expectations of my employers and myself.

No sooner had I rendered myself indispensable to Messrs. B. H. Schröder & Co. in my new career, and thus obtained a practically independent position, than I hastened to write to the friend of the Meincke family, Mr. C. E. Laué of Neu Strelitz, describing to him all my adventures, and begging him to ask Minna at once for me in marriage. But, to my horror, I received a month later the heartrending answer, that she was just married.[12] I considered this disappointment at the time as the greatest disaster which could have befallen me, and I was for some time utterly unfit for any occupation and sick in bed. I constantly recalled to mind all that had passed between Minna and myself in early childhood, all our sweet dreams and vast plans, for the ultimate realization of which I now saw such a brilliant chance before me; but how could I think of realizing them without her participation? Then again I bitterly accused myself for not having demanded her in marriage before proceeding to St. Petersburg; but again I recollected that I could not have done so without exposing myself to ridicule, because while in Amsterdam I was only a clerk, and my position was a dependent one, subject to the caprice of my employers; besides, I was not sure of succeeding at St. Petersburg, where instead of success I might have made a complete failure. I fancied that neither could she be happy with anyone else besides me, nor

Street scene, St. Petersburg

III
AMERICAN INTERLUDE
1850–1852

Sacramento, where Schliemann established,
during the California Gold Rush, a prosperous
business dealing in gold bullion.

SCHLIEMANN HAD BARELY SET FOOT on Russian soil on January 30, 1846, when he blossomed into an enterprising commodity dealer. Nothing in his demeanor betrayed that only a few months before the poised international merchant had been a subaltern pen-pushing clerk. Attending to his transactions with dispatch as well as with Teutonic *Gründlichkeit*, he was soon recognized as an up and coming man in the St. Petersburg import market. Within little over a year (1847) he was admitted to the First Guild of Merchants, which greatly enhanced his stature and credit rating. His Russian peers took to him as one of their own. Not only could they converse freely with him in their own language, but they also appreciated his expansive, imaginative style and the verve with which he launched his business deals. Millionaires would invite him to their homes and country estates and present their daughters or nieces. Several offers of partnership were forthcoming. Meanwhile, Schliemann made bigger and bigger plans.

Though at least nominally an agent of the house of Schröder-Amsterdam (at 0.5 percent rate of commission) and of their affiliates in London, Hamburg, and elsewhere, Schliemann astutely built up his connections with other firms, some of which he had already contacted before going to Russia. He lost no time in casting out for more commodities in addition to his mainstay, indigo. Within a few months he was arranging for a large shipment of saltpeter from Chile, and with varying success he began to dabble in Rhine wine, jewels, sugar, tea, coffee, and dyewoods. Despite the subarctic cold, seven days after his arrival in St. Petersburg, he rushed to Moscow in an open sleigh. Three more visits followed the same year. Soon he was off to Western Europe.

On October 1, 1846, Schliemann went on what was to be one of his many long business trips via Lübeck and Hamburg to Amsterdam and then to the British Isles. In England, the industrial workshop of the world, technologically ahead of all other nations, he was overawed by the

59

machine shops, ironworks, steel bridges, locomotive factories, and shipyards. In the diary he began keeping then and kept during all his voyages, he espoused the ideology of progress evoked by this ingenuity of engineering that, he was certain, would transform the affairs of men on the planet within a few decades.

Schliemann felt very much at home in London. Forgetting for once the concerns of business and the noisy harbingers of progress, he discovered the British Museum. There he was, above all, spellbound by the "Egyptian things"—the mute mummies lying in their sarcophagi—and by the graceful ceramics from classical Greece and Rome. The Louvre in Paris further stimulated his newly reawakened antiquarian interests.

On the return trip he again touched German soil, but despite its proximity he refrained from visiting his native ground. Indeed, when passing the Mecklenburg coastline by boat, he had to confess, to his own amazement, that "it was with the utmost indifference that I gazed upon my native country."[1]

During the first year in St. Petersburg, Schliemann seems to have been in a state of euphoria. But there were also reverses. Not all the schemes he hatched came off. No wonder Messrs. Schröder got alarmed. His senior employer in Amsterdam wrote him unmistakably in June 1846: "Our worst fears have unfortunately come true. In your correspondence you take on a tone which no businessman would use. . . . Never tell us what we should do. . . . You have an opinion of your influence and power which we by no means share. . . ."[2] And a short while later J. W. Schröder of Hamburg really laid it on the line when he heard of the failure of one of the young man's projects: "We are not the least bit surprised, rather did we expect it all along. . . . You lack all knowledge of men and the world, prattle too much, have too high expectations, and are infatuated with brainless chimeras. . . . Because you think you have reached your goal, you become rude and arrogant toward your friends. . . . Take pains to become a sensible human being, acquire good, unassuming manners, don't dream of Spanish castles in the sky. . . . However, since I am confident that you will mature, I will give you another chance. I only hope that my associates agree with me. . . ."[3]

As in his later archaeological ventures, Schliemann was not one to be crushed by reverses for long. Neither would he admit his own inadequacies. He knew he was marked for success and somehow never failed to believe in his lucky star. But in both business and exploration, his periods of exuberance were rapidly replaced by moments of bleak despair. Soon it was the Schröders' turn to beg him not to be discouraged. "The world will not come to an end. Besides, we shall not let you down. . . . If, while you are with us, you experience a bad year, all necessary assistance shall be given you."[4]

Schliemann maintained good relations with the Schröders and remained their agent for many years. Long after he left the business he would keep in amicable contact with the scions of the great merchant family. However, observing due courtesies, he increasingly dealt with them as an equal; they became "associates" and "friends" rather than employers. When he thought the time was ripe, he asked, and was granted, a raise of his commission to 1 percent. His own enterprises flourished on the whole, even though he would spend anxious days when goods were delayed or prices fell on the world market. To his father he wrote with a shot of cynicism in February 1848: "Standing at my work desk from early morning to late at night, I am constantly racking my brain how I can fill my money bag through profitable speculations, no matter whether they will benefit or harm colleagues and competitors."[5]

With father, sisters, brothers, uncles, aunts, and cousins he constantly exchanged letters. Loyalty to his family, even though he had been cast adrift and left to his own resources at a tender age, was to Schliemann an article of faith. To the father to whom he owed next to nothing he wrote faithfully (though sometimes sounding himself like a father addressing a wayward son), sent presents, and supported him. Thus he reported to his father on the state of his youngest brother, Paul, born in 1831 and still a child, who was helping him with minor chores at his St. Petersburg office.[6]

Another younger brother, Louis (Ludwig), who resembled Schliemann in many ways but was more high-strung and erratic, had followed his example and emigrated to the Netherlands. For a while he worked for Schröder and supplied Heinrich with motley business intelligence. When Schliemann declined to take him into his Russian firm, Louis threatened to kill himself but then changed his mind and in June 1848 was off to America, "which, if I can help it, I never want to leave again. . . . Where a man counts only as man and only work bestows honor. And where those are present there is nobility."[7]

After drifting about in New York, Louis went to California via Cape Horn. He had been caught by gold fever and soon struck it rich. "Men coming to this country should bring every cent along, instead of leaving it at home. Independent fortunes have been made here in a few months and remain to be made for more than half a century. . . . Gold is all over the country and even in the mountains around San Francisco . . . ," he wrote Schliemann.[8] With his gold, Louis opened an inn which appears to have done very well. Within a few months he promised to send money to his family in Mecklenburg and to provide for his unmarried sisters.

The thought that his ne'er-do-well younger brother was accumulating a fortune faster than he may have ruffled Schliemann. Possibly he began to plan on going to California himself. But then came a thunderbolt: Louis, at the age of twenty-seven, had died on May 21, 1850, in Sacramento, allegedly of typhus (the immediate cause was an overdose of mercury given by the attending physician).

Schliemann decided to go to America, and in his "autobiography," which devotes only a paragraph of six lines to his American adventures, he wrote: "Not having heard of my brother, Louis Schliemann, who in the beginning of 1849 had emigrated to California, I went thither in the spring of 1850, and found that he was dead."[9] But this reference was patently wrong in almost every respect. Schliemann, evidently much shaken by the news, stayed on several months in St. Petersburg and did not leave for America until December 1850 to settle his brother's estate, look after his grave, and retrieve what he could for the benefit of his sisters.[10] He took his time to unwind his own affairs and convert his assets (some 50,000 German thalers) into transferable legal tender. In addition, he wrote to America to inquire about economic opportunities. He hinted that he was never to return to St. Petersburg. Despite his flourishing business in Russia, in the back of his mind he obviously had resolved to seek new opportunities in the gold-rich Pacific Eldorado.

Schliemann's journey to America was almost as eventful as his last attempt to cross the Atlantic. After brief stopovers in Amsterdam, to arrange his business affairs, and London, where he admired the Crystal Palace, "this stupendous masterpiece of modern art," he set sail from Liverpool in the elegantly appointed steamer *Atlantic*. But severe westerly gales struck the ship in midocean, both engines were disabled and she threatened to capsize. Provisionary sails were rigged and the ship was driven before the wind until the Irish coast was sighted. Schliemann and the other passengers disembarked at Queenstown and traveled to Dublin; about a week later, they set sail once again on the *Africa*. Schliemann complained that his accommodations were far inferior to those of the *Atlantic*, but with only moderately unfavorable weather to contend with, the *Africa* proved to be far more reliable, and he reached his destination safely.

Like so many Germans of his and a later generation, Schliemann felt drawn to America. Plans to emigrate as a very young man faltered only because of his father's intransigence. But once in command of his own resources, visits of long duration followed in swift succession. After being a Russian and before rediscovering his German ties, Schliemann thought of himself as American. While he would eventually renounce his Russian citizenship, he stayed an American to the end. One of his major works,

Mycenae—signed Dr. Henry Schliemann—bears the proud subscript "Citizen of the United States of America" in the American edition. Whenever in America, he seems to have felt like an American and was prone to speak of Americans as "we." California he was wont to call "our state." Even after archaeology claimed him for good, many of his projects (and investments) centered on America. To reside in New York, to farm in the prairie states, to own a factory or residential properties in Indianapolis—all these were at one time or another the focus of his ambition.

On all his travels in America, Schliemann wrote voluminous diaries which, unfortunately, remain largely unpublished, with the exception of his journal of his first residence in the United States in the years 1851 to 1852.[11] The eighty-page narrative was written in English, apart from a few Spanish insertions, and in addition to its fascinating picture of that tumultuous and colorful period in America's history, it reveals Schliemann's chameleon-like ability to instantly adopt, even in writing, the language of the environment he happened to find himself in. However, he probably "edited" his American diary after his return to Mother Russia. The frequent references to beautiful and peaceful St. Petersburg, "our" Czar's

The mail steamship *Atlantic*

wise rule, and Schliemann's firm intention to return to that blessed land undoubtedly represent later insertions.

Contrary to what he wrote in *Ilios,* Schliemann was not in California when that state was admitted to the Union (1850)—he got there a year later—and hence did not automatically acquire U.S. citizenship as he avowed. (He was naturalized in New York in 1869.)

Schliemann's picture of California ranges from the idyllic to the squalid, and, at last, his disillusionment with the golden state was complete. He had his fill of American sharpshooters and con men, who, however, he was proud to say, never got the better of him. Though he succeeded in doubling his money, he found everything around him precarious; he abhorred the climate, the crime in the streets, the moral latitude, and increasingly yearned for the law and order of St. Petersburg. And, erroneously as it turned out, he became convinced that an inevitable glut of gold production would lead to an economic setback which would be fatal to the Western state's prosperity and to his own business interests. That conviction may have sealed his decision to return to St. Petersburg, or at least to the Old World. On the first leg of that journey, recrossing the Isthmus of Panama, Schliemann would once again come close to disaster.

The rest of the trip proved less eventful. Schliemann visited Cuba, tarried in New York, and after crossing the Atlantic, took his leisure in England and France. In England, he befriended Dr. G. F. Collier, who was very impressed by Schliemann's ability to recite verbatim a speech he had heard the Hungarian patriot Kossuth make in Washington, D.C., but thought such feats a waste of intellect, which Schliemann should put to better use. Why not try his hand at writing?

JOURNEY TO CALIFORNIA

from *Schliemann's First*
Visit to America

On the 15th [February 1851] at 4 o'clock in the afternoon we came in sight of Zandy-hock [Sandy Hook] and entered the Bay of New York. . . . When about 3 miles from New York City we began to fire can[n]ons and to throw rockets, in order to give the inhabitants to understand that we brought some highly joyful intelligence. It was about 9 o'clock P.M. when we got into the steamer's resting-place at New Jersey-City [Jersey City]. . . .

I stopt at the Astor House, the grandest and most gigantic hotel I ever saw; it is provided with more than 300 bedrooms, besides many large saloons, smoking and private chambers. There is a large reading-room for the sole use of the boarders of the house, furnished with papers from all States of the Union. Patriotism does not allow any foreign papers. Each boarder pays $2½ a day for bedroom and attendance, breakfast, dinner, tea and supper. Wine is paid extra. I find the American table extremely comfortable and tasteful to me; in the morning I used to take ham and eggs, buckwheat cakes, fried hominy and chocolate. At dinner, oysterpies, soup, roastbeef, roast turkey, game and pudding. At 6 o'clock P.M. weak tea, and at 11 o'clock at night for supper cold turkey and ham.

The 16 Febry. was a Sunday and I went to church. . . . Afterwards I went to C. D. Behrens, 335 Houston Street, the former partner of my unfortunate brother, who was very much surprised to see me; I invited him to dine with me in the Astor House. . . .

New York is a very regularly built, nice, clean town and has many many elegant and even colossal buildings; but as a new city it can in no way be compared in architectural point of view to any of the grand European capitals. The houses are generally of brick, not covered with chalk [lime]. Of the streets, which are all very regular and well paved, the broadest and most elegant is the Broadway, which is about 3½ miles long, and passes [through] the whole town. There are four theatres, all of which are small, badly decorated, and little attended, for the bustling busy spirit of the Americans does not permit them to think of theatres. The only place of amusement most attended to is Barnum's Museum, where all sorts of ludicrous humbug is represented. Fellow's minstrels' concerts are also much visited; the musicians

Astor House, New York City

are all Negroes, who contrive to amuse the public by their music, their songs, and by all sorts of burlesque humbug. I cannot say that I like these American amusements, in which the Yankees find so great delight. On Monday, the 17th Feby. I visited the various houses for which I had letters of recommendation. On the 18th I was invited to a grand ball, which the Light-Guard gave in the Astor House, and which lasted till 5 o'clock in the morning.

There was a large congregation of Yankees' ladies. Be it that the American beauties do not take enough exercise in the open air, or be it for the quick change of the temperature, the fair sex fades here extremely soon, and usually at the age of 22 they look just as old and worn out as they are beautiful and symmetrical at 16 and 18. The men are with few exceptions of good constitution, but thin and weak as compared to the English; they are, if properly approached, very frank and communicative, and regarding industry and assiduity, there is hardly a people on the earth's surface who surpass them; the fair sex, though a little more solid than the French, is here by far lighter than the daughters of fair England, and an overvivacity and a very great tendency to the frivolous and amusing are the chief characteristic of the Yankees' daughters.

Having after most careful investigation ascertained that the best investment for funds for exportation to California is gold coin, I entrusted all my funds to the care of Messrs. James King & Son, giving them at the same time all necessary instructions how to act in my behalf. On the 20th Febry. at 9 A.M. I left by the railway for the south, and arrived at 1½ o'clock at Philadelphia and at 7½ o'clock in the evening at Baltimore, where I stopt for the night at Barnum's Hotel. The American railroads are merely laid out with the design to make money, and not the least notice is taken as to convenience and accommodations for passengers; you see here neither stationhouses nor watchmen, and everywhere only one track of rail on the railroads. Alas! but too frequently great misfortunes happen in consequence. . . .

The cars are very long, and the entrance is from both ends; in the midst of each car is a small iron stove. There is little or no regularity prevailing, which is the more awkward and proves the more frequently fatal, as there are numerous broad rivers to pass, where the cars stop and the passengers are taken over by steamers; on these occasions the rush is always immense, and as if a race were to be won, the passengers storm on with mad fury out of the cars on the steamers, and from these again into the cars. These latter are roughly made . . . and a long corridor as it were, conducts through the cars, so that you can walk through 10 or 12 cars without interruption. The seats are on both sides, and on each bank sit 2 persons. The leaning can be turned over, so that 4 can sit together if they choose proper. In each train there is a smoking car.

In Baltimore I enjoyed a good oyster supper, and the following morning a good oyster breakfast, and on the 21st February at 9 A.M. I started by rail for Washington. . . .

On my arrival at Washington, I went immediately to the sessions of Congress in the Capitol, a magnificent building on the top of a hill. With the most vivid interest and the sincerest delight, I heard the powerful speeches of Henry Clay, Senator of Kentucky, [John Parker] Hale of New Hampshire, [James Murray] Mason of Virginia, [Stephen A.] Douglas of Illinois, [John] Davis of Massachusetts, etc. The chief topic of discussion was the late Negro riot at Boston. . . . In the evening at 7 o'clock I drove to the President of the United States, to whom I made my introduction by stating that the great desire to see this beautiful country of the West, and to make the acquaintance of the great men who govern it had induced me to come over from Russia, and that I now deemed it my first and most agreeable duty to pay my respects to the President. He received me most kindly presented me to his wife, daughter, and father, and I had 1½ hours conversation with them.

The President is a very plain and friendly looking man of about 50; his name is Fillmore. His wife is about 46, a very noble and friendly looking lady; his daughter may be 17 years and is looking rather green [pale?]. At 8½ opened the "levee" with the President, and there assembled more than 800 persons, from all parts of the Union, all eager to see and speak to the President. This latter introduced me to Mr. Webster, Secretary of State; to Mr. Clay, Senator of Kentucky; and to several others. The President's palace is a most magnificent mansion; there are no sentinels to watch and bar the doors; there exist no ceremonies to which the stranger has to submit to be presented to the first magistrate. I staid there till 11 o'clock.

On Saturday, 22nd Febry. I visited the great Patent Office, where patterns are exhibited of all inventions upon which a patent has been granted by the United States government. At 10 o'clock A.M. I went in a coach from the Capitol to the Potomac River, where I embarked on board a steamer to go down and see Mount Vernon. It being Washington's birthday, there were numerous passengers. We arrived at Mount Vernon at 12 o'clock, and remained there about 1½ hours. Washington's mansion is a plain building, 2 stories high, erected in his plantation called Mount Vernon; close to the house are the tombs of him and his wife. He died in 1799. The house is occupied and guarded by a Negro family, slaves to W. Here and there in the gardens are stationed Negro boys, offering for sale lemons and sticks, which, according to their assertions, were pluck[ed] and cut from trees planted by the great Washington. My fellow-passengers bought of these objects with great eagerness, and were anxious to pick out from the wall which surrounds Washington's tomb little stones which they . . . were going to preserve as holy relics. We then visited Fort Washington, a small fortress on the Potomac River, and returned to town at 3½ o'clock. After dinner I went to the National Theater, which had only been recently erected for the concerts of Jenny Lind; a roughly made building, with still worse decorations. The house was thronged, for the celebrated actress Davenport was to play. The actors and actresses knew their parts very well by heart, and I must avow that I never amused myself better. In the American theaters there is no prompter.

On Sunday the 23rd Febry. I went 2 times to church, and visited also the grand marble monument which is now being erected by wilful [voluntary?] contributions to the memory of great Washington. As the necessary funds can be collected but very slowly, the construction of the monument proceeds also very slowly, and it will take still more than 21 years to complete it. Every state of the Union has contributed one large piece of marble, upon which is marked the name of the state. When completed the monument will be 576 feet high, and will resemble an immense pyramid. . . .

[Back in New York] on the 26th Febry. I went again to the sev-

Washington, D.C.

eral parties to whom I had been introduced by letters from Europe, gathered from everyone some subsequent introductions for San Francisco, settled my money matters . . . and on the 28th Febry. at 3 o'clock in the afternoon I went on board the *Crescent City* with destination for Chagres [Panama]. Thousands had gathered on the pier, partly to bid a last farewell to their parting friends, and partly led by curiosity. Such was the throng of the multitude, that with the utmost difficulty only I could get on board the steamer. . . . [The trip to California, part of which was accomplished by crossing on foot the Cordilleras de los Andes at the Isthmus of Panama, was full of discomforts and dangers, and took more than a month.]

Monday 31 March. This morning at 10½ we stopt in the port of San Diego, a miserable little place. San Diego is divided into 3 parts, of which a few wooden houses are built on the bank of the harbour, a few more a little farther up the coast, and the bulk of the town about 4 miles from the stopping [landing] place of the vessels. The harbour is but small, however 30 to 50 feet deep and enclosed by huge rocks. The surface of the water is covered with a sort of very long yellow seaweed, called kelp, which grows sometimes hundred feet long. Having only one passenger to put ashore, and to deliver the mail, we did not throw the anchor and went on again after 1½ hours stoppage. . . .

Tuesday 1 April. This morning at 5 we passed the beautiful island Santa Barbara, consisting of 7 huge rocks, and presenting the most grand and picturesque sight. At first comes a high quadrangular rock forming an immense arch or thoroughfare, large and deep enough for any man-of-war to pass, then comes a high rock in the form of an immense cone, then a mountain, then again a cone, again a mountain, again a cone and again a mountain. Shortly after this we saw the island [of] Santa Cruz, then San Miguel, and then Santa Rosa, all of them consisting of high rocks. . . .

Wednesday 2 April. We see this morning the Californian coast involved in a thick fog, which is said to be peculiar to the environs of S.F. [San Francisco].

In the afternoon at 2½ o'clock we entered the Golden Gate (consisting of 2 immense pieces of rock in the form of a gate), and proceeded at a fast rate into the harbor of San Francisco, which is enclosed and sheltered by huge mountains, and large enough to contain all the fleets of the globe. Soon we saw the outskirts of the city of S.F. and soon afterwards the city itself. More than 800 large 3-mast ships of all nations were lying close to the city, and presented a grand and beautiful appearance. Owing to the innumerable masts, little could be seen of the town ere we landed in a boat.

The rush of the passengers to get off was so great, that not without difficulty and danger could I get away. . . . For putting ashore I was to pay

$1.50; for carrying the luggage to the hotel, $2.50. I put up at the Union Hotel, which is the best in this city. For a small bedroom on the 4th floor, 6 feet long by 5 feet broad, I have to pay $7 per day, board included. The streets are paved with planks; the houses, for the most part, are of wood. The new arrival is amazed when he looks upon this bustling, busy city of 40,000 inhabitants, and when he thinks that it has taken [come into] existence only 18 months ago, for before that there were only a few frame buildings.

GOLD RUSH DAYS

*from Schliemann's First
Visit to America*

Sacramento City, April 26 [1851]. Almost four weeks have past since [my arrival in California], and great changes have taken place. . . . After having looked around and come to the conviction that I ought to take several weeks in order to get well acquainted with the locality and the mode of doing business in this quarter, I thought I should do as well to go for a couple of days to Sacramento, to look after the affairs of my unfortunate brother, who died here May 21 last year. I therefore crossed again the bay on a steamer and went up the Sacramento River. . . . After much difficulty I found out the tomb of my brother, and gave $50 to the undertaker to get made a beautiful marble tombstone with inscription thereon, which has since been executed in San Francisco, and the tombstone stands now on the grave.

Having looked here to business and ascertained that I [would] do better to invest my capital in this city than at San Francisco, I decided to settle down here and therefore went back to S.F. on the 7th April to fetch my luggage. On the 9th inst. I returned to Sacramento and have lived here ever since. I must avow that the climate agrees perfectly well with me—the days are hot, the nights cool and refreshing, and I like it much better than at S.F., where a strong gale blows all day long.

Sacramento lies in the midst of the Sacramento Valley, which comprizes abt. 360 square miles and resembles an immense garden covered with beautiful trees and green underwood at all seasons of the year. An immense levee or dike has been erected at great expense to protect the city from inundation, which would otherwise occur almost every year, for from the melting of the snow in the mountains the waters of the river assume a vast magnitude. Though this city is still in its infancy, it contains already abt. 10,000 inhabitants and the population is daily increasing. The streets are broad and very regular, but of course not paved and with very few exceptions all houses are of wood. The Americans are extremely smart in the art of tracing out towns, and to this city they have given 55 immense streets, commencing northward by A and terminating southward by Y; beginning westward by 1st and terminating eastward by 31. Thus it is no wonder that most part of our city is covered with meadows, trees, and underwood, and offers to the sportsman an inexhaustible stock of rabbits, coyotes, and quails. The great plague of this place are the rats, of which there are millions.

I thought to find here great wealth, but I was much mistaken; the wild speculations of various kind, but especially those in real estate, have killed almost everybody, and men worth a year ago hundred thousands have now nothing. . . . In no country of the world have I found so much selfishness and such immense love of money as in this Eldorado. With an American, money goes over [above] everything in the world, and the desire to attain it as fast as possible brings forth his indescribable, his boundless energy. His enterprising spirit, too hot for mature consideration, boldly goes ahead, and however frequently defeated by miscalculations, he as often tries to go ahead again; an American can never become daunted. . . .

The foreigner who comes to this country is lost in admiration and esteem for the American race, in contemplating the wonder works, which have been achieved here in less than two years. But these sentiments soon disappear, when the new arriver becomes thoroughly acquainted with the character of the Californian Yankees, when he sees himself surrounded by a gang of scoundrels, when he sees that all is based here on swindling, that all is abominable falsehood, fraud and humbug, or in plain Californian: that all is calculated to "shave."

May 2d. Every day furnishes me new and striking proofs of the sharp and cunning character of the people I am doomed to live with. At first they surround me with politeness and civilities; make me the trustee of a thousand little confidences and when they think they have inspired me with the fullest confidence then they make an attempt to cheat me. As I used to think every one here to be a rogue, and as I have all my eyes about me, so they fail in their attempt, but not yet daunted they try a second time to impose upon me. Being again frustrated in their hopes, they leave me entirely. . . .

14 May. Having determined to settle down permanently in Sacramento City, I thought it the greatest duty incumbent upon me to travel through the country, to visit the various towns and villages in the mining districts, to inspect the diggings and the different ways in which gold is won, in order to gather at least some superficial idea of this country's wealth and to see the resources of this city. With this intention I started on the 14 May at 9½ o'clock in the morning by the steamer *Dana* to Marysville.

It was a fine but very cold day and I froze, though wrapped up in 2 blankets. After having gone up the Sacramento River for 30 miles and left to the right hand the American River, we went up the Feather River, leaving the Sacramento to the left. Having proceeded on the former for 20 miles, we entered the Yuba and after having run in it for ½ m. we landed at Marysville. Fare on the steamer, $5. We passed on the road the cities of Nicolaus, Plumas and Suttersville, of which a year ago were entertained very high ideas, but which have never become and will never become anything. At Suttersville I saw a great many of the native Indians, who half or entirely naked were running about their dwellings, consisting of heaps of earth. . . .

Wishing to see the beautiful Sonoma Valley, which I had heard highly praised, I went to San Francisco on Monday, May 26, at 2 o'clock in the afternoon, and put up at the Hotel Rassette-House [Russ House?]. . . . The steamer having been announced in the newspaper as sailing on the 27th, I arrived at the place from which it was to start at six in the morning, but there was no steamer there, and they told me that I had come a day early. And so I was forced to wait in San Francisco the entire day. I had nothing to do, and was completely bored. We left finally at 9 o'clock in the morning, May 28. There being a strong contrary wind, we proceeded very slowly, and I should have been bored to death if I had not met on board Prof. F. G. Reeger of Sonoma, a very interesting man, who had traveled a great deal and seen much of the world. I don't think I have ever seen a man so likeable, affable and wise as Mr. Reeger. With equal facility he spoke English, French, German, Italian, Portuguese, Spanish, Dutch, and without doubt is as deeply conversant with the Greek and Latin languages. Inasmuch as foreign languages have always given me great pleasure, I took extraordinary delight in speaking with Mr. Reeger in different idioms, and thus the time passed very quickly. We arrived at the landing-place at five in the evening, and were taken in a carriage to Sonoma, a little village with four or five hundred inhabitants.

The beautiful Sonoma Valley delighted me with its millions of flowers and the fresh healthy air that one breathes there. The land is very fertile, and Señor Vallejo produced in a small garden more than fifteen thousand pesos worth of wine. Certainly if the gold-mines had not been discovered, the land here would sell at a very high figure, but since labor now costs very much, no one thinks of agriculture, and the land has no price at all. For my part, I would not wish to live in Sonoma, but there are some who prefer the quiet of the fields to the bustle of the large cities.

I departed from Sonoma on Saturday the 31st of May by the stage for Napa where we had lunch, and at five in the evening arrived at Benicia, which I left at half past six in the evening by the steamer *Senator*, and arrived at Sacramento at half past one.

My only occupation here being to lend money on mortgages on land and houses, I have nothing to occupy myself with, and since from my youth I have become accustomed to work from morning till night, I cannot describe the impatience and boredom which torment me. At the same time the heat during the day is unbearable, and causes me to suffer a great deal, because I am very full-blooded. The society of Sacramento is composed of adventurers, whose sole ambition and desire is to enrich themselves at another's expense. There is no company here to my taste, there are no ways of amusing myself, and with all my heart I wish to return to Europe as soon as possible. But since the journey from St. Petersburg and the transportation of the money here has cost me so much, I should like to recover the large expense, and return via China. . . .

San Francisco, June 4th, 1851. A most horrible disaster has befallen this City! a conflagration greater than any of the preceding fires has reduced nearly the whole city to ashes.

I arrived here last night at 10½ o'clock and put up at the Union Hotel on the Plaza. I may have slept a quarter of an hour, when I was awoke by loud cries in the street: "fire, fire" and by the awful sounds of the alarm-bell. I sprung up in all haste and looking out of the window I saw that a frame building only 20 or 30 paces from the Union Hotel was on fire. I dressed in all haste and run out of the house, but scarcely had I reached the end of

The San Francisco fire of 1851

Clay Street when I saw already the Hotel on fire from which I had just run out. Pushed on by a complete gale the fire spread with an appalling rapidity, sweeping away in a few minutes whole streets of frame buildings. Neither the iron houses nor the brickhouses (which were hitherto considered as quite fireproof) could resist the fury of the element; the latter crumbled together with incredible rapidity, whilst the former got red-hot, then white-hot and fell together [collapsed] like card-houses. Particularly in the iron houses people considered themselves perfectly safe and they remained in them to the last extremity. As soon as the walls of the iron houses [were] getting red-hot, the goods inside began to smoke, [and] the inhabitants wanted to get out, but usually it was already too late, for the locks and hinges of the doors having extended [expanded] or partly melted by the heat, the doors were no more to be opened. Sometimes by burning their hands and arms people succeeded to open the doors and to get out, but finding themselves then surrounded by an ocean of flames they made but a few paces, staggered and fell, rose again and fell again in order not to rise any more. It was tried in vain to arrest the progress of the fire by the blowing up of houses with gunpowder.

Wishing to avoid dangers I went up Montgomery Street and ascended Telegraph Hill which is a mountain abt. 300 feet high close to the city. It was a frightful but sublime view, in fact the grandest spectacle I ever enjoyed. The fire continued to spread in all directions sweeping away the whole of Washington, Kearny, Montgomery, California, Sansome, and many other streets, and, except a few houses on Battery Street, Bush Street, and on the Hillside, the whole beautiful city was burned down. The roaring of the storm, the crack[l]ing of the gunpowder, the cracking of the falling stonewalls, the cries of the people and the wonderful spectacle of an immense city burning in a dark night all joined to make this catastrophe awful in the extreme.

A report having spread out among the people that the fire had been caused by French incendiaries, the scorn of the enraged populace fell upon the French and many a poor French chap was thrown headlong in the flames and consumed.

I remained for the night in the restaurant on Telegraph Hill and went at 6 in the morning down to the city. It was a horrible sight to see the smouldering ashes and ruins of this a day before so flourishing city. Whilst I saw a great many Germans, Frenchmen, Englishmen and other foreigners half in despair sitting and weeping on the ashes of their destroyed property, the Americans never daunted, laughing and joking among themselves just as if nothing had happened, went boldly ahead to construct new houses and I saw them in many places at 6 o'clock in the morning busy to lay on the still hot ashes of their former buildings the foundations for new ones. In the morning from 6 till 10 it is very hot in San Francisco; then all at once a strong gale springs up and from 10 A.M. off the cold increases till 3 o'clock in the morning, so that it is impossible to walk here during the day after 10 or during the night without a very thick overcoat.

July 31. Since writing the foregoing pages my position in the world has undergone a most memorable change to my advantage.

Having during my recent excursion in the mining districts fully satisfied myself as to the enormous wealth of this country and the immense resources of Sacramento City, I established here already in the beginning of June a banking-house for the purchase of gold dust and the sale of "exchange" on the United States and Europe. I have got two clerks, one an American of the name of A. K. Grim and native from Cleveland in Ohio; the other a Spaniard, Miguel de Satrustegui, native of San Sebastian in Biscaya (Old Spain); to each of them I pay $250 (abt. 360 rubles silver) per month. My office is in the house on the corner of Front and J. Streets, which being built entirely of stone and iron, is considered perfectly fireproof. . . .

Gold dust comes in plentifully and I buy on an average 5 puds [about 150 pounds] per day. My purchases go for the most part to the house of Rothschild at London, whose branch-establishment at San Francisco supplies me by every night's steamer with the necessary coin.

The continued great heat from 100 to 125 degrees Fahrenheit which accelerates the decomposition of animal and vegetable matter, and the exhalation of the many swamps and ponds with stagnant water all around the town—all this contributes to infest the air and to produce much sickness. Ague, isthmus-fever, diarrhea, dysentery, erysipelas, etc., are taking away hundreds of hopeful men and quickly people our cemetery, whose number of graves is several times larger than the number of the population of our city, though the latter was only founded some 3 years ago.

The thieves of this country having invented the sling shot, which ensures additional success to their criminal industry, great caution is now requisite and my 2 clerks and myself go night and day armed with Colt's revolving-pistols (each of which can kill 5 men in as many seconds) and long bowie-knives. I always get up at 5 o'clock in the morning, take at 5½ my breakfast at the Orleans Hotel and open my office at 6 o'clock to shut it at 10 o'clock in the evening. During the whole day my office is crowded with people and I seldom get my dinner before 8 o'clock at night.

1 September. . . . My business is now on an enormous scale and my profits are large. If in former years I had known that I should one day gain only one quarter of what I earn now, I should have thought myself the happiest of men, but now I feel myself very unfortunate, since I am separated by a

distance of 18,000 versts [some 11,000 miles] from St. Petersburg where all
my hopes, all my desires are concentrated. In fact, in the midst of the hurricanes on the roaring oceans, in dangers and hardships, in toil and difficulties,
in the whirlwind of amusements and in the bustle of business my beloved
Russia, my charming St. Petersburg is constantly before my eyes. Whilst
here in Sacramento I can every moment expect to be murdered or robbed,
I can in Russia sleep tranquilly in my bed without any fear for my life or
property, for thousand eyes of justice watch there over the peaceful inhabi-
tant. Whilst nearly the whole western Europe is constantly alarmed by
impending disturbances, Russia (by far the most powerful and the largest
of all empires that ever existed or that will ever exist) beams with the
bright ray of eternal peace thanks to its wise and most glorious Emperor
Nicolas. It is not without immense gratification and pride that I witness
the great admiration and reference [reverence] with which the Americans
speak of our great monarch.

My bank is from early till late constantly jammed, crammed and
rammed full of people from all nations and I have to speak all the day long
in 8 languages. In fact if I knew a hundred languages it would not be sufficient
to speak to every one in his native tongue. The people I have most to deal

A California mining town during the Gold Rush

with are Americans, Mexicans and Chinamen, but the last mentioned bring but little gold to market and I have never been able to buy from a Chinaman more than 5 oz. at a time. The Chinamen who come to this country are a very harmless, honest and industrious set of people, and I never heard of any fraud being committed by any one of them. . . .

The Mexicans are a lazy and false [deceitful?] class of people without the least education and I never saw any one of them who was able to write his name; the lower and middling classes of Mexicans cover themself instead of coat and waistcoat with gaudy colored, embroidered blankets called "sarapes," which mode of dress is peculiar to all Spanish races of South America, but of different color. . . . From New Granada,[1] Peru and Chile there have also many thousands come over to California. The New Granadians are of the same character and habits as the Mexicans, whereas the Peruvians and Chileans are a good natured very industrious race of people, particularly the latter who are celebrated for their great assiduity, perseverance and gentlemanly behaviour. Alas! the Chileans are the only nation which has derived great profit by their independence from Spain.

The Kanakas, inhabitants of the Sandwich Islands, of which likewise thousands have made this country their asylum, are of brown color; their extreme laziness and ignorance does not allow them to apply themselves to any work whatever and they live from robbing and marauding. But the meanest and most disgusting people I ever saw are the Californian Indians, who are of copper-red color and stand but very little above the beasts, of which they have the habits. They are of small height and have most deformed features; they have thick black hair of which also the forehead is overgrown as far as the eyes. They are extremely dirty and live like ants in heaps of earth in which they literally roast, the fire being kindled in the midst of the earthen hut and only a small opening practiced at the top for the passage of the smoke. They are constantly armed with bows and quivers filled (stuck) with arrows and are a thievish miserable race. All of them are attacked by venerian sickness, which the baby sucks with the milk of the mother, or, as medical men affirm, of which he is attacked in the mother's womb.

1 November. I have just recovered from a severe fever which has confined me to bed for nearly 3 weeks. I caught it on the 4th [of] October with frequent vomiting and chills [alternating] in quick succession with great heat. On the 5th my whole body was covered with yellow spots and from the 6th to the 20th I was lying in continual ravery. My accommodation and attendance was most miserable indeed my bed being in the office of which the fore- and back-doors are constantly open. My physicians did not administer me anything but quinine and calomel, but in spite of this poisonous medicine my strong constitution triumphed at last and I am now again

feeling quite smart [chipper]. My brother died here 1½ year ago from the very same sickness and according to the doctors' assertions there is no chance for my recovery if the fever catches me a second time. . . .

Sacramento, February 17th. A heavy rain storm has set in upon us a fortnight ago and has continued since without intermission, in consequence of which the miners in the dry-diggings have now a great abundance of water and are reaping rich harvests. The waters both in the American and Sacramento Rivers are rising rapidly and if the storm continues but for a few days longer, the artificial embankments which surround the city will be put to a severe test.

I believe that nowhere in the world gambling is carried on to a more alarming extent than in this city and the gambling houses, of which there are a dozen, are night and day crowded with people, principally miners, who are losing here in a few minutes what they have accumulated during years of hard labor and privations. How immense the persons are who make gambling their profession is evident from the fact that when I first came to this city $8,000 *monthly* rent was paid for one gambling-table in the Eldorado Saloon. . . .

Sacramento, March 8th. Since writing the above the incessant rain had caused the waters of the rivers to rise uninterruptedly, till they reached last night an awful height being in different places level with the "levee." Last night at 12½ o'clock we were suddenly awoke by the tolling of the alarm bell and made aware of the impending danger. The levee on the Sacramento had given way in one small place, and the opening became every moment larger. I ran to the place of the disaster and assisted in stopping the opening, but all endeavors were fruitless and the water widened it every moment more and more and gushed through with increasing impetuosity. All at once a large piece of the levee on which we stood was loosened under our feet and gave way with a tremendous crash. I was with a number of others thrown into the water and taken away with the current for a considerable distance. We had some difficulty to get out after a most disagreeable bath of muddy water and some bruises and contusions. The streets of the city filled with great rapidity; in some places the water stood 10 to 12 feet deep and people had to save themselves on the 2d floor of the houses. The loss of goods damaged or lost by the fire was most enormous. The house where I lived being built upon a small elevation, I had in the bank no water, the latter coming only up to the level of the ground floor.

As soon as the terrors of the first impression caused by the flood had passed, people thought of diverting themselves and to make the best of it. A great number of small flat boats were made in all haste of planks; rafts were put together and soon the communication was everywhere restored.

The streets presented a most burlesque appearance; here a horse dragging a raft with people, there a man in a cask rowing with some pieces of wood, there some boats capsizing, etc. Some people are said to have made a hundred dollars in a single day by conveying people across the streets. . . .

San José, March 30. I was fortunate enough to catch the fever again on the 17 inst., and after having for several days been tormented by chills and vomiting, with yellow spots over all my body and in the impossibility to get up from bed, finding [I found] myself in a complete state of exhaustion and frequent ravery. My clerks in conformity to the directions previously given by me for such an event, wrapped me up in blankets and sent me in a senseless [unconscious] state under the attendance of a servant by the steamer down to San Francisco and thence by a coach to San José. Till the 28 inst. I have been lying in a most desperate state and in almost continual ravery, but at last my strong constitution bore off the victory and already today I have been able to get up for a couple of hours. If my convalescence continues I shall probably return the day after tomorrow to Sacramento, give over my business to Mr. B. Davidson, agent for Rothschild at San Francisco and return as soon as possible to my beloved Russia, for I feel I should not survive if I caught another time the fever.

Sacramento, April 7th. On passing through San Francisco on 2 inst. I represented to Mr. B. Davidson the impossibility of my remaining any longer in the poisonous climate of Sacramento and requested him to take over my business without any further responsibility for myself, to which he

San Jose, California

consented and he came up yesterday to settle our accounts. Everything having now been settled and arranged between us, I go by this day's steamer with aforesaid friend down to San Francisco and leave to morrow by the steamer *Golden Gate* for Panama. . . .

In spite of my frequent severe illness and the frequently pretty large deficiencies which I found in my cash [box], and which I can only attribute to the dishonesty of my clerks, I have all reason to be perfectly satisfied with my success in California and most assuredly among those who leave this country there is hardly one in a hundred thousand who has done as well as myself. Nothing exceeds my joy and exultation in finding myself away from California, which seemed destined to become my grave. . . .

Panama, April 24th. We anchored this afternoon at 6 o'clock in the bay of Panama abt. 2 miles from the city and were immediately surrounded by a large number of boats to take us off. But we could not leave the steamer before the harbor-master came on board, which lasted till 7½ o'clock. I did not get away before 8 o'clock. I was with six other passengers in one boat. When we were abt. 200 paces from the shore some 20 naked natives threw themselves in the water, and approached us swimming tendering their services to carry our luggage to any place in the town where we might wish to stop. But when we refused to let take it before reaching the shore, they seized our things with impetuosity, the one taking a trunk, the other a carpetbag, the other a hatbox, and having swum with them ashore they run then away with them and disappeared in the dark of the night. Several of my fellow-passengers were robbed in this way of all they had earned in California. But as to myself, I was prepared for these tricks and sitting on my luggage with my revolving pistol in one hand and my dagger in the other I threatened to shoot or stab the first man who attempted to carry off anything of my luggage. After having fairly landed I engaged two men at 1 dollar each to take my trunks to the hotel and watching them closely and menacing to blow out the brains of the first who would attempt to run away, I at lost [last] got safely to the American Hotel, where I got very bad accommodation for the night and stinking victuals.

Hoping to find a steamer on the Atlantic side and being afraid that the rainy season would soon render the roads across the mountains impassible, I and Mr. Livingston [a fellow passenger from California] in company of many hundred others set off on the slippery and perilous way. I had 3 mules, for which I paid $40. The rain continued to pour down in torrents so that soon we had not a bit of dry cloth on. The small mountain gulches, brooks, and rivulets had grown up to rapid streams, and the narrow mule track was slippery in the extreme, particularly on the declivity of the mountains. The

Panama Railroad

mule is a wonderfully clever beast; when we came on mules' back to a mountain gulch or rivulet resting on large slippery stones, then the mule looks attentively for a few seconds in the water, draws his four legs together and slips down the stone, and then putting his foot on some crevice or unequality of the opposite stone he jumps out of the dilemma with great agility. Sometimes my bridle tore and then the mule feeling himself free, immediately jumped into the thicket to feed on some foliage and I had then to glide instantly backward down to avoid certain destruction, for I should have been litterally hanged in the thick branches entertwined with ivy.

Quite exhausted by fatigue we at last reached Gorgona by 6½ P.M., and I with many others put up at the Railroad Hotel, where I slept on my trunks. Next morning (26 April) at 5 o'clock I was awoke by the cries of an Irishman who, having drunk rather too big a draught the night before, was robbed of his trousers containing a purse with sum [the sum of] 500 dollars. The city police was called in, but all searches were in vain. . . . At abt. 8 o'clock I with some 7 other passengers hired at the rate of 2 dollars each a boat made of a hollow tree and went down on the Chagres River to Frijol, whence we proceeded by the railway to a spot called Aspinwall on Navy Bay which is part of the Carabian [Caribbean] Sea. . . .

We expected for certain to find a steamer in Navy Bay, but to our utmost vexation and disappointment there was none, the *Crescent City* having gone the same morning. We found ourselves in the most miserable situation imaginable, for the rain poured down in torrents and no house was there to give us shelter, only one house having as yet been erected for the American consul. Thus we made the best of it and camped under palm trees.

I spread my blankets on my trunks and slept on them in spite of the incessant rain.

Next morning, our first care was to obtain something to eat, for not having got anything since we left Gorgona, all of us experienced an awful hunger. But, alas, food was nowhere to be got and in the extremity of our position we killed an immense lizard, which we ate raw with the same voracious appetite as if it had been a roasted turkey. . . . On the 27th we made of palm leaves and palm branches some huts or shelters, through which however the rain filtered incessantly. On the same day at 6 o'clock P.M. the railway train brought the remainder of the passengers per *Golden Gate* amounting in all to abt. 1,300 persons, which number was increased by the arrival at Panama of two more steamers, the passengers of which were brought down on the 28th and 30th April by the railwaycars and thus on the 30th our number altogether might amount to abt. 2,600.

The incessant rain rendered it utterly impossible for us to kindle fire and unable to procure us any other victuals we fed on the raw meat of lizards, monkeys, turtles, mules, and crocodiles, which latter is considered as a great delicacy among the natives of this country and particularly the tail.

Crossing the Isthmus.

Our position was the most horrible imaginable and our sufferings increased every moment. Ever since we left Panama none of us had any dry clothes on and we had no means to protect ourselves against the rainstorm which continued to pour upon us in all its intensity. Hundreds of us were attacked by the isthmus-fever, diarrhea, dysentery and [the] ague, and died after a day or two of cruel suffering. The dead remained where they were, because none of us could or would bury them. The fetid odor and poisonous miasma arising from the quick putrification and decomposition of the dead bodies of men and beasts infested still more the unwholesome state of the atmosphere. But all the above torments and sufferings were but trifling to the pain we had to endure from the mosquitos, which surrounded us night and day by myriads and did not cease to torment us by their atrocious sting.

Like a crazy man have I frequently weltered in the mud without being able to free myself of this most horrible of plagues. Many of my fellow-passengers rubbed themselves the whole body with mercury in order to get rid of the mosquitos, but I would not do it. Already at the end of January, in consequence of the great deal of mercury which had been administered to me by the Californian physicians, a small wound sprung up on my left leg, to which however I paid no attention to it as it did not cause me any pain. Even when I left California the wound was but trifling; but as soon as we passed Cape Lucas on the Pacific Ocean and entered the tropics the wound became much worse and grew daily more dangerous until the Isthmus of Panama, where it assumed a most serious character and caused me the most atrocious pains, which I contrived to linger a little by rubbing with mercury. The wound enlarged daily and the flesh fell off for a considerable distance and the bare bone was visible.

Many of my fellow-passengers were killed by the bite of scorpions and snakes (particularly rattlesnakes) which abound in these regions.

Thus I spent fully 14 days in wet clothes and camped 12 days (from 26 April till 8th May) on a swamp, being night and day exposed to the rain which continued to fall upon us in torrents and against which we had no means to protect ourselves; being deprived of all food except the raw meat of lizards, crocodiles, turtles, monkeys, etc., with which my fellow-passenger Livingston supplied me; being brought to despair by the mosquitos; expecting every moment death either by gangrene which seemed going to join [attack] my wound in the leg, or by the multitude of sicknesses to which I saw hundreds of my fellow-passengers falling victims, or by the bite of snakes and scorpions, of which I saw so many a poor fellow perish—thus thousands of miles from my beloved St. Petersburg, thousands of miles from those dear to my heart. I lay more dead than alive and without being able to move on account of my leg wound. In this horrible situation all human feeling forsook us and we sunk below the beast. We became so familiarized with death, that it lost for us all its terror, that we began to like it and to look upon it as a lingering of our sufferings. Thus it came that we laughed and amused ourselves at the convulsions of the dying and that crimes were perpetrated among us; *crimes so terrible!* that now at a later date I cannot think of it without cold and trembling horror.

At last on the 8th May at abt. 4 o'clock in the morning a cannonshot apprised us of that a steamer was approaching and nothing could exceed our joy and enthusiasm. It was the United States steamer *Sierra Nevada.* . . . With the assistance of some seamen I was brought on board the *Sierra Nevada* where I took a stateroom with two beds in the upper cabin entirely by myself and had to pay $130. I gave the wet clothes which I had on and those which were in my trunks to one of the waiters to get them dried, and having got my wound dressed by the ship's physician and taken some beef tea and wine I slept for the first time since the 24th April in dry bedclothes. We left the same evening for Kingston, capital of the British island Jamaica, where we arrived on the 11th May in the morning. . . .

After a quick run of 6½ days we arrived on the 18th at 4 o'clock in the morning at New York, where I put up at the New York Hotel on Broadway. New York is a paradise for a man who comes from California, and full of enthusiasm I cried out, Oh New York! New York! . . .

[The following day] I left by the steamer *Europa* for Liverpool. . . .

Our passengers were for the most part fine people and formed the best

Broadway, New York City, in the 1850s

society I ever met with on board a steamer, and if not my wound in the leg
had caused me so much pain, I should certainly have enjoyed this trip very
much. . . .

[Docking at Liverpool on the evening of 30th May, Schliemann spent
the night at the Adelphi Hotel, and left the next morning for London on the
mail train.] After having given over to Baring Brothers & Co., what funds I
had brought with me from California in gold dust and bills of exchange, I
applied to Dr. G. F. Collier of Spring Gardens, London, who after having
burnt out the foul flesh of the wound with *lapis infernalis* dressed it and
ordered me to remain quiet in my room, keeping the leg always in a horizontal
situation. . . . I took at the doctor's advice a private lodging just opposite
his country-seat at Chiswick. But being accustomed to active life, the inac-
tivity and particularly the loneliness brought me nearly to despair, and thus
after having lived 7 days at Chiswick, I left by the steamer via Boulogne for
Paris. . . .

[Later in July 1852, proceeding via Hamburg to Mecklenburg] I met
two of my sisters, of whom I recognized only the one who had been with
me two years ago in St. Petersburg; but the other I did not recognize at all,
not having seen her for more than 20 years. My two sisters were going to
enjoy the sea-bath on the island [of] Rügen . . . whilst I went over Wismar and
Grevismulen to Kalkhorst to visit my uncle the Reverend F. Schliemann. . . .
I then left by way of Boltenhagen, Wismar, [etc.] to Ankershagen, the little
village where I was born and raised.[2]

It is impossible for me to describe the impression produced upon me
by the sight of the places, where I spent the happy years of my early childhood,
and where every house, every tree, every stone and every bush brought to my
memory a thousand agreeable reminiscenses of years long gone bye. It must
be that every object appears in gigantic proportion to the eye of the child,
because the church-steeple which formerly appeared to me of immense height
and which I always thought the highest in the world, the linden tree in the
midst of the orchard which formerly seemed to touch the clouds—in fact
everything appeared now only in miniature to me, except the balsam-poplars
and the cherrytrees before the door, which must have grown up considerably,
for they seemed to me of the same height as 21 years ago. I found the initials
H. S. of my name a hundred times on the glass panes of our former dwelling-
house, or on the trees in the garden and in the court, where I had the habit
to cut it when a child, and on the large linden tree where I had perpetuated
myself with a hatchet in 2 feet long initials, the latter appeared so fresh as if
made only a month ago. On the door of the pavilion in the garden I still
found an inscription made with pencil by my father and dated 7 May, 1827.
The present vicar Conradi showed me every kindness, accompanied me to

the church and to my mother's grave, the railing of which was in a very decaying state, and having satisfied my curiosity as much as I could in a couple of hours, I hired from the innkeeper a wagon with a pair of horses and left for the village Viperow on the lake Muritz to visit another sister of mine, who lives there in the family of my uncle Wachenhusen. . . . I started the ensuing morning by the steamer *Erbgrossherzog Friederich Franz* for Cronstadt and St. Petersburg. . . .

July 24th, 1852. I was today on [at the ex]change, where all my old friends received me with enthusiasm. I also visited Miss Catherine Lyschin [Ekaterina (Petrovna) Lyshin], to whom I vainly paid my addresses in former years, but who now received me most kindly and everything appears to promise fair.

December 31, 1852. . . . I have travelled much and seen certainly a great deal of the world, but never have I seen a country which pleased me so much as my heartily beloved Russia, never have I seen a city which pleased me one thousandth part as much as my charming St. Petersburg, never have I met with a people for whom I felt only one thousandth part of the liking and love which I cherish for my adopted brethren the Russians. I shall therefore make St. Petersburg my home for the remainder of my life and never think of leaving it again.

IV
MIDAS TOUCH
1852–1864

The Exchange at St. Petersburg, the capital of Imperial
Russia and the site of Schliemann's most successful
business transactions.

AFTER LEAVING AMERICA, Schliemann wrote his sisters from the transatlantic steamboat how much he had enjoyed New York, which he found to be "a thousand times more lovely than on my first visit." Not only were the buildings remarkably large and beautiful, but everybody's face, he swore, "showed the imprint of liberty and freedom." He concluded this French epistle: "The truth is that I have such enthusiasm for New York that I desire nothing better than staying on; and as soon as I complete my European voyage I have the intention to settle here [*de m'y fixer*]."[1]

Yet back in the Old World, he seems to have wavered. Passing through his native Mecklenburg for the first time in more than a decade, he conceived a plan to buy an estate there and become a landlord-farmer. During his most hectic commercial transactions in the following years, he continued to toy with acquiring country property in his homeland. He kept friends and real estate agents on the lookout and carried on an extensive correspondence regarding it. Apart from Mecklenburg, Schliemann also considered the Rhineland, as well as various Mediterranean countries and Russia. (Language, he assured his confidants, was no obstacle no matter where he settled, since he would master the foreign tongue in no time—that is, if he did not know it already.) In between, there flared up southern Brazil and, of course, America—once in the form of a cotton plantation in Louisiana. Indeed, the United States, despite Schliemann's outspoken opinion on the low business morale and corruption of justice, continued to loom as the ultimate escape, particularly when things got tough elsewhere.[2] Characteristically for this driven man, when in America he had yearned for Russia; once back in Russia, America was constantly on his mind. He stayed in touch with friends in Sacramento and San Francisco and was ever eager to learn how things were going in "our" state.

With the capital he had doubled in a few months in California, Schliemann returned to St. Petersburg in August 1852. This time he came as a man of substance. His former associates and colleagues welcomed him with open arms. Before long, all the wheels of the import trade were turning for Heinrich Schliemann, merchant of the First Guild. Though he renewed his connections with the Schröders, he set himself up as an independent dealer, also building up a branch in Moscow. His wealth and reputation grew. To his father he could boast that "here [in St. Petersburg] and in Moscow I am considered the most clever, crafty, and competent merchant."[3] In June 1855, he reported, there suddenly came to him one night the intuition that saltpeter was bound to rise in prices. He immediately got up and dispatched telegrams to Hamburg, Berlin, and Königsberg commissioning his agents to buy up all the supplies available. The result was a profit of about 40,000 thalers. By 1856 he declared that he controlled a third of all the indigo imported into Russia. When he happened to hear that the Russian government was planning to issue a new law code, he bought up fine-quality paper in the knowledge that it had to be printed on durable stock. Needless to say, he persuaded officials to accept his bid.

Once again Schliemann seized every commercial opportunity. Yet if he was ever fortunate in his business dealings, his choice of a wife proved to be a disaster. Even before going to America, he had courted several Russian women. Two of them he came close to marrying. With one, named Sophia, he apparently was head over heels in love. He advised his family of his betrothal with "the most adorable creature it is possible to imagine. . . . I am at the utmost peak of happiness. What sweet compensations after so much suffering! . . . She is an accomplished pianist and can speak three European languages fluently. . . . Sophia is very thrifty and so we shall grow rich."[4] But Schliemann's passion soon cooled when at a party his bride-to-be shamelessly flirted with a handsome officer. He consoled himself with the knowledge that a man of his position rated as a highly eligible bachelor in St. Petersburg. There were adorable creatures galore eager for his advances.

In fact, another girl stood in the wings whose acquaintance he had made before Sophia's, "a beautiful and very clever Russian girl, but [one] who has little or no fortune."[5] He admitted his "regrettable" impatience to get married. Yet this new suit also came to nought. There was another candidate, an "angel of virtue and beauty," the sixteen-year-old niece of his old friend Zhivago, whom he had known from his Dutch days. She, too, soon vanished from the stage, why we do not know. Their courtship ended shortly before Schliemann left for America and may have played a part in his departure.

As described at the end of his American travel journal, immediately upon his return to St. Petersburg, Schliemann resumed his search, and his attentions fell upon Ekaterina Petrovna Lyshin, "a very good, simple, clever, and sensible girl," whom he had met during his first St. Petersburg stay. She was related to a fellow merchant, but alas, had no money of her own, nor could she be considered a beauty. Besides, she already had turned him down. (She may have been the same girl he courted after Sophia.) But now, two years later, when a more affluent, self-assured, and somewhat dandified Schliemann knocked again at her door, she accepted him.

In October 1852, only two months after his return to Russia, Schliemann could report his recent marriage to his father and sisters. It did not take him long, however, to regret the rash step. Ekaterina seems to have been a selfish creature. For her husband at least, she had no sympathy whatever. Before long Schliemann had to admit to himself that she did not love him. They had no common interests. She grew to hate everything about him: his mannerisms, his temper, his parsimony, his passion for languages. On one occasion, she was joined by her brother in laughing in his face at his antiquarian interests. His dream of sharing with a loving wife his joys and sorrows was totally shattered.

But distressingly, the more she rejected him, the higher rose his ardor. For the sensual man Schliemann believed himself to be, his wife's tantalizing coldness drove him to the brink of insanity. For a while, the birth of a son, Sergei, in 1855, on whom the father doted, brought them closer. But this domestic peace did not last long. Two more children were born, both girls, whom, as Schliemann conceded, he had to "steal" from his wife.[6] The marriage would drag on for fifteen years, and to escape its hell, Schliemann sought refuge in his work and lengthy travel. Yet most of the time he hoped for reconciliation and appeared to remain desperately infatuated with his wife. His letters to her through the years, full of entreaties, accusations, bribes and promises, attempts of reconciliation, and threats, read like a case history of human bondage.

While cursed with an unrequited love, Schliemann flourished materially as never before. Plans for travel and dreams of settling down in another country were forgotten. He admitted that during the Crimean War (1853-1856), he thought of nothing but money. To a German friend who was still trying to find a latifundium for him, he confessed that, as long as hostilities were to last, "there was not the slightest chance that he would tear himself away from Mammon."[7] His father and even an old aunt were fed figures of his rising annual income. His capital, he announced from time to time, had doubled again (already in the first year of his return) or tripled or quadrupled. When he got back from a lucrative business trip to the Nizhni Novgorod trade fair, he wrote to the same German friend: "The result of the fair, favorable against all my expectation, has with one stroke wiped out my plans and has urged on me the firm decision never again to leave Russia."[8]

His autobiographical notes (and even more so his letters) tell a lot about his commercial operations during the period of the Crimean and, later, the American Civil Wars. To him wars were opportunities, little else. The political and moral issues they raised did not concern him in the least. In the Crimean War he specialized as a dealer in war material, some of which was contraband, and he was not above running blockades. The Civil War enriched him, when he cornered scarce cotton. He also knew how to turn a quick profit from bad harvests of sugar, indigo, and olive oil. With smug serenity he saw the hand of providence steer his wartime enterprise. The dubious morality of such a claim he apparently never woke up to. However, he was always ready to shed tears over business worries and financial setbacks. There is no evidence (and no mention) that because of wartime hostilities he felt himself cut off from Russia's enemies, England and France, or that he discontinued his relations with the Schröders' London branch.

Despite his prosperity, however, apprehension of eventual failure or disaster began to haunt him. Could the goddess Fortuna, who had bestowed such bounteous favors on him, be trusted in the future? As usual, Schliemann's moods were liable to change from elation to gloom, and from arrogance to humility. Ever-growing wealth carried the seeds of discontent and caution. Schliemann clearly saw that the aftermath of the Crimean War would bring serious financial dislocations, if not an economic crisis of major proportions, and tried to prepare astutely for this by withdrawing most of his capital from the market and putting it into conservative dividend-paying investments. In time, he trained himself to make the difficult transition from enterprising trader and speculator to careful investor in relatively safe securities for steady income.

More than anything, the financial setbacks and uncertainties of the years right after the Crimean War, particularly the 1857 crisis, made Schliemann decide to retire from business. By standing on the sidelines during his extended travels and "clipping coupons," he was sure he would make more money than by engaging in hazardous commerce. His thoughts had turned to liquidating his business before. Now, in 1858, he was ready. He had accumulated enough to live in affluence for the rest of his life. His capital he now estimated to be six times the sum he had brought back from California.

During the years of his second St. Petersburg residence Schliemann had, whenever his commercial activities allowed him, returned to one of his earlier loves—languages. His fascination with linguistic studies again appears in his autobiographical notes of this period, and nothing gave him greater joy than taking up modern and ancient Greek (in that order). With his growing proficiency in the classical languages and literature, Schliemann now turned longingly toward the Mediterranean lands connected with his "darling Homer." These, he had told his father in 1856, he must visit before acquiring a country estate.

His decision to retire permitted him to undertake an extended trip, from November 1858 to July 1859, that included Jerusalem, where he claimed to have visited all the places mentioned in the Old and New Testaments, Damascus, where he found nothing to attract him but the "coy beautiful Jewesses," the Aegean islands (namely the island of Syros), and, at last, Athens. He mailed a brief summary of his travels in the Bible lands to *The Times* of London, which published it on May 27, 1859. On the brink of taking a ship to Odysseus' island, Ithaca, he fell ill. Then he received bad tidings from Russia, necessitating his speedy return.

Thus, Schliemann's intended retirement turned out to be short-lived. He resumed his business, and his wealth grew even larger. He may have become impatient with a life of leisurely and seemingly aimless travel, and he yearned for his children. However, his letters of the time deplored his own inveterate greed and reiterated that commerce no longer gave him any pleasure. By the same token, he was ready to resign himself to the fact that "nature has meant me for trade" and that he should stick to his last.[9]

Despite such fatalistic thoughts, his letters, as in past years, were filled with new plans for retirement. To eventually retreat to his own well-appointed country place was still much on his mind. Sometimes he would fantasize about settling in the vicinity of a university town such as Bonn or Rostock. Still, he remained ridden by doubts about whether an active person such as himself, who throve under the excitement of the marketplace, could really adjust to the rural pace. But what else would be there for him to do? If only he had been younger, he could have taken up an academic career.

In one of his blue moods, Schliemann even took a dim view of his mania for the learning of languages, which appeared to him all of a sudden unproductive. Later he was to say, "Languages help to educate, but by themselves do not make an educated person."[10] He may have been thinking of Dr. Collier's admonition that feats of memory should not be mistaken for intellectual efforts.

Granted, however, that he would be always barred from scholarship, could he not perhaps make a name for himself as a writer? But a writer of what? And did he have any real ability for that demanding calling?

Schliemann's extensive diaries and letters are possible proof that he had for a long time harbored a secret ambition to write, enjoyed writing, and consciously worked on his prose. Eventually he came to choose models, like the revered Ernest Renan, whom he cultivated in Paris. But as yet he did not take his efforts seriously. The lines he wrote in 1856 to his aged aunt in Kalkhorst, at whose household he had stayed in his early youth (1832), are quite revealing. In them he admitted candidly: "I have often tried to compose some writing but no sooner have I completed a page than I tear it up in disgust over my own stupidity and come to the decision never to try again, for like a house without foundation my scribblings collapse within themselves."[11] He still had to learn what Thomas Mann once said about his craft: "A writer is someone to whom writing does not come easily." Regretfully, Schliemann never took sufficient pains when later composing his many archaeological works.

By the end of 1863, he at last felt able to liquidate his business. Commerce in Russia was again at a low ebb, and for some time he had turned to investing in Cuban and American railroad bonds, as well as buying apartment houses in Paris. To his friends Schröder & Co. in Hamburg, he served notice that he definitely was giving up his St. Petersburg business "because the lamentable causes which render my stay here intolerable persist."[12] This cryptic comment may refer to either economic conditions or his agonizing marital life, or both. With Schröder in London he now deposited his last will, leaving instructions that it was to be opened only in the event that they should not receive any word from him for six months. In St. Petersburg he entrusted two bankers to look after his still pending business affairs. His life had reached a watershed. He was still only forty-two. What he was ultimately to do, he was as uncertain about as ever. Would a trip around the world give him peace and direction? For as the German philosopher Hermann Keyserling remarked, travel may well be "the shortest way to oneself."

WEALTH AND ITS DISCONTENTS

from *Ilios*

At the end of 1852 I established a branch-house at Moscow for wholesale dealing in indigo, first under the direction of my excellent agent, Mr. Alexei Matweieff, and after his death under the direction of his servant

Jutchenko, whom I raised to the dignity of a merchant of the Second Guild, considering that an able servant may easily become a good director, whilst a director can never become a good servant.

As I was always overwhelmed with work at St. Petersburg, I could not continue my linguistic studies there, and it was not until the year 1854 that I found it possible to acquire the Swedish and Polish languages.

Divine Providence protected me marvellously, and on more than one occasion I was saved from apparently certain destruction by a mere accident. All my life long I shall remember the morning of the 4th of October, 1854. It was at the time of the Crimean War. The Russian ports being blockaded, all the merchandise intended for St. Petersburg had to be shipped to the Prussian ports of Memel or Königsberg, thence to be forwarded overland. Some hundreds of chests of indigo, as well as large quantities of other goods, had been thus shipped by Messrs. J. Henry Schröder & Co. of London and Messrs. B. H. Schröder & Co. of Amsterdam, on my account, by two steamers to my agents, Messrs. Meyer & Co. of Memel, to be sent on by the latter overland to St. Petersburg. I had just returned from the indigo auctions at Amsterdam in order to see after my goods at Memel, and had arrived late in the evening of the 3rd of October at the Hôtel de Prusse in Königsberg, when, happening to look out of the window of my bedroom on the following morning, I saw the following ominous inscription, written in large gilt letters on the tower of the gate close by, called "das Grüne Thor":

> Vultus fortunae variatur imagine lunae,
> Crescit decrescit, constans persistere nescit.
> ("Fortune's face changes with the phases of the moon,
> Waxing and waning, it does not know how to stay still.")

Though I am not superstitious, the inscription made a profound impression upon me, and I was seized with a kind of panic, as though an unknown disaster were hanging over me. In continuing my journey by the mail-coach, I was horror-stricken to learn, at the first station beyond Tilsit, that the whole city of Memel had been consumed on the previous day by a fearful conflagration; and I saw this but too well confirmed on my arrival before the city, which resembled an immense graveyard on which blackened walls and chimneys stood out like tombstones, mournful monuments of the fragility of human things. Almost in despair, I ran among the smouldering ruins in search of Mr. Meyer. At last I found him, and asked him whether my goods were safe: by way of answer, he pointed to his smouldering warehouses and said, "There they are buried."

The blow was tremendous: by eight and a half years' hard labour in St. Petersburg I had only saved 150,000 thalers, or £22,500, and this was now all lost. But no sooner had I acquired the certainty that I was ruined, than I recovered my presence of mind. It gave me great comfort to think that I had no debts to pay, for it was only at the beginning of the Crimean War, and business being then very unsafe, I had bought only for cash. So I thought Messrs. Schröder of London and Amsterdam would give me credit, and I felt confident that I should make up the loss in course of time. In the evening, when on the point of leaving by the mail for St. Petersburg, I was telling my misfortune to the other passengers, when a bystander suddenly asked me my name, and, having heard it, exclaimed: "Schliemann is the only man who has not lost anything! I am Meyer & Co.'s first clerk. Our warehouse being crammed full of goods when the steamers arrived with his merchandise, we were obliged to build close to it a wooden barrack, in which all his property lies perfectly safe."

The sudden transition from profound grief to great joy is difficult to bear without tears: I was for some minutes speechless; it seemed to me like a dream and incredible that I alone should have escaped unhurt from the universal ruin. But so it was. The strangest thing was that the fire had originated in Meyer & Co.'s stone warehouse, at the northern extremity of the town, whence, owing to a furious gale which was blowing from the north at the time, the flames rapidly spread over the whole city; whereas, under the protection of the same storm, the wooden barrack remained unhurt, though it was not more than a couple of yards north of the warehouse. My goods having thus been preserved, I speedily sold them to great advantage; turned the money over and over again; did a large business in indigo, dyewoods, and war material (saltpetre, brimstone, and lead); and, as capitalists were afraid to do much business during the Crimean War, I was able to realize large profits, and more than doubled my capital in a single year. . . .

My wish to learn Greek had always been great, but before the Crimean War I did not venture upon its study, for I was afraid that this language would exercise too great a fascination over me and estrange me from my commercial business; and during the war I was so overwhelmed with work that I could not even read the newspapers, far less a book. When, however, in January 1856, the first tidings of peace reached St. Petersburg, I was no longer able to restrain my desire to learn Greek, and at once set vigorously to work, taking first as my teacher Mr. Nicolaos Pappadakes and then Mr. Theokletos Vimpos, both from Athens, where the latter is now archbishop [1879]. I again faithfully followed my old method; but in order to acquire quickly the Greek vocabulary, which seemed to me far more difficult even than the Russian, I procured a modern Greek translation of *Paul et Virginie*, and read it through, comparing every word with its equivalent in the French original. When I had finished this task, I knew at least one-half the Greek words the book contained, and after repeating the operation I knew them all, or nearly so, without having lost a single minute by being obliged to use a dictionary. In this manner it did not take me more than six weeks to master the difficulties of modern Greek, and I next applied myself to the ancient language, of which in three months I learned sufficient to understand some of the ancient authors, and especially Homer, whom I read and re-read with the most lively enthusiasm.

I then occupied myself for two years exclusively with the literature of ancient Greece; and during this time I read almost all the classical authors cursorily, and the *Iliad* and *Odyssey* several times. Of the Greek grammar, I learned only the declensions and the verbs, and never lost my precious time in studying its rules; for as I saw that boys, after being troubled and tormented for eight years and more in schools with the tedious rules of grammar, can nevertheless none of them write a letter in ancient Greek without making hundreds of atrocious blunders, I thought the method pursued by the schoolmasters must be altogether wrong, and that a thorough knowledge of the Greek grammar could only be obtained by practice—that is to say, by the attentive reading of the prose classics, and by committing choice pieces of them to memory. Following this very simple method, I learnt ancient Greek as I would have learnt a living language. I can write in it with the greatest fluency on any subject I am acquainted with, and can never forget it. I am perfectly acquainted with all the grammatical rules without even knowing whether or not they are contained in the grammars; and whenever a man finds errors in my Greek, I can immediately prove that I am right, by merely reciting passages from the classics where the sentences employed by me occur.

Meanwhile my mercantile affairs in St. Petersburg and Moscow went on steadily and favourably. I was very cautious in my business; and although I received severe blows during the fearful commercial crisis of 1857, they did not hurt me much, and even in that disastrous year I made, after all, some profits.

In the summer of 1858 I renewed with my friend, Professor Ludwig von Muralt,[1] in St. Petersburg, my study of the Latin language, which had been interrupted for nearly twenty-five years. Now that I knew both modern and ancient Greek, I found the Latin language easy enough, and soon mastered its difficulties.

I therefore strongly recommend all directors of colleges and schools to introduce the method I have followed; to do away with the abominable English pronunciation of Greek, which has never been in use outside of England; to let children first be taught modern Greek by native Greek professors, and only afterwards begin ancient Greek when they can speak and write the modern language with fluency, which it can hardly take them more than six months to do. The same professors can teach the ancient language, and by following my method they will enable intelligent boys to master all its difficulties in a year, so that they will not only learn it as a living language, but will also understand the ancient classics, and be able to write fluently on any subject they are acquainted with.

This is no idle theory, but a stubborn fact, which therefore ought to be listened to. It is a cruel injustice to inflict for years upon an unhappy pupil a language of which, when he leaves college, as a general rule he knows hardly more than when he first began to learn it. The causes of this miserable result are, in the first place, the arbitrary and atrocious pronunciation of Greek usual in England;[2] and in the second place the erroneous method employed, according to which the pupils learn to disregard the accents entirely, and to consider them as mere impediments, whereas the accents constitute a most important auxiliary in learning the language. What a happy effect would be produced on general education, and what an enormous stimulus would be given to scientific pursuits, if intelligent youths could obtain in eighteen months a thorough knowledge of modern Greek, and of that most beautiful, most divine, and most sonorous language, which was spoken by Homer and Plato, and could learn the latter as a living tongue, so as never to forget it! And how easily, at how small an expense, could the change be made! Greece abounds with highly-educated men, who have a thorough knowledge of the language of their ancestors, who are perfectly acquainted with all the classics, and who would gladly and at moderate salaries accept places in England or America. How greatly the knowledge of modern Greek assists the student in mastering ancient Greek I could not illustrate better than by the fact, that I have seen here in Athens office-clerks who, feeling no inclination for commerce, have left the counting-house, settled down to study, and been able in four months' time to understand Homer, and even Thucydides.

Latin should, in my opinion, be taught not before, but after, Greek.

In the year 1858 I thought I had money enough, and wished to retire from commercial pursuits. I travelled in Sweden, Denmark, Germany, Italy, and Egypt, where I sailed up the Nile as far as the Second Cataracts. I availed myself of this opportunity to learn Arabic, and I afterwards travelled across

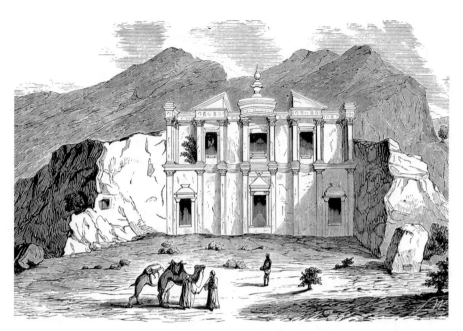
The ruins at Petra

the desert from Cairo to Jerusalem. I visited Petra, and traversed the whole of Syria; and in this manner had abundant opportunity of acquiring a practical knowledge of Arabic, the deeper study of which I continued afterwards in St. Petersburg. After leaving Syria I visited Smyrna, the Cyclades, and Athens, in the summer of 1859, and I was on the point of starting for the island of Ithaca when I was seized with fever. At the same time I received information from St. Petersburg that a merchant, Mr. Stepan Solovieff, who had failed, owing me a large sum of money, and with whom I had agreed that he should repay it in the course of four years by annual instalments, not only had not made his first payment, but had brought a suit against me in the Commercial Court. I therefore hurried back to St. Petersburg, was cured of fever by the change of air, and promptly gained my cause. But my antagonist appealed to the Senate, where no lawsuit can be terminated in less than three and a half or four years; and my presence on the spot being necessary, I went into business once more, much against my will, and on a much larger scale than before.

My imports from May to October 1860 reached as high a sum as £500,000. Besides indigo and olive oil, I also in 1860 and 1861 embarked largely in cotton, which gave great profits, owing to the Civil War in the United States of America, and the blockade of the Southern ports. But when cotton became too dear, I abandoned it, and in its stead went into tea, the

importation of which by sea was permitted from May 1862 and onwards. . . .
But when in the winter of 1862–1863 the insurrection broke out in Poland,
and the Jews, profiting by the disorder then prevailing there, smuggled immense quantities of tea into Russia, I could not stand this competition,
being obliged to pay the high import duty. I therefore retired again from the
tea trade, but it took me a long time to sell at a small profit the 6,000 chests
which had remained on my hands. But my staple commodity always remained indigo; for, as I knew the article well, and was always favoured by
Messrs. John Henry Schröder and Co. of London with choice and cheap
purchases, and as I also imported large quantities direct from Calcutta, and
never confided the sale of indigo to clerks or servants, as others did, but
always stood myself in my warehouse, and showed and sold it personally
and wholesale to the indigo dealers, I had no competition to fear, and my
net profit on this article was on an average £10,000 annually, with 6 per cent
interest on the capital employed.

Heaven continued to bless all my mercantile undertakings in a wonderful manner, so that at the end of 1863 I found myself in possession of a
fortune such as my ambition had never ventured to aspire to. But in the midst
of the bustle of business I never forgot Troy, or the agreement I had made
with my father and Minna in 1830 to excavate it. I loved money indeed, but
solely as the means of realizing this great idea of my life. Besides, I had
recommenced business much against my will, and merely in order to have
some occupation and distraction while the tedious lawsuit with the merchant
who had attacked me was going on. When therefore his appeal had been
rejected by the Senate, and I had received from him the last payment, in
December 1863, I began to liquidate my business. But before devoting myself
entirely to archaeology, and to the realization of the dream of my life, I
wished to see a little more of the world. . . .[3]

The Great Wall of China, a highlight of Schliemann's
trip around the world.

OFTEN TOUTED AS THE EPITOME of undiluted pleasure and relaxation, travel is many things to many people. Among other things, it is hard work. It can also be an opiate and an escape. To be sure, it may provide a liberal education. But to those who have become addicted to it and who wander feverishly about the globe like another Flying Dutchman, it is foremost a state of mind. To the middle-aged Schliemann, it was all these. And to no mean degree, it was a measure of his despair. As always, his motives were hopelessly mixed.

Despite what the "autobiography" says, he had not firmly—if at all— decided on an archaeological career in 1863. Just as in previous years, he continued to go through bouts of indecision, of self-doubt, of plans for retirement and counterplans that even included new commercial ventures. To J. W. Schröder of Hamburg, he wrote from Aachen, where he spent five weeks in the spring of 1864 to take the waters: "Since commerce is now at a low ebb in St. Petersburg and I am hardly able to tame my thirst for knowledge, I intend to go on the 25th [May 1864] via Genoa to Tunis . . . and from there on to Egypt, East India, China, Japan, California, Mexico, and Cuba. Afterwards I shall return to St. Petersburg to renew my business, should, in the meantime, conditions have taken a turn for the better. . . ."[1] Thus he left his options open. Commercial considerations were still very much on his mind.

His two-year world trip served, then, as a convenient stopgap. To take up almost continuous wandering suited the active man not just as a grand opportunity for universal study but as a palliative, and the path of least resistance—without forcing a major decision.

Had Schliemann's eyes already been firmly set on Greece and Troy, as some of his biographers would have us believe, he would have gone there first to resume the journey so abruptly cut off in 1858. Instead he undertook a long absence from Europe, far away from home and his obstreperous wife.

Infatuation with antiquity had not yet taken full possession of him, and Schliemann, the American, remained from his young days an *europamüder* (tired-of-Europe) adventurer, ever eager to get away from it all.

Still, Schliemann was not really a "traveler." For that he was too cantankerous—constantly complaining about hotel accommodations; haggling with servants, innkeepers, and shopkeepers; bemoaning uncleanliness; ever susceptible to all kinds of tourists' diseases and laid up for weeks in the most unlikely places; too prejudiced in sizing up unfamiliar peoples; rather indifferent to art and scenery (apart from his invariable intoxication with mountain views and panoramas);[2] pathetically oblivious of the political and social upheavals then taking place in various countries; and inattentive to anything but standard textbook sites.[3] He was adrift without his Pausanias and Homer, who were to stimulate him to original and heterodox observations. Egypt, the Near East, and the Far Orient did not provoke him to any adventurous forays as they had some of his great Victorian contemporaries.

But he had a natural curiosity, nevertheless. Ruins, particularly in the Near East and northern India, attracted his attention and drew judicious comments that anticipate Schliemann's later archaeological tastes. The voluminous journals he kept of all his trips are occasionally lit by a few perceptive, colorful flashes. Japanese and Chinese theaters, which he sought out wherever he could, delighted him. The perverse ancient fashion of binding women's feet in China and the mixed bathing establishments and institutionalized prostitution in Japan he investigated with the laudable detachment of the social scientist. Also on this trip, as throughout his life, he showed a somewhat morbid taste for graveyards. On arriving in a provincial town in India, he immediately made his way to the burial ground of the victims massacred in the recent Sepoy revolt.

China and Japan, long goals of his, impressed him considerably. The result was his first book, *La Chine et le Japon au temps présent*, written in French on his fifty-day voyage across the Pacific to California and issued in a small edition by an obscure Paris publisher in 1867. It was never translated into another language, but Schliemann had made his literary debut.

His ability to put a book together (from his diary entries) and see it published and even reviewed made Schliemann once more think that his future might be as an author. After all there was nothing incongruous in becoming a writer of books at the age of forty-five. To be an author did a lot for his self-esteem and was a steppingstone to more ambitious undertakings.

La Chine et le Japon deals with only a part of his lengthy trip around the world that started in the middle of April 1864. From Aachen he proceeded at a leisurely pace via Paris and Genoa to Tunis, where he gathered economic data for the Schröders and stopped over at the Carthaginian ruins. A short trip took him to Malta. For once he was nonplussed by the local idiom. In Egypt, his next goal, he suffered much from the heat of summer, which, as he wrote a sister, made him literally drink several buckets of Nile water a day. No wonder he fell ill and was bedridden for weeks with an irritating skin disease. At last he returned to Italy to seek a cure at the spa of Porretta (Terme) near Bologna.

Fully recovered, he moved on to Florence and Naples and from there to the ruined sites at Capri, Paestum, and Pompeii. His fanatic belief in the therapeutic benefits of sea bathing, which he had embraced in his youth at Rostock and Hamburg and which he maintained, despite physicians' warnings, to his last days, was probably responsible for his first bout with an ear ailment that was ultimately to kill him. Again tormented by pain, he consulted a doctor in Naples—the same city where he collapsed and died in 1890. Not getting any relief, he rushed to Paris and from there to a specialist at Würzburg recommended by the Schröders. After three weeks he was ready to reembark for Egypt, stopping on the way at Vienna, Trieste, and Corfu. Thence he boarded an English boat through the Red Sea to India. All the time he industriously kept his journal (some five hundred pages of it), written in his usual polyglot fashion—mostly in English, but also in German, French, Italian, modern Greek, Russian, Spanish, Dutch, and even Arabic. (On the way to India he studied Hindustani.)

Soon after arriving in Calcutta on December 13, 1864, he attended an auction of indigo, the vegetable dye to which he owed the bulk of his fortune. Then he boarded a train on the thousand-mile ride to Delhi. There he admired Islamic mosques and Mogul palaces but was surprised by the devastation left from the 1857 rebellion. From Delhi he ascended the Himalaya foothills, taking in a changing picture of natural vegetation and cash crops (tea, sugar cane, cotton) up to the pleasant village of Landur at about seven thousand feet. The mountain scene provoked him to an obbligato purple passage on the majestic view.

His Indian itinerary also included Lucknow, which won the crown of all Indian cities because of its cleanliness; Agra, with the nearby Taj Mahal and the great Akbar's tomb; and Benares, along the Ganges, whose waters teemed with droves of pilgrims.

On his return to Calcutta, Schliemann shipped out in another English steamer to Penang (Malaya) and Singapore, reaching Batavia (Jakarta), the chief port of Java, on February 19. In Java he traveled through the luxuriant tropical landscape and visited the unsurpassed botanical garden of Buitenzorg (Bogor), apart from riding up a nearly ten-thousand-foot volcano to enjoy

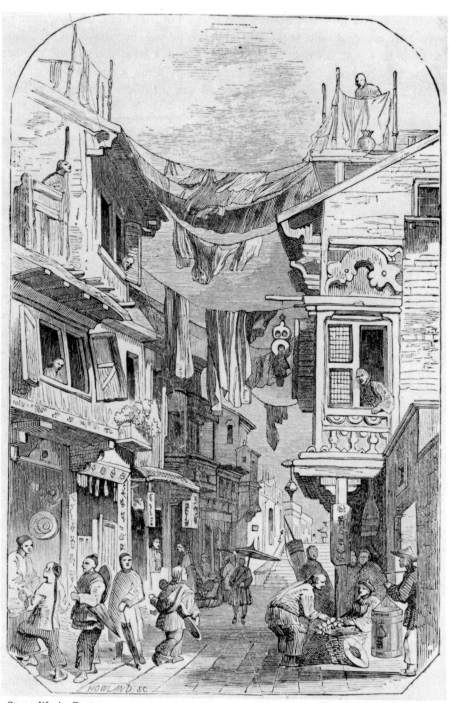

Street life in Canton

another "unique" panorama. This time Schliemann was plagued by digestive troubles, besides a recurrence of his ear complaint that necessitated an operation in Batavia for the removal of internal bony growths. After passing through Saigon, where he took a dim view of the recently established French control and had even less kind things to say about the native people, he landed in Hong Kong on April 1, 1865. Oddly enough, for the Chinese, whom he considered almost a master race when observing them in Singapore or Java (and even California), he had little respect in their own country. There they seemed to him mostly decadent, depraved, and dirty. Much of their degradation he attributed to the curse of opium.

Schliemann stayed in China for two months. From Hong Kong (he noted its "splendid panorama") he passed to the bustling cities farther north, such as Canton, Amoy, Foochow (Minhow), Shanghai, Tientsin, and Peking.[4] He was not overly impressed by any of these places. Peking, for which he had such high hopes, was a letdown. His jaundiced views probably are due to his own discomfort in that strange and at the time torn country, for whose political predicaments he lacked understanding. He thought it barbaric to drink green tea and, to add insult to injury, not to use any sugar and milk. Robert Payne, an old China hand himself who wrote a perceptive book on Schliemann, suggested that "nearly all his conclusions were wrong." What Schliemann has to say of the dilapidated state of Peking was totally muddleheaded and is not borne out by any contemporary visitors. Nor did he ask any questions that may have put him straight. Instead he performed, as Payne put it, "miracles of improvisation on the theme of the ruined city slowly sinking into the mud. . . . He thought the shining palaces of the Forbidden City were in ruins, when they were nearly invisible behind a green flood of summer trees."[5] As to the paved streets, stone sewers, mutilated cornices, and granite bridges Schliemann conjures up in their state of decay, there were none to start with.

However, the Great Wall amply made up for Schliemann's disappointments. The formidable monument, which, contrary to his assertion, was mainly constructed during the Ming dynasty around A.D. 1400, overawed him. It also happened to be located in an area to whose physical and human landscape he could respond.

Japan, shortly before the opening of the Meiji era, when the power of the Shogun, or "secular emperor" Schliemann talks of, was abolished and only twelve years after Perry had opened it with a bang to the West, cast a magic spell on Schliemann and produced his most interesting comments. Though he was not blind to the virulent xenophobia, which he thought was largely incited by the daïmyos (barons), his grasp of the virtues of the people is as sensitive as his visual impressions. But then he always did his best by people who cultivated cleanliness, such as the Indians of Lucknow, the northern Chinese at the Manchurian border, or the black Nubians of the upper Nile.

In July of 1865 he embarked on the *Queen of Avon*, a sailing vessel, for a long voyage to San Francisco. Back in California after an absence of fourteen years, he inspected familiar sites, gauged the development that had taken place since his previous stay, and tried to locate his brother's grave at Sacramento. He was shocked to learn that the cemetery had been leveled and the tombstone he had erected was lying around in broken pieces. Worse still, the corpse underneath, which he intended to have shipped home for reburial, turned out to be not his brother's at all. Though the gold fever had petered out, California appeared to him more solid and wholesome. He took his time to survey it anew and came to appreciate its attractions as never before. In his journal he noted: "This beautiful land has the climate of Italy, the soil of Egypt, the silver of Peru, and as energetic a population as New England."[6] He also had occasion to visit the natural wonders of the Yosemite Valley and, not unexpectedly, waxed ecstatic.

After California he took ship for Nicaragua to avoid the Panamanian hell and continued on the Atlantic side for New York. By now he was beginning to lose his animus for travel. The beauties of tropical Nicaragua left him cold. Even New York had lost its glow. All alone in his hotel room he was laid low with malaria, but a German doctor put him on his feet with a strong dose of quinine and coffee. In his diary he now tended to become more introspective and self-questioning. He nurtured a sneaking suspicion of the futility of travel and raged against his own restlessness. Once again he was apprehensive—and indecisive—about his future.

Despite such passing sentiments, Schliemann extended his itinerary from New York to Niagara Falls, into Canada, and then down to New Orleans and on to Mexico. None excited him. Cuba, where he made some investments, and the smaller Caribbean islands, including St. Thomas, where he met the Mexican general and former President Santa Anna, were the last stops in the New World. Meanwhile he had learned to again enjoy the gypsy life, so that soon after, somewhat complacently, he could assure his old friend Hepner: "I like traveling; for everywhere I find interesting and educated travel companions, from whom I can acquire useful knowledge."[7]

At last, early in 1866, he was back in Europe, making his landfall in England. In London he examined an exhibit of prehistoric cave artifacts from the Dordogne at the Crystal Palace. A few days later he returned to Paris, where he now intended to make his home.

THE GREAT WALL OF CHINA

from *China and Japan*
at the Present Time

[After arriving in Peking] my desire to see the Great Wall was as intense as was my apprehension of the hardships of the road. Hence I decided to get started right away and to spend another eight days in Peking on my return. I sent At-shon [Schliemann's servant] the same evening to rent two carts and a saddle horse for the trip to Ku-pa-ku (Ku-pei-k'ou) and back. The next day at 4 A.M. I took leave . . . and set out for the north. . . .

At-shon drove in a cart with the baggage, and far from admiring the walls of Peking or the open countryside, he just slept. I rode horseback, while the other cart followed so that I could seat myself there in case my mount defaulted—which actually happened around noon the next day. The horse, seized by fatigue, started to limp, and I was forced to tie it to the cart, while I took my place on the pole. The sun shone mercilessly. I suffered much, even though I wore a large Arab turban.

Eventually, at six in the evening, we entered the large town of Ku-pa-ku, which is considered the cleanest in all of China. It lies just at the Man-churian border, in a valley surrounded by high mountains. The arrival of a stranger is there a rare occurrence and hence a special event. If a dressed orangutan or gorilla were suddenly to walk along the boulevards of Paris, he would not be the object of greater curiosity than excited my person among these mountain people. Barely had I passed through the city gate than I was surrounded and trailed by an immense crowd which accompanied me to the hostelry and even stood sentry in my room. The latter could, of course, not accommodate everybody, and some climbed from the outside to the window and tore the paper to scrutinize me. Nobody could understand why I wasn't dressed in the Chinese manner and why I had short hair instead of a long pigtail. However, one might have forgiven me even that mark of bad taste, but to see me write from left to right in unknown characters with a pencil or a steel pen (instruments completely unknown in China) rather than drawing Chinese hieroglyphs with a brush from top to bottom and right to left—that was such an unheard-of event that one could not believe one's eyes in contemplating the miracle.

I found the people's attention rather annoying but did not know what to do. Five or six individuals I chased away by scaring them with my un-loaded pistol, but I did not dare to play the same trick on sixty or seventy people who could very well turn on me. When asked about the purpose of my trip, At-shon unfortunately told them that it was to see the Great Wall. Thereupon all of them broke into an uproarious laughter, because no one could understand how I could be so mad as to undertake a long and weary voyage for the sole reason of viewing stones. I should mention on this occasion that it is contrary to the Chinese character to submit to the least strain unless absolutely necessary. . . .

After taking breakfast, I left with my guide to climb the wall. An immense crowd of curiosity seekers again kept me company as soon as I put a foot in the street and they trailed me even right to the wall until we got to the first steep slope. There, the fear of exerting themselves got the better of their inquisitiveness, and everybody left me, except for At-shon, who chivalrously accompanied me right up to a dangerous juncture where, on both sides, the wall was falling off into the abyss. Here the rampart had crumbled to a width of only thirty-four centimeters—that is, to so narrow a space that one could hold on only by walking on all fours. At-shon's courage gave way, and he stayed behind. Thenceforth I continued all alone.

At a distance of about eight kilometers I saw that the wall crossed a very high ledge. I wanted to climb it at all costs. This was, however, not an easy matter, because the passage appeared to be blocked by five precipitous rocks, where the wall rose at angles of fifty, fifty-four, and sixty degrees. . . . To scale the steep slopes I had to keep close to the parapets and not look back. I then proceeded to cross a dangerous col with closed eyes and on all fours.

By dint of perseverance I reached at last the longed-for goal, but how great was my shock when I realized that the wall traversed within two kilometers another mountain which was at least two hundred meters higher and which blocked the view to the west. I had to get there, no matter what, and bravely went to work. After climbing several smaller slopes, I got finally to the large precipice which was probably some 130 meters high and rose at an angle of sixty degrees. The steps were barely three inches wide and were strewn with debris so that the climb was more difficult than all the preceding ones put together. Yet by and by I moved on to the top and then ascended to the roof of a crenelated watchtower. By now it was noon, I had been five and a half hours on the road. But the panorama that unfolded before my eyes compensated me amply for my troubles. . . .

Casting a glance toward the north, I saw above the mountains the high plateau of Manchuria. Below me, at a depth of nine hundred meters, I perceived a long straight valley. A river from the north traverses its entire length, fertilizing the rice fields, meandering in various curves, and dividing the beautiful city of Ku-pa-ku in two parts so that one of them is placed on a peninsula; it sends out one arm of its limpid waters into an eastern valley. With an optical aid I could see the crowds in the city streets, and I recognized At-shon sitting on the threshold of my inn. The city was surrounded by lovely gardens, everything was enveloped by the lively green of spring, except for the fruit trees which had not yet begun to sprout. Near the city a battalion of soldiers was drilling with guns; I could hear a threefold echo from their firing. . . .

I have enjoyed magnificent views from the heights of the volcanoes of Java, from the crest of the Sierra Nevada in California, from the summits of the Himalayas in India and the altiplanos of the South American Cordilleras, but I have never seen anything that could compare with the splendid picture that now unfolded before my eyes.[1] . . . That Great Wall of China of which, since my infancy, I had never been able to hear people talk without feeling a lively curiosity, I now held before me a hundred times more grandiose than I had imagined. And the more I gazed upon this immense barrier with its formidable crenelated turrets always positioned on the highest mountains, the more it seemed to me the fabulous creation of an antediluvian race. But knowing from history that this wall was constructed about 220 years before our era, I could not comprehend how mortal hands were capable of raising it—how they could transport and place on these enormous precipitous rocks the materials, the granite blocks, and the billions of tiles which had to be manufactured in the valleys below. It seemed to me obvious that the wall had been started in the valleys and all the materials were transported along the wall during construction.

But how is it, I asked myself, that that generation of giants, who had been able to complete in the middle of rugged mountains such an enormous barrier, had any real need for it? Were not the chests of that race of Hercules the most formidable wall which could be brought up against the invasion of the enemy from the north?

Yet granting the necessity of building such a wall, how then could one conjure up so many millions of workers needed for the manufacture of tiles and cement, the cutting of granite, and the conveying of the materials to these heights? Furthermore, how could one marshal so many soldiers to invest a large enough garrison in the twenty thousand towers of the wall, which, counting all its bends, amounts to a length of no less than three thousand two hundred kilometers? . . .

For centuries now the Great Wall has been neglected and abandoned. Instead of garrisons of warriors, the crenelated towers are today inhabited by peaceful pigeons who build their nests here, while the wall itself teems with inoffensive lizards and is covered by yellow flowers and violets announcing the coming of spring. It is without doubt the largest work ever raised by the hands of men. The gravestone of past greatness, cutting through abysses and clouds, it silently protests against the corruption and decadence that has fallen on the Chinese Empire.

I would have loved to stay on the tower until the evening, because my eyes could not get enough of this magnificent panorama, but the sun was burning and a terrible thirst eventually compelled me to leave the inhospitable region. I descended the sixth and fifth slope backward, supported by my hands. Then I followed a narrow winding path to the foot of the mountains. Many places were so steep that I had to slide down on my belly. Nevertheless, I managed to carry with me not only my telescope but also a big tile of sixty-seven centimeters length by fastening both objects to my back.

Once I got below, I stuck the telescope in my belt and took the tile in my arms. But no sooner had I entered town than I was once again surrounded by a crowd of men, women, and urchins who, by pointing with their fingers to the tile and shouting, made amply known how mad they thought I was to take pains in carrying away a miserable stone of fifty pounds. I uttered the word *shuaiat* (water) and expressed in sign language that I was dying from thirst. The people rushed to me fresh water in a basket but would not accept any remuneration. I had never encountered in China such a fine demonstration of generosity.

In addition, I should say that the inhabitants of this town stand out for their kindness, just as their curiosity ranks them above all other Chinese. These mountain people seemed quite content, and strange as it may seem, one does not see a single beggar in town. Ku-pa-ku may well merit its reputation of being the cleanest town in China. The neat garments of the people, though of plain cloth, do not lack a certain elegance. As everywhere in China, the women are not particularly coquettish except for their mutilated small feet. Moral corruption has not yet reached these mountain people, and men, women, and children are all strong and robust, and their rosy cheeks testify to the healthfulness of the climate and their abstinence from opium. The passion for this poison is widespread in the southern provinces, where one sees all over livid faces devoid of all expression. The vice diminishes as one approaches the north. In Tientsin and in Peking one notices the ravages of this drug among but a small fraction of the population. . . .

JAPAN

from *China and Japan*
at the Present Time

In Shanghai I booked passage for Yokohama (Japan) on the steamboat *Peking*, which belongs to the Peninsular and Oriental Company. I paid 100 taels (900 francs) for a crossing that a good steamer can easily make in three days.

After a very agreeable voyage we got, on June 1 [1865] at six in the morning, in view of the first little rocky island of Japan. I saluted it with lively pleasure, for all voyagers had talked to me of that country with such enthusiasm that I burned with desire to visit it. . . .

On June 3, at around ten o'clock in the morning, we saw at a distance of some 150 English miles the famous volcano Fujiyama, which has an altitude of 4,725 meters, lifting its eternally snow-covered summit above the clouds. . . . In the afternoon we entered the large Gulf of Yedo and cast anchor outside Yokohama at ten in the evening.

The following morning I rose early to go ashore. On climbing the bridge, I had no difficulty in convincing myself that I was no longer in China: instead of the many dirty embarcation boats, with two eyes painted on their bows, which surround in China all newly arrived ships and which are almost invariably rowed by two women carrying little infants bound to their backs . . . there was only a single bark. It was manned by two sturdy Japanese who wore nothing but a very narrow belt barely hinting at an intention to be dressed. Instead, their whole bodies from neck to knees were tatooed with red and blue pictures of dragons, lions, tigers, and male and female divinities so that one could say of the men what Julius Caesar said of the ancient Britons: "Though they may not be clothed, they are at least well painted." Their hair dress also differed from that of their neighbors of the Celestial Empire, because their heads were shaven from the forehead to the top. . . .

Barely had I arrived when two porters tried to put my belongings on two bamboo rods to carry them. But when looking at these men, I noticed that they were covered with infections of the skin . . . and after waiting for half an hour, I obtained the services of two other healthy men who carried my things to the customs. Two customs officers appeared. With a smile on their lips they said on meeting me, "*Ohayo* [Good day]," bowed almost to the floor, and stayed in this position for half a minute. Then they signaled to me to open my suitcases so that they could examine them. Since this is a

The Yoshiwara district of Tokyo

rather tiresome matter, I offered each an *itzebu* (2½ francs), if they would dispense with it. But to my surprise, they refused to accept the money and touching their chest said, *"Nippon musko,"* which means that a Japanese man considers it beneath his human dignity to neglect his duty for the sake of a compensation. Hence I had to open my trunks. But far from harassing me, they satisfied themselves with a superficial examination. In short, they proved to be most obliging and amiable, and then said, *"Sayonara* [Goodbye]," with another deep curtsy.

From there I went with my two coolies, who carried the baggage to the Colonial Hotel. The hotel is located in the middle of a garden of camellia bushes. . . .

After settling down in my new abode, I went into the city of Yokohama, which in 1859 was still a little village and counts today [1865] fourteen thousand inhabitants. The streets are all macadamized. They are ten to twenty meters wide and are lined by wooden two-story houses with the roofs covered by bluish tiles. The ground floors of the houses are always kept open toward the street during the day but are closed at night by large boards. . . .

The Japanese are most certainly the cleanest nation in the world, and nobody, no matter how poor he may be, will fail to visit at least once a day one of the many bathhouses with which the towns are amply provided. . . .

The public baths consist of a large hall whose walls are furnished with niches for the storing of the visitors' clothes. In one corner stands a large vat with hot water which is piped from a kitchen. The hall opens in its entire length to the street. Here, in daily life prevails the absence of any [separation of] genders so typical for the Japanese language, which fails to express the difference between masculine, feminine, and neuter. From dawn to dusk all the public baths are filled with a confusing mixture of the two sexes of every age—all totally reduced to the sole costume of our first ancestors before they bit into the fatal apple. Each one takes a bucket of hot water, washes his whole body carefully, then dresses, and leaves.

"Oh, *sancta simplicitas!*" I exclaimed when I passed for the first time in front of one of these bathhouses and saw thirty or forty men and women, completely in the nude, rushing outside to examine at closer range a large, bizarrely shaped piece of coral suspended from my watch. Oh holy simplicity which does not fear the opprobrium of the rest of the world; uncensored by any code of decorum, it does not register any shame over the absence of clothes! . . .

As to establishments of prostitution, they are always grouped together in an isolated part of town. Their number in Yedo [Tokyo] is so staggering that they form a town by itself called Yoshiwara, separated from the rest of the capital by walls and embankments. One cannot enter there but through a single gate which is guarded day and night by many police officers. Yoshiwara has a circumference of at least two English miles and forms a parallelogram. . . . There are more than one hundred thousand courtesans in Yoshiwara, none of whom can leave without a pass for which she has to pay a considerable sum. City for city the trade of prostitution is always leased by the Japanese to the highest bidder as a monopoly for a certain number of years, thus assuring immense revenues which form one of the largest resources of the Japanese treasury.

On June 7 and 8, the government announced in the foreign press of Yokohama, and by means of numerous posters in the streets, that on the tenth of the month the Shogun (the secular emperor) would leave with a large retinue from Yedo via the Tokaido, the principal highway, for Osaka in order to pay a visit to the Mikado (the spiritual emperor), whose sister he had married. The Japanese were asked to close all the shops along the Tokaido and to remain in their houses until the procession had passed. But on June 9, the English consul of Yokohama announced that he had succeeded in obtaining permission for foreigners to watch the procession from a grove of trees four miles outside Yokohama and several steps away from the Tokaido.

I went there on foot to better survey the countryside. The road led almost continually over small dikes through rice paddies. The soil of the fields consisted of excellent black earth, which probably originated from lava or igneous rock. In addition, it has been fertilized in the course of centuries by liquid manure. The most widely cultivated product is, of course, rice, taking the place of bread, which is unknown in Japan. . . .

Along both sides of the road I saw many flowers—foremost roses without thorns. (Never have I come across any flower in this country which had the least scent, nor a fruit which had any taste.) One is certain to always find in any well-placed grove one or two small wooden temples decorated with beautiful sculptures.

After a march of one and a half hours I came to the grove that had been set aside for foreigners desirous of watching the parade of the Shogun. Some one hundred foreigners assembled there, with about thirty policemen to keep order. After another hour and a half of waiting, the procession began to pass. At first came a great many coolies carrying baggage on bamboo rods; then a battalion of soldiers, dressed in long white or blue blouses, black or dark-blue trousers tied at the ankles, blue stockings, straw sandals, and lacquered bamboo hats, a haversack on the back, and armed with bows and quivers or rifles and swords. The officers were garbed in fine yellow calico with a sky-blue or white robe falling to their knees and decorated with small white marks as a sign of nobility. . . . Attached to their belts were two swords and a fan. Their horses wore instead of iron shoes straw sandals.

Next came more coolies carrying baggage and then higher officers on horse, robed in long white garments with large red hieroglyphs on the back. They were followed by two battalions of lancers on foot, two cannons, two battalions of foot soldiers, coolies carrying large lacquered boxes, then again lancers on foot in white, blue, or red robes, high dignitaries on horse in white with red hieroglyphs, a battalion of white-bloused soldiers, four stable boys who led four saddle horses caparisoned with black trappings, four splendid black-lacquered *norimons* (litters in the form of carriages without wheels), and behind them a carrier with a fleur-de-lis standard of gilded metal. At last arrived the Shogun, riding a beautiful brown horse with straw sandals like all the other horses. His majesty appeared to be about twenty years old. Of royal demeanor, he had a face of somewhat dark complexion. That prince was dressed in a white gold-embroidered robe and a lacquered gilded hat. Two swords were attached to his belt. Some twenty high dignitaries, also in white robes, formed his escort and closed the procession.

When horseback riding the next morning along the Tokaido, I saw in the middle of the road near the place where we had watched the procession, three corpses which were mangled to such a degree that it was impossible to judge by their clothes to which class of society they had belonged. I made inquiries in Yokohama and learned that a peasant, who probably had not known at all of the coming of the Shogun, had crossed the highway some steps ahead of the first battalion of soldiers. This so incensed one of the officers that he ordered one of his men to punish the audacity of that man and to cut him to pieces. But the soldier hesitated to obey, and the angry officer cracked his skull with one stroke of his sword. Then he killed the peasant. At that moment a superior officer intervened. After he was informed of the facts, he thought the executing officer had gone mad and ordered another soldier to kill him with a blow of the bayonet. The order was carried out immediately. The three corpses remained on the great highway, and the entire procession, which must have counted some 1,700 persons, passed over them without being concerned about them or even noticing them. . . .

I had heard so much of the wonders of Yedo that I was itching to go there. After the treaties of 1858 that capital should have been opened to foreign commerce in 1862, but the Western governments had consented, at the solicitation of the Shogun, to defer the opening of that port indefinitely. Hence no one could visit Yedo except for the ambassadors of the great foreign powers and their guests. However, some time ago ambassadors withdrew from Yedo on account of the many outrages committed against their lives and those of their staff. All had left but for the plenipotentiary of the United States of America, Mr. Pryune [Robert H. Pryun], and even he had been absent for several months while leaving Mr. Portman in charge. I had to receive an invitation from the latter to be able to visit Yedo—there was no other way. As elsewhere it is very difficult for a foreigner in Japan to obtain an invitation from the chargé d'affaires of a great power, particularly if one has no opportunity to make his personal acquaintance [beforehand]. Nevertheless, thanks to the kind intervention of my esteemed friends Messrs. W. Grauert & Company of Yokohama, I succeeded at last on June 24. The consul-general at once sent a pass for Yedo on my name to the Japanese central police office in Yokohama with the request to put an escort of five *yakunins* (mounted police officers) at my disposal at eight the following morning.

With the aid of the American consulate I forwarded my baggage the same evening to Yedo . . . and rented for the duration of my trip for 6 Mexican piasters (36 francs) a day a horse from Mr. Clark. The latter was a Jamaican Negro. At first a carpenter, he became a sailor, then a hotel steward, later a baker, and at last the owner of a stable of nine horses which he rented out. He intended to resume the baking trade as soon as the house he was about to build was completed.

Imperial Palace, Tokyo

It had been raining almost continually since my arrival in Japan, but on Sunday, of June 25, it seemed as if all the sluices of heaven had been opened. Nevertheless, covered with a coat and an impermeable paper cap, which the Japanese make from a tree bark and which is so solid that it can be sewn only with difficulty, I started out at 8:45 A.M. with the five *yakunins* who had to accompany me in the torrential rain without being permitted to accept the least gratuity. Yet they submitted to their fate with that stoic resignation which removes half the bitterness from the saddest adversity. . . .

We left on horse: the two officers of superior rank preceding, while the three others formed the rear guard. Six *bettos* (stableboys), all naked, though covered from neck to ankles with artful and lively body paintings of gods, birds, elephants, dragons, or landscapes, accompanied us on foot and competed with the horses in speed. One of them was tatooed on his back and chest with a scene of the eruption of the sacred volcano Fujiyama. . . .

Toward noon we arrived in the port of Yedo, which is defended by six immense forts built into the sea two miles from the coast. Still more than by these forts, Yedo is protected by the shallow water of its bay, where not even the tiniest boat can approach the shore at low tide. . . .

Around two o'clock in the afternoon we arrived at the American legation located at the great temple of Dsen-fu-si, which means "eternal bliss." One enters there through an enormous granite gate, whence a paved road leads across a large court to the great temple. To the left is another, much smaller temple as well as an extensive building inhabited by the forty priests attached

Schliemann's father, Ernest, in his later years. The elder Schliemann was a Lutheran pastor, whose scandalous conduct compelled his son to leave home at an early age.

Heinrich Schliemann's birthplace in Neubukow (Mecklenburg) in East Germany. A plaque on the wall commemorates Schliemann as a "great scholar" and "the discoverer of Troy."

Schliemann as a prosperous young merchant in St. Petersburg, where he amassed his great fortune as a trader in commodities.

Schliemann in middle age in the late
1860s—the turning point of his career.
Divorced from his Russian wife, Catherine,
and dissatisfied with merely making money,
he decided to devote himself to travel and a
life of learning.

Sophia Engastromenos, Schliemann's
second wife, on their wedding day in
September 1869. A Greek girl thirty years
his junior, she shared his enthusiasm for
archaeological exploration and became his
invaluable companion and co-worker.

The hill of Hissarlik, believed to be the site of the ancient city of Troy.

A view of the great trench which Schliemann cut through the hill of Hissarlik. The methods he used in his early excavations of Troy aroused a storm of controversy among fellow archaeologists.

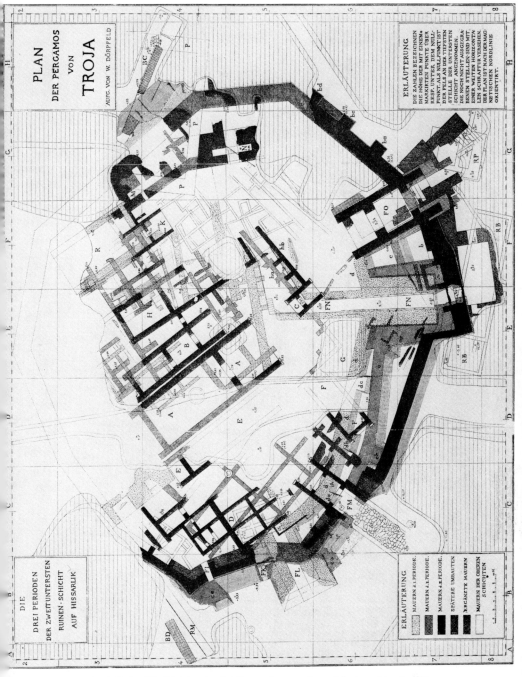

A map drawn by Wilhelm Dörpfeld showing Schliemann's excavations of the lowest levels of Troy.

A contemporary sketch of the Great Treasure found by Schliemann in 1873 at Troy, the discovery that brought him worldwide fame.

Sophia Schliemann wearing a golden diadem and necklace from the Great Treasure.

Golden vessels from the Great Treasure, including the famous two-handled "sauceboat."

to the sanctuary. . . . The American legation is installed in a similar building to the right. It was here that I enjoyed for three days the hospitality of the chargé d'affaires, Mr. Portman, who lavished his attention on me. . . .

Mr. Portman guided me, to start with, around the two temples and the adjoining two bastions in order to show me what he called "his fortifications." These consist of two bamboo palisades and numerous guard posts and sentry boxes from which watch during the day more than two hundred and during the night three hundred *yakunins*, armed with swords and bows, rifles and daggers. Every evening the password for the coming night is chosen, and anyone who attempts to enter without being able to name it will be immediately cut to pieces.

It continued to rain profusely, but my wish to see Yedo was so great that I could not be held back. After refreshing myself with a bath, I left again on horse in company of five other police officers. We rode, as before, in a file, one behind the other. In the course we passed through several of the many quarters of the *daïmyos*. Their palaces are invariably placed in the center of a vast quadrangle measuring from three hundred to six hundred meters and surrounded by a huge wooden two-storied battlement that serves as habitation for the *daïmyos'* men and their families. . . .

The *daïmyos* are obliged by law to live in their Yedo palaces during six months of the year and to leave behind their families as hostages during their absence. They leave Yedo and return to it with a great train of followers whose size is in proportion to their properties. Among the richest it is in excess of fifteen thousand men. . . .

Nowhere in Yedo did I see a butcher or a dairy shop, nor a furniture store, for all these articles are unknown in Japan. However, I noticed a sizable number of stores selling objects of lacquered wood. . . . Above all, I was astonished by the quantity of stores offering Japanese silk, each of which has more than one hundred employees, men and women, and which can rival the grandeur and wealth of the most opulent emporiums of Paris. . . . Several bookstores sell textbooks and the sacred works of Confucius and Mencius at so reasonable a price that they are within reach of the poorest.[1] I was also struck by the many toy stores. The Japanese manufacture toys at so low a cost and with such perfection and often with such ingenious mechanisms inside that they leave behind the craftsmen of Nürnberg and Paris. . . . The toy in the manufacture of which the Japanese particularly excel is the whip top. They make more than one hundred different kinds, one always stranger than the other. . . .

In the spacious courtyard of the temple of Asakusa Kannon there are displayed figures that resemble those of Madame Tussaud's in Baker Street in London. The grounds have also tea gardens, bazaars, ten galleries for practice shooting with bow and arrow, several theaters, exhibits by jugglers, etc. However, I cannot believe that such a mixture is compatible with sincere religious convictions. . . .

Afterward I visited the great theater, called in Japanese Taïsibaya, even though my five *yakunins* tried their utmost to keep me away. . . . On the program was a dramatic piece followed by burlesque sketches, which were so admirably acted that one could understand everything without knowing Japanese. . . .

Admittedly, I cannot imagine how sentiments of purity and piety are able to exist in the life of a people where not only the two sexes attend the same public baths, but where also women of all ages amuse themselves to the highest degree with watching obscene shows.

VI
HELLENIC PILGRIMAGE
1868

The coastline of the island of Ithaca, site of the
legendary kingdom of Ulysses and a major goal of
Schliemann's Homeric pilgrimage.

On February 1, 1866, Schliemann, now forty-four years old and looking definitely middle-aged, enrolled as a part-time student at the Sorbonne. To gain admittance to the venerable institution, he had obtained a special permission from the French Ministry of Education. The graying millionaire must have cut an odd figure among the young scholars who shared their benches with him. The courses he took were Modern French Language and Literature, French Poetry of the Sixteenth Century, Petrarch and His Travels, Comparative Linguistics, Arabic Language and Literature, Greek Philosophy, Greek Literature, and Egyptian Philology and Archaeology. So wide-ranging a curriculum mirrored his interest in languages and literature and philology in general but hardly indicated a concentration on archaeology. There is no evidence that he decided to specialize in the study of antiquities or was preparing himself for actual excavation. Rather, he tried to fill the gaps in his education. Probably he envisioned a career as a writer of books which were to reflect a cultured, well-informed mind—as he hoped the forthcoming French volume on his travels in the Orient would. As yet, he did not dare to aspire to pioneering scholarship.

For a while he was absorbed in his studies. After ten days of attending classes he wrote to his sister Doris: "Paris with all its glories has no attraction for the traveler who has sailed around the globe and who has seen the wonders of India, the Sunda archipelago, Indochina, Japan, Mexico, etc. What interests and keeps me here are the lectures of the great university professors on literature, philosophy, hieroglyphic writing, etc., in addition to museums and theaters, for nowhere in the world does one find anything as sublime."[1] His ardor brought him the attention of his professors, whom he treated with profound reverence. By and by, he gained entrance to the intellectual circles of the city. Ernest Renan, the celebrated scholar of religion and an elegant writer, he counted as a much admired friend.

Schliemann's Parisian life indeed offered amenities and stimulations as he moved with ease between the fashionable Left Bank apartment on place

Saint-Michel overlooking the Seine, classes at the Sorbonne, visits to the races, dining at fine restaurants, meetings of learned societies, nights at the opera, and soirées with the city's great men. Had he then made a clean break with the past? He may have thought so.

In all the whirl of his new existence he was lonely, and anything but calm. Perhaps to let off steam, he studied Persian on the side. He still entertained the hope of luring his estranged wife to join him, imploring her with extravagant inducements and promises—as well as warnings that he would cut her off financially. And, of course, he could not keep away completely from the pursuits of money-making, even though he wrote a banker friend in St. Petersburg: "I am in a state of utter happiness, away from commerce and the exchange, eagerly bent on perfecting myself in the sciences so that I do not have the slightest intention ever to become again a merchant."[2]

True enough, one of his feet was already planted in another world, the world of learning, to which he was so much attracted and for which Paris seemed to him the universal fulcrum. No longer did he stand at his desk all day writing or dictating letters and trading commodities from far-flung corners of the world. But he was only a dabbling student who was by no means sure where he was going. And while he was through with being a merchant, he still had to look after his capital. Preserving one's millions, he was wont to echo the old adage, was at least as difficult as making them. It could be equally time-consuming. In this spirit, and not just as a pastime, he bought up valuable Paris real estate, which he considered a reasonably safe way to make his money work for him. Soon he was busy bickering with tradesmen, examining plumbing, complaining about his tenants' gas consumption, and renovating and converting his newly purchased properties. At the same time he continued following the stock exchanges of London, Paris, and New York. There were even moments when he thought of starting all over again in St. Petersburg. Besides, his substantial American and Cuban investments beckoned.

Came the summer of 1866 and university recess, and Schliemann turned up in St. Petersburg. He stayed only briefly before taking off for Moscow and Nizhni Novgorod. Then he boarded a Volga boat and traveled toward the Caspian Sea. On the way he disembarked at Samara to take a one-month cure in a sanitarium (the spas and health establishments he visited during his lifetime make an endless list) but suffered such ill effects from drinking too much koumiss, an Asiatic beverage usually made from fermented mare's or camel's milk, that he had to give up the planned trip into the Caucasus and Persia. Instead, he ambled around the Crimea and looked over the newly created monuments to man's destructiveness at such places as Sebastopol, which had been pulverized in the Crimean War. Crossing the Black Sea and traveling up the Danube he continued into Central Europe. His goal was Dresden, the beautiful baroque residential city of Saxony, which he had visited before and where he owned property. He investigated a modern educational institution and decided that it would make an ideal progressive school for his children. For this purpose he was ready to leave Paris and settle in that mecca on the Elbe. He implored his wife to move the family to the large villa he had bought. But Ekaterina brusquely rebuffed him. She was adamant that her children should be brought up in Russia and within the Orthodox faith. To join a husband whom she despised was out of the question. Yet even now Schliemann would not give up and prayed for a domestic reunion. Though he must have realized how futile it was, he now began to beseech his wife to move with him and the children to America.[3] There they would make a new beginning.

The next year, in October 1867, he was back—all alone—in the United States and Cuba. To his personal concerns had been added crises in the international money market. Schliemann had read in *The Times* of London of the possibility that certain American government securities would be redeemed in paper money, which might well amount to their repudiation and, as a consequence, would precipitate the soaring of the value of gold. Since a sizable part of his capital was involved, he had to find out for himself. He was also eager to know how American railroads, in which he was heavily invested, were doing. It was to be his third trip to the United States—and this time it was mainly devoted to business and economics. A declared goal of his was to collect "precise data on chances for the reconstruction of the Southern States, the labor market, and the cultivation of sugar, rice, and cotton."[4] To his consternation, he found the South destitute. He was appalled by the many crippled veterans and the profusion of soldiers' graveyards, which he made a habit of visiting. On these strange promenades he took a curious interest in finding out the ethnic backgrounds of the buried men.

Schliemann's itinerary covered a good part of the United States east of the Mississippi. A highlight was his attending a lecture by Dickens. From New York he went again to Niagara Falls and then into the Midwestern heartland. All the time he was gathering information on the various railroad companies. Hence he proceeded to and from Chicago, and via Buffalo, Cleveland, Toledo, and Detroit on the New York–Central, the Toledo-Cleveland, Michigan-Central, Illinois-Central, Chicago-Burlington-Quincy, and the Pittsburgh–Fort Wayne, in each of which he owned stock. He was happy to report to Europe: "I am entirely satisfied with these roads, they all yield 10% dividends. . . ."[5]

No longer captivated by New York, he complained that its streets were unkempt, narrow, and badly lit. Of course, it had to compare unfavorably with Haussmann's grand design of the Paris of Napoleon III. Since Schliemann thrived on enthusiasm, he now went overboard about Chicago and its explosive growth from barely 3,500 in the year 1838 to 250,000. In a letter to his son he noted: *"La ville la plus merveilleuse que j'ai visité dans le voyage, c'était la fameuse Chicago."*[6] Other correspondents were treated to statistics on that city's phenomenal exports of cereals, hogs, lard, and bacon. He found "so many wonderful things there," he confessed, that one could write "ten books about them."[7] He saw both the hog butcher and a new Athens. Since his Dresden days, a special interest of his was local schools. Chicago he did not find wanting in this respect either. All schools were "splendid." What impressed him more than anything were coeducational—he called them in English "promiscuous"—classes, in which "boys and girls sit pêle-mêle together. . . . The continuous association of children of both sexes has a very beneficial effect. . . ."[8] As a proof of the intellectual benefits of such a system he mentioned admiringly that "girls and boys of 12 and 13 years translate Horace from Latin and Homer and Sophocles from Greek into English and German[!]."[9]

Eventually Mr. Schliemann went to Washington. There he headed for the Treasury Department, buttonholed the secretary, and afterward called on Lincoln's successor, President Andrew Johnson. "He is a fairly simple man, of about 55. I told him I wished to pay him my respects, and said that his latest message to Congress had pleased me very much . . . and he said, 'Yes, Cuba has a leaning towards the United States, and the time will come when it will be absorbed into them.' "[10] The indiscretion concerning Cuba, unlikely to have been made in those rather blunt words by a chief executive to an utter stranger, sounds a bit like wishful thinking on Schliemann's part.

Aside from the President and cabinet secretaries, he also visited "the famous General Grant." They all, Schliemann declared, "put him at rest over the economic situation and prospects of the country."[11] The government did not intend to withdraw the gold backing of federal bonds. Nevertheless, Schliemann was disturbed by the enormous outflow of gold and the excessive import of European goods—possibly amounting to what we would call today a "dollar gap"—so that he took a dim view of the American monetary situation and instructed his London broker to sell two-thirds of the government bonds he held. With some of the money he bought shares in the Illinois and Jersey Central Railroads; some he sank into Parisian real estate.

Of Andrew Johnson's abilities he took away a favorable impression and lamented the talk of impeachment. He felt the public clamor for Grant—

who, he was convinced, could not hold a candle to Johnson—to be raised to the highest office in the land reminiscent of the glorification of the military by an autocracy like Russia but unworthy of the Western democracy.

During his stay in the United States, Schliemann crisscrossed the South through the Virginias, Tennessee, Alabama, Mississippi, and Louisiana down to New Orleans. His journey on the New Orleans–Jackson and the Great Western Railroads again was undertaken for gathering information, which he reported extensively to the Schröders. In these letters he touched on the devastations wrought by the war, abuses of a tyrannical military government, prospects for the raising of crops and livestock, soil conditions, labor supply, and the need for immigrants (preferably Germans) to speed up development.

A recurring theme of his correspondence was the Negro question. It redounds to his credit that firsthand knowledge had completely changed his mind on the subject. "All complaints from here [the South] and the Northern States as to the former slaves' and present freemen's laziness . . . and [their] total incapacity to be educated, are *downright falsehoods*," he stated in an English letter to Schröder in Hamburg. "Since I left Washington . . . I have seen the latter work in the plantations, on the railroads . . . and I can assure you that they are as willing and eager to work and as energetic and perseverant in their labour as any workmen I have yet seen and that, both morally and intellectually, they stand much higher than their former tyrants and present calumniators! In fact in seeing the other day at Jackson (Mississippi) and now in New Orleans in the state conventions Negro delegates, who but 2½ years ago were ignorant, abject slaves, gesturing gracefully and making most able speeches, in deliberating on framing a constitution for the state, I could not help regretting that I was not myself a Negro to be able to speak as they did. . . ."[12] Apart from being convinced of the Negroes' equality in every respect, he was charmed by their music. His affection, communicated with his usual extravagant rhetoric, was genuine and was nurtured by many personal contacts.

New Orleans he thought a beautiful city, but he felt that, as a result of the Civil War, it had lost its vitality and was sinking into poverty.

On Russian Christmas Eve, which fell a day before his forty-sixth birthday, he found himself alone in a hotel room. "My heart and thoughts," he wrote in his journal, "have been constantly with my little darlings, Sergei, Natalie, and Nadja. I see them rejoicing over the Christmas tree. I weep bitter tears that I cannot share their joy and increase their happiness with presents. . . . I would give 100,000 dollars to spend the evening with them. Truly it requires much more strength and philosophy than I possess to pass this day without tears."[13] Odysseus was as far away from home as he could ever be.

In Cuba he continued with his economic inquiries. Here, likewise, his main concern was railroads—and labor. As always he was charmed by that tropic island and could not praise enough its benign midwinter climate. He was now certain that on all his voyages he never enjoyed any of his stays as much as this one in Cuba. Indeed, he had been so happy, he announced on leaving the Caribbean island, that it cost him the greatest effort to tear himself away. (He was to say much the same on his last transatlantic voyage in 1885/86.)

However, the Cuban bliss was tarnished by the horrible conditions of the nonwhite population, particularly the Negroes (some still slaves) and, even more so, of the Chinese who were being brought in by the shipload to replace the latter in the cane fields. He estimated that at least ten thousand Chinese had committed suicide and even more were killed by epidemics. Schliemann devised a plan to bring over "Hindus from the Malakka coast," whom he judged better geared to the conditions.[14] Somewhat like early Spanish missionaries, who, out of their love for the Indians, advocated the introduction of Negro slaves, Schliemann insisted that he acted from unselfish, humanitarian motives alone. Indeed, he promoted this project with missionary zeal and offered to go himself to India and arrange for the shipment until his old Amsterdam mentor and friend Hepner wrote to him unmistakably: "Do not go to Bombay to trade in human flesh, rather try to make those people happy to whom you are tied by the bonds of nature."[15] Though he did not seem to see the connection and even less the moral implications, Schliemann's prime concerns were the two Cuban railroads (the Havana-Matanzas and Matanzas-Sabanilla) he and the Schröders were heavily invested in, and he knew that their success depended entirely on the prosperity of the sugar plantations, which, in turn, required cheap and efficient labor.

Paris and the Sorbonne reclaimed Schliemann early in 1868. It was back to his studies, his books, his houses, and the social and cultural life of the capital of the jaded Second Empire dizzily speeding to its collapse. But already he was planning another trip.

Come spring he was to travel to southern Italy and Sicily, and then, at last, he would tour the sites linked with the great Homeric epics, culminating in a search for Troy, the embattled fortress of the heroes of Hellenic dawn. Unlike any previous voyage, his peregrinations among ancient ruins of the Mediterranean world would be in the main devoted to antiquarian studies. They were to be the overture to his own archaeological operations. His passion for Homer, so long in the making since the fleeting encounters with Greek mythology in his childhood, had been rekindled and never burned brighter.

The superannuated student of the Sorbonne did not deliberately adopt a new profession or follow in the footsteps of his scientific-minded, intellectually disciplined professors. Even when in later years he used the standard tools of learning with greater skill, groped for excavation techniques, and enriched scholarship, he was impelled first and foremost by his enthusiasm. Homer was his beloved sun, who never set; cold, skeptical analysis could not obscure or eclipse him. In this sense Schliemann's 1868 Hellenic trip was conceived as the pilgrimage of a pious believer. Like the Bible fundamentalist, he *knew* beforehand that Homer was holy writ, and what was needed was someone to provide the proof to counter modern irreligious assailants.[16] Perplexed and rudderless in middle age, Schliemann took Homer to be his guide. His life gained new meaning. From now on, both his romantic yearning and realistic activism would be directed to a search through throbbing ancient landscapes. At last he had found a theme big enough for his energy and fervor.

In the introduction to his book *Ithâque, le Péloponnèse, et Troie,* written immediately after his return from the Homeric sites, Schliemann gave his father the main credit for putting him on the sacred path.[17] But he stated that he would not have published a book on the subject had it not been for the "error which almost all archaeologists had perpetrated about the site of Ithaca's capital, the stables of Eumaeus, ancient Troy, etc."[18] This oddly critical stance, employed by a novice against seasoned scholars, became his specialty. No matter how long-standing the controversy or farfetched his own position, when it concerned the credibility of Homer, he dared to differ from all recognized authorities. In this respect *Ithaka* (*Ithâque*) points the way to all his future work. Here, in his first "archaeological" book, he not only described the three main sites—Mycenae, Tiryns, and Troy— where he was later to score his greatest triumphs, but he already proposed wayward views which were to be the basis for his revolutionary explorations. While it may be doubtful that he wrote the book as a kind of prologomenon to excavations already planned, he at least professed the confidence of an author who had found a promising theme that rose beyond the mere conventions of a talkative travelogue.

Ithaka, Schliemann's second book, which he wrote in French like the first and which he simultaneously released in a German translation, is actually a strange mixture of travel book, first-person narrative, cut-and-dry tourist information, chatty anecdotal episodes, and abstruse academic debate.[19] With its childlike infatuation with Homeric antiquity, it might well be called "Schliemann's Sentimental Journey to the Homeric Lands."

Though he will later affect some restraint, the book mirrors much the same naïve enthusiasms that were also to become a trademark of his writings.

The moment he set foot on Ithaca, in July 1868, Schliemann moved onto a bewitched island. Homer was present everywhere. Indeed, Schliemann was sure that nowhere else in Greece had traces of the remote heroic age managed to survive in such profusion. To him the lovable local people were clearly Odysseus' descendants. No doubt about it, on Mount Aëtos he *was* inside Odysseus' castle. It took little physical evidence to persuade him that he had located the place where the Phaeacians had deposited the sleeping Odysseus, the very site where the faithful dog Argos expired on recognizing his master, Laertes' fields, and Eumaeus' stables. In his first actual excavation, he dug up vases he was sure were filled with human ashes, possibly containing no less than the remains of Odysseus and Penelope themselves or—as he added as cautious afterthought—"of their descendants."[20]

Thus *Ithaka*, for all its endearing naïveté, is a telling document of Schliemann's romanticism, his dilettantism, and his conceit. But in a letter to his sisters he defines it as "less a description of travel than critique of works written on Ithaca and Troy."[21] Criticism of some sort was indeed implied when he took issue with scholars over the true site of Troy or the location of the royal graves in or outside the "acropolis" of Mycenae. In the main, however, he was simply critical of all who dared to disagree with the Homeric gospel, starting with Strabo and the Alexandrine skeptics. Whether one may call it critical or naïvely dogmatic, it was his literal interpretation of the bard that bore fruit.

After Ithaca, Schliemann took a ship for Corinth on the Peloponnese. From there he visited the ruins of ancient Corinth and, towering above it on a steep rock, Acro-Corinth, which afforded a unique bird's-eye view over the plain of Argolis and the Aegean inlets. Then he made his way to the preclassical fortress cities, foremost Mycenae and Tiryns. He left Nauplia to visit the isles of Hydra, Poros, and Aegina. On the last he climbed up to the well-preserved temple of Aphaia. Then he went on to Athens to spend a few days with his former teacher Theokletos Vimpos, by now an archbishop and professor at the University of Athens. In August he sailed for Constantinople and Çanakkale, entrepôt to the Troad.

Schliemann's adventures at Ithaca were paralleled by similar experiences on the Peloponnese and in the Troad. By debunking Bunarbashi (the Ballidagh) as the site of Homer's Troy, a then fairly recent though popular hypothesis apparently first advanced by the French explorer Jean-Baptiste Lechevalier (or Le Chevalier) in the late eighteenth century, he undoubtedly magnified his own originality. In fact, he almost certainly owed it to Frank

Calvert, a British resident who served as American vice-consul (later consul) at the Dardanelles, that Hissarlik and its probable identity were first brought to his attention.

Hissarlik, then, was by no means as dark a horse in Homeric scholarship as Schliemann would have us believe. Charles Maclaren, a Scottish classicist and explorer, had written a treatise upholding the site of Hissarlik, *Dissertation on the Topography of the Plain of Troy*, as early as 1822. George Grote, the English historian of Greece, and a number of leading authorities, both in England and on the Continent, had opted for it. Nobody had ever challenged the view that the hill of Hissarlik and its environs had been the site of Novum Ilium of Hellenistic and Roman days. And the assumption that those worshipers of Troy's glory, such as Xerxes, Alexander the Great, and Julius Caesar, had picked the "wrong" location to honor and rebuild the city, lacked plausibility. Even more so, basic facts relating to the Trojan War, as described in the *Iliad*, could not be squared with the location (some eight miles from the Hellespont) and terrain of Bunarbashi.

Nevertheless, it was Schliemann's merit that already on his first inroad into the Troad he tested the material evidence. At Ballidagh he sank some thirty shafts to prove the impossibility of any ancient fortress being buried underneath. For Hissarlik, though he examined the hill closely and gauged its geographic setting within the region, he had to defer archaeological investigation for the time being.

After his return to Paris, he at once concentrated on whipping the journal of his antiquarian junket into shape for book publication. The project took him three months of intensive labor. As yet he was striving above all for literary laurels. To his son Sergei he wrote on November 1, 1868: "I worked day and night on my archaeological work, for I have the hope to create for myself with this book a reputation as author. . . . If it is successful, I shall continue to write books all my life, because I cannot imagine a more interesting career than that of author of serious books. Writing one is always so happy, so content, and when going into society one has always thousands of things to tell . . . which entertain everybody. In fact, an author is always sought after and he is everywhere welcome; and even though I am but a novice in that métier, I have at least ten times more friends than I would want to have. . . ."[22]

For a lonely man, this was a rather strange boast. Perhaps it was meant to deceive his family in St. Petersburg, besides making the boy feel proud of his absentee father and look up to him as a model. Overconfident and exuberant, Schliemann disregarded the agonies of authorship. He would tackle archaeology in the same spirit.

As to the book, its unsophisticated faith in Homer and hasty conclusions were ridiculed by the few who reviewed it. It hardly made a reputation for its author. But it had the merit to lay the foundation for Schliemann's future profession.

The book completed, suddenly, on Christmas 1868 (Russian calendar), loaded with presents for his children, Schliemann arrived in St. Petersburg, only to find his family gone. When they returned, his wife gave him the cold shoulder, treating him, he wrote, as if he were a "Tartar invader," so that he quickly beat retreat and fled forever from his Russian home. At last he became convinced that reconciliation with Ekaterina was impossible.

ODYSSEUS' ISLAND—ITHACA

from *Ithaca, the Peleponnese* *and Troy* and *Ilios*

At last I was able to realize the dream of my life and to visit at my leisure those eventful places that had continued to hold my intense interest.[1] I set out in April 1868, by way of Rome and Naples, for Corfu, Cephalonia, and Ithaca, visiting in succession the sites where vivid poetic memories of antiquity still prevail. . . .

I arrived in Corfu, the capital of the same-named island, on July 6 at six in the morning. There I stayed for two days to explore the land.

We have unanimous testimony from antiquity that Corfu is identical with the island of Scheria or Homer's land of the Phaeacians. . . . Tradition mentions a large stream, Cressida Brisis (Fountain of Cressida), flowing from the west into Lake Kalichiopulos, as the river at whose banks Nausicaa washed the laundry with her maids and where she encountered Odysseus.

King Alcinous' daughter is among the noblest characters drawn by Homer. The grace of her manners has never ceased to enchant me. No sooner had I gone ashore in Corfu than I rushed to Cressida Brisis in order to look over the place which is the setting for one of the most touching episodes in the *Odyssey*.

My guide led me to a mill built one kilometer from the mouth of a small river. From here I had to proceed on foot. Barely had I ventured a few hundred paces than I hit several obstacles. Irrigation canals, dug at the river's right and left, were too wide to jump across. In addition, the fields were partly under water. But these difficulties only increased my desire to go ahead. I peeled off to my shirt and left my clothes in the care of the guide. Then I steadily advanced along the river, frequently up to my chest in the water and mud of the canals and inundated fields. At last, after a harassing walk of half an hour, I perceived two large crudely hewn stones which tradition assigns to the wash troughs of the inhabitants of the ancient city Corcyra and to the site where Nausicaa came upon Odysseus. The location corresponds perfectly to Homer's description, for Odysseus landed at the the river mouth while Nausicaa came to the washbasins near the river. . . . These basins, of necessity, had to be by the sea, because after Nausicaa and her servants had washed the laundry, they spread it out for drying on the pebble beach along the seashore. Then they bathe, anoint themselves, eat, and play ball. But the princess, throwing the ball to one of her ladies, misses and the ball falls into the river current. Whereupon the young girls raise a loud scream which awakens Odysseus.

It is clear from this that the place where Odysseus had camped in the bushes near the stream was located close by the washbasins and the river bank where the girls were playing ball.

There can be no doubt about the identity of that river with the one described by Homer, for it is the only one in the ancient town's environs. In fact, there is just one other river on the whole island, but that one is some 12 kilometers from ancient Corcyra, while the Cressida Brisis is within three kilometers. No doubt a road led in ancient times from town to the wash troughs. But today there are everywhere cultivated fields and not a trace is left of such a route. . . .

I rented for 11 francs a bark to cross from Cephalonia to Ithaca. Alas, the wind was unfavorable so we were forced to tack. The voyage took us six hours instead of a mere hour had conditions been better. At last, at around eleven o'clock at night we disembarked in the small port of St. Spiridon on the south side of Mount Aëtos. We had entered Odysseus' kingdom.

I must confess that, despite fatigue and hunger, I was filled with tremendous joy to find myself in the fatherland of the very hero whose adventures I had read and reread with such fervent enthusiasm.

On landing I had the pleasure to make the acquaintance of Panagis Astroieraka, a miller from whom I rented an ass for 4 francs to carry my luggage, while he himself acted as guide and cicerone to the capital Vathi (βαθύ). When he heard that I had come to Ithaca to do archaeological research, he strongly applauded my plan and on the way retold the adventures of Odysseus from beginning to end. The ease with which he recited them proved to me clearly that he had told the same story thousands of times. His zeal to inform me about the heroic deeds of Ithaca's king was so great that he would not suffer any interruption. In vain did I ask him, Is this Mount

Aëtos? Is this the harbor of Phorcys? On which side is the Grotto of the
Nymphs? Where is Laertes' field?—all my questions remained unanswered.
The road was long, but the miller's narrative was just as long, and when
at last, half an hour after midnight, we crossed the threshold of his house in
Vathi, he had just arrived in the underworld with the souls of the Suitors
accompanied by Hermes.

I congratulated him enthusiastically for having read the Homeric poems
and memorized them so well that he could render the main events of the
24 chapters of the *Odyssey* with such facility in modern Greek.

To my great surprise he replied that not only was he ignorant of the
ancient tongue, but he could neither read nor write modern Greek: the
adventures of Odysseus were known to him solely from [oral] tradition. To
my question whether that tradition was widespread among the people of
Ithaca or whether it was the special domain of his family, he replied that his
family was indeed the guardian of the same, that no one else on the island
knew the story of the great king as well as he. All the others had only a dim
concept of it. . . .

There is no inn in Ithaca's capital. However, with little effort I obtained
a nice room in the house of two amiable young sisters, Misses Helene and
Aspasia Triantafyllides, whose father, a scholar, had been dead for several
years.

The white houses of that town of some 2,500 inhabitants line
the southern section of the long, narrow harbor. The latter, called Vathi
($\beta\alpha\theta\acute{\upsilon}$ = deep), itself a part of the Gulf of Molo, has given the town its name.
The harbor is one of the best in the world, because it is ringed by mountains
and its waters, even within one meter off the shore, are so deep that vessels
can anchor outside the shipowners' houses. . . .

Nearly all archaeologists who have visited the island equate it with
Homeric Ithaca.[2] . . . The island consists of a chain of limestone rocks. The Gulf
of Molo cuts it in two almost equal parts which are joined by a narrow
eight-hundred-meter-wide isthmus. There are extensive ruins on that isthmus
called "Old Castle," generally held to be the remains of Odysseus' Palace. . . .

Despite the sultry summer heat, the island has a very healthy climate and
deserves Homer's epithet "well suited for the training of excellent men."

It has been said quite rightly that nowhere else is the memory of classical
antiquity preserved as vividly and purely as on the island of Ithaca. . . . Here
all our associations are tied in with the heroic age: every hill, rock, and spring,
every olive grove reminds us of Homer and the *Odyssey*, and we leap with
ease across more than one hundred generations into the most glorious epoch
of Greek knighthood and poetry.

As soon as I was settled in my new habitation, I rented a guide and a

horse and asked to be taken to the small port of Dexia, which is at the foot
of Mount Neion and shares a part of the large inlet of Molo. Dexia is the
site of Phorcys harbor, where the Phaeacians first put the sleeping Odysseus
ashore with his treasures (afterward they deposited him under an olive tree
away from the road). . . .

The location is described in such detail in the *Odyssey* that one simply
cannot go wrong, for one sights outside the cove two small precipitous head-
lands, inclined toward the entrance, and nearby, on the slope of Mount
Neion, at fifty meters above sea level, the Grotto of the Nymphs. On the
northwesterly side of the grotto there is, indeed, a kind of natural doorway,
two meters high and forty centimeters wide, through which one can comfortably gain access to the cavern. On its south side is a round opening which
represents the entrance of the Gods, because at this point the cave is seventeen meters deep so that a man cannot very well enter.

The interior is completely dark. But my guide lit a large fire with a
brush in order that I could thoroughly examine the grotto. It is almost
circular, with seventeen meters in diameter. On entering it, one has to descend
three meters to reach the bottom. There one notices traces of rock-carved
steps. A very mutilated altar emerges on the opposite side. From the ceiling
protrude masses of stalactites in bizarre shapes. Little imagination is needed
to recognize in them urns, jars, and the looms on which [according to Homer]
the Nymphs wove purple fabrics. It was in this grotto that Odysseus, upon
Athene's advice, hid the treasures he had been given by the Phaeacians.

We returned down to the gulf (Phorcys harbor) and then continued to
the foot of the one-hundred-fifty-meter-high Mount Aëtos, which is separated
in the south from the Neion by a very fertile valley cutting across the narrow
isthmus. . . .

The ascent of the Aëtos causes the stranger many difficulties, particularly
in the heat of summer, because the mountain rises in a steep angle of forty-
five to fifty degrees and is covered with boulders. For lack of a path, one often
has to crawl on all fours. But the natives, used to climbing up the rock, scale
the Aëtos quite easily. They even cultivate the mountain to its top where
soil appears only between stones. . . .

We went up the Aëtos from the west. There the slope is gentler than on
the other sides, and one comes across numerous traces of an old road which
must have led from Odysseus' palace to the small westerly port between
Aëtos and Neion called today St. Spiridon.

It took half an hour to reach the southerly peak. Here were ruins of
a tower of coarsely cut stones of about one and a half meters in length and
nearly the same width, which are piled upon each other without cement. . . .
Inside it is a subterranean basin, perhaps a cistern, since all stones of the

structure converge toward the center, thus forming a kind of vault. . . .

A thick circuit wall of similar construction lies 10 meters below, while Cyclopean walls with defense towers extend downward southwest and southeast, their impressive ruins crowding the slope at a distance of sixty meters from the peak.[3] [Still other Cyclopean ruins adjoin.] . . . Beyond them the peak expands to a perfect plateau of thirty-seven by twenty-seven meters.

Here stood Odysseus' palace. Unfortunately, all that is left are two parallel outer walls, apart from a small cistern for domestic use. . . . The royal palace was large, because Odysseus said to Eumaeus: "This, doubtless, is the magnificent house of Odysseus. It is easy to recognize even among a multitude of houses. . . . Nobody could take it by assault." According to the *Odyssey* it was adorned with columns. The 108 Suitors sat around the table in the great hall. . . . In addition we read that Penelope climbed the high staircase in the palace, took a key, and let herself and her maids into a remote storeroom. Thus, we have little reason to doubt that the palace occupied the entire flattened area of the peak and that the court was situated in the thirty-meter-wide space between the parallel circuit walls. The altar of Zeus stood on this court.

The top of Aëtos is studded with large horizontally lying stones. But here and there I noticed patches covered by bushes and shrubs which indicated the presence of soil. At once I decided to excavate wherever the nature of the soil would permit it. However, I had no tools with me and had to postpone my explorations to the following day.

The heat was oppressive. . . . I was dying of thirst but had brought neither water nor wine along. Yet, so excited was I by the knowledge of being among the ruins of Odysseus' palace that I was oblivious of heat and thirst. Now I searched the area, now I reread in the *Odyssey* the description of the touching scenes which took place at this very spot, now I admired the splendid panorama which unrolled before my eyes. . . .

In the north I spotted the island of Santa Maura or Leucadia with Cape Doukato, greatly renowned in antiquity for the famous rock, called Leap of Sappho, from where the lovesick jumped into the sea in the hope that the bold leap would cure them of their passion. Among the most eminent victims of this folly are counted the celebrated poetess Sappho, the poet Nicostratos, Deucalion, and Artemisia, the queen of Caria. . . .

According to Strabo, every year, on the feast day of Apollo, the Leucadians used to cast a criminal down the rock into the sea as atonement for the crimes of the people. They tied feathers and live birds to the victim in order to cushion the fall.[4] Down below, fishing boats grouped in a circle stood by for a possible rescue.

In the south I sighted the glorious mountains of the Peloponnesus; in

Port of Vathi, Ithaca

the east the jagged ranges of Arcania; and at my feet in the west the splendid straits beyond which rise almost perpendicularly the beautiful heights of Cephalonia.

At last I descended the eastern slope and discovered at about thirty-eight meters below the top further vestiges of a road. . . . I also came across ruins of small houses whose Cyclopean build betrayed their great antiquity. When I reached the foot of the mountain, a peasant approached me and offered for sale an earthenware vase and a fine Corinthian silver coin with an Athene head on one side and a horse on the other. He had just discovered these objects in a crude rock-carved tomb which was devoid of human bones. I bought them for 6 francs.

At my return to Vathi I engaged four workers for the following day to carry out excavations on the Aëtos. I also hired a boy and a girl to carry water and wine up the mountain. In addition, I rented a horse for myself and an ass to transport tools.

Having had a swim in the sea and a cup of black coffee, I started out with my workers on July 10 at five o'clock in the morning. Perspiring profusely, we reached the peak at seven.

At first I had the four men tear out the underbrush by their roots, then I put them to excavating in the northeastern corner, where I suspected the splendid olive tree to have stood from which Odysseus built his marriage bed and around which he constructed his bedroom. . . . However, we found nothing but scattered pieces of tile and pottery. At a depth of sixty-six centimeters we hit bare rock. To be sure, we came across many crevices into which the olive tree could have sent its roots, but I had lost all hope of finding archaeological objects here. . . .

While my workers were occupied with this excavation, I was closely examining the entire area of the palace. In the course I encountered a thick partly curved stone. Scraping it with a knife to remove the soil, I saw that it formed a semicircle. I now continued to dig with my knife, and I soon noticed that the circle had been completed on the other side by small stones piled upon each other, thus forming a kind of miniature wall. Initially I attempted to carve out the whole circle but failed in this, because the soil—mixed with a white substance which I recognized as ashes from calcinated bones—was nearly as hard as the stone itself. Hence, I began to dig with a pickax. But as soon as I had reached a depth of ten centimeters, I smashed a beautiful, though quite small, vase filled with human ashes. I now continued to excavate with utmost care and discovered twenty vases, each one of a different bizarre shape. Some were lying on their sides, others were standing. Unfortunately I broke most when extricating them because of the hard soil and lack of adequate tools. Only five were undamaged. Two of the vases had pleasantly painted decorations when I took them out of the ground. But these almost vanished when exposed to the sun, though I hope to make the painting reappear by rubbing the vases with alcohol and water. All of the vases were filled with the ashes of human bones.

In addition I found in the small cemetery the curved blade of a sacrificial knife, thickly covered with rust, but otherwise well preserved; an earthenware idol representing a goddess with two flutes in her mouth; also the remains of an iron sword, a boar's husk, several animal bones, and, finally, an implement, from braided bronze filaments. I would have gladly given five years of my life for an inscription, but, alas, there was none.

Though it is difficult to determine the age of these objects, I am yet certain that the vases are far older than the most ancient vases from Cumae in the Naples Museum. It is quite possible that my five vases preserve the ashes of Odysseus and Penelope, or those of their descendants. . . .

On the following day, July 11, I rose at four o'clock in the morning and once more climbed the Aëtos with the four men. On its southern slope, about twenty meters above sea level, I was shown a number of ancient rock-hewn tombs which had been excavated in 1811 and 1814 by Lieutenant Guitara, bringing to light many golden bracelets, rings, and earrings.

But these graves cannot have been very ancient, for we know from Homer that the dead were cremated in the heroic age.[5] Since one frequently finds in the graves of Ithaca and Corfu scarabs with Egyptian hieroglyphs and Phoenician idols, together with Greek coins and ceramics, one has good reason to assume that the custom of burying the dead was introduced into the Ionian Islands by Egyptians and Phoenicians several hundred years after Homer. . . .

The only interesting discovery I made that day was parts of an ancient track which wends from the palace to the north side. Unfortunately I could not follow this lead on account of the briars and other considerable difficulties of terrain. But when I learned from my workers that they had seen traces of an old road in the rock at about four kilometers farther north, I concluded at once that this must be the same track.

The next day, July 12, I started with my guide as usual at five o'clock in the morning—first of all to examine the old road and afterward to visit the north side of the island. . . . When I learned that the ancient route led through the village of St. John to vineyards along the seashore, which tradition calls the field of Laertes, I sent my guide ahead with the horse. Meanwhile, I had another man take me via the old road to the country estate of Odysseus' father. . . .

Once I got to the field of Laertes, I sat down to rest and read the twenty-fourth chapter of the *Odyssey*. The arrival of a stranger is quite an event in the capital of Ithaca, but even more so in the countryside. No sooner had I sat down than the villagers crowded around me and besieged me with questions. I thought it best to read to them verses 204 to 412 from the twenty-fourth chapter and to translate word for word into their dialect.

Their enthusiasm knew no bounds when they listened to the terrible suffering of ancient King Laertes as told in the melodious language of Homer, the language of their glorious ancestors of three thousand years ago. Breathlessly they followed the description of Laertes' great joy when, at this very spot where we were assembled, he was reunited, after twenty years' separation, with his beloved son Odysseus, whom he had thought dead.

All eyes were bathed in tears when I had finished my reading. Men, women, and children came up to me and embraced me with the words: "You have given us immense pleasure. Many, many thanks!" They carried me triumphantly to the village. There each outdid the other in lavishing on me hospitality without accepting the least compensation. They would not let me depart without my promising them to revisit their village. . . .

Classical antiquity is alive in every farmhouse on the island of Ithaca, and one is constantly reminded of the description Homer gives of the homestead of Eumaeus, the divine swineherd. . . . As soon as I approached one of the island's scattered homesteads to buy grapes or drink water, I was attacked by dogs. Until now I had always been successful in keeping them at respectful distance by throwing stones at them or at least acting as if I were about to do so. But when I wanted to enter a farm in the island's south, four dogs hurled themselves furiously at me, and neither stones nor any other threats intimidated them. I cried for help. My guide had remained behind, and it seemed that nobody was at home. Fortunately I recalled the desperate situation Odysseus found himself in under similar circumstances:

"As soon as the barking dogs saw Odysseus, they rushed toward him howling. Odysseus, however, wisely sat down on the ground and let his staff slip from his hand."

I thus followed the clever king's example by lowering myself to the ground and keeping still. The dogs, who had just wanted to devour me, now circled around me and continued to bark but did not touch me. At the slightest move they would have bitten me. My playing humble calmed their savagery. . . .

My guide, seeing my precarious state, hollered loudly, thus bringing to the scene the owner, who had been at work in a vineyard near his farm. At once he called the dogs, and I was set free. He was a seventy-year-old man of mild mien, large intelligent eyes, and aquiline nose. His white mane formed a strange contrast to the blackish color of his tanned face. As peasants are wont to, he walked barefoot and wore the white cotton fustanella, which is fastened above the hips around the belly, falling in innumerable folds to the knees. . . .

I sharply reproached the old man for the wildness of his dogs, who would have torn me to pieces or, at least, would have viciously bitten me, had I not at that moment of threatening danger been reminded of the manner which the great king of Ithaca employed.

He repeatedly asked my forgiveness, saying that his dogs knew all the inhabitants of the area very well and rarely barked when any of them approached. As long as he could remember, no stranger had ever come to his home, which was situated in the midst of fields at the tip of the island. Therefore, he could not have anticipated such a danger.

To my question why, despite his obvious poverty, he kept four dogs, that ate as much as two men, he answered angrily: His father, his grand-father, and all his ancestors down to Telemachos, Odysseus, and Penelope had kept as many dogs, and he would rather suffer privation than to be separated from his faithful guardians.

I could not offer any counterargument to the honest old man's reasoning. His profuse patriotism was shocked by the very thought of having fewer dogs in his home than his illustrious ancestors at the time of the Trojan War. Convinced that his explanation had appeased me, he brought a basketful of peaches and grapes. And as another proof of his sense of pride and dignity, he categorically declined to accept any recompense. . . .

But since by all means I wanted to show him my appreciation of his hospitality, I read him the first 113 verses of the fourteenth chapter of the *Odyssey*. . . . He listened to me attentively. When, after finishing my recitation, I wanted to leave, he urged me to read to him also from the *Iliad*, of which he had but a hasty knowledge. However, I thought I had sufficiently paid my debt and could not be held back. Yet the old man's curiosity had been aroused to such a degree that he would not let the opportunity pass to learn of the events of the Trojan War. Therefore, he accompanied me on foot for the rest of the day and gave me no peace until I had told him the main incidents from the twenty-four chapters of the *Iliad*.

We wandered through the southern and southeastern part of the island, finding on two small plateaus along the steep coast ruins of several buildings which, judging from their manner of construction, may very well belong to the end of the Roman Republic or the beginning of the Empire. The most thorough search failed to yield a single Cyclopean building block. . . .

I left Ithaca with deep emotion. Long after I had lost sight of the island, my eyes were still gazing in its direction. Never in all my life shall I forget the happy days spent among those sterling, amiable, and virtuous people.

AEGEAN CITADELS—ARGOS TO ILIUM

from *Ithaca,*
the Peloponnese and Troy

We finally arrived in Corinth at six in the evening. Except for a travel bag, I sent my baggage on to Athens.

Modern Corinth exists only since 1859. In that year an earthquake totally destroyed the former city, which had been built over the ruins of ancient Corinth. It was then decided to abandon the site on account of the unhealthy air and contagious fevers from which the inhabitants perpetually suffered during the hot season. The new city was founded seven kilometers northeast at a site where the isthmus is relatively flat and a strong wind between the two seas keeps the air fresh and healthy.

I stayed three hours at ancient Corinth to examine the few ruins which are left. At first I was shown an oval amphitheater, wholly cut into the rock, of ninety-seven meters in length and sixty-four meters in breadth, equipped with a subterranean entrance for gladiators and wild animals. It was probably built after the age of Pausanias [2nd century A.D.], because he fails to mention it. Furthermore, I inspected the celebrated Seven Doric Columns, supposedly belonging to the temple of Athene Chalinitis, which Pausanias described. The columns carry the mark of great antiquity and appear to be much older than the seventh century B.C. temple of Paestum.

There is a one-story building in close proximity to these columns. It is carved entirely from stone such that the rock around it has been cut away and the remaining wall been given a thickness of thirty-three centimeters. The house stands all by itself. Since it is one with the rock on which it stands and from which it is hewn, it is, without doubt, one of the most curious monuments of ancient times.[1]

All around the area of the old town I noticed artificial hills. According to Pausanias' description, Corinth had a considerable number of temples and other magnificent monuments, and I have no doubt whatever that well-planned excavations would lead to important archaeological discoveries. But such excavations are unfortunately—and to the detriment of scientific progress—not about to be launched because Greece is short of money. It is hard to believe that until now no remains have been found of the order of columns that is named for that town—either in Corinth itself or its environs. Even the characteristic acanthus has vanished from the flora of the isthmus.

Although Corinthian farmers, when working their land, dig the soil only superficially, they quite often come across tombs with beautiful urns of fired clay. Antiquities are found here in such profusion that I was able to purchase a splendid vase for 3 francs and 25 centimes. From this follows that substantial results can be expected if excavations were executed on a large scale and with adequate funds. . . .

Above Corinth I climbed up to the famous fortress of Acro-Corinth, poised on a nearly perpendicular rock of 629 meters, which rises so steeply in its lonely majesty that neither the formidable fortress of Aden nor that of Gibraltar can stand comparison with this giant citadel. . . .

Since I had taken my Pausanias along, I read on the summit of Acro-Corinth his description of Corinth. I had difficulty believing that 629 meters below in the plain, now a picture of devastation and desolation, there was once a large, powerful, and famous city, the pride of Greece and the emporium of its trade—a city whose wealth, splendor, and luxury had become proverbial; a city that founded innumerable colonies, among them powerful and magnificent Syracuse; a city which long withstood the ambitions of Rome and which Mummius gained only through treason in 146 B.C.

I returned to New Corinth in the evening. There the commander of the small garrison had the extraordinary kindness to give me an escort of two soldiers to accompany me to Argos [the next morning].

The night I had to spend on a wooden bench in a wretched inn because the town did not have a hotel. Though I was thoroughly worn out, I was unable to close my eyes, since mosquitoes kept pestering me constantly. In vain did I try to protect myself against them by covering my face with a cloth: they bit me through my garments. I ran to the door in despair, but it was locked. The innkeeper had gone out and taken the keys with him. The place had, instead of windows, wall openings protected by iron rods. Thanks to hard and long labor I managed to rip out two rods. At the risk of being taken for a thief by night watchmen, I jumped into the street and made my bed on the beach along the seashore, where, luckily, there were no mosquitoes. Right away I fell asleep and enjoyed at least three hours of most pleasant rest.

At four o'clock in the morning I got up, swam for half an hour in the ocean, and to the great surprise of my landlord I showed up at his house. He had just started to search through my belongings, because realizing that I had made a getaway, he had assumed that I had robbed him. He was satisfied with a 2 franc coin I gave him as payment for the damaged iron rod.

At five we continued our trip to Argos—the two soldiers and a guide on foot—I on a bad horse, a veritable Rosinante. Despite my great efforts, I had been unable to get hold of either bridle, saddle, or stirrups. Such "luxury" articles are unavailable in Corinth. . . .

The trail, barely a footpath, crosses very mountainous terrain. After continuous climbing and descending, we came to the ruins of the ancient city of Cleonae. There we camped at a bubbling spring to have a frugal meal of dry bread, water, and wine. My guide and the two soldier escorts rested for an hour while I explored the ruins of Cleonae. Unfortunately there was nothing much to see but a few columns and the foundations of ancient buildings. Next to these ruins is a swamp whose evaporations poison the air and produce dangerous fevers from which almost all the people of the area suffer.

At half past twelve we arrived at the dirty, poor village of Charvati, which occupies part of the site of ancient Mycenae, the former capital of King Agamemnon once celebrated for its enormous wealth. My guide and the two soldiers, who had come all the way from Corinth on foot, were so tired that they could not accompany me to the citadel, a distance of three kilometers from Charvati. They had my permission to rest in the village until my return, the more so now that we had crossed the mountains and there was little reason to fear robbers. They had never even heard of Mycenae, had no idea of the heroes to whom this city owes its fame, and thus could not have been of any use to me, either to show me the monuments or to spur my enthusiasm for archaeology. Therefore I took along only a farmboy, who knew the citadel under the name of "Fortress of Agamemnon" and the treasury as "Tomb of Agamemnon."[2]

Mycenae's fame belongs exclusively to the heroic age, for the city lost its importance after the return of the Heraclides and the conquest of Argos by the Dorians. But it maintained its independence and took part in the national war against the Persians. . . .

Entrance to the Treasury of Atreus

When Thucydides visited the city half a century later, he found it in ruins. Strabo wrote, "Mycenae is no more," though apparently he was never there; otherwise he would have mentioned its ruins and citadel. On his visit Pausanias saw part of the citadel, the Lion Gate, the "treasuries" of Atreus and his sons, the tombs of Cassandra, Agamemnon, Agamemnon's companions murdered by Aegisthus, the charioteer Eurymedon, the sons of Cassandra, Electra, Aegisthus, and Clytemnestra.

Since the two latter tombs were, as Pausanias says, "some distance away from the wall, because Aegisthus and Clytemnestra were considered unworthy to be buried inside where Agamemnon and those who were murdered with him rested," one may conclude that Pausanias had seen all the mausoleums within the fortress itself and that those of Aegisthus and Clytemnestra were situated outside the circuit walls of the citadel.

Not a trace is left now of all these funerary monuments. But, no doubt, excavations could recover them. The fortress is, however, so well preserved and indeed even today in much better condition than one might conclude from Pausanias' remark, "There survive yet remains of the citadel, among them the gate above which the lions are." As a matter of fact, all circuit walls of the citadel are still visible today. At many places they have a thickness of five to seven meters and, according to the elevation or depression of the ground, a height of five to twelve meters. Here and there the walls were constructed from enormous irregular blocks, with gaps in between which were filled with pebbles. . . .

The entire ground within the citadel is covered with pieces of tile and pottery. Some fragments are found to a depth of six meters, as I was able to observe in a pit a peasant had just dug (for what purpose I do not know). Hence one has good reason to infer that the whole fortress was inhabited in antiquity. Considering its commanding location and large size, one may well conclude that it contained the palaces of the family of Atreus. That Sophocles was of the same opinion follows from his *Electra.*

From the fortress I made my way to the Treasury of Agamemnon, which is one kilometer away. It is dug into the slope of a hill across from a ravine. A gallery fifty meters long and nine meters wide, formed by parallel walls ten meters in height . . . leads to the big portal. . . . In the jambs one can spot holes for bolts and hinges. Aligned with those are a number of smaller circular holes of about five centimeters in diameter at the bottom of which one can see two very tiny holes. The latter, at all events, were pierced by bronze nails, of which some remains have been preserved. . . .

The treasury consists of two rooms. The first major one is conical with a sixteen-meter diameter and sixteen-meter height. It is joined by a door with the other room in the back, which, cut into the rock, is only seven and a half meters long and wide.[3] That chamber is completely dark, and unfortunately I had not taken any matches along. I asked the boy who had accompanied me from Charvati to go and fetch some, but he assured me that there were none in the village. Persuaded of the contrary, I promised him half a drachma for three matches. The boy was quite dumfounded by my generosity and would not believe me. Three times he asked me whether I was really going to give him 50 leptas if he brought me matches.[4] Twice I said yes, the third time I swore by the ashes of Agamemnon and Clytemnestra.

No sooner had I taken this oath than the boy ran quickly to Charvati, which is more than two kilometers distant from the Treasury of Agamemnon. He returned in no time, carrying in one hand a faggot, in the other ten matches. When I asked him why he had brought three times more matches than I requested, he initially gave an evasive answer. But pressed by repeated queries he finally confessed he had been worried that one or the other match would not light, and in order to be quite certain and to receive the promised reward, he fetched ten instead of three. He now kindled a large fire in the inner room. Its glow set numerous bats domiciled here aflutter. Whizzing their wings they tried to escape, but blinded by the glow of the fire they could not find the exit, flew from one side of the chamber to the other, and molested us a great deal by crashing into our faces and clinging to our clothes. This scene vividly reminded me of Homer's verses describing how Hermes leads the souls of the Suitors into the underworld and how they follow him "as bats flutter, producing a whirring noise inside the divine cave. . . ."

Near the citadel one sees the ruins of two other treasuries of smaller dimensions but built in the same style. The vaults of both have collapsed, but the walls are well preserved. When I closely examined blocks from these edifices, I found traces of bronze nails—clear proof that the interior had been dressed with copper plates. The whole surface of ancient Mycenae is covered with broken tiles and pottery . . . and just by looking at the soil one realizes that this must have been the site of a great city.

On my return to Charvati at four in the afternoon, I found my escorts and the guide fast asleep. The only way I could rouse them was by splashing their faces with water. Once fully awake, they tried to persuade me to stay in the village for the night, because it would be too late to get to Argos. However, I had little desire to spend the night in this village, the dirtiest and most miserable I had so far seen in Greece: a village without a spring, devoid of bread and fruit, with only brackish rainwater. I therefore ordered our departure. When my people raised further objections, I dismissed the two soldiers with a gift and mounted my Rosinante. With whip and spur I eventually succeeded in getting the horse to almost gallop and thus advanced toward Argos. Under the circumstances, my guide, who owned the horse, had no choice but to follow. But he did not have an easy time keeping up with me. . . .

The following morning, after breakfasting in an Argos public house, I climbed the fortress, which lies on a conically shaped 334-meter-high rock. Two street urchins offered me their services as guides for a compensation of 10 lepta each.

In antiquity the citadel was called by the Pelasgian name Larissa or, on account of its circular shape, Apsis—i.e., shield. However, I noticed few Cyclopean remains among its walls, and even of Hellenic construction there is little left. Almost all the walls were built by Venetians or Turks. Today, the citadel is abandoned and is in visible decay. The view from above is splendid. . . .

I stayed for an hour at the highest point of the fortress, surveying the Argos plain and visualizing the events that took place in ancient days. Here, in 1856 B.C., Inachos settled, and in 1500 B.C. Danaus arrived with Egyptian colonists. Here ruled Pelops and his descendants, Atreus and Agamemnon, Adrastos, Eurystheus, and Diomedes. Here Heracles who killed the lion in the Nemean Cave and Hydra in the Lernaean Swamps, was born. . . .

Argos, one of ancient Hellas' largest and most powerful cities, was noted for its people's love for the fine arts and especially music. The city had, as Pausanias reports, thirty magnificent temples, superb tombs, a stadium, gymnasium, and many other fine monuments. Now only a few ruins remain.

No sooner had I descended from the citadel with my two young guides than about twenty other boys joined me, and as much as I tried to rid myself of this noisy lot, I did not succeed. It was in such company that I inspected the remaining old town walls, then the ancient theater. . . . Nearby are the ruins of several temples. In one of the latter I bought from a farmer for 30 drachma a small marble bust of Zeus which he had allegedly found when plowing.

Since there were no more antiquities around, I returned to the city. But the twenty boys, who had accompanied me against my will, shouting loudly, demanded to be paid. Each one maintained he had been my guide. To disengage myself from them, I gave each 10 leptas. With that they were satisfied. . . .

Toward two o'clock in the afternoon I boarded a public coach bound for Nauplia. Seven kilometers from Argos and four from Nauplia I got off at the citadel of Tiryns, which lies on the plateau of a small hill and is surrounded by eight- to twelve-meter-high and eight- to nine-meter thick crudely cut walls. Pausanias reports that the hero Tiryns, who gave the town its name, was a son of Argos and a grandson of Zeus. He continues, saying that nothing was left of the ruins but a wall built by the Cyclopeans, blocks of which are of such enormous size that a team of mules could not move even the smallest one as much as an inch.[5] . . .

Throughout antiquity these walls were considered a miracle. . . . And Pausanias compares their magnificence to that of the Pyramids of Egypt. In any case, their construction goes back to the mythical age of Greece. Tradition related that Proitos [the king for whom the walls were built] ceded Tiryns to Perseus. The latter left it to Electryon, whose daughter Alkmene, the mother of Hercules, married Amphytrion. . . . Hercules conquered Tiryns and for a long time made here his domicile, wherefore he is frequently called the Tirynthian. . . . Homer calls Tiryns "girded by walls." Since he does not use this epithet for other cities, he obviously wanted to state that . . . Tiryns had a special claim to this title. . . .

I continued my trip on foot alone in the direction of Nauplia and arrived within an hour at the city gate, above which one can still see the Lion of St. Mark's. On my way to the inn I passed several fountains with Turkish inscriptions which indicate that they were laid out in the twelfth century after the Hegira.[6]

The steamboat had just left for Piraeus, and it was a full week until the next sailing. . . . [Schliemann visited instead the islands of Hydra, Poros, and

Aegina. From the last he chartered a boat to Piraeus and stayed in Athens for eight days before setting out for the Dardanelles.]

At one o'clock in the morning of August 6, 1868, I sailed on the *Nile*, a steamboat of the Messageries Impériales, from Piraeus to the Dardanelles. Unfortunately we arrived there as late as the following evening at ten. Since Turkish law forbids landing after sunset, we had to continue our voyage by the same ship to Constantinople . . . which we reached on the eighth at ten A.M. The same day I returned on the *Simoïs* to the Dardanelles. . . . I immediately looked up the Russian consul, M. Fonton, to whom I announced my wish to visit the plain of Troy. He offered excellent advice and engaged for me a guide with two horses for 90 piasters (20 francs). Without any further delay we started out for Bunarbashi, which we reached at six in the evening.

The entire land that we crossed was, with few exceptions, undeveloped. It is covered by pine and oak. The latter belong to the species *Quercus aegilops*, whose acorns are used in European tanneries and represent virtually the only export article of the land. The road was quite good. From time to time we found springs with drinking water.

Bunarbashi, presumably occupying the site of ancient Troy, is a dirty village of twenty-three hovels, fifteen of which are occupied by Turks and the rest by Albanians. Every flat roof harbors several stork nests. I counted up to twelve on one. These birds are of considerable benefit because they destroy serpents and frogs, with which the nearby swamps teem.

After my guide led me to the house of an Albanian who spoke some Greek, I paid him off. But right on entering the Albanian's house I realized

that I could not possibly stay here. Bedbugs swarmed on the walls and the wooden bench on which I was supposed to sleep. The whole place was disgustingly filthy. When I asked for milk, I was given a bowl which apparently had not been rinsed in ten years. I would have rather perished of thirst than touch it.

Hence I was forced to spend the night in the open air. I made an agreement with the Albanian to store my baggage for 5 francs a day and to supply me each morning with a loaf of barley bread. I was thus also spared watching how they prepared it.

My next concern was to secure for a few days a horse and a guide who spoke some Greek. It was anything but easy to find one. The one I got hold of demanded 45 piasters or 10 francs. I searched in vain, however, for bridle and saddle. Such things were, it seemed, not even known by name. . . .

I readily confess that I could hardly control my emotions when I saw before me the vast plain of Troy—an image that had haunted the dreams of my early childhood. Yet at first sight it seemed to me too far-flung and Troy too distant from the sea, Bunarbashi had really been built within the confines of the ancient town as almost all archaeologists who have visited the place maintain. But when I examined the ground more closely and failed to discover anywhere the least remains of tiles and pottery, I reached the conclusion that an error had been made about the actual site of Troy. My doubts increased when, accompanied by my Albanian host, I visited the springs at the foot of the hill on which Bunarbashi is located. These springs have always been equated with those mentioned by Homer as the sources of the turbulent Scamander. From one, he reports, "flows lukewarm water and steam forms above it like from a burning fire. The other runs during the summer like hail or cold snow or freezing water. Nearby are beautiful broad stone basins where the Trojan wives and their lovely daughters used to wash their gorgeous dresses—long ago, when peace reigned and ere the sons of the Achaeans had come."

But Homer's description does not fit the springs I visited. . . . Since all these springs, except one, rise next to each other at the foot of two rocks, no marked difference in temperature is likely to occur among them. Also, Homer when pointing out these springs, would not have spoken of just two, considering there were thirty-four or forty within a small area. . . .

The archaeologists who mention only two springs and keep silent over the other thirty-two or thirty-eight, look upon the brook rising here as the source of the Scamander. The large stream Menderes, which crosses the Trojan plain, they hold to be the Simoïs. This is, however, a great fallacy. For that small brook in no way corresponds to Homer's description of the Scamander as the region's main river. . . .

On our return to Bunarbashi, my host gave me the ordered loaf of bread. While my guide busied himself with the horse, I lost no time exploring the whole extent of the area which, erroneously, is considered the location of ancient Troy. In my opinion, I could best fulfill my purpose by following the same road by which, according to Homer, Achilles and Hector ran three times around the city. Assuming that the springs at the foot of the hill of Bunarbashi are really the very same Homer talks of—with which, however, I disagree—it would then be very easy to establish the circumference of Troy and the route taken by the two heroes. . . .

To start with, I went to the Scamander, taking it for the main stream. From here I walked aside the Bunarbashi hill straight to the two springs, following constantly westward the same route which Achilles must have necessarily passed in order to meet Hector before the Scaean Gate. After reaching the springs, I turned southeast, trailing a crevice between Bunarbashi and the adjacent rock. . . . After a strenuous one-hour march I reached a precipitous slope. . . . There the two heroes would have had to descend in order to get to the Scamander and to round the city. I left my guide and the horse on the hill, climbed down the precipice [so steep] that I was forced to crawl on all fours. I needed almost a quarter of an hour to get to the bottom. I then became fully convinced that no mortal, not even a goat, would have been able to descend in a speedy trot . . . and that Homer, who is so meticulous in his topographic details, could never have entertained the thought that Hector and Achilles in their race around the city had run three times down this slope—which is an absolute impossibility.

Thereupon I continued along the bank of the Scamander, the present Menderes, always following the same route which the heroes would have had to pass three times. . . . After a hike of three quarters of an hour along the river, I returned to the place from where I had started and from where, of necessity, Achilles had to leave if he were running aside the walls of Troy to the Scaean Gate. Altogether it took me two hours to encircle the site which one assigns to ancient Troy.

Once more I turned toward Ballidagh [Bali Dagh] (the name of the southeastern section of the Bunarbashi highland) by wandering from north to south through the area equated with Troy. Even though I intensely gazed in all directions for any hewn stone, a potsherd, or anything else that might indicate a former settlement, all effort was in vain: there was not the slightest sign of former human activity. . . .

Since, nevertheless, the theory of the site of Troy in the Bunarbashi highlands is gaining ever new adherents who blindly believe in it as dogma and discuss it with complete confidence, I considered it my duty to science to excavate at a few places. . . .

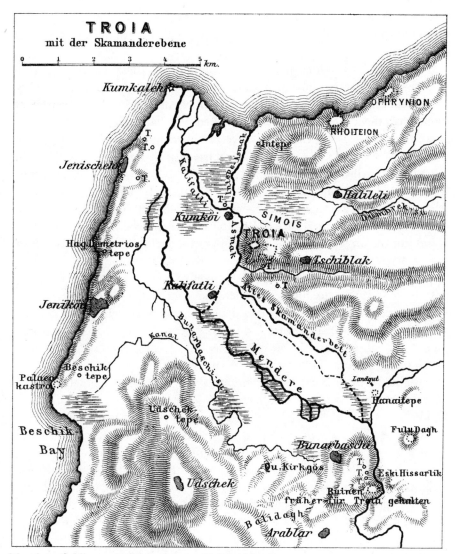

Map from *Schliemann's Excavations* by C. Schuchhardt

Should the evidence given above still be held insufficient to prove that Troy could never have stood on the Bunarbashi hills, I may add that neither from the top nor from any other place is it possible to see [Mount] Ida. This is in contradiction to Homer, who has Zeus looking down from Ida at the city of Troy. . . .

[The next day] we began our excavations in the southeast of Bunarbashi. My five workers, the guide, and myself positioned ourselves in a line of about one hundred meters. There we examined the ground by digging holes, which we intended to expand into ditches should we find ruins of ancient buildings or even potsherds.

As a rule, excavations are made at places where there is a good chance of finding antiquities. Though by now I had become completely and firmly convinced that I would not discover anything of the kind, I nevertheless shouldered the expense and gladly suffered the hardships connected with excavations. In truth, I could not have mustered more zeal had I been impelled by the certainty of digging up archaeological treasures. All I had in mind was the selfless goal of stamping out at the root the inane and erroneous belief that Troy could have been situated on the Bunarbashi highlands. I selected a shovel, ax, and bucket for myself and, despite the oppressive heat, worked with the same industry as the best of my workers.

At almost any point we hit the bedrock at a depth of half a meter. There were not the slightest traces of pottery and tiles, nowhere the least indication that the place had ever been settled by men. Nevertheless, we energetically pushed on eastward to the Scamander and continued our excavations the following day when we turned toward the rock of Ballidagh in the north—yet without any success, so that I will now swear an oath that no town has ever existed here. . . .

Indeed, it seems incomprehensible how anyone could have ever taken the heights of Bunarbashi for the site of Troy. The only explanation I can offer is that travelers have come here with preconceived ideas which, literally, blinded them. For a clear and unbiased glance could have made them realize immediately that it is altogether impossible to bring the location of these highlands into harmony with the references given in the *Iliad*. . . .

The day after, August 14, I set out with my guide and workers at five o'clock in the morning. We first walked east to the Scamander and thence north along the sandy river bed. The heat had rendered the soil so dry and powdery that it could not support my horse. Therefore I handed it over to my guide with the instruction to lead it across the fields to Hissarlik (New Ilium), while I continued on foot with the five workmen.

After an hour's difficult walk through the sand we reached the point where the small river Kimar-Su, the ancient Thymbrius, coming down from the Callicalone hills, flows into the Scamander. The banks are so thickly overgrown by trees that it is difficult to see the brook. . . . The climate is very unhealthy because, during the great heat of summer, the swamps emanate pestilential miasmas which generate dangerous fevers. . . . However, we have it from ancient authors that the region has always been marshy, even at a time when its population had been far more numerous and vigorous. Even right by the wall of Troy was a swamp, as Odysseus told Eumaeus. . . .

At about ten in the morning we came upon an extensive high terrain which was covered with potsherds and rubble from worked blocks of marble. The site of a great temple was indicated by four freestanding marble pillars which were half-buried in the soil. The vast expanse of the rubble-sown field left no doubt that we were within the confines of a large once-flourishing city. In fact, we found ourselves at the ruins of New [Novum] Ilium, known today as Hissarlik, a name that means "palace."

After walking around the ground for half an hour, we came to a hill of about forty meters in altitude which descends in the north almost perpendicularly to the plain and which is about twenty meters higher than the spur of the mountain range whose last outlier it is.

All doubts concerning the identity of Hissarlik with New Ilium vanish at the sight of this mountain range, which completely corresponds to Strabo's words, "continuous mountain ridge."

The peak of the hill of Hissarlik consists of a square, flat plateau of some 233 meters in length and width. The ingenious Frank Calvert, by exploring the hill, has established that it was, in the main, raised artificially from ruins and rubble of temples and palaces which through the course of centuries were successively built on its ground.[7] During excavation of the eastern section of the top he laid bare a part of a large edifice, a palace or temple, constructed from square blocks piled upon each other without cement. Even from the meager remains of this structure one can deduce that it was once of large size and had been executed with perfect artistry.

After having twice thoroughly examined the entire plain of Troy, I completely shared Frank Calvert's conviction that the plateau of Hissarlik marks the site of ancient Troy and that on this very hill stood its Pergamus fortress. . . .

In order to reach the ruins of the palaces of Priam and his sons, as well as the temples of Athene and Apollo, it will be necessary to remove the entire artificial part of the hill. Then it will undoubtedly transpire that the citadel of Troy extended considerably beyond the adjacent plateau. For the ruins of the palace of Odysseus [in Ithaca] and those of Tiryns and Mycenae, as well as the large, yet untouched, Treasury of Agamemnon, prove clearly that the buildings of the heroic age were quite extensive. . . .

The site of New Ilium, five kilometers in circumference, is well marked by circuit walls of which ruins are in evidence even today. The slopes, which have to be climbed and descended when circling the city, are so gentle that one can cross them in swift pace without being likely to fall. Hector and Achilles running three times around the city covered some fifteen kilometers, and such a stretch is nothing out of the ordinary. . . .

Though I have explained at length why Hissarlik fully agrees with the description Homer gives of Ilium, I will yet add that as soon as one sets foot on the Trojan plain, the view of the beautiful hill of Hissarlik grips one with astonishment. That hill seems to be destined by nature to carry a great city with its citadel. Indeed, such a position, if well fortified, is bound to wield control over the entire plain of Troy. There is no other place in the whole region which can compare with it.

From Hissarlik one can also see the Ida, from whose peak Zeus watched over Troy. . . .

On leaving Hissarlik I moved on to the town of Yenitsheri at Cape Sigeum, a promontory rising about eighty meters above sea level. Here one can take in a splendid panorama of the entire Trojan plain. When, with the *Iliad* in hand, I sat on the roof of a house and looked around me, I imagined seeing below me the fleet, camp, and assemblies of the Greek; Troy and its Pergamus fortress on the plateau of Hissarlik; troops marching to and fro and battling each other in the lowland between city and camp. For two hours the main events of the *Iliad* passed before my eyes until darkness and violent hunger forced me to leave the roof.

I went to a coffeehouse. Then I dismissed the workmen. Contrary to my expectation, I had had no occasion to use them at Hissarlik, for even without any trial digs I had become fully convinced that it was here that ancient Troy had stood. Besides, the season was unfavorable for major excavations, because the climate in August is pestilential in the plain and the soil gets too dry. April and May are the best time. . . .

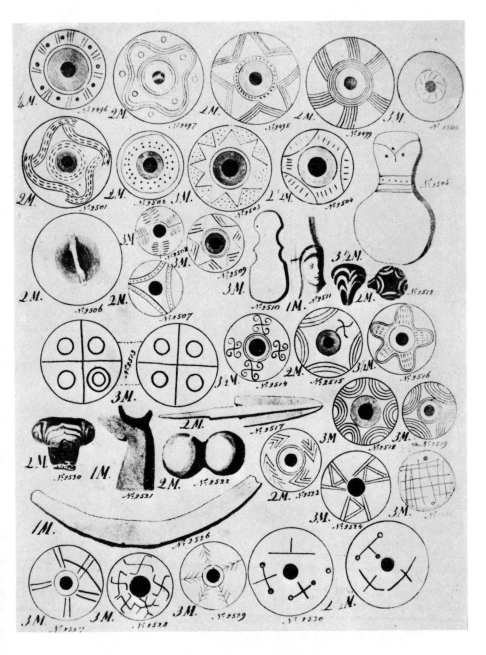

A page from Schliemann's journal of his first major excavations at Hissarlik, showing the decorations on earthenware objects discovered at what may have been the site of the ancient city of Troy.

His TRIAL DIGS at Ithaca and in the Troad whetted Schliemann's appetite for further archaeological exploration, and he began to form projects to excavate Hissarlik and Mycenae. Late in December 1868, after completing the manuscript of *Ithaka*, he wrote Frank Calvert from Paris to announce the forthcoming publication of his work and to thank him for the invaluable information he had contributed.[1] On that occasion he told him: "It gives me pleasure to inform you that I am now quite *decided* to dig away the whole artificial mount [*sic*] of Hissarlik."[2] Realizing only too well his near-total ignorance of archaeological techniques and the general conditions at Hissarlik, he bowed to Calvert's superior knowledge and point-blank presented him with a lengthy questionnaire that opened:

"Please inform me:

"When is the best time to begin work?

"Is it not advisable to commence as early as possible in spring?

"I am very susceptible to fever; is there much apprehension of same in spring?

"What medicines have I to take with me?

"Must I take a servant with me? or can I get a very trustworthy one at Athens? Probably it is better to have a faithful Greek who speaks Turkish? . . ."

Among other commonplace points he raised were:

"Have I to take a tent and iron bedstead and pillow with me from Marseille? for all the houses in the plain of Troy are infested with vermin.

"Please give me an *exact* statement of *all the implements* of whatever kind and of *all the necessaries* which you advise me to take with me.

"Do I require pistols, dagger and rifle?

"Can I get laborers enough, where and at what wage? . . ."

157

Then he went on to pose more strictly archaeological questions such as:

> "In how much time do you think I can dig away the artificial mount?
> At what cost?
> "What had led you to conclude that the hill is artificial?
> "What is the high [sic] of the artificial mount to be taken away? . . ."[3]

Within a few days, Calvert, extraordinarily chivalrous and forbearing, returned a numbered list, giving extensive answers to all Schliemann's queries, which certainly bespoke his unselfish expertise. It also showed how much Schliemann's procedure at the Hissarlik hill would owe to Calvert's counsel. Nevertheless, chances are that had Calvert had the funds and Homeric ardor to launch major operations of his own, he might have proceeded more carefully and caused less destruction.[4]

Schliemann did not immediately act upon Calvert's information. Christmas and New Year intervened. Other matters claimed his attention, and for a while Troy seemed to fade into the background. Finally, in April 1869, Calvert had word from Schliemann about the delay: "With the excavations at Hissarlik I think we must wait till next spring for I cannot hope to obtain my divorce here before the beginning of June and the terrible heat, the pestilential fevers and the dryness of the soil make the works next to impossible in the summer months."[5]

The letter was written from, of all places, Indianapolis in the Midwestern American state of Indiana.

The year 1869 was a decisive one in Schliemann's life, even though it did not advance his archaeological projects. It had started miserably enough for him, with the disastrous homecoming to his family in early January. But with the publication of *Ithaka* soon after, he had—at least in his own eyes—not only established himself as an author, but, more important, had also found a field of studies which was wide open to an outsider and which could enlist a man who was an entrepreneur and activist as well as an aspiring savant.

Schliemann felt that he now deserved admission to the republic of letters and learning. Basically insecure, in the manner of brash and outwardly successful people, he was the more eager for official recognition to legitimize his transition from merchant to writer-scholar. Upon the advice, and with the active help, of a lawyer cousin he campaigned at the University of Rostock in his native Mecklenburg for the title of Doctor of Philosophy without having to undergo the usual bench-warming rigors of a student's curriculum.[6] For that purpose, he presented, together with his two published books, a vita—written in both an ancient Greek and Latin version—that was to be considered his actual thesis.[7] This rather irregular academic wire-pulling, so typical of many of Schliemann's transactions, worked, and he received his doctorate the same year from his home university. He was to take considerable pride in the title. Thenceforth, he wanted to be known and addressed as Dr. Heinrich (or Dr. Henry) Schliemann.

The unfortunate Christmas incident at St. Petersburg may have persuaded Schliemann that, before preparing for the resurrection of Homer's Troy, he should make a clean slate of his personal life and write finis to his marital disaster. He set about getting a divorce. Learning that proceedings would be much simpler and faster in the United States, he again sailed across the Atlantic in March 1869. A first and mandatory step was to acquire American citizenship. Since he had already declared his intention to become an American citizen in 1851 during his first stay, the only other requirement was proof of a five-year residence. New York friends graciously obliged by testifying to that effect and, within three days of his arrival in New York, on March 29, 1869, Schliemann became an American citizen in fact rather than make-believe.

Alas, New York proved to be a less easy and tractable ground for ending his marriage. Inquiries as to which state could best accommodate him led to Indiana.[8] On April 1, 1869, Henry Schliemann, American citizen, took up residence in Indianapolis. The proceedings did not turn out to be as smooth and expeditious as expected, however, particularly since they hinged on the Indiana state legislature, which was about to reform its all-too-loose divorce laws. Despite his insistence on wanting to stay within the law (only a few days after friends had to perjure themselves to make him an American citizen), Schliemann, who boasted of having five lawyers working for him, was not beyond using his "influence" to sway the right honorable legislators. He got his divorce on June 30, and the decree became final on July 14. His legal aides promptly presented him with a bill for $1,500. One may speculate into whose pockets part of that money went. Thanks to Schliemann's politicking, the reformed divorce bill did not take effect until 1873.

Schliemann was far from idle during the long wait of more than three months in Indianapolis. At first he wanted to make it quite clear that he was, and would remain, a bona fide resident of the ("our") city by acquiring a house to live in and even purchasing a share in a starch factory.[9] With his customary verve he highly praised the growing Midwestern center of forty thousand inhabitants, for whose incredibly rapid progress in commerce and industry, he asserted, European standards of comparison were meaningless. "No less than 12 mighty railways cross the little town and their number will grow to 15 by the end of the year."[10] He also took a lively interest in the passing parade of Negro servants he hired to keep house for him. His cook, who was half-black, half-Indian, he reported, read three newspapers every day and was thoroughly familiar with American politics, history, and geography—the more surprising since "in the whole state of Indiana there is not a single school for colored people."[11] Keeping his eye on the American economy, he further reported that the Southern states, "which were but three years ago covered with gore and anarchy," were now "flourishing."[12]

During his stay in Indianapolis, he read widely and sent out a steady stream of letters to friends and relatives in Europe. Even the venerable Ernest Renan he tried to delectate with little pieces of Americana he had observed. The London Schröder was supplied with a report on American business and the affairs of Cuba, which, he kept insisting, once annexed to the United States, will be "a vast and beautiful garden, crossed in all directions by well-paying railroads."[13] In addition, he discovered a special fascination for polar exploration and the Northwest Passage and even pledged financial support for such research. He also found time to further his study of the Arabian language and its literature and composed an essay on the *Arabian Nights,* rejecting the thesis of its alleged Chinese literary origins. Another lengthy paper delivered to the Convention of American Philologists at Poughkeepsie summarized his views on the learning of languages in colleges. It opened with Charles V's remark: "With every language one acquires a new life."[14]

While his divorce case was progressing, Schliemann's thoughts turned toward remarriage. In fact, even before suing for divorce and while still in Paris, Schliemann had written in February 1869 to his former teacher and Athenian friend, the Archbishop of Mantineia and Kynouria, Theokletos Vimpos, asking him to find a wife among the black-haired beauties of Hellas. The request was accompanied by two copies of his recent book with liberal checks to cover binding costs and a "donation for the poor." (More money followed later to help the archbishop, who had asked his assistance, pay off debts.)

His future bride had to be Greek. He allowed that there was no lack of witty and beautiful Parisiennes who would jump at a chance to "heal his sufferings," but he was apprehensive of the morals of French ladies. His specifications for a wife were that she have the same lovable character as Vimpos' sister, who, unfortunately, was already married. Preferably poor and without dowry, she should be intelligent and have a good education. Above all, "she must be enthusiastic about Homer and about a rebirth of my beloved Greece."[15]

Vimpos, apparently, was not the least floored by the mission his former pupil entrusted to him and straightaway went scouting for a made-to-order bride. By early May, Schliemann had several photographs of eligible women. To one Polyxanna he took exception because of her Italianate surname. Also, her physiognomy seemed to betray the character of a bossy, ill-tempered virago. However, he reacted quite differently to the likeness of a young schoolgirl by the name of Sophia Engastromenos, who turned out to be the daughter (the youngest of seven children) of the archbishop's favorite cousin, a formidable lady of Cretan origin.[16] The girl's father, who had fought with distinction in the Greek War of Independence, was a draper of moderate means.

Sophia struck the mature would-be suitor as not only extraordinarily beautiful (of the dark, sultry Mediterranean type) but splendid in all respects. Alas, she was much too young for him. Wouldn't it be better for him to marry a widow who knew what marriage was all about than a ripe young girl who was likely to put too much value on the physical aspect of a conjugal relationship? Though he had been of a hot-blooded, sensuous nature, he confessed, companionship was now uppermost in his mind. He wanted a wife who could be his student and assistant, who was to share his antiquarian interests and accompany him on his travels. Schliemann was, indeed, possessed by the Platonic eros to teach and direct a young person. Throughout the correspondence pertaining to his remarriage, this is a recurrent theme. In a way he hoped to have his wife take the place of his faraway children, whose education he so passionately had wanted to guide and whom he wanted for pupils and comrades.[17] His conclusion in reply to Vimpos' pictorial prospectus was a renewed solicitation: "Try to find me a wife with a Greek name and a soul impassioned for learning."[18]

No sooner had he written this letter in Indianapolis than he had second thoughts. Within a day he sent off another missive to Vimpos. Now he declared, "Already have I fallen in love with Sophia Engastromenos . . . so that I swear she is the only woman who shall be my wife."[19] But then he conjured up reasons why he might not be able to marry her after all: "First, I am not sure yet that I shall get the divorce; second, because of my matrimonial difficulties I have had no relations with a woman for six years."[20] However, he soon after reassured Vimpos that he was "in every respect most fit to marry a Greek wife."[21]

A few weeks later, though the divorce had not yet been granted, Schliemann's mind had been made up. He wrote to his old father:

The Archbishop of Greece [a Schliemannesque exaggeration], my former teacher, has sent me the portraits of several Athenians for selection; I have chosen from these Sophia Engastromenos as the most lovable and it appears that the Archbishop, before he was promoted to the higher clergy and still thought of remaining a sinner, intended to marry her. At any rate I intend, if everything goes well, to go to Athens in July to marry her and with her to come to you, since as I am enthusiastic about the Greek language I believe that I can be happy only with a Greek, I will, however, take her only if she has a liking for sciences because I believe that a beautiful young girl can respect and love an old man only in the event she has enthusiasm for sciences in which he is much more advanced than she is. I have ordered 12 copies of Sophia's photograph and will send you one today or tomorrow. . . .[22]

Schliemann wasted no further time. His divorce granted, he left Indianapolis for New York and on August 7 was bound for France. He took another ship from Marseille and arrived in Athens on September 4 in "the fatherland of gods and heroes."[23]

It wasn't all smooth going. The Engastromenos clan, it seems, was a grasping lot. With Sophia, however, he was delighted from the beginning. He knew he had chosen well when, watching her in class at a school for gifted Athenian girls, he heard her recite Homer and reveal a good command of ancient history. He also saw her move with natural grace among her family. To his chagrin, however, he was soon to realize that the girl's relations looked upon the whole affair as mainly a financial arrangement. And when, at long last, he had a chance to be alone with Sophia and asked her why she wanted to marry him, he got the disconcerting answer that her parents wanted her to take a rich husband. That almost ended the courtship. Schliemann announced that he was leaving for good. Notes flew to and fro between the Hôtel d'Angleterre and the Engastromenos home. Undoubtedly coached by her family, Sophia sent sweet, conciliatory lines which, in the end, melted the middle-aged Lothario. Schliemann pressed for an early wedding. They were married by the archbishop on September 23. The greed of Sophia's family did not diminish, however. It would become a considerable source of irritation to Schliemann in the early years of his marriage and almost led to another divorce.

The newly married couple left Piraeus on their wedding night en route to Messina and Naples and eventually Paris, where they were to make their permanent home. On the way, at the art centers of Western Europe, Schliemann, with little regard for his bride's own wishes and her delicate constitution, began Sophia's "scientific education." (Indoctrination in foreign languages followed in Paris.) For hours on end he would drag her through the great galleries and museums. At last he had gained the "lifetime student" he had looked for. Yet, he loved Sophia sincerely and fiercely. While still on his honeymoon he reported to his family in Germany: "Sophia is a splendid wife, who could make any man happy, for, like almost all Greek women, she has a kind of divine reverence for her husband. . . . She loves me as a Greek, with passion, and I love her no less. I speak only Greek with her, for this is the most beautiful language in the world. It is the language of the gods."[24]

The luxury apartment in Paris, high living, opera, and chic clothes made little impression on Sophia. She was homesick. The force-feeding with foreign languages (French and German) was too much for her. When Schliemann learned of the death of his daughter Natalia from a rare disease and in grief withdrew into himself, Sophia began to suffer from uncontrollable crying spells.[25] At last, upon doctor's orders, he had to take her back to Athens, which from then on was to be his home port. The shock over Sophia's nervous state brought him to his senses. He also learned to treat his young wife with greater consideration and to forswear his role as Prussian schoolmaster.

Sophia, indeed, would become a wonderful wife and companion. She gave Schliemann two bright children (Andromache and Agamemnon), took an active part in his researches, developed into an able assistant at his excavations, and with her diplomatic skill helped smooth many a difficult impasse that her impatient, hotheaded husband precipitated with officials. When, years later, the couple visited Ankershagen in Mecklenburg, Schliemann's old love, Minna, remarked that Sophia was the greatest treasure the world-famous archaeologist had ever discovered. In a moving letter a few weeks before his death, Schliemann would write Sophia—in classical Greek, of course:

> . . . On our wedding anniversary it is my wish that the gods will let us spend this day together in health and well-being not only in the coming year but on each of the following 21 years. Today I look back at the long time that we have shared with each other and I see that the fates have bestowed on us much suffering but also many sweet joys. . . . Words fail me to celebrate our marriage. At all times you were to me a loving wife, a good comrade, and a dependable guide in difficult situations, as well as a dear companion on the road and a mother second to none. It has always been a pleasure to me to watch you in the panoply of your virtues. Therefore, today, I promise that I shall marry you again in a future life.[26]

Less than four months after his wedding, Schliemann's thoughts were once again focused on Troy. Aboard the steamboat *Niemen* bound from Marseille to Piraeus he mailed on February 17, 1870, an urgent letter to Frank Calvert. In it he begged the American consul to inform him, "by the first opportunity," whether he now had obtained the *firman* (official permit by the Turkish government to excavate), for "in that case I should like to commence at Hissarlik at once."[27] Schliemann had as yet no concept of how slowly the bureaucratic mills grind in the Orient. All his fuming, pressuring, arm-twisting, flattering, bribing, and cajoling would make little difference. The diplomatic battle for Troy had barely begun.

While Sophia convalesced at her parents' home, Schliemann dashed off alone on a sailing trip (on which he again came close to shipwreck several times) among the Cyclades—glorious dots not only in the dark-blue Aegean but in Greek mythology, history, and art. He stopped over at Syros (Syra), the most populous; Delos, birthplace of Apollo and Artemis; Naxos, sacred to Dionysos; Paros, famous for its marble; and Thera (Santorin), part of a once highly active volcanic cone under whose lava beautiful vases had been dug up, older than anything from classical Greece.[28] Schliemann, who acquired some, thought that they were at least four thousand years old.

When he got back to Athens, there was no word from Constantinople. To pass time, he went with Sophia for brief visits to Delphi, Marathon, and Eleusis, regions that were then judged unsafe because of widespread brigandage. Then his patience, always at a breaking point, came to an end as far as the Turkish government was concerned, and within a few days he was off to the plain of Troy. *Firman* or no *firman* he had a date with King Priam. Sophia refused to come along.

For twelve days, from April 9 to 21, he rummaged around the Hissarlik hill with indifferent results, though with typical Schliemann zest. Apart from a few building foundations, he collected masses of potsherds, stone lance points, bronze nails, and veritable garbage heaps from food leftovers. He was not overimpressed. His enthusiasm grew, however, when there cropped up a vase with the inevitable "human ashes." Nor did he hesitate to identify as Helen of Troy a terra-cotta bust one of his workers extricated from a trench. In personal letters and lengthy articles he dispatched to the Institut de France and the *Augsburger Allgemeine Zeitung* he asserted that the subterranean walls he hit upon belonged to Priam's Palace. And one of the silver pieces found, though late Roman, was inscribed in Greek, "Hector of Troy"—a welcome message from the gods that boosted the fledgling excavator's spirits.

But then came the showdown. The Turkish peasants who owned the land vigorously protested—and not without provocation—Schliemann's illegal operations on their property. None of his pronouncements on his scientific mission impressed them in the least. Only when he agreed to their carrying away some of the blocks from the ruins he had unearthed were they temporarily mollified. After a few days they reappeared. The argument started anew, and exorbitant demands were made. Schliemann proposed to buy the land from them, but in vain. In addition, there loomed a threat from the Turkish authorities who, once alerted, surely would make short shrift of his freebooting enterprise. So, in a huff, Schliemann dismissed his workmen and returned to Athens. From now on he would try legal means. He hoped that, while waiting for the Turks to comply, he could switch his activities to Mycenae. But the Greek government threw cold water on that project, giving as reason for its refusal the rampant banditry in the land.

Meanwhile news of Schliemann's Hissarlik raid got to Constantinople, no doubt aided by his voluble utterances. Calvert and the American ambassador to the Sublime Porte, Wayne MacVeagh, who was also trying to help Schliemann, were taken aback. Wrote Calvert: "I cannot conceal how injudicious I think it is of you to have made a boast of what you did—and we must suffer the consequences and get the Firman when the Government are in a better humour."[29] Those virtues of the well-bred Anglo-Saxon such as fair play, sportsmanship, and understatement were rather alien to Schliemann. A man like Calvert he would never comprehend.

That Schliemann eventually got his permit was in itself almost miraculous. His obsequious letters to Turkish officials, his frequent *démarches* at Constantinople—while antechambering there he learned Turkish—his petitions and interviews, his exaggerated promises to turn over all the precious metal objects he might find, his pestering of foreign diplomats and of Calvert himself, whom he once promised "an excellent commission" if he could effect the land sale, hardly advanced his cause.

Though he was as yet unable to tackle either Troy or Mycenae, Schliemann kept himself busy otherwise. He undertook several trips to Paris, vacationed with his wife at Boulogne-sur-Mer on the eve of the Franco-Prussian War (in which his sympathies were wholly with the French), and went for a two-month tour through England and Scotland. When Paris was besieged by German troops, Schliemann became alarmed by rumors that much of the city was devastated and feared the worst for his houses. The substantial income he derived from their rents was at stake. But the German bigwigs, including Prince Bismarck, refused to let him through the lines to Paris. Never one to be discouraged by a rebuff or at a loss to circumvent regulations, Schliemann got hold of a postmaster's passport for 5 francs and put on his uniform. Charles Klein from Lagny, the postmaster, was listed as thirty and Schliemann was about fifty, though he looked even older. Three times, he told a friend later, the Germans were about to arrest him and would have surely shot him, had he not put to good use the German mania for titles. "By addressing every lieutenant as general and every common soldier as colonel, I managed to overcome all obstacles."[30]

To his happy surprise, all his Paris property was unscathed. He shed tears of joy, he reported, when he got to 6, place Saint-Michel, and saw that all the valuables he had thought destroyed were intact. "I gave the books in my library as many kisses as I would have given a child snatched from death's door."[31]

Barely had he returned from his wartime adventure to Athens when his wife gave birth to a daughter on May 18, 1871. Then on August 12, when Schliemann was in London, he at last received the coveted *firman* through the good services of the American embassy in Constantinople. With the season already far advanced and the move to his own house in Athens under way, he made plans with Sophia to go to Hissarlik at their earliest convenience. But once they got to the Dardanelles at the end of September, they were faced with more delays and chicaneries. Finally, on October 11, the path was cleared, and work could start in earnest.

The *firman* contained three main provisions: (1) all the finds had to be divided—one half going to the new Turkish archaeological museum, the other to Schliemann; (2) uncovered ruins must be left in the state they had been recovered; (3) all expenses connected with the excavation had to be borne by Schliemann. In addition, he was given a government supervisor who was to watch over the operations. Such a person was always a thorn in Schliemann's side, and he would taunt the poor man, who after all was only doing his duty.

With winter approaching, it was to be a short dig of barely six weeks (October 11–November 24) and not a particularly rewarding one. Sophia soon returned to their infant daughter in Athens, while Schliemann continued his excavations rather erratically. More than one fair-minded scholar has, in fact, compared them to outright rape. The problems of stratification and chronology completely baffled him. Most of the artifacts he collected—such as so-called carrousels, volcanoes, humming tops, or plain spindle whorls—were new to him and almost anybody else. At this stage, Schliemann was a rank amateur who lacked sound method and insight. As often as not, his workers stood in each other's way. Their employer, overwrought and huffing and puffing, ran to and fro over the lacerated hill to keep them in line and to put them to work hacking into the mound.

In truth, Schliemann felt mostly bewildered, and, strange for so assertive a man, at times even he realized that he was only a neophyte groping in the dark. He begged others for advice, and in one of his reports on his excavations, he inserted the appeal: "I therefore consider it necessary to describe everything as minutely as possible, in the hope that one or other of my honoured colleagues will be able to give an explanation of the points which are obscure to me."[32]

Still, he was as ready as ever to jump to hasty conclusions, some of which he would stick to with religious zeal. Since he was convinced that the ancient Trojans worshiped Athene, he saw her alleged owl image in primitive vases, urns, and shards, just as he was later to detect Hera effigies among the pottery of Mycenae and Tiryns. Throughout his operations, Schliemann's faith in the absolute accuracy of Homer (in whom, as he proclaimed, he

"Owl-faced" terra-cotta vase and stone object from Troy

believed "as in the Gospel itself") also remained steadfast. Homer inspired his overall excavation plan, which was oddly at cross-purposes with itself. It rested on two assumptions derived from the *Iliad*, namely that the temple of the Trojan Pallas Athene occupied the highest point of the hill, while the defense wall with Priam's citadel (the former allegedly built by Apollo and Poseidon) had to be at the very bottom. Hence he aimed at simultaneously locating the towering temple—which he never found—and the virgin soil some fifty feet below, where, as he was to learn later, Homeric Troy could not be found either. No wonder this schizophrenic scheme created chaos. His master strategy, simple in its brutality, to cut a wide north-south trench, a man-made Grand Canyon, through the entire mound and in the course mercilessly demolish practically everything in its way, without properly recording or photographing it, is a sad story for which even Schliemann's greatest admirers have come up with only feeble excuses. Wilhelm Dörpfeld, who became an assistant and good friend, was forced to concede again and again in the authoritative compendium of his own later work at Hissarlik that missing edifices (some probably of that very Troy Schliemann had been looking for) had been dismantled by the master without a trace.

During his 1871 labors, Schliemann agonized most over implements from the so-called Stone Period. Since they were encountered in top layers as high as Hellenistic and Roman remains, they presented him with a total mystery. How could he ever hope to find Homer's bronze or iron city if he had already hit near the surface a neolithic culture of presumably much older date? Exuberance gave way to despair. Thus he confided to his diary on November 1, 1871, that now he had lost all hope of ever finding Troy.[33] But the mercurial man rebounded, particularly after Frank Calvert and his equally knowledgeable brothers—most important James Calvert—furnished him with plausible explanations for the aberrant Stone Age deposits. Digging beyond this disconcerting layer, Schliemann met again with metal objects and ancient ware of greater sophistication. The Homeric sun broke through the clouds. His report toward the close of the 1871 season could sign off with an affirmative coda.

The onset of cold weather with its slashing rainfall and chilling north winds put an end to the excavations of the brief 1871 season. Schliemann could not immediately return to his new home in Athens for he was detained by quarantine for eleven days on Samos. He was keen on getting home, seeing his little daughter, and burying himself in archaeological and philological literature in order to clear up vexing questions raised by his excavations.

Foremost on his mind was the swastika that he found scratched or painted on some objects found at Hissarlik. The symbol intrigued him. Like the "owl" vases, which he was to come across in ever greater profusion during his 1872 dig and which he convinced himself were definite proof for Homeric connections with the Hissarlik site, the swastikas had to assume a fundamental significance, and he was prone to link them with the Indo-European "ancestral" races of Bactria and India. First carried away by flights of fancy, he would then look for academic authorities to bear him out.[34] Unlike the far-fetched equation of Pallas Athene with crudely shaped anthropomorphic vessels, he did not have to improvise a grand theory all by himself. The scholars who subscribed to it were consulted, and the upshot for Schliemann was a highly pleasing notion of the Aryan kinship of the Trojans with the Hellenic people (and Mecklenburgers). Ever ready to leap to sweeping conclusions, he planned a grand tome on swastikas as "religious symbols of the very greatest importance among the progenitors of the Aryan races," which might well have earned him honorable citation by the latter-day racist apostles of Nordic supremacy.[35]

Happily he decided to remain a practicing archaeologist. There was an increasing correspondence to take care of. His notes had to be reworked into articles for the press. And to broaden his understanding of the unusual artifacts he had encountered in the Troad, Schliemann also felt the need to inspect various prehistoric collections in museums and to personally contact colleagues in Western Europe. This gave him a welcome excuse to travel. In Paris he looked up Ernest Renan, who remained skeptical about Troy. Afterward, in London, he was introduced to Gladstone, then serving his first term as Prime Minister. "I found to my astonishment and delight," Schliemann wrote to the wife he had left behind in Athens, "that he has followed my work with keen interest. Although we disagreed on many points of view, in general he seems certain that my major premise is sound."[36]

Schliemann started the new season of 1872 earlier than the previous year, on April 1. Despite the somewhat sober mood with which he concluded his 1871 labors at Hissarlik, he had put some of his doubts aside and resumed his great task with buoyant energy. The more modest goals he had charted only a few months ago ("I shall be perfectly contented, if by my labours I succeed only in penetrating to the deepest darkness of prehistoric times . . .")[37] may have sounded as if he had become converted to the detached, plodding attitude of the scientific researcher. Yet he went overboard as soon as he had the vaguest hunch that he might be close to Homeric sites. The will to believe almost always got the better of brute, recalcitrant facts. But then, it may be argued, some of the great insights are made of just such dubious stuff. Nevertheless, the pendulum could as easily swing the other way. Whenever faced with reverses, Schliemann easily gave in to perplexity and even resignation.

His basic plan (and assumptions) remained much the same during his 1872 excavations: in order to reach the virgin soil where Homer placed Priam's citadel, he had to drill all the way through the man-made hill. In this enterprise Schliemann developed the skills of a demolition engineer—at the expense of archaeological responsibility.

This time his working methods were vastly more efficient. In line with his large-scale undertaking, he hired a railroad engineer, who also helped with the drawing of maps. (The fleeting notion to invite seasoned excavators from Pompeii or Rome was quickly abandoned.) He was provided by his "honoured friends, Messrs. John Henry Schröder & Co. of London, with the very best English wheelbarrows, pickaxes, and spades."[38] Special equipment also included battering rams (!), as well as screw-jacks, chains, and windlasses. In the course of excavation Schliemann removed gigantic masses of soil and building blocks and never tired of estimating the hundred thousands of cubic feet or yards he disposed of. No wonder that such drastic operations led to near-fatal cave-ins and rock slides. Still he continued.

On occasion he would humbly canvass the opinions of even skeptical scholars, such as the illustrious German classicists Ernst Curtius and Alexander Conze, on literary and cultural questions ("I sometimes lack the sound counsel of a man like you, and if you could advise me, I would be tremendously obliged to you"[39]). But he never seemed bothered about his lack of exacting excavation techniques. Frank Calvert tried to impress on him the advantage of digging a web of smaller trenches instead of gaping "platforms," but he made little dent. And Emili Burnouf could not help admonishing him ("*Tenez bien compte de cela!*") to always indicate the precise site where an object has been found, because only then could one assemble what belongs together. "Solely the knowledge of the location occupied by the object during excavation can truly indicate its epoch," Burnouf wrote sagaciously.[40] But such wisdom, though at times piously echoed in Schliemann's writings, was rarely honored in actual procedures.

The 1872 season had its share of tribulations. Schliemann was particularly irked by the bad habits of his Greek workmen. Obviously, they lacked the capitalistic impulse that raises North German pastors' sons to hereditary membership in the St. Petersburg merchant guild. He also took exception to shrieking owls (he ordered his men to gun down Athene's sacred bird) and to croaking frogs, not to mention poisonous snakes and motley insects. In midsummer he and most of the crew succumbed to "marsh fever" and had to call a halt to their operations on August 14.

His excavations, however, particularly if measured by volume of soil displaced, made great strides in several parts of the hill. As was his custom, Schliemann had contingents of workers digging simultaneously at several places. Up to one hundred fifty were enlisted. In addition to his engineer, Schliemann recruited three overseers. Sophia, who did not stay the entire season, held her own command. But nothing really earthshaking was brought forth for a long time. By early May he had confessed to a society of Greek philologists, "It seems that the Olympic gods wished to withhold forever prehistoric traces in the Troad from the eyes of men."[41] Somewhat discouraged, Schliemann toyed with Calvert's original suggestion to hand over operations, including his *firman*, to a society or institution. He became more and more alarmed by the costliness of the enterprise, quite out of proportion to its returns. In the future, he hinted, he might confine himself to choice Greek sites like Delphi, Mycenae, Olympia, and Delos.

Was he ever going to solve the Trojan Question? Short of coming across Trojan inscriptions, nothing but Cyclopean walls as part of a royal stronghold deep down on the natural rock would suffice. Only a few days after the gloomy communication to the Greek philologists, he advised Burnouf that he had indeed reached the rock bottom, but it is doubtful whether he actually did. Here, at or near the bottom, he saw ample testimony of a high archaic civilization and what he considered magnificent pottery represented by the Homeric *dépas amphikypellon* (an elongated two-handled goblet).

At the time he had also cut a wide trench in the eastern half of the hill belonging to Calvert, and almost immediately discovered a beautiful, probably Hellenistic, piece of relief sculpture, which may have once adorned a temple frieze. It became one of Schliemann's most cherished trophies. After compensating Calvert for his half-ownership, he was determined to take it to Greece—in disregard of Ottoman laws and his *firman*. There was then enacted a prologue or dress reheasal to his later scheme to smuggle a still greater hoard out of the country. Because of the unwieldy size of the sculpture,

Schliemann proposed to saw off pieces on both sides, which he declared would stand to improve its artistic quality, but Calvert talked him out of this vandalism, and the relief was surreptitiously shipped in toto on a Greek caïque to Piraeus to be deposited in Schliemann's garden. He sent plaster copies of it to Rostock and to classical departments in Berlin, Munich, and Vienna and the British Museum in London. Later on he donated the original to the Berlin Ethnological Museum.

Meanwhile, Schliemann's Homeric enthusiasm was further fired by the appearance of a very ancient wall and what he baptized the "Great Tower of Ilium," which, a few years later, turned out to be just a section of the emerging double circuit wall of the second prehistoric city. Though it was neither a tower nor even on the prime rock, he needed little convincing that this was a glorious historic landmark. He proclaimed that Troy of the Trojans had at last been found. Raising his (imaginary) Homeric standard on Priam's citadel, he officially announced that he was restoring to Hissarlik the sacred name of which Lechevalier and his skeptical predecessors and followers had so pettily deprived it.[42] Henceforth his bulletins were to be signed from the Pergamus (citadel) of Troy or Ilium.

The excavation of these structures marked Schliemann's "definitive" identification of the city of *Iliad* fame. From this view he would never veer. So much was he impressed by the formidable wall and lofty "tower," to-

gether with the pottery and a few specimens of precious metal he collected, that eventually he saw himself compelled to give up his dogma that Homer's Troy had to be laid out at the very bottom. At this stage of his campaign, however, his ideas about the successive strata of the Hissarlik hill remained vague and confused. Gradually he came to distinguish four layers—usually equated with "four nations"—preceding the classical Greek colony, "Aeolic Ilium," of around the 7th century B.C. As to the "tower," it was fortunate that during its discovery in 1872 he thought it to rest on the lowest level. Otherwise, as he insinuated in his report, he might have dismantled it, too.

Throughout his 1871 and 1872 seasons at Hissarlik, as well as during his third season in 1873, Schliemann mailed frequent progress reports to the *Augsburger Allgemeine Zeitung* and *The Times* of London. The world was kept well informed of his excavations. These dispatches were later collected in Schliemann's third book, *Troy and Its Remains* (1875); and just as his excavations were erratic, there was little order in these compositions. Even the edited book lacks unity and consistency, though it possesses an endearing freshness. Schliemann frequently changed his interpretations and theories from report to report, and he candidly conceded in the introduction to the book that "if my memoirs now and then contain contradictions, I hope that these may be pardoned when it is considered that I have here revealed a new world of archaeology, that the objects which I brought to light by thousands are of a kind hitherto never or but rarely found, and that consequently everything appeared strange and mysterious to me."[43]

THE CAMPAIGN BEGINS

from *Troy
and Its Remains*

*On the Hill of Hissarlik, in the Plain of Troy,
October 18th, 1871.*

. . . The site of Ilium is upon a plateau lying on an average about 80 feet above the plain, and descending very abruptly on the north side. Its northwestern corner is formed by a hill about 26 feet higher still, which is about 705 feet in breadth and 984 in length, and from its imposing situation and natural fortifications this hill of Hissarlik seems specially suited to be the acropolis of the town.

Ever since my first visit, I never doubted that I should find the Pergamus of Priam in the depths of this hill. In an excavation which I made on its north-western corner in April 1870, I found among other things, at a depth of 16 feet, walls about 6½ feet thick, which, as has now been proved, belong to a bastion of the time of Lysimachus.[1] Unfortunately I could not continue those excavations at the time, because the proprietors of the field, two Turks in Kum-Kaleh, who had their sheepfolds on the site, would only grant me per-mission to dig further on condition that I would at once pay them 12,000 piasters for damages, and in addition they wished to bind me, after the con-clusion of my excavations, to put the field in order again. As this did not suit my convenience, and the two proprietors would not sell me the field at any price, I applied to his Excellency Safvet Pasha, the [Turkish] Minister of Public Instruction, who at my request, and in the interest of science, man-aged that Achmed Pasha, the Governor of the Dardanelles and the Archi-pelago, should receive orders from the Ministry of the Interior to have the field valued by competent persons, and to force the proprietors to sell it to the government at the price at which it had been valued: it was thus ob-tained for 3,000 piasters.

In trying to obtain the necessary firman for continuing my excavations, I met with new and great difficulties, for the Turkish Government are col-lecting ancient works of art for their recently established Museum in Con-stantinople, in consequence of which the Sultan no longer grants permission for making excavations. But what I could not obtain in spite of three journeys to Constantinople, I got at last through the intercession of my valued friend, the temporary *chargé d'affaires* of the United States to the Sublime Porte— Mr. John P. Brown, the author of the excellent work *Ancient and Modern Constantinople* (London, 1868).

So on the 27th of September [1871] I arrived at the Dardanelles with my firman. But here again I met with difficulties, this time on the part of the before named Achmed Pasha, who imagined that the position of the field which I was to excavate was not accurately enough indicated in the document, and therefore would not give me his permission for the excavations until he should receive a more definite explanation from the Grand Vizier. Owing to the change of ministry which had occurred, a long time would no doubt have elapsed before the matter was settled, had it not occurred to Mr. Brown to apply to his Excellency Kiamil Pasha, the new Minister of Public Instruc-tion, who takes a lively interest in science, and at whose intercession the Grand Vizier immediately gave Achmed Pasha the desired explanation. This, however, again occupied 13 days, and it was only on the evening of the 10th of October that I started with my wife from the Dardanelles for the Plain of Troy, a journey of eight hours. As, according to the firman, I was to be watched by a Turkish official, whose salary I have to pay during the time of my excavations, Achmed Pasha assigned to me the second secretary of his chancellery of justice, an Armenian, by name Georgios Sarkis, whom I pay 23 piasters daily.

At last, on Wednesday, the 11th of this month, I again commenced my excavations with eight workmen, but on the following morning I was enabled to increase their number to 35, and on the 13th to 74, each of whom receives 9 piasters daily (1 franc 80 centimes). As, unfortunately, I only brought eight wheelbarrows from France, and they cannot be obtained here, and cannot even be made in all the country round, I have to use 52 baskets for carrying away the rubbish. This work, however, proceeds but slowly and is very tiring, as the rubbish has to be carried a long way off. I therefore employ also four carts drawn by oxen, each of which again costs me 20 piasters a day. I work with great energy and spare no. cost, in order, if possible, to reach the native soil before the winter rains set in, which may happen at any moment. Thus I hope finally to solve the great problem as to whether the hill of Hissarlik is—as I firmly believe—the citadel of Troy.

As it is an established fact that hills which consist of pure earth and are brought under the plough gradually disappear—that for instance, the Wartsberg, near the village of Ankershagen in Mecklenburg, which I once, as a child, considered to be the highest mountain in the world, has quite vanished in 40 years—so it is equally a fact, that hills on which, in the course of thousands of years, new buildings have been continually erected upon the ruins of former buildings, gain very considerably in circumference and height.[2] The hill of Hissarlik furnishes the most striking proof of this. . . . In addition to the imposing situation of this hill within the circuit of the town, its present Turkish name of Hissarlik, "fortress" or "acropolis"—the word . . . has passed from the Arabic into the Turkish—seems also to prove that this is the Pergamus of Ilium; that here Xerxes (in 480 B.C.) offered up 1,000 oxen to the Ilian Athena; that here Alexander the Great hung up his armour in the temple of the goddess, and took away in its stead some of the weapons dedicated therein belonging to the time of the Trojan War, and likewise sacrificed to the Ilian Athena. I conjectured that this temple, the pride of the Ilians, must have stood on the highest point of the hill, and I therefore decided to excavate this locality down to the native soil.

But in order, at the same time, to bring to light the most ancient of the fortifying walls of the Pergamus, and to decide accurately how much the hill had increased in breadth by the débris which had been thrown down since the erection of those walls, I made an immense cutting on the face of the steep northern slope, about 66 feet from my last year's work. This cutting was made in a direction due south, and extended across the highest plateau, and was so broad that it embraced the whole building, the foundations of which, consisting of large hewn stones, I had already laid open last year to a depth of from only 1 to 3 feet below the surface. According to an exact measurement, this building, which appears to belong to the first century after Christ, is about 59 feet in length, and 43 feet in breadth. I have of course had all these foundations removed as, being within my excavation, they were of no use and would only have been in the way.

The difficulty of making excavations in a wilderness like this, where everything is wanting, are immense and they increase day by day; for, on account of the steep slope of the hill, the cutting becomes longer the deeper I dig, and so the difficulty of removing the rubbish is always increasing. This, moreover, cannot be thrown directly down the slope, for it would of course only have to be carried away again; so it has to be thrown down on the steep side of the hill at some distance to the right and left of the mouth of the cutting. The numbers of immense blocks of stone also, which we continually come upon, cause great trouble and have to be got out and removed, which takes up a great deal of time, for at the moment when a large block of this kind is rolled to the edge of the slope, all of my workmen leave their own work and hurry on to see the enormous weight roll down its steep path with a thundering noise and settle itself at some distance in the plain. It is, moreover, an absolute impossibility for me, who am the only one to preside over all, to give each workman his right occupation, and to watch that each does his duty. . . .

Notwithstanding all these difficulties the work advances rapidly, and if I could only work on uninterruptedly for a month, I should certainly reach a depth of more than 32 feet, in spite of the immense breadth of the cutting.

The medals hitherto discovered are all of copper, and belong for the most part to Alexandria Troas; some also are of Ilium, and of the first centuries before and after Christ.

My dear wife, an Athenian lady, who is an enthusiastic admirer of Homer, and knows almost the whole of the *Iliad* by heart, is present at the excavations from morning to night. I will not say anything about our mode of life in this solitude, where everything is wanting, and where we have to take four grains of quinine every morning as a precaution against the pestilential malaria.

All of my workmen are Greeks, from the neighbouring village of Renköi; only on Sunday, a day on which the Greeks do not work, I employ Turks. My servant, Nikolaos Zaphyros, from Renköi, whom I pay 30 piasters a day, is invaluable to me in paying the daily wages of the workmen, for he knows every one of them, and is honest.[3] Unfortunately, however, he gives me no assistance in the works, as he neither possesses the gift of commanding, nor has he the slightest knowledge of what I am seeking.

I naturally have no leisure here, and I have only been able to write the above because it is raining heavily, and therefore no work can be done. On the next rainy day I shall report further on the progress of my excavations.

On the Hill of Hissarlik, October 26th 1871.

Since my report of the 18th I have continued the excavations with the utmost energy, with, on an average, 80 workmen, and I have to-day reached an average depth of 4 meters (13 feet). At a depth of 6½ feet I discovered a well, covered with a very large stone, and filled with rubbish. Its depth I have not been able to ascertain; it belongs to the Roman period, as is proved by the cement with which the stones are joined together. Ruins of buildings, consisting of hewn stones joined or not joined by cement, I only find at about a depth of 2 meters (6½ feet). In the layers of *débris* between 2 and 4 meters deep (6½ to 13 feet), I find scarcely any stones, and to my delight the huge blocks of stone no longer occur at all. Medals belonging to Ilium and to the first and second centuries before Christ, and the first two centuries after Christ, as well as coins of Alexandria Troas and Sigeum, the age of which I do not know, were found almost immediately below the surface, and only in some few cases as deep as 1 meter (3¼ feet). . . .

In the depth we have now arrived at I also find very many of those elegant round vertebrae which form the backbone of the shark, and of which walking-sticks are often made. The existence of these vertebrae seems to prove that in remote antiquity this sea contained sharks, which are now no longer met with here. To-day I also found upon a fragment of rough pottery the representation of a man's head with large protruding eyes, a long nose, and a very small mouth, which seems clearly to be of Phoenician workmanship.

I also constantly come upon immense quantities of mussel-shells, and it seems as if the old inhabitants of Ilium had been very fond of this shell-fish. Oyster-shells are also found, but only seldom; on the other hand, I find very many fragments of pottery. As far as the depth yet reached, all the buildings which have stood upon this hill in the course of thousands of years seem to have been destroyed by fire. . . .

On the Hill of Hissarlik, November 3rd, 1871.

My last communication was dated the 26th of October, and since then I have proceeded vigorously with 80 workmen on an average. Unfortunately, however, I have lost three days; for on Sunday, a day on which the Greeks do not work, I could not secure the services of any Turkish workmen, for they

Hellenistic coins depicting scenes from Homer

are now sowing their crops; on two other days I was hindered by heavy rains.

To my extreme surprise, on Monday, the 30th of last month, I suddenly came upon a mass of *débris*, in which I found an immense quantity of implements made of hard black stone (diorite), but of a very primitive form. On the following day, however, not a single stone implement was found, but a small piece of silver wire and a great deal of broken pottery of elegant workmanship, among others the fragment of a cup with an owl's head. I therefore thought I had again come upon the remains of a civilized people, and that the stone implements of the previous day were the remains of an invasion of a barbarous tribe, whose dominion had been of but short duration. But I was mistaken, for on the Wednesday the stone period reappeared in even greater force, and continued throughout the whole of yesterday. To-day, unfortunately, no work can be done owing to the heavy downpour of rain.

I find much in this stone period that is quite inexplicable to me. . . .

In the first place, I am astonished that here on the highest point of the hill, where, according to every supposition the noblest buildings must have stood, I come upon the stone period as early as at a depth of 4½ meters (about 15 feet). . . . Next, I cannot explain how it is possible that I should find things which, to all appearance, must have been used by the uncivilized men of the stone period, but which could not have been made with the rude implements at their disposal. Among these I may specially mention the earthen vessels found in great numbers, without decorations, it is true, and not fine, but which however are of excellent workmanship. Not one of these vessels has been turned upon a potter's wheel, and yet it appears to me that they could not have been made without the aid of some kind of machine, such as, on the other hand, could not have been produced by the rude stone implements of the period.

I am further surprised to find, in this stone period, and more frequently than ever before, those round articles with a hole in the centre, which have sometimes the form of humming-tops or whorls (*carrousels*), sometimes of fiery mountains. . . .

Again, to my surprise, I frequently find the priapus, sometimes represented quite true to nature in stone or terra-cotta, sometimes in the form of a pillar rounded off at the top (just such as I have seen in Indian temples, but there only about four inches in length). . . .

With the exception of . . . silver wire and two copper nails, I have as yet found no trace of metal in the strata of the stone period. . . .

As in the upper strata, so in those of the stone period, I find a great many boars' tusks, which, in the latter strata, have without exception been pointed at the end, and have served as implements. It is inconceivable to me how the men of the stone period, with their imperfect weapons, were able to kill wild boars. Their lances—like all their other weapons and instruments—are, it is true, made of very hard black or green stone, but still they are so blunt that it must have required a giant's strength to kill a boar with them. . . .

My expectations are extremely modest; I have no hope of finding plastic works of art. The single object of my excavations from the beginning was only to find Troy, whose site has been discussed by a hundred scholars in a hundred books, but which as yet no one has ever sought to bring to light by excavations. If I should not succeed in this, still I shall be perfectly contented, if by my labours I succeed only in penetrating to the deepest darkness of pre-historic times, and enriching archaeology by the discovery of a few interesting features from the most ancient history of the great Hellenic race. The discovery of the stone period, instead of discouraging me, has therefore only made me the most desirous to penetrate to the place which was occupied by the first people that came here, and I still intend to reach it even if I should have to dig another 50 feet further down.

On the Hill of Hissarlik, November 18, 1871.

Since my report of the 3rd of this month I have continued my excavations with the greatest zeal, and although interrupted sometimes by the rain, and sometimes by Greek festivals, and also in spite of the continually increasing difficulty in removing the rubbish, I have now reached an average depth of 10 meters or about 33 English feet. Much that was inexplicable to me has now become clear, and I must first of all correct an error made in my last report, that I had come upon the stone period. I was deceived by the enormous mass of stone implements of all kinds which were daily dug up, and by the absence of any trace of metal, except two copper nails, which I believed to have come in some way from one of the upper strata into the deeper stratum of the stone period. But since the 6th of this month there have appeared not only many nails, but also knives, lances, and battle-axes of copper of such elegant workmanship that they can have been made only by a civilized people. Hence I must not only recall my conjecture that I had reached the stone period, but I cannot even admit that I have reached the bronze period, for the implements and weapons which I find are too well finished. I must, moreover, draw attention to the fact, that the deeper I dig, from 7 meters (23 feet) downwards, the greater are the indications of a higher civilization. . . .

When, at the time of writing my last report, I saw stone implements and weapons brought to light, and none but stone, and was forced to believe that I had penetrated into the stratum of the people belonging to the stone period, I really began to fear that the actual object of my excavations, to find here the Pergamus of Priam, had failed; that I had already reached a period long anterior to the Trojan War, and that the colossal sepulchral mounds in the Plain of Troy were perhaps thousands of years older than the deeds of Achilles. But as I find ever more and more traces of civilization the deeper I dig, I am now perfectly convinced that I have not yet penetrated to the period of the Trojan War, and hence I am more hopeful than ever of finding the site of Troy by further excavations; for if there ever was a Troy—and my belief in this is firm—it can only have been here, on the site of Ilium. . . .

November 21st.—The heavy rainfall of yesterday and the day before, which continued till this morning, rendered it impossible to dispatch this report before the evening; for I am here living in a wilderness at eight hours' distance from the nearest post-office, that is, from the Dardanelles. I hope that the ground will have become sufficiently dry by to-morrow morning for me to proceed with my work. I intend, at all events, to continue the excavations till the appearance of winter, and then to begin again in April.

The constant warm damp weather produces a very malignant fever, and my services as a doctor are daily sought. Fortunately, I have a large stock of quinine by me, and can thus help everyone. . . . I am also daily called upon not only to cure wounded men, but camels, donkeys, and horses. I have hitherto been successful in all cases by using tincture of arnica. I have also, thus far, cured all the fever patients who have applied for my help. Not one of them, however, has ever come to thank me; indeed gratitude does not appear to be one of the virtues of the present Trojans. . . .

Of the terrible difficulties of the excavations, where such large pieces of stone are met with, only those can have any idea who have been present at the work and have seen how much time and trouble it takes, especially during the present rainy weather—first to get out the small stones round one of the many immense blocks, then to dig out the block itself, to get the lever under it, to heave it up and roll it through the mud of the channel to the steep declivity.

But these difficulties only increase my desire, after so many disappointments, to reach the great goal which is at last lying before me, to prove that the *Iliad* is founded on facts, and that the great Greek nation must not be deprived of this crown of her glory. I shall spare no trouble and shun no expense to attain this result. . . .

On the Hill of Hissarlik, April 5th, 1872.

On the first of this month, at 6 o'clock on the morning of a glorious day, accompanied by my wife, I resumed the excavations with 100 Greek workmen from the neighbouring villages of Renkoï, Kalifatli, and Yenishehr.[4] Mr. John Latham, of Folkestone, the director of the railway from the Piraeus to Athens, who by his excellent management brings the shareholders an annual dividend of 30 per cent., had the kindness to give me two of his best workmen, Theodorus Makrys of Mitylene, and Spiridion Demetrios of Athens, as foremen.[5] Mr. Piat, who has undertaken the construction of the railroad from the Piraeus to Lanira, has also had the kindness to let me have his engineer, Adolphe Laurent, for a month. . . .

Now in order to be sure, in every case, of thoroughly solving the Trojan question this year, I am having an immense horizontal platform made on the steep northern slope, which rises at an angle of 40 degrees, a height of 105 feet perpendicular, and 131 feet above the level of the sea. The platform extends through the entire hill, at an exact perpendicular depth of 14 meters or 46½ English feet, it has a breadth of 79 meters or 233 English feet, and embraces my last year's cutting. M. Laurent calculates the mass of matter to be removed at 78,545 cubic meters (above 100,000 cubic yards): it will be less if I should find the native soil at less than 46 feet, and greater if I should have to make the platform still lower. It is above all things necessary for me to reach the primary soil, in order to make accurate investigations. . . .

In spite of every precaution, however, I am unable to guard my men or myself against the stones which continually come rolling down, when the steep wall is being picked away. Not one of us is without several wounds in his feet.

During the first three days of the excavations, in digging down the slope of the hill, we came upon an immense number of poisonous snakes, and among them a remarkable quantity of the small brown vipers called *antelion*, which are scarcely thicker than rain worms, and which have their name from the circumstance that the person bitten by them only survives till sunset. . . .

On the Hill of Hissarlik, April 25th, 1872.

I have continued the excavations most industriously with an average of 120 workmen. Unfortunately, however, seven of twenty days were lost through rainy weather and festivals, one day also by a mutiny among my men.

I had observed that the smoking of cigarettes interrupted the work, and I therefore forbade smoking during working hours, but I did not gain my point immediately, for I found that the men smoked in secret. I was, however, determined to carry my point, and caused it to be proclaimed that transgressors would be forthwith dismissed and never taken on again. Enraged at this, the workmen from the village of Renkoï—about 70 in number —declared that they would not work, if everyone were not allowed to smoke as much as he pleased; they left the platform, and deterred the men from the other villages from working by throwing stones. The good people had imagined that I would give in to them at once, as I could not do without them, and that now I could not obtain workmen enough; that moreover during the beautiful weather it was not likely that I would sit still a whole day. But they found themselves mistaken, for I immediately sent my foreman to the other neighbouring villages and succeeded (to the horror of the 70 Renkoïts, who had waited the whole night at my door) in collecting 120 workmen for the next morning without requiring their services.

My energetic measures have at last completely humbled the Renkoïts, from whose impudence I had very much to put up with during my last year's excavations, and have also had a beneficial effect upon all of my present men. Since the mutiny I have not only been able to prohibit smoking, but even to lengthen the day's work by one hour; for, instead of working as formerly from half-past five in the morning to half-past five in the evening, I now always commence at five and continue till six in the evening. But, as before, I allow half an hour at nine and an hour and a half in the afternoon for eating and smoking.

According to an exact calculation of the engineer, M. A. Laurent, in the seventeen days since the 1st of the month I have removed about 8,500 cubic meters (11,000 cubic yards) of *débris*; this is about 666 cubic yards each day, and somewhere above 5⅓ cubic yards each workman.

We have already advanced the platform 49 feet into the hill, but to
my extreme surprise I have not yet reached the primary soil. . . . At all
depths from 3 meters (10 feet) below the surface we find a number of flat
idols of very fine marble; upon many of them is the owl's face and a female
girdle with dots; upon one there are in addition two female breasts. The
striking resemblance of these owls' faces to those upon many of the vases
and covers, with a kind of helmet on the owl's head, makes me firmly convinced that all of the idols, and all of the helmeted owls' heads represent
a goddess, and indeed must represent one and the same goddess, all the
more so as, in fact, all the owl-faced vases with female breasts and a navel
have also generally two upraised arms: in one case the navel is represented
by a cross with four nails. The cups (covers) with owls' heads, on the
other hand, never have breasts or a navel, yet upon some of them I find
long female hair represented at the back.

The important question now presents itself:—What goddess is it who
is here found so repeatedly, and is, moreover, the only one to be found,
upon the idols, drinking-cups and vases? The answer is:—She must necessarily be *the tutelary goddess of Troy*, she must be *the Ilian Athena*, and
this indeed perfectly agrees with the statement of Homer, who continually
calls her θέα γλαυκῶπις Ἀθήνη [*Théa glau-kōpis Athéne*] "the goddess Athena
with the owl's face."[6]

Of pottery we have found a great deal during the last weeks, but unfortunately more than half of it in a broken condition. Of painting upon
terra-cotta there is still no trace; most of the vessels are of a simple brilliant
black, yellow, or brown colour; the very large vases on the other hand are
generally colourless. . . .

To my great regret, the excellent engineer Adolphe Laurent leaves me
to-morrow, for his month is up, and he has now to commence the construction of the railroad from the Piraeus to Lamia. He has, however, made me
a good plan of this hill.

I must add that the Pergamus of Priam cannot have been limited to
this hill, which is, for the most part, artificial; but that, as I endeavoured to
explain four years ago, it must necessarily have extended a good way further
south, beyond the high plateau. But even if the Pergamus should have been
confined to this hill, it was, nevertheless, larger than the Acropolis of
Athens. . . .

I have just built a house with three rooms, as well as a magazine and
kitchen, which altogether cost only 1,000 francs (40l.), including the
covering of waterproof felt; for wood is cheap here, and a plank of about
10 feet in length, 10 inches in breadth, and one inch thick, may be got for
two piasters, or 40 centimes. . . .

To-morrow the Greek Easter festival commences, during which unfortunately there are six days on which no work is done. Thus I shall not be able to continue the excavations until the 1st of May. . . .

On the Hill of Hissarlik, May 23rd, 1872.

There have again been, including to-day, three great and two lesser Greek church festivals, so that out of these twelve days I have in reality only had seven days of work. Poor as the people are, and gladly as they would like to work, it is impossible to persuade them to do so on feast days, even if it be the day of some most unimportant saint. "The saint will strike us" is ever their reply, when I try to persuade the poor creatures to set their superstition aside for higher wages.

In order to hasten the works, I have now had terraces made at from 16 to 19 feet above the great platform on its east and west ends; and I have also had two walls made of large blocks of stone—the intermediate spaces being filled with earth—for the purpose of removing the *débris*. The smaller wall did not seem to me to be strong enough, and I kept the workmen from it; in fact, it did not bear the pressure, and it fell down when it was scarcely finished. Great trouble was taken with the larger and higher wall: it was built entirely of large stones, for the most part hewn, and all of us . . . thought it might last for centuries. But nevertheless on the following morning I thought it best to have a buttress of large stones erected, so as to render it impossible for the wall to fall; and six men were busy with this work when the wall suddenly fell in with a thundering crash. My fright was terrible and indescribable, for I quite believed that the six men

 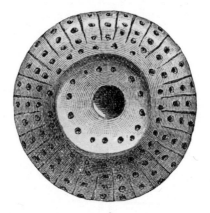

Terra-cotta spinning whorls

must have been crushed by the mass of stones; to my extreme joy, however, I heard that they had all escaped directly, as if by a miracle.

In spite of every precaution, excavations in which men have to work under earthen walls of above 50 feet in perpendicular depth are always very dangerous. The call of "*guarda, guarda*" is not always of avail, for these words are continually heard in different places. Many stones roll down the steep walls without the workmen noticing them, and when I see the fearful danger to which we are all day exposed, I cannot but fervently thank God, on returning home in the evening, for the great blessing that another day has passed without an accident. I still think with horror of what would have become of the discovery of Ilium and of myself, had the six men been crushed by the wall which gave way; no money and no promises could have saved me; the poor widows would have torn me to pieces in their despair —for the Trojan women have this in common with all Greeks of their sex, that the husband, be he old or young, rich or poor, is everything to them, heaven and earth have but a secondary interest.

Upon the newly made western terrace, directly beside my last year's excavation, we have laid bare a portion of a large building—the walls of which are 6¼ feet thick, and consist for the most part of hewn blocks of limestone joined with clay. None of the stones seem to be more than 1 foot 9 inches long, and they are so skillfully put together, that the wall forms a smooth surface. This house is built upon a layer of yellow and brown ashes and ruins, at a depth of 6 meters (20 feet), and the portion of the walls preserved reaches up to within 10 feet below the surface of the hill. . . . It is with a feeling of great interest that, from this great platform, that is, at a perpendicular height of from 33 to 42 feet, I see this very ancient building (which may have been erected 1,000 years before Christ) standing as it were in midair. To my regret, however, it must in any case be pulled down, to allow us to dig still deeper. . . .

On the Hill of Hissarlik, June 18th, 1872.

Since my report of the 23rd of last month I have been excavating, with the consent of my honoured friend, Mr. Frank Calvert, on that half of the hill which belongs to him, on condition that I share with him the objects I may find. Here, directly beside my large platform, and at a perpendicular depth of 40 feet below the plateau, I have laid out a third platform about 109 feet broad, with an upper terrace 112 feet broad, and I have seventy men digging there. . . .

I had scarcely begun to extend this third platform horizontally into the hill, when I found a block of triglyphs of Parian marble, about 6½ feet long, nearly 2 feet 10 inches high, and nearly 22 inches thick at one end, and a little over 14 inches on the other. In the middle there is a piece of sculpture in high relief, a little above 2 feet 10 inches long and nearly the same height, which represents Phoebus Apollo, who, in a long woman's robe with a girdle, is riding on the four immortal horses which pursue their career through the universe. Nothing is to be seen of a chariot. Above the splendid, flowing, unparted, but not long hair on the head of the god, there is seen about two-thirds of the sun's disc with ten rays 2⅓ inches long, and ten others 3½ inches long. The face of the god is very expressive, and the folds of his long robe are so exquisitely sculptured that they vividly remind one of the masterpieces in the temple of Νίκη ἄπτερος [Níke ápteros] in the Acropolis of Athens. But my admiration is especially excited by the four horses, which, snorting and looking wildly forward, career through the universe with infinite power. Their anatomy is so accurately rendered that I frankly confess that I have never seen such a masterly work. . . .

The discovery of this work of art upon the steep declivity of the hill —whereas it must necessarily have stood on the opposite side above the entrance to the temple—can only be explained by the fact that the Turks who came here in search of monumental pillars despised this sculpture because it represented living creatures, the imitation of which is strictly forbidden in the Koran. . . .

On the Hill of Hissarlik, July 13th, 1872.

As the great extent of my excavations renders it necessary for me to work with no less than 120 men, I have already been obliged, on account of the harvest season, to increase the daily wages to 12 piasters since the 1st of June; but even this would not have enabled me to collect the requisite number of men, had not Mr. Max Müller, the German Consul in Gallipoli, had the kindness to send me 40 workmen from that place. In consequence of this, even during the busiest harvest season, I have always had from 120 to 130 workmen, and now that the harvest is over, I have constantly 150. . . . Besides battering-rams, chains, and windlasses, my implements consist of 24 large iron levers, 108 spades, and 103 pickaxes, all of the best English manufacture. From sunrise to sunset all are busily at work, for I have three capital foremen, and my wife and I are always present at the works.

But for all this I do not think that I now remove more than 400 cubic yards of *débris* in a day, for the distance is always increasing, and in several places it is already more than 262 feet. Besides this, the continual hurricane from the north, which drives the dust into our eyes and blinds us, is exceedingly disturbing. This perpetual high wind is perhaps explained by the fact that the Sea of Marmora, with the Black Sea behind it, is connected with the Aegean Sea by a strait comparatively so narrow. Now, as such perpetual high winds are unknown in any other part of the world, Homer must have lived in the Plain of Troy, otherwise he would not have so often given to his 'Ίλιος [Ilios] the appropriate epithet of "ἠνεμόεσσα" [enemóessa] (the "windy" or "stormy"), which he gives to no other place. . . .

As every object belonging to the dark night of the pre-Hellenic times, and bearing traces of human skill in art, is to me a page of history, I am, above all things, obliged to take care that nothing escapes me. I therefore pay my workmen a reward of 10 paras (5 centimes, or a half-penny) for every object that is of the slightest value to me; for instance, for every round terra-cotta with religious symbols. And, incredible as it may seem, in spite of the enormous quantities of these articles that are discovered, my workmen have occasionally attempted to make decorations on the unornamented articles, in order to obtain the reward; the sun with its rays is the special object of their industry. I, of course, detect the forged symbols at once, and always punish the forger by deducting 2 piasters from his day's wages; but, owing to the constant change of workmen, forgery is still attempted from time to time.

As I cannot remember the names of the men engaged in my numerous works, I give each a name of my own invention according to their more or less pious, military or learned appearance: dervish, monk, pilgrim, corporal, doctor, schoolmaster, and so forth. As soon as I have given a man such a name, the good fellow is called so by all as long as he is with me. I have accordingly a number of Doctors, not one of whom can either read or write. . . .

Our greatest plague here, after the incessant and intolerable hurricane, is from the immense numbers of insects and vermin of all kinds; we especially dread the scorpions and the so-called Σαραντοπόδια ([sarantopódia] literally "with forty feet"—a kind of centipede), which frequently fall down from the ceiling of the rooms upon or beside us, and whose bite is said to be fatal. . . .

Pergamus of Troy, August 4th, 1872.

On the south side of the hill where, on account of the slight natural slope, I had to make my great trench with an inclination of 14 degrees, I discovered, at a distance of 197 feet from the declivity, a Tower, 12 meters or 40 feet thick, which likewise obstructs my path, and appears to extend to a great length. I am busily engaged in making large excavations to the right and left of it, in order to lay bare the whole. . . .

I believe that the Tower once stood on the western edge of the acropolis, where its situation would be most interesting and imposing; for its top would have commanded, not only a view of the whole Plain of Troy, but of the sea with the islands of Tenedos, Imbros, and Samothrace. There is not a more sublime situation in the area of Troy than this, and I therefore presume that it is the "Great Tower of Ilium" which Andromache ascended because "she had heard that the Trojans were hard pressed and that the power of the Achaeans was great." After having been buried for thirty-one centuries, and after successive nations have built their houses and palaces high above its summit during thousands of years, this Tower has now again been brought to light, and commands a view, if not of the whole plain, at least of the northern part and of the Hellespont. May this sacred and sublime monument of Greek heroism for ever attract the eyes of those who sail through the Hellespont! May it become a place to which the enquiring youth of all future generations shall make pilgrimage and fan their enthusiasm for knowledge, and above all for the noble language and literature of Greece! May it be an inducement speedily and completely to lay bare the walls of Troy, which must necessarily be connected with this Tower and most probably also with the wall laid open by me on the north side, to uncover which is now a very easy matter.

The expenses of excavating Ilium are, however, too great for private means, and I hope that a company will be formed, or that some government will decide to continue my excavations, so that I may proceed to the excavation of the acropolis of Mycenae. Meanwhile I shall continue the excavations at my own expense, but I shall in future confine myself to gradually uncovering the large surrounding walls, which are sure to be in a more or less good state of preservation at a great depth below the city wall built by Lysimachus. . . .

In conclusion, I flatter myself with the hope that, as a reward for my enormous expenses and all my privations, annoyances, and sufferings in this wilderness, but above all for my important discoveries, the civilized world will acknowledge my right to re-christen this sacred locality; and in the name of the divine Homer I baptize it with that name of immortal renown, which fills the heart of everyone with joy and enthusiasm: I give it the name of "TROY" and "ILIUM," and I call the acropolis, where I am writing these lines, by the name of the *Pergamus of Troy.*

Pergamus of Troy, August 14th, 1872.

I am now compelled to stop the works this evening, for my three foremen and my servant, who is also my cashier, have been seized by the malignant marsh-fever, and my wife and I are so unwell that we are quite unable to undertake the sole direction throughout the day in the terrible heat of the sun. We shall therefore leave our two wooden houses and all our machines and implements in charge of a watchman, and to-morrow we shall return to Athens.

The admirers of Homer, on visiting the Pergamus of Troy, will find that I have not only laid bare the Tower on the south side, along the whole breadth of my trench, down to the rock upon which it stands . . . but that by my excavations on the east and west I have uncovered it considerably further, without having found its end. . . .

In stopping the excavations for this year, and in looking back upon the fearful dangers to which we have continually been exposed since the 1st of April, between the gigantic layers of ruins, I cannot but fervently thank God for His great mercy, that not only has no life been lost, but that none of us has even been seriously hurt.

Now, as regards the result of my excavations, everyone must admit that I have solved a great historical problem, and that I have solved it by the discovery of a high civilization and immense buildings upon the primary soil, in the depths of an ancient town, which throughout antiquity was called Ilium and declared itself to be the successor of Troy, the site of which was regarded as identical with the site of the Homeric Ilium by the whole civilized world of that time. The situation of this town not only corresponds perfectly with all the statements of the *Iliad*, but also with all the traditions handed down to us by later authors. . . .

Schliemann's Trojan antiquities ("Priam's Treasure") as they were displayed at the South Kensington Museum in London.

Schliemann's oft-expressed wish during the 1872 season to yield his costly Hissarlik excavations to an archaeological society barely got beyond the debating stage. Nobody came forth with an offer, though Curtius of Berlin, on behalf of the German government, expressed some interest.[1] Schliemann himself failed to act decisively upon it, even though he was itching to conquer other buried cities. Furthermore, after suffering frequent bouts of disease in the unhealthy climate of the Troad ("that pestilential desert"[2]), he had recurrent premonitions of early death. Troy loomed like another Sacramento: to survive, he had to get away from it. There was so much left to accomplish. However, the certainty that he had at last located Homeric Troy made him cling to Hissarlik after all.

He had high expectations. The previous season he had discovered a small cache of precious metal objects near a skeleton that he identified as "a Trojan woman" who had been burned alive. Would those objects usher in more important and valuable finds? Somehow, both he and Sophia felt that they were on the verge of great discovery. Now, more than ever, he was sure to be on the right track. He had uncovered what he insisted were unmistakably Trojan sites. King Priam himself, "that mythical king of a mythical city, in the mythical heroic age," as he would say with scornful irony, was about to materialize.[3] Thus, he cheerfully reconciled himself to serve one more season at Hissarlik. His explicit purpose was to lay free the "Great Tower" and the ringed wall of Priam's citadel.

However, another crisis was in the making. The Sublime Porte, apparently pressured by the director of the Imperial Museum, threatened to revoke his *firman*.[4] To Schliemann this was, of course, just another example of Turkish infamy, and he could not for the world see any reason why he should be victimized. He brushed off the accusation that he had carried away the bulk of all artifacts, though it is easy to surmise that Ottoman officials had gotten wind of his abduction of the Apollo triglyph and were outraged. Now, naturally, it was Schliemann's turn to act the injured party. It was always he who was being persecuted by vindictive officials. He never gave them any provocation. On the contrary, they owed him nothing but gratitude. The fame of his fabulous archaeological discoveries would even boost the country's tourism.

Schliemann let it be known that by hook or crook he had to continue his sacred mission at Troy, which by the right of discovery was his and which, in the name of science, needed him. Immediately he mobilized his Constantinople contacts. The diplomatic cabal he brought into play was successful. The Turkish government, though not formally renewing his *firman*, let it transpire that he could proceed with digging. But this, as we shall see, was not the end of it.

Even before Schliemann resumed excavation, reports of major archaeological coups in the Troad had brought learned visitors to the scene—the vanguard of a growing number.[5] Curtius, whom Schliemann eagerly courted, though he declared himself for Bunarbashi, had already turned up the year before. Schliemann regretted his absence when the English banker-prehistorian Sir John Lubbock, whose career was not unlike his own, examined the riddled hill and excavated a nearby tumulus on his own. Another pilgrim was the young Hereditary Prince of Saxe-Meiningen, a close relation of the German Imperial house, who later became a personal friend. Early in 1873 there also arrived Count Ludolf, the Austrian ambassador at Constantinople, and Professors Alexander Conze and Georg Niemann from Vienna. However, even when Troy made dramatic news, Schliemann's grandiloquent prediction that his discoveries would cause such a sensation throughout the civilized world that admirers of Homer would come in the hundreds of thousands to worship at the sacred relics was never fulfilled.

So impatient was he to get back—and so ill-advised—that he appeared on the scene with Sophia as early as January 31, when the icy Boreas lashed mercilessly from Thrace across the Dardanelles. The temperature sank below the freezing point. But in barely a week the days became warmer and spring seemed in the air. Cranes and storks now appeared in droves, the latter to recolonize the roofs of Turkish houses, a token of spring that never ceased to delight Schliemann. By the beginning of March, one hundred and sixty men were at work. Yet there were reverses, both in weather and morale, and Schliemann remained mystified by the mixed lot of articles that turned up in the same deposit: whorls, coins, owl-faced vases, stone weapons, copper utensils, and the like, which could not possibly be all of the same age.

As usual, Schliemann had his people work at several places at the same time, and in his reports one meets with bewildering references to the northwest corner, the northern slope, the southern section, the eastern half, this platform, and that trench, and so on. There is little evidence that he was wresting order from the chaos of layers and sublayers, of ditches and depressions, not to speak of a hodge-podge of artifacts and the labyrinthine network of building fundaments and walls. If anything, Schliemann added to the confusion. At one moment he was occupied with the Greek temple of Athene, then he was on to Lysimachus' rampart, suddenly switching to segments of the "Homeric" wall, only to wander off into another layer somewhere above or below. As before, he evidenced little discernment of successive strata. He scattered his laborers and energies. By trying to do too much, much escaped him—including a treasure his men dug up and absconded with. He also continued to believe that the Troy of the *Iliad* was the original settlement at the bottom.

As the season advanced Schliemann began to register formidable finds. Nearly all of them, he was certain, pertained to the Troy of the heroes: foremost, extensions of ancient circuit walls, a sacrificial altar attributed to the cult of Athene, a paved road (ramp) that Schliemann rightly guessed would lead him to a city gate—the Scaean Gate no less—and nearby an unimpressive building of a few smallish rooms that had to be King Priam's Palace.

A curious incident happened during the unearthing of the well-constructed ramp. Schliemann was worried that the local people would dismantle the fine structure by removing its paving stones. So he made the announcement that Christ had proceeded up this way on his visit to King Priam. He even installed a picture of Jesus on top to frighten away impious looters of both the Greek Orthodox and Islamic persuasions. The episode is told at length in the German edition of his book *Trojanische Altertümer* but was dropped in the English version, *Troy and Its Remains*, perhaps in the belief that such pragmatic invocation of the Christian deity would offend the Victorian sense of propriety.

After such an *embarras* of Homeric riches, Schliemann felt his assignment nearly completed. In drawing a balance sheet of his three-year labors, he claimed, in a letter of May 30, 1873, to his son Sergei, that he had uncovered more than half of the ancient city, carried away more than 250,000 cubic meters of debris, dug up most, if not all, of the monuments of immortal glory, and collected enough unique antiquities to fill a museum. "But now we are tired," he confessed, "and because we have attained our goal and have realized the great idea of our life, we will forever terminate our excavations here at Troy on June 15."[6]

For some time Schliemann had thought about writing a book on his excavations at Hissarlik which would announce to the world the ideas and efforts that contributed toward his recovery of the Troy of the *Iliad*. He was already in touch with the reputable publishing house of Brockhaus in Leipzig, who agreed to put out a work which narrated the progress of his researches. It was to be accompanied by ample illustrations (engravings and woodcuts) of artifacts, based on some ten thousand pictures taken by a professional photographer, in addition to a pictorial atlas. Schliemann mailed advance copy to Leipzig while still in Athens. From Troy, in March 1873, he told his publisher that he lacked time, but not subject matter, to submit more manuscript pages. He also assured him, maybe as excuse for the loose organization over which Brockhaus fretted, that he had "no literary plans. My sole wish is to make the subject widely known, to destroy false theories, and produce general enthusiasm for Ilium."[7]

While writing to Brockhaus, he reported on his work at the Hellenistic-Roman temple of Athene and the extensive Greek inscriptions therein. Other letters to the publisher followed during the season, announcing further notable finds. Eventually, in early summer, Schliemann broke the news of an unexpected windfall which was to add a dramatic chapter to his Trojan saga and was bound to make the publisher's mouth water. Meanwhile, in May, Sophia had rushed to Athens to her dying father. But her husband persuaded her to return quickly. She came just in time.

To this day it has not been possible to determine the date that the golden objects that Schliemann called the "Treasure" (or Priam's Treasure) were found. Nor is the exact place known.[8] Schliemann's various accounts, of which there are many, are by no means clear on these points. In fact, in his later *Troja* (1884) he rescinded the account given in his earlier book. Further confusion is added by the use of Western and Eastern calendars. However, the discovery was most likely made between eight and nine o'clock in the morning, late in May or early June, a few days before the planned closing of the campaign. The site was somewhere northwest of the "Scaean Gate," at or near the large circuit wall (maybe in a niche within) or inside the "royal palace" itself. Schliemann quite possibly wanted to remain vague about the location so that he could keep the place to himself should more valuables remain buried there. A triangle symbol on Emile Burnouf's map in *Ilios* (1880/1881) marks the approximate spot.

To Schliemann the fabulous treasure was the ultimate proof. So rich a trove could come only from the wealth of great King Priam himself. It confirmed the Trojan riches in gold Homer had spoken of. Furthermore, by being hastily gathered, as he occasionally claimed (actually there is little evidence of haste in the careful assembly of the pieces), it showed that one member of the King's family or a faithful servant had tried to save the treasure from the flaming city but must have been overcome in the attempt. The glittering articles—Schliemann estimated their gold value alone at over one million francs—bore out Homer's descriptions of such Trojan ware.

We know, of course, today that all the objects were some one thousand years older than Schliemann thought, and despite their sumptuousness, they are, on the whole, of a rather simple design and craftsmanship of the early metal age. Somewhat similar pieces (and entire treasures) have not only been found later in Troy, but also at other Asia Minor sites (for example, Dorak close to the Troad) and on Aegean islands (Polióchni on Lemnos, Thermi on Lesbos.)[9] Indeed, caches of that kind are not uncommon in the area. Some of the vases and drinking vessels (like the famous double-spouted "sauce boat") also have affinities with copper and bronze age deposits on the Greek mainland and may have been imported from there or the islands to Troy. Other articles seem to relate to central Anatolian (for example, Alaca Hüyük in the bend of the Halys River) and Cypriot pre-historic cultures, whose treasures come mainly from tombs. The two delicate diadems and a filigree are reminiscent of Mesopotamian jewelry. All in all, the different pieces thus point to a complex, multicultural world in the Eastern Mediterranean even at that early age. As to the origin of the objects, one cannot be sure. It is at least doubtful that any were of local Trojan manufacture. A few scholars have suggested that they represent "pirate loot."

It may be unfair to refer to Schliemann, the pioneer archaeologist, as a mere gold seeker. Even the most scientific-minded modern excavator will not express disdain if his spade should bring forth beautifully wrought objects from a remote age. But it cannot be denied that Schliemann rejoiced in his discovery, relished its material worth, and, despite his and others' avid disclaimers of mercenary intention, seriously considered selling the treasure for cash. It should be said in his defense, however, that scholars and laymen alike are quite justifiably spellbound by the glow emanating from ancient gold with its aesthetic, sensuous, and almost mystical connotations. Precious objects may distill the artistic and even religious sensibilities of an ancient race. And a fascination with them is in itself an element of culture.

Besides, it was one of Schliemann's unstated dogmas that worked gold and other fine metals and gems were an unmistakable touchstone of great prehistoric epochs. The glory of the ages was enshrined in precious images and articles. Gold, not necessarily for its own sake, was never far from his mind when he later returned to Troy and when he campaigned at Mycenae, Orchomenos, or Tiryns. One might very well argue that nine-teenth century archaeology was in need of such dazzling finds in order to prove its worth and electrify a wide audience. It is doubtful whether without such spectacular discoveries many people would have taken seriously Schliemann's claim to have unearthed the palaces, fortresses, tombs, and belongings of the Homeric heroes. However, it must be added that quite a few scholars and professional archaeologists were not blinded by gold. Particularly in Germany, many remained unconvinced. To Schliemann, however, any such doubt was nothing but base jealousy. Seldom would he tolerate a rational debate.

It never seemed to have seriously bothered Schliemann's mind that the treasure could belong to anybody but him. Despite the contractual obligation he had entered, he chose to subscribe to the law that the spoils belonged to the discoverer alone. The view that it might be a national legacy of the people of Turkey he would have considered a ridiculous proposition, even though the new Imperial Museum at Constantinople had been installed in this spirit.[10] Nor did it bother his conscience that the Turks had already been irritated over his illegal export of the Apollo relief. As to the *firman*, he marshaled all the rationalizations he could think up to prove that the Turks, rather than he, were lawbreakers. Anyhow, by eluding those devious Orientals he only served the cause of science and helped to preserve these ornaments of ancient Troy for future generations. (Another defense frequently advanced on Schliemann's behalf is that "they all did it"—which *may* be historically correct but is morally invalid.)

His main task after the great discovery was then a delicate, though not entirely novel, one (to him): to get the treasure out of the country. Again, we are not fully informed how he proceeded. Probably the earliest hint of his bonanza was a cryptic letter he sent to Frank Calvert's brother Frederic, accompanying a bulk shipment to the family estate at Thymbria. It may have been written on the very day of the discovery, since it is dated only a day after (if referring to the same calendar) Schliemann wrote his son of his intention to close the campaign. In it he tells Frederic: "I am sorry to inform you that I am closely watched, and expect that the Turkish watchman, who is angry at me, I do not know for what reason, will search my house tomorrow. I, therefore, take the liberty to deposit with you six baskets and a bag, begging you will kindly lock them up, and not allow by any means the Turks to touch them.[11] . . ." Undoubtedly, the shipment contained the treasure, which a few days later was safely on its way to Greece. Ever suspicious Schliemann would not even tell the Calverts of the contents.

The Schliemanns now made haste to get home themselves. For one, they had to escape the wrath of the Turks. To his friends Schröder & Co. of London he wrote in Caesarean conciseness: "My hopes have been surpassed, my mission is fulfilled, and within eight days I shall part from Troy forever."[12]

On June 17 he and Sophia left Hissarlik. In Schliemann's opinion, all the work had been done, and no major problem remained to be cleared up. The strenuous three-year campaign had been brought to a brilliant conclusion.

However, in reflecting on the results, Schliemann, in the moment of his greatest triumph, was compelled to admit in his last report that the Troy that had finally emerged from his spadework was not quite what he had imagined. Of course, there was not the slightest doubt in his mind that he had uncovered the one and only Troy. Yet, painfully and reluctantly, he had to allow that Homer was after all a poet and not a historian, who lived at least three hundred years after the Trojan War. As an inspired bard, he was entitled to poetic license and, as a spiritual ancestor of Heinrich Schliemann, to exaggeration. The critics, on whom Schliemann had poured mockery for their little faith, could have told him that all along. Indeed, they had put it more pithily and epigrammatically by saying that Homer knew little about the Homeric Age.

Schliemann would not go that far. (Neither do the majority of modern Homer scholars, who continue debating the issue to this very day.) As a matter of fact, he was quite ready to reverse himself (and did!) if only he could come up with the slightest ground for restoring Troy to its full glory. But as of now, in order to clean up the contradictions within his own thoughts and notes, he stated flatly, and with cool honesty, that he had to withdraw some of his previously held opinions. But even after he had done so, there was still enough left to sustain his Homeric faith. His excavations had, he declared, achieved their main purpose by showing that Troy really existed. There was a Scaean Gate, a Great Tower, and Priam's Palace. The great epics were based on historical events. He took pride in having solved "the greatest and most important of all historical riddles."[13]

A MOMENTOUS DISCOVERY

from *Troy and Its Remains*
and *Ilios*

Pergamus of Troy, February 22nd, 1873.

I returned here on the 31st of January with my wife, in order to continue the excavations, but we have been repeatedly interrupted by Greek church festivals, thunderstorms, and also by the excessive cold, so that I can scarcely reckon that I have had as yet more than eight good days' work.

Last autumn, by the side of my two wooden houses, I had a house built for myself of stones from the old Trojan buildings, the walls of which were two feet thick, but I was compelled to let my foremen occupy it, for they were not sufficiently provided with clothes and wrappers, and would have perished through the great cold. My poor wife and I have therefore suffered very much, for the strong icy north wind blew with such violence through the chinks of our house-walls which were made of planks, that we were not even able to light our lamps of an evening; and although we had fire on the hearth, yet the thermometer showed 23° F., and the water standing near the hearth froze in solid masses. During the day we could to some degree bear the cold by working in the excavations, but of an evening we had nothing to keep us warm except our enthusiasm for the great work of discovering Troy. Fortunately this extreme cold lasted only four days, from the 16th to the 19th of this month, and since then we have had glorious weather. . . .

I have also brought with me an artist, that I may have the objects found copied immediately in Indian ink, and the drawings multiplied in Athens by means of photography. This will, however, render it impossible for me to state the depths at which the objects were found upon distinct plates, as I have hitherto done. The articles discovered in the different depths are now mixed together, but in each case the depth, as well as the relative size, is stated in meters, in addition to the number in the catalogue.[1] . . .

On the north side of the hill, at a distance of 131 feet from the declivity and at a depth of 51 feet . . . I am having five terraces made on two sides simultaneously, and the *débris* carried away in man-carts and wheel-barrows. In the northeastern excavations this *débris*, from the surface to a depth of 10 feet, consists of black earth, mixed with splinters of marble; and among them I find very many large and beautifully-sculptured blocks of marble, which evidently belong to the temple of the time of Lysimachus, which stood here, but are of no further value to archaeology. . . .

The other cutting—which I opened to reach the supposed site of the very ancient temple of Athena—is at the east end of my large platform, upon which I am again throwing the greater part of the *débris* which is being dug down there, because to remove it beyond the platform would be too difficult. In the mean time I have only had this cutting made 42½ feet broad, but I intend to widen it as soon as I find any prospect of advantage to archaeology from doing so. In the lower terrace of this cutting I find the continuation of that Trojan wall which also shows itself in the more eastern cutting. This wall is here only 3¼ feet high, but the stones lying below it leave no doubt that it was at one time much higher. Every visitor to the Troad confirms my observation of the remarkable fact, that this wall continues on the two sides of my large cutting through the entire hill, to the right and left of the entrance, at a depth of 39½ feet. . . .

Terra-cotta hippopotamus

Among the interesting objects discovered in this excavation, I must especially mention a brilliant red terra-cotta hippopotamus, found at a depth of 23 feet. It is hollow, and has a ring on the left side, and therefore may have served as a vessel. The existence of the figure of a hippopotamus here at a depth of 23 feet is extremely remarkable, nay, astonishing; for this animal, as is well known, is not met with even in Upper Egypt, and occurs only in the rivers of the interior of Africa. It is, however, probable that hippopotami existed in Upper Egypt in ancient times; for, according to Herodotus, they were worshipped as sacred animals at the Egyptian town of Papremis. At all events, Troy must have been commercially connected with Egypt; but even so, it is still an enigma, how the animal was so well known here as to have been made of clay in a form quite faithful to nature. . . .

Simultaneously with these excavations I had 22 men working in a north-westerly direction, from the southeastern corner of the Acropolis, in order to lay bare the Great Tower still further on that side, an operation that has become impossible to effect from my great trench. . . .

Pergamus of Troy, March 15th, 1873.

I have continued the excavations with great zeal, favoured by glorious weather and an abundance of workmen. . . . The leaves of the trees are only now beginning to sprout, while the plain is already covered with spring flowers. . . . One of the discomforts of our life in this wilderness is the hideous shrieking of the innumerable owls which build their nests in the holes of the walls of my excavations; their shrieks sound mysterious and horrible, and are especially unendurable at night.

I have proceeded with the excavation of the site of the [Greek or Macedonian] Temple of Athena with the greatest energy. . . . As the tower, which I partly uncovered last year, extends directly below the temple at a great depth, and as I wish at all events to lay bare its entire breadth, I shall leave only the ruins of the north and south walls of the temple standing, and break away all the rest. . . . Down to the present depth of 4½ meters (14¼ feet) below the surface, that is, from 7 to 10 feet below the foundations of the temple of Athena, I find nothing but yellow wood-ashes, and among these an immense number of enormous earthen jars (πίθοι) [pithoi] from 3¼ to 6½ feet long, and pointed below, which must have served not only as wine and water jars, but as cellars for keeping provisions, for there are no walled cellars. . . .

I find very many copper coins of Ilium and Alexandria Troas, and Roman ones from the time of Augustus to Constantine the Great, especially the latter, directly below the surface, and at most down to a meter (3¼ feet) deep. Iron I do not find at all, not even in the temple, but a number of copper nails, which, however, I begin to think could not have been used for driving into wood; for this purpose they seem to be far too long and thin. . . .

The many thousands of stones which I bring out of the depths of Ilium have induced the inhabitants of the surrounding villages to erect buildings which might be called grand for the inhabitants of this wilderness. Among others, they are at present building with my Ilian stones a mosque and a minaret in the wretched Turkish village of Chiplak, and a church-tower in the Christian village of Yenishehr. A number of two-wheeled carts, drawn by oxen, are always standing by the side of my excavations, ready to receive the stones which can be of any use as soon as they have been brought to the surface; but the religious zeal of these good people is not great enough for them to offer to help me in the terrible work of breaking the large, splendidly hewn blocks so as to make them more convenient to remove.

Although spring is only just commencing, there is already a great deal of malignant fever in consequence of the mild winter, and the poor people of the neighbourhood are already daily beginning to make large claims upon my stock of quinine.

I found myself obliged to raise the men's wages to 10 piasters or 2 francs, eight days ago. . . .

The life in this wilderness is not without danger, and last night [March 28, 1873], for instance, my wife and I and the foreman Photidas had the narrowest escape of being burnt alive. In the bedroom on the north side of the wooden house which we are inhabiting, we had had a small fireplace made, and, owing to the terrible cold which has again set in during the last six days, we have lighted a fire in it daily. But the stones of the fireplace rest merely upon the boards of the floor, and, whether it was owing to a crevice in the cement joining the stones, or by some other means, the floor took fire, and when I accidentally awoke this morning at 3 o'clock, it was burning over a space of two yards long by a yard broad. The room was filled with dense smoke, and the north wall was just beginning to catch fire; a few seconds would have sufficed to burn a hole into it, and the whole house would then have been in flames in less than a minute, for a fearful north wind was blowing from that side. In my fright I did not lose my presence of mind. I poured the contents of a bath upon the burning north wall, and thus in a moment stopped the fire in that direction. Our cries awoke Photidas, who was

Jug with long neck

asleep in the adjoining room, and he called the other foremen from the stone house to our assistance. In the greatest haste they fetched hammers, iron levers and pickaxes; the floor was broken up, torn to pieces, and quantities of damp earth thrown upon it, for we had no water. But, as the lower beams were burning in many places, a quarter of an hour elapsed before we got the fire under and all danger was at an end. . . .

Pergamus of Troy, April 5th, 1873.

Amidst cold but glorious spring weather most favourable for the workmen, who now number 150 on the average, I have this week continued the excavations with the greatest energy and with good results.

The most interesting object that I have discovered here in these three years is certainly a house which I brought to light this week, and of which eight rooms have already been laid open; it stands upon the Great Tower, at a depth of 7 and 8 meters (23 to 26 feet), directly below the Greek Temple of Athena. Its walls consist of small stones cemented with earth, and they appear to belong to different epochs. . . .

To the east side of the house is a sacrificial altar of a very primitive description, which is turned to the northwest by west, and consists of a slab of slate granite about 5¼ feet long, and 5½ feet broad. The upper part of the stone is cut into the form of a crescent, probably for killing upon it the animal which was intended for sacrifice. About 4 feet below the sacrificial altar I found a channel made of slabs of green slate, which probably served to carry off the blood. . . . Of course I leave the altar *in situ*, so that visitors to the Troad may convince themselves by the nature of its pedestal and of the *débris* of the earthen wall, beside which it stands, of the correctness of all these statements, which might otherwise appear too incredible. The remarkable substructure of this sacrificial altar, the curious *débris* in which it was buried, the preservation of the great house, which has evidently been burnt, and the walls of which were built at different epochs, and lastly, the fact that its spaces were filled with heterogeneous *débris* and with colossal jars—all this is a puzzle to me. I confine myself, therefore, to stating the facts merely, and refrain from expressing any kind of conjecture. . . .

Pergamus of Troy, April 16th, 1873.

Since my report of the 5th of this month I have had, on an average, 160 workmen, and have brought many wonderful things to light, among which I may especially mention a street of the Pergamus, which was discovered close to my house, at a depth of 30 feet, in the Great Tower. It is 17¼ feet broad, and is paved with stone flags [flagstones], from 4¼ to 5 feet long, and from 35 inches to 4½ feet broad. It runs down very abruptly in a due southwestern direction towards the plain. I have as yet only been able to lay bare a length of 10 meters (33⅓ feet). It leads, without doubt, to the Scaean Gate, the position of which appears to be accurately indicated, on the west side at the foot of the hill, by the direction of the wall and by the formation of the ground; it cannot be more than 492 feet distant from the tower. . . .

This beautifully paved street leads me to conjecture that a grand building must at one time have stood at the top of it, at a short distance on the northeast side; and therefore, seven days ago, when the street was discovered, I immediately set 100 men to dig down the northeastern ground lying in front of it. . . . In order to extract from this excavation all the objects of the greatest use to archaeology, I am having the walls made perpendicular, as in fact I have had them made in almost all of the other cuttings. As the work of removing this gigantic block of earth is carried on both from above and from below, I confidently hope to have finished it in twenty days' work. . . .

Pergamus of Troy, May 10th 1873.

I have had many interruptions, for the Greek Easter festival lasts six days, then the feast of Saint George and its after celebrations again took away several days, so that during all this time I have had only four days of actual work; however, on these days, with on an average 150 men, I have continued the works with great energy.

As we have had continual fine weather since the beginning of April, my men no longer go to the neighbouring villages for the night as they have hitherto done; but they sleep in the open air and even in the excavations, which is very convenient for me, as I now have them always at hand. Besides this, the long days are of great advantage to me, for I can continue work from a quarter to five till a quarter past seven in the evening. . . .

Today I finished the excavations above the paved tower-road. They have brought to light two large buildings of different ages, the more recent of which is erected upon the ruins of the more ancient one. Both have been destroyed by terrible fires, of which the walls bear distinct traces; moreover all the rooms of both houses are filled with black, red, and yellow wood-ashes and with charred remains. . . .

I was firmly convinced that this splendid street, paved with large flags of stone, must proceed from the principal building of the Pergamus, and I therefore confidently carried on the excavation in order to bring that edifice to light. To accomplish this, I was most unfortunately compelled to break down three of the large walls of the more recent house. The result has, however, far surpassed my expectations, for I not only found two large gates, standing 20 feet apart, but also the two large copper bolts belonging to them. . . . I now venture positively to assert that the great double gate which I have brought to light must necessarily be the Scaean Gate . . . [for] the street which runs down abruptly at an angle of 65 degrees towards the plain, in a southwestern direction from the double gate and the Great Tower, cannot possibly have led to a second gate, so that the double gate which I have laid bare must necessarily have been the Scaean Gate; it is in an excellent state of preservation, not a stone of it is wanting.

Here, therefore, by the side of the double gate, upon Ilium's Great Tower, at the edge of the very abrupt western declivity of the Pergamus, sat Priam, the seven elders of the city, and Helen; and this is the scene of the most splendid passage in the *Iliad*. From this spot the company surveyed the whole plain, and saw at the foot of the Pergamus the Trojan and the Achaean armies face to face about to settle their agreement to let the war be decided by a single combat between Paris and Menelaus. . . .

This gate, as well as the large ancient building, stands upon the wall or buttress already mentioned as leaning on the north side of the tower. At this place the buttress appears to be about 79 feet thick, and to be made of the *débris* which was broken off the primary soil when the tower was erected. The site of this building, upon an artificial elevation directly above the gate, together with its solid structure, leave no doubt that it was the grandest building in Troy; nay, that it must have been the PALACE OF PRIAM. I am having an accurate plan made, so far as I can, of the portion that has been laid bare; I cannot, however, bring to light the whole of it, for in order to do this I should have to pull down both my stone and my wooden house, beneath which it extends; and even if I did pull down my own houses, I should still be unable to make a complete plan of the house till I had removed the building which stands upon it, and this I cannot at once make up my mind to do. . . .

It has now become evident to me that what I last year considered to be the ruins of a second storey of the Great Tower are only benches made of stones joined with earth, three of which may be seen rising behind one another like steps. From this, as well as from the walls of the tower and those of the Scaean Gate, I perceive that the tower never can have been higher than it now is.

The excavations of the north side of the field belonging to Mr. Calvert, which I opened to discover other sculptures, have been stopped for some time, as I can no longer come to terms with him. . . .

I must also add that I now positively retract my former opinion, that Ilium was inhabited up to the ninth century after Christ, and I must distinctly maintain that its site has been desolate and uninhabited since the end of the fourth century. . . .

Troy, June 17th, 1873.

In the new large excavation on the northwest side . . . I have convinced myself that the splendid wall of large hewn stones, which I uncovered in April 1870, belongs to a tower, the lower projecting part of which must have been built during the first period of the Greek colony, whereas its upper portion seems to belong to the time of Lysimachus. To this tower also belongs the wall. . . , 9 feet high and 6 feet broad, and as continuous with the surrounding wall of Lysimachus; and so does the wall of the same dimensions,

Excavation of "Homeric" Troy

situated 49 feet from it, which I have likewise broken through. Behind the latter, at a depth of from 26 to 30 feet, I uncovered the Trojan city wall which runs out from the Scaean Gate.

In excavating this wall further and directly by the side of the Palace of King Priam, I came upon a large copper article of the most remarkable form, which attracted my attention all the more as I thought I saw gold behind it. . . . In order to withdraw the treasure from the greed of my workmen, and to save it for archaeology, I had to be most expeditious, and although it was not yet time for breakfast, I immediately had "*paidos*" called. This is a word of uncertain derivation, which has passed over into Turkish, and is here employed in place of ἀνάπαυσις [*anápausis*], or time for rest.

While the men were eating and resting, I cut out the treasure with a large knife, which it was impossible to do without the very greatest exertion and the most fearful risk of my life, for the great fortification-wall, beneath which I had to dig, threatened every moment to fall down upon me. But the sight of so many objects, every one of which is of inestimable value to archaeology, made me foolhardy, and I never thought of any danger. It would, however, have been impossible for me to have removed the treasure without the help of my dear wife, who stood by me ready to pack the things which I cut out in her shawl and to carry them away.[2]

The first thing I found was a large copper shield (the ἀσπὶς ὀμφαλόεσσα [*aspis omphalóessa*] of Homer) in the form of an oval salver, in the middle of which is a knob or boss encircled by a small furrow (αὔλαζ [aúlax]).[3] This shield is a little less than 20 inches in length; it is quite flat, and surrounded by a rim (ἄντυζ [ántyx]) 1½ inch high; the boss (ὀμφαλός [omphalós]) is 2⅓ inches high and 4⅓ inches in diameter; the furrow encircling it is 7 inches in diameter and ⅖ of an inch deep.

The second object which I got out was a copper caldron with two horizontal handles, which certainly gives us an idea of the Homeric λέβης [lébes]; it is 16½ inches in diameter and 5½ inches high; the bottom is flat, and is nearly 8 inches in diameter.

The third object was a copper plate ⅖ of an inch thick, 6⅓ inches broad, and 17⅓ inches long; it has a rim about 1/12 of an inch high; at one end of it there are two immovable wheels with an axle-tree. This plate is very much bent in two places, but I believe that these curvatures have been produced by the heat to which the article was exposed in the conflagration; a silver vase 4¾ inches high and broad has been fused to it; I suppose, however, that this also happened by accident in the heat of the fire. The fourth article I brought out was a copper vase 5½ inches high and 4⅓ inches in diameter. Thereupon followed a globular bottle of the purest gold, weighing 403 grammes (6,220 grains, or above 1 lb. troy); it is nearly 6 inches high and 5½ inches in diameter, and has the commencement of a zigzag decoration on the neck, which, however, is not continued all round. Then came a cup, likewise of the purest gold, weighing 226 grammes (7¼ oz. troy); it is 3½ inches high and 3 inches broad.

Next came another cup of the purest gold, weighing exactly 600 grammes (about 1 lb. 6 oz. troy), it is 3½ inches high, 7¼ inches long, and 7⅕ inches broad; it is in the form of a ship with two large handles; on one side there is a mouth, 1⅕ inch broad, for drinking out of, and another at the other side, which is 2¾ inches broad, and, as my esteemed friend Professor Stephanos Kumanudes, of Athens, remarks, the person who presented the filled cup may have first drunk from the small mouth, as a mark of respect, to let the guest drink from the larger mouth. This vessel has a foot which projects about 1/12 of an inch, and is 1⅓ inch long, and ⅘ of an inch broad.[4] It is assuredly the Homeric δέπας ἀμφικύπελλον [dépas amphikýpellon]. But I adhere to my supposition that all of those tall and brilliant red goblets of terracotta, in the form of champagne-glasses with two enormous handles, are also δέπα ἀμφικύπελλα, and that this form probably existed in gold also. I must further make an observation which is very important for the history of art, that the above-mentioned gold δέπας ἀμφικύπελλον is of cast gold, and that the large handles, which are not solid, have been fused on to it. On the other hand the gold bottle and the gold cup mentioned above have been wrought with the hammer.

The treasure further contained a small cup of gold alloyed with 20 per cent. of silver, that is, the mixed metal called *electrum*. It weighs 70 grammes (2¼ oz. troy), and is above 3 inches high, and above 2½ inches broad. Its foot is only ⅘ of an inch high and nearly an inch broad, and is moreover not quite straight, so that the cup appears to be meant only to stand upon its mouth.

I also found in the treasure six pieces of the purest silver in the form of large knife-blades, having one end rounded, and the other cut into the form of a crescent; they have all been wrought with the hammer. . . .

Upon and beside the gold and silver articles, I found thirteen copper lances, from nearly 7 to above 12½ inches in length, and from above 1½ to 2⅓ inches broad at the broadest point; at the lower end of each is a hole, in which, in most cases, the nail or peg which fastened the lance to the wooden handle is still sticking. The pin-hole is clearly visible in a lance-head which the conflagration has welded to a battle-axe. The Trojan lances were therefore quite different from those of the Greeks and Romans, for the latter stuck the shaft into the lance-head, the former fastened the head into the shaft. . . .

As I found all these articles together, forming a rectangular mass, or packed into one another, it seems to be certain that they were placed on the city wall in a wooden chest (φωριαμός [*phoriamós*]), such as those mentioned by Homer as being in the palace of King Priam. This appears to be the more certain, as close by the side of these articles I found a copper key above 4 inches long, the head of which (about 2 inches long and broad) greatly resembles a large safe-key of a bank.[5] Curiously enough this key has had a wooden handle; there can be no doubt of this from the fact that the end of the stalk of the key is bent round at a right angle, as in the case of the daggers.

It is probable that some member of the family of King Priam hurriedly packed the treasure into the chest and carried it off without having time to pull out the key; that when he reached the wall, however, the hand of an enemy or the fire overtook him, and he was obliged to abandon the chest, which was immediately covered to a height of from 5 to 6 feet with the red ashes and the stones of the adjoining royal palace.

Perhaps the articles found a few days previously in a room of the royal palace, close to the place where the treasure was discovered, belonged to this unfortunate person. These articles were a helmet, and a silver vase 7 inches high and 5½ inches broad, containing an elegant cup of electrum 4⅓ inches high and 3½ inches broad. The helmet was broken in being taken out, but I can have it mended, as I have all the pieces of it. . . .

That the treasure was packed together at terrible risk of life, and in the greatest anxiety, is proved among other things also by the contents of the

largest silver vase, at the bottom of which I found two splendid gold diadems
κρήδεμνα [krédemna]);[6] a fillet, and four beautiful gold ear-rings of most
exquisite workmanship: upon these lay 56 gold ear-rings of exceedingly curious form and 8,750 small gold rings, perforated prisms and dice, gold buttons,
and similar jewels, which obviously belonged to other ornaments; then followed six gold bracelets, and on the top of all the two small gold goblets. . . .

The person who endeavoured to save the treasure had fortunately the
presence of mind to stand the silver vase, containing the valuable articles
described above, upright in the chest, so that not so much as a bead could
fall out, and everything has been preserved uninjured. . . .

As I hoped to find other treasures here, and also wished to bring to light
the wall that surrounded Troy, the erection of which Homer ascribes to
Poseidon and Apollo, as far as the Scaean Gate, I have entirely cut away the
upper wall, which rested partly upon the gate, to an extent of 56 feet. Visitors
to the Troad can, however, still see part of it in the northwestern earth-wall
opposite the Scaean Gate. I have also broken down the enormous block of
earth which separated my western and northwestern cutting from the Great
Tower; but in order to do this, I had to pull down the larger one of my
wooden houses, and I had also to bridge over the Scaean Gate, so as to
facilitate the removal of the *débris*. The result of this new excavation is very
important to archaeology; for I have been able to uncover several walls, and
also a room of the Royal Palace, 20 feet in length and breadth, upon which
no buildings of a later period rest.

Of the objects discovered there I have only to mention an excellently
engraved inscription found upon a square piece of red slate, which has two
holes not bored through it and an encircling incision, but neither can my
learned friend Émile Burnouf nor can I tell in what language the inscription
is written.[7] Further, there were some interesting terra-cottas, among which is
a vessel, quite the form of a modern cask, and with a tube in the centre for
pouring in and drawing off the liquid. There were also found upon the wall
of Troy, 1¾ feet below the place where the treasure was discovered, three
silver dishes (φιάλαι [phiálai]), two of which were broken to pieces in digging down the *débris*; they can, however, be repaired, as I have all the pieces.
These dishes seem to have belonged to the treasure, and the fact of the latter
having otherwise escaped our pickaxes is due to the above-mentioned large
copper vessels which projected, so that I could cut everything out of the hard
débris by means of a knife.

I now perceive that the cutting which I made in April 1870 was exactly
at the proper point, and that if I had only continued it, I should in a few
weeks have uncovered the most remarkable buildings in Troy, namely, the

Palace of King Priam, the Scaean Gate, the Great Surrounding Wall, and the Great Tower of Ilium; whereas, in consequence of abandoning this cutting, I had to make colossal excavations from east to west and from north to south through the entire hill in order to find those most interesting buildings. . . .

But Troy was not large. I have altogether made twenty borings down to the rock, on the west, southwest, south, southeast and east of the Pergamus, directly at its foot or at some distance from it, on the plateau of the Ilium of the Greek colony. As I find in these borings no trace either of fragments of Trojan pottery or of Trojan house-walls, and nothing but fragments of Hellenic pottery and Hellenic house-walls, and as, moreover, the hill of the Pergamus has a very steep slope towards the north, the northeast, and the northwest, facing the Hellespont, and is also very steep towards the plain, the city could not possibly have extended in any one of these directions. I now most emphatically declare that the city of Priam cannot have extended on any one side beyond the primeval plateau of this fortress, the circumference of which is indicated to the south and southwest by the Great Tower and the Scaean Gate, and to the northwest, northeast and east by the surrounding wall of Troy. The city was so strongly fortified by nature on the north side, that the wall there consisted only of those large blocks of stone, loosely piled one upon another in the form of a wall, which last year gave me such immense trouble to remove. This wall can be recognized at once, immediately to the right in the northern entrance of my large cutting, which runs through the entire hill.

I am extremely disappointed at being obliged to give so small a plan of Troy; nay, I had wished to be able to make it a thousand times larger, but I value truth above everything, and I rejoice that my three years' excavations have laid open the Homeric Troy, even though on a diminished scale, and that I have proved the *Iliad* to be based upon real facts.

Homer is an epic poet, and not an historian: so it is quite natural that he should have exaggerated everything with poetic licence. Moreover, the events which he describes are so marvellous, that many scholars have long doubted the very existence of Troy, and have considered the city to be a mere invention of the poet's fancy. I venture to hope that the civilized world will not only not be disappointed that the city of Priam has shown itself to be scarcely a twentieth part as large as was to be expected from the statements of the *Iliad*, but that, on the contrary, it will accept with delight and enthusiasm the certainty that Ilium did really exist, that a large portion of it has now been brought to light, and that Homer, even although he exaggerates, nevertheless sings of events that actually happened. Besides, it ought to be remembered that the area of Troy, now reduced to this small hill, is still as large as, or even larger than, the royal city of Athens, which was confined to the Acropolis. . . .

But this little Troy was immensely rich for the circumstances of those times, since I find here a treasure of gold and silver articles, such as is now scarcely to be found in an emperor's palace; and as the town was wealthy, so was it also powerful, and ruled over a large territory.

The houses of Troy were all very high and had several storeys, as is obvious from the thickness of the walls and the colossal heaps of *débris*. But even if we assume the houses to have been of three storeys, and standing close by the side of one another, the town can nevertheless not have contained more than 5,000 inhabitants, and cannot have mustered more than 500 soldiers; but it could always raise a considerable army from among its subjects, and as it was rich and powerful, it could obtain mercenaries from all quarters. . . .

Homer can *never* have seen Ilium's Great Tower, the surrounding wall of Poseidon and Apollo, the Scaean Gate or the Palace of King Priam, for all these monuments lay buried deep in heaps of rubbish, and he made no excavations to bring them to light. He knew of these monuments of immortal fame only from hearsay, for the tragic fate of ancient Troy was then still in fresh remembrance, and had already been for centuries in the mouth of all minstrels.

Homer rarely mentions temples, and, although he speaks of the temple of Athena, yet, considering the smallness of the city, it is very doubtful whether it actually existed. . . .

I formerly believed that the most ancient people who inhabited this site were the Trojans [of Homer], because I fancied that among their ruins I had found the δέπας ἀμφικύπελλον, but I now perceive that Priam's people were the succeeding nation. . . .

In consequence of my former mistaken idea, that Troy was to be found on the primary soil or close above it, I unfortunately, in 1871 and 1872, destroyed a large portion of the city, for I at that time broke down all the house-walls in the higher strata which obstructed my way. This year, however, as soon as I had come by clear proofs to the firm conviction that Troy was not to be found upon the primary soil, but at a depth of from 23 to 33 feet, I ceased to break down any house-wall in these strata, so that in my excavations of this year a number of Trojan houses have been brought to light. They will still stand for centuries, and visitors to the Troad may convince themselves that the stones of the Trojan buildings can *never* have been used for building other towns, for the greater part of them are still *in situ*. Moreover, they are small, and millions of such stones are to be found upon all the fields of this district.

Valuable stones, such as those large flags which cover the road leading from the Scaean Gate to the plain, as well as the stones of the enclosing wall and of the Great Tower, have been left untouched, and not a single stone of the Scaean Gate is wanting. . . .

In closing the excavations at Ilium for ever, I cannot but fervently thank God for His great mercy, in that, notwithstanding the terrible danger to which we have been exposed owing to the continual hurricanes, during the last three years' gigantic excavations, no misfortune had happened, no one has been killed, and no one has ever been seriously hurt. . . .

In December of the same year [1873] the Turkish authorities of Kum-Kaleh seized many gold ornaments which two of my workmen had found in three different places in the preceding March, whilst working for me in the trenches of Hissarlik, at a depth of nearly 30 ft. below the surface of the hill. Most of these jewels were contained in a vase with an owl's head. . . . But as the statements of the labourers differ as to the particular objects contained in each treasure, I can only describe them here conjointly. The two workmen had stolen and divided the three treasures between themselves, and probably I should never have had any knowledge of it, had it not been for the lucky circumstance that the wife of the workman of Yeni Shehr, who had got his share of the plunder, besides two more pendants, had the boldness to parade one Sunday with the earrings and pendants. This excited the envy of her companions; she was denounced to the Turkish authorities of Kum-Kaleh, who put her and her husband in prison; and, having been threatened that her husband would be hanged if they did not give up the jewels, she betrayed the hiding-place, and thus this part of the treasure was at once recovered and is now exhibited in the Imperial Museum of Constantinople. The pair also denounced their accomplice at Kalifatli, but here the authorities came too

Gold earrings

late, because he had already had his part of the spoil melted down by
a goldsmith in Ben Kioi, who, at his desire, had made of it a very large,
broad, and heavy necklace, with clumsy flowery ornaments in the Turkish
fashion. Thus this part of the treasure is for ever lost to science. . . . As
both thieves declared separately on oath before the authorities of Kum-
Kaleh that the owl-vase, with part of the gold, was found by them immediately to the west of the wall, and that the two other treasures were found
close by, and indicated the exact spot of the discovery, there can be no doubt
as to its accuracy. . . .

All these gold ornaments, both genuine and re-made, are now in the
Imperial Museum at Constantinople. The genuine ones . . . are nearly all of
the same type as those contained in the great treasure discovered by me,
though similar types had never before been found elsewhere. . . .

This treasure of the supposed mythical king Priam, of the mythical
heroic age, which I discovered at a great depth in the ruins of the supposed
mythical Troy, is at all events a discovery which stands alone in archaeology,
revealing great wealth, great civilization and a great taste for art, in an age
preceding the discovery of bronze, when weapons and implements of pure
copper were employed contemporaneously with enormous quantities of
stone weapons and implements. This treasure further leaves no doubt that
Homer must have actually seen gold and silver articles, such as he continually describes; it is, in every respect, of inestimable value to science,
and will for centuries remain the object of careful investigation. . . .

As the Turkish papers have charged me in a shameful manner with
having acted against the letter of the firman granted to me, in having kept
the treasure for myself instead of sharing it with the Turkish Government,
I find myself obliged to explain here, in a few words, how it is that I have
the most perfect right to that treasure.

It was only in order to spare Safvet Pasha, the late Minister of Public
Instruction, that I stated in my first memoir, that at my request, and in
the interest of science, he had arranged for the portion of Hissarlik, which
belonged to the two Turks in Kum-Kaleh, to be bought by the government.
But the true state of the case is this. Since my excavations here in the
beginning of April 1870, I had made unceasing endeavours to buy this
field, and at last, after having travelled three times to Kum-Kaleh simply
with this object, I succeeded in beating the two proprietors down to the
sum of 1,000 francs (40l.). Then, in December 1870, I went to Safvet
Pasha at Constantinople, and told him that, after eight months' vain endeavours, I had at last succeeded in arranging for the purchase of the
principal site of Troy for 1,000 francs, and that I should conclude the

bargain as soon as he would grant me permission to excavate the field. He knew nothing about Troy or Homer; but I explained the matter to him briefly, and said that I hoped to find there antiquities of immense value to science. He, however, thought that I should find a great deal of gold, and therefore wished me to give him all the details I could, and then requested me to call again in eight days. When I returned to him, I heard to my horror that he had already compelled the two proprietors to sell him the field for 600 francs (24*l.*), and that I might make excavations there if I wished, but that everything I found must be given up to him. I told him in the plainest language what I thought of his odious and contemptible conduct, and declared that I would have nothing more to do with him, and that I should make no excavations.

But through Mr. Wyne McVeagh [Wayne MacVeagh], at that time the American Consul, he repeatedly offered to let me make excavations, on condition that I should give him only one-half of the things found.[8] At the persuasion of that gentleman I accepted the offer, on condition that I should have the right to carry away my half out of Turkey. But the right thus conceded to me was revoked in April 1872, by a ministerial decree, in which it was said that I was not to export any part of my share of the discovered antiquities, but that I had the right to sell them in Turkey.[9] The Turkish Government, by this new decree, broke our written contract in the fullest sense of the word, and I was released from every obligation. Hence I no longer troubled myself in the slightest degree about the contract which was broken without any fault on my part. I kept everything valuable that I found for myself, and thus saved it for science; and I feel sure that the whole civilized world will approve of my having done so. The new-discovered Trojan antiquities, and especially the treasure, far surpass my most sanguine expectations, and fully repay me for the contemptible trick which Safvet Pasha played me, as well as for the continual and unpleasant presence of a Turkish official during my excavations, to whom I was forced to pay 4¾ francs a day.

It was by no means because I considered it to be my duty, but simply to show my friendly intentions, that I presented the Museum in Constantinople with seven large vases, from 5 to 6½ feet in height, and with four sacks of stone implements. I have thus become the only benefactor the museum has ever had; for, although all firmans are granted upon the express condition that one-half of the discovered antiquities shall be given to the museum, yet it has hitherto never received an article from anyone. The reason is that the museum is anything but open to the public, and the sentry frequently refuses admittance even to its director, so everyone knows that the antiquities sent there would be for ever lost to science. . . .

An early nineteenth-century view of the fortress of Mycenae, the city which, according to Homeric tradition, was once ruled by Agamemnon.

Schliemann's excavations of the Grave Circle near the Lion Gate, the site of his sensational discoveries of Mycenaean art and treasures in 1876.

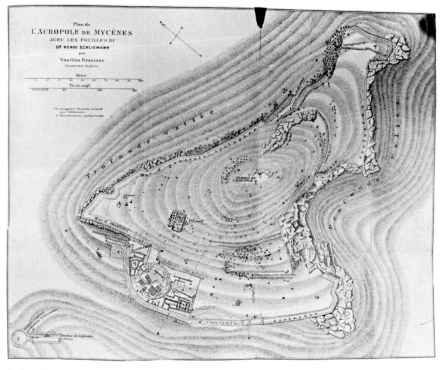

A plan of Mycenae showing the famous Grave Circle and the five shaft graves excavated by Schliemann. Excavations at a "treasury," shown at the lower left corner, were supervised by his wife Sophia.

A recent view of the Grave Circle of Mycenae with the Argolis beyond.

Courtesy of Mrs. Gray Johnson Poole

A party of archaeologists at the Lion Gate in Mycenae. Schliemann has been identified as the figure standing on top of the gate, his assistant, Wilhelm Dörpfeld, as the man sitting in the niche at the upper left, and Sophia Schliemann as the woman in the white hat on the right.

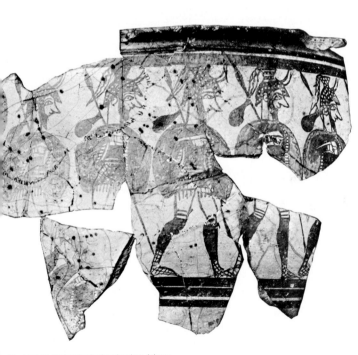

A selection of the treasures discovered by Schliemann at Mycenae: a golden diadem from Grave III (upper left); the "Mask of Agamemnon" from Grave V (lower left); a richly decorated golden cup from Grave V (upper right); a fragment from the famous Warrior vase discovered in a ruin near the Lion Gate (lower right); and a dagger inlaid with three golden lions from Grave IV (extreme right).

Schliemann, aged sixty, at the height of his fame, the friend of statesmen and princes, both acclaimed and vilified by the scholars of his age.

Sophia Schliemann with her children Andromache and Agamemnon, about 1880.

The Italianate mansion in Athens, called
"The House of Troy," where the
Schliemanns lived in regal but austere
splendor.

The English Prime Minister William E.
Gladstone, himself a Homeric scholar, was
one of Schliemann's most faithful friends
and a staunch defender of his controversial
theories.

Rudolf Virchow (1821-1902), the prominent German scientist who joined Schliemann during his second campaign at Troy and instilled in him sound principles of archaeological investigation.

Wilhelm Dörpfeld (1853-1940), the brilliant young architect who became Schliemann's principal assistant in 1882 and applied his meticulous methods to the later excavations at Troy and Tiryns.

The Treasury of Atreus at Mycenae.

IF ANYTHING, Priam's Treasure proved a mixed blessing to Schliemann. It was the Midas touch all over again. The gold enriched him, but it also possessed him. He was haunted by worries over the treasure's safety. The possibility that thieves might break into his house caused him sleepless nights. He did not dare to leave his Athens home or travel lest the treasure be stolen. Yet it was also a source of immense satisfaction to him. He alone had found the Golden Grail. The story of his quest and triumph would echo through the ages. Proudly he wrote to his sisters in Germany of the "great glory" that the discovery would bring the name Schliemann.[1]

On his return from Hissarlik, he began to pour forth a veritable avalanche of letters and articles on his crowning achievement. It was not in his character to be secretive for long. As soon as he got to Athens, he had to share his excitement with the rest of the world. Anything that stood to enlarge his fame, no matter what the consequences, he was unable to keep to himself. Schliemann was always his own publicity agent. To friends and relatives he sent a portrait of his young Hellenic wife wearing a Trojan diadem and other jewels from the treasure. Predictably, the latest news from Troy spread with lightning speed all over Greece and beyond. His house was besieged by people who wanted to set eyes on Priam's gold. Foreign cities asked to exhibit the treasure. He had no restful minute. Work on his archaeological book stalled. In the great centers of Europe and America people talked about Schliemann and Troy. He was an instant celebrity.

But, predictably too, Turkey was not going to take the adventurous excavator's latest coup lying down. In the beginning Schliemann was certain that the Turks would and could do nothing. Anyhow, he knew how to deal with them. Outside Turkey no law court would interfere in the dispute between two foreign parties. However, he was mistaken.

He had a first taste of Turkish intransigence when the authorities ordered the arrest of the governmental overseer at Troy, Amin Effendi (Efendi), who was accused of negligence. At heart a kindly and compassionate man, Schliemann was deeply disturbed that he was the cause of the man's misfortunes. Hence he wrote a letter to the Dardanelles governor appealing to him "in the name of humanity" not to punish an innocent.

> If he did not supervise me well, it is because we always worked at the same time at five different places and no mortal has yet been born who is able to split himself in five to keep simultaneous watch over five diggings. . . . I wish you had seen the despair of the poor fellow when he later heard from the workers that I had found and removed a treasure. You should have seen with what rage he stormed into my room and with loud voice demanded, in the name of the Sultan, that I shall instantly open all my boxes and all my closets, while, in reply, I just threw him out of the house—you would take pity on him. . . . The only fault of Amin Effendi is that he is not an archaeologist, and to watch five excavation sites you need five archaeologists. . . .[2]

When Schliemann was offered a peace branch by Dr. P. A. Déthier, director of the Turkish Imperial Museum, who asked for but a few token "owl-faced" vases accompanied by a friendly, conciliatory letter, he advised his intermediary, the then U.S. Ambassador George H. Boker, that he would do no such thing. Instead he made the counteroffer "to continue diggings at Troy at my expense for three more months in his, Mr. Déthier's, company, solemnly binding myself to let him have everything we may find."[3] The director did not bother to answer.

Turkey now used political pressure on Greece, which in turn ordered confiscation of the treasure. But before such action was taken, Schliemann had distributed the labeled pieces among Sophia's relatives for safekeeping. Priam's Treasure was to be reburied in the stables and backyards of private houses all over Greece and Crete. No one kept a written record of its whereabouts that could fall into "enemy hands." Schliemann sent a special messenger to his wife, then taking the baths in Ischia, to give her an oral account of the various hiding places. Meanwhile he was harassed by the Greek authorities wherever he went. During an inquest he did not buckle and refused to give any information. For a while he was put under virtual house arrest. His assets were blocked. When later going abroad, he found his hotel rooms ransacked, apparently by Turkish agents.

Eventually the affair came before a Greek court in April 1874 and was settled the next April. The court decided against Schliemann.[4] He was ordered to pay the Turkish government, with the Imperial Museum as beneficiary, 50,000 francs. In a grand gesture, he advanced instead five times the amount and, to boot, sent along a load of (nonprecious) Trojan antiquities.[5] The treasure was fully his. To safeguard it until he made further dispositions, he now stored it in the vaults of the Greek National Bank. With his donation to the Turks, he requested a speedy renewal of his *firman*. Whenever giving anything to governments or institutions, Schliemann expected handsome returns. Such transactions were to him essentially barters rather than outright donations.

From the start he considered the treasure not just an archaeological or material asset but a "weapon" in his dealings with governments. Previously he had singled out the Apollo metope for such a pawn in power politics. His strategy was simple. In exchange for the promise of turning over the precious objects to the Greek nation after his death, he wanted to be given a free hand to dig at Mycenae and Olympia. Occasionally other sites were also mentioned, such as Delphi and Delos. All along he reiterated in the press, in letters, and in his book on Troy that he would bequeath the collection to Greece but said in private that such a pledge did not entail any final commitment.[6] At one time or another—and often at the same time—the Trojan haul was offered for sale to the British Museum, the Louvre, the Museo Nazionale in Naples, and even the Hermitage in St. Petersburg. Miffed by the less than enthusiastic Greek reactions to his proposals, Schliemann sent out feelers to Italy as early as July 1873 through the noted archaeologist Giuseppe Fiorelli to let him dig a prehistoric city in Italy or Sicily.[7] For that privilege he was prepared to set up a museum to display his Trojan collection. He intimated that he would move his family and build himself a house in Naples or Palermo.

While such negotiations went on, Schliemann's opus on Troy—*Troy and Its Remains*—was completed. Published in German and French editions in the spring of 1874 (the English edition came out a year later), it was hardly the success author and publishers had hoped for. The unscholarly approach to the material, lack of organization and analysis, and hasty conclusions were widely faulted. The accompanying "Atlas" fared even worse; the illustrations were technically weak and inadequately arranged and captioned. In general, there was little opposition to Schliemann's identification of Hissarlik with Troy, but his fanciful equations of Hissarlik structures with Homeric references (*e.g.*, Scaean Gate, Priam's Palace) were challenged. In Germany a veritable storm rose among the professional guild of classicists. Schliemann was held to ridicule in the press. The popular comic paper *Kladderadatsch* poked fun at his Trojan mania.

Schliemann took such criticism with anything but equanimity. To him it was in the main an expression of the pettiness of academic pedants. Rarely did he bother to examine properly an opponent's thesis. He bombarded newspapers and journals with vehement retorts, harming his cause

A contemporary German cartoon: "After Mr. Schliemann found the Trojan treasure as a result of his Homeric studies, he happens to read the Saga of the Nibelungen and immediately sets out with wife and her apron to search for the Rheingold."

rather than furthering it by their lack of reasoned argument. Only a few scholars, like Max Müller and Ernst Curtius, could take exception with some of his wilder hypotheses without being banished to limbo. Yet in letters to third parties, they, too, were dressed down for their totally mistaken views. In a rare change of mood, Schliemann himself would, once in a while, admit the shortcomings of his archaeological expertise: "It was an entirely new world for me; I had to learn everything by myself and only by and by could I attain the right insight."[8] But he was slow to understand that scholars can disagree, debate, and compromise without dealing in personalities, that, indeed, a healthy discourse is the very catalyst of intellectual progress.[9]

After Troy, Mycenae had always been next on Schliemann's list of potential sites. Actual plans to excavate there as early as the spring 1870 had gained Greek encouragement. And during the 1873 season, when he thought he had done all there was to do in Troy, Schliemann again approached the Greek authorities.

In an application to the Greek government he asked for the right to carry on excavations at Olympia and Mycenae at his own expense. All the finds were to remain in his possession until his death, when they would pass to the Greek nation. He promised to set aside a sum of at least 200,000 francs for the construction of a public museum to house his collection, with the understanding that it was to bear his name. Thus he wrote in January 1873 to the Greek minister of education, underlining his request with the remarks: "I have settled in Athens, married a Greek wife, and am unremittingly working for the glory of Greece. . . . Since I have been fortunate enough to discover the real site of Ilium and marvellous ruins, and I have found a quantity of things of archaeological value, of which I am making a unique prehistoric collection, as any one can see who visits my house, where it is all exhibited. . . . I shall bring to Athens any further finds that I may make. . . ."[10]

Despite the Greek parliament's initially friendly reaction, the plan was rejected by the government, probably upon the advice of the Greek Archaeological Society, the main reason being that according to Greek law any antiquities taken from the Greek soil were the inalienable property of the nation and hence could not be held by any private person. Schliemann renewed his threats to abandon the country for good ("La vie à Athènes nous dégoute et nous reviendrons habiter à Paris"),[11] all the while contemplating ways of persuading parliament—just as he had the Indiana legislature—to change the law to accommodate Dr. Schliemann.

His annoyance with the Greek authorities was to rise to a fever pitch when he learned that permission to excavate Olympia had been granted to the German Empire. To his friends he announced his firm resolve to search for cities of the "heroic age" in the Campania of Italy. But then he petitioned the minister of education once more to be given Mycenae. How this strange man could be both shifty and stubborn, adamant and uncompromising, arrogant and meek, indecisive and fast acting, wavering in his concepts yet rigidly dogmatic! Nothing now would deter him from Mycenae. The only trouble was that no permission was forthcoming.

To tackle Mycenae, the "city" of the Achaean overlord Agamemnon—called by Homer "rich in gold" (πολύχρυσος)—had been on Schliemann's mind since his antiquarian trip through Greece in 1868. On his first visit a reading of Pausanias had led him to the novel theory that the tombs of the royal house of Atreus were located within the Cyclopean ramparts of the ancient citadel rather than the outer walls of the lower city, as the experts had usually deduced from the Pausanias passage. Schliemann, ever the impatient man of action, was eager to prove his controversial theory, as he had done in the Troad, by no less a discovery than the tombs of Agamemnon, Cassandra, and their companions murdered on their return from the sack of Troy by Clytemnestra and her lover Aegisthus.

Indeed, Mycenae was made for him. The rambling amorphous mound of Hissarlik—devoid of any notable surface structures to orient oneself by, with its fathomless aggregate of millions of cubic feet of debris and complex jumble of strata—was archaeological quicksand. In Mycenae, on the other hand, there was not much need to worry about stratification and which layer was which. Within a few feet or a yard or two one was likely to hit virgin rock; thus Schliemann's propensity to cut through deposits would do relatively little harm. A fairly extensive number of references from Homer and the great Attic dramatists to Hellenistic historian-geographers like Pausanias and Strabo could offer guidance.

Furthermore, there was never the slightest doubt about the identity of the formidable ruins. Mycenae stood there, its name and physical presence had persisted through millennia. Its walls, raised from enormous blocks, though exposed to everybody's sight, were, because of their weight and size, not as vulnerable to blunderers as the buried structures of Troy that, no sooner laid free, were coveted as building material by local people. (Schliemann himself used such blocks for building his stone hut on top of the hill and, on the whole, tolerated with a certain amount of amusement the carting away of material from the structures he had dismantled.)

Without notifying the Greek authorities, Schliemann left in late February 1874 for Mycenae—allegedly for a "survey," but in fact to dig. He thus repeated the same illegal stratagem that he used in 1870 at Hissarlik and which had caused him nothing but headaches. Now, when he was already in hot water with the Turks and was looked upon with suspicion by the Greeks, it seemed sheer folly. Apparently he even tried to mislead officialdom about his intentions by preparing for foreign travel. On arrival in the Argolis he pretended that he already had the government's consent; as he later declared in the Ilios autobiography, "Having obtained from the Greek government permission to excavate at Mycenae, I began operations there in February 1874."[12] The events of the following days quickly dissipated such a claim.

Instead of the planned nine days, Schliemann excavated at Mycenae for five days with twenty-odd men. Apart from Sophia, he was accompanied by his friend Émile Burnouf and Burnouf's daughter, a gifted artist who was to draw the finds. He dug thirty-four small trenches, mainly within the citadel ("acropolis"), where debris was abundant, and brought forth a number of terra-cotta idols and ancient pottery in addition to an undecorated stela. The idols, he maintained, represented the goddess Hera, thereby confirming his hypothesis that Homer's Hera *bo-ōpis*, a patron goddess of Mycenae (and the entire Argolis), was originally conceived as cow-eyed—an analogy to the Trojan owl-faced or owl-eyed Athene. Further evidence for this he found at the nearby Heraion shrine. During the short stay he became fully convinced that Mycenae was indeed worthy of his archaeological energies. Possibly he had already fixed his eye on the circular terrace southeast of the Lion Gate as the most propitious target. Early in his archaeological career he had formed the principle that sites with the greatest accumulation of pottery shards and other miscellaneous debris were the ones likely to yield the highest returns. At places where such deposits were absent or slight, he did not, as a rule, bother to turn his spade.

Excavations were brought to an abrupt end when the local prefect received instructions to stop the unauthorized operation. A basket with

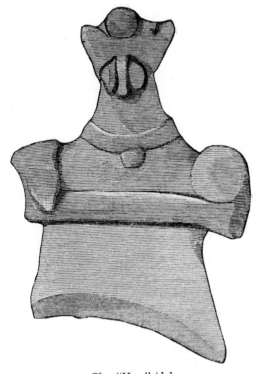

Clay "Hera" idol

Schliemann's artifacts was confiscated, but since they were seemingly worthless, it was given back by the Nauplia chief of police. This largesse, however, raised the displeasure of the capital's authorities, and telegrams flew to and fro while Schliemann had no choice but to return to Athens.

Despite the unfortunate foray, the Greek government bore no permanent grudge and on March 29, 1874, agreed to let Schliemann continue his investigation at Mycenae. However, just then Turkey was suing Schliemann in the Greek courts, and the pending trial forced him to stay in Athens. By July the Greek government withdrew the permit. Mycenae had to wait.

There followed difficult months for Schliemann, relieved in the summer during court recess by travel in central Greece and the Peloponnese. In the former he scouted—but refrained from digging—around Orchomenos in Boeotia, according to Homer once a mighty city as rich in gold as Troy and Mycenae. Orchomenos was the site of the so-called Treasury of Minyas, a preclassical underground vault resembling the "beehive" tombs or treasuries of Mycenae. In the Peloponnese his main goal was Olympia, which his fellow Germans had snatched away from him. A side trip took him to the waterfall of the Styx.

To offer new proof of his dedication to Greece and its heritage. Schliemann proposed to tear down at his own expense the Venetian "Frankish" Tower on the Acropolis of Athens, a fourteenth century monstrosity that had been built over the Propylaea and blocked out part of the Parthenon. The offer was accepted. Schliemann purchased wood for putting up a scaffold, but then the Greeks took over the demolition work, though he had to shoulder the bill of 10,000 francs.

Incensed, he sent off a letter to King George, remonstrating against the shabby treatment he received from the Greek government. In a tone of self-pity he assured the Greek monarch—apparently to squelch rumors—that he had come to Greece with his "honestly earned fortune," which he intended to put to use for the benefit of science. He also declared, once again, that, unless given satisfaction, he would be forced to leave the country for good.

When the trial with Turkey was over in April 1875, Schliemann at last was free to break out of his Athenian confinement. He needed to get away, renew relations with colleagues in Western Europe, and examine collections of ancient artifacts there. His first goal was Paris, where he lectured on his Trojan researches before the Société Géographique. However, the attending members were unimpressed by his extravagant assertions and gave him the cold shoulder. His reception in England was more cordial. For some reason, the English took Schliemann to their hearts and made a public figure of him. No other country was as responsive to his theories or applauded his successes so generously. Perhaps the long-standing association of gentleman amateurs with archaeological pioneer work, ranging from John Aubrey, William Stukeley, and the famous Dilettanti to such prominent nineteenth century figures as Austen Layard and the prehistorians John Evans and John Lubbock, made Schliemann, the self-taught outsider and merchant-adventurer, welcome in learned and social circles. British fair play rather than the arrogance of a closed academic shop also had a part. Schliemann's career was the stuff Victorian heroes were made of. The great Gladstone, a statesman and himself a Homeric scholar, applauded his achievement. Schliemann's June 1875 lecture, "The Discoveries at the Site of Troy," before the London Antiquarian Society (which in 1876 made him an honorary member), followed by a brief talk by Gladstone, was a complete triumph. He became the toast of the town, a most sought-after dinner and house guest of high society. In London, he wrote, he had been treated "as if I had conquered a new continent for England."[13]

From London he went to The Hague as guest of the cultured Queen Sophie of the Netherlands, who had a strong interest in antiquity. Later he sent her as a tribute several Tanagra figurines from Greece, which he commissioned his brother-in-law to acquire ("buy anything very nice and very cheap"[14]) and which he then, with the knowledge of the Queen, undertook to smuggle out of the country, since all export of antiquities was forbidden.[15]

During his stay in Holland he was full of praise for the prehistoric and Egyptian exhibits at the University of Leiden. Consecutively he then inspected collections of early European antiquities in Copenhagen, Stockholm, Danzig, and elsewhere. In August he went as guest speaker to his home university, Rostock. The topic, of course, was Troy. At the time he made the acquaintance of Professor Rudolf Virchow, the famous Berlin physiologist and prehistorian who was recommended to him by Gladstone. Virchow, a close friend in Schliemann's later years, had excavated archaic sites in Eastern Germany, where he came up with pottery that strongly resembled the facial and figurative vases of Hissarlik.

Toward the end of his European tour, Schliemann was at a loss over where to turn and again toyed with the idea of making ancient Italy the focus of his archaeological appetite. He was hopeful that archaic settlements comparable to Troy or Mycenae might be found in the southern peninsula and Sicily. Within a few weeks he made his way through a staggering number of towns but found them all wanting. Hence he arrived at the decision to quit Italy in order "to remain with the prehistoric age and to continue excavation in Asia Minor," as he wrote to Burnouf in December

1875 from Naples.[16] He concluded that he would do everything in his power to obtain a new *firman* from the Turks.

His mind made up, he went by ship from Naples straight to Constantinople to reestablish contacts with the Sublime Porte. He stayed for two months and got the government to sanction a return engagement at Hissarlik. Alas, the *firman*, valid for two years, was not enough. Insurmountable obstacles were raised by the imperious governor of the Dardanelles, Ibrahim Pasha. After repeated attempts to come to terms with the local satrap, Schliemann had to abandon Troy once more without having had a chance to resume exploration. He renewed his application to the Greek government, and at long last he obtained permission to dig at Mycenae. He set out immediately, stopping on the way for a few days at Tiryns.

The Greeks had stipulated the same conditions as they had in 1874. That is, everything Schliemann excavated belonged to the nation and had to be handed over. He alone had to defray the costs. However, he was given exclusive rights of first publication. Knowing Schliemann's inclinations only too well, the authorities were particularly concerned that no existing structures be demolished. Operations were to be confined to realistic proportions by limiting the number of laborers and excavations at one time. Specific terms as to the sites and excavation procedures were to be worked out during the campaign with officials of the Greek Archaeological Society. The Society sent to Mycenae one of its trusted officers (ephor), Panagiotes Stamatakes, was wos to be assisted by overseers.

Styles of Mycenaean masonry walls

To Schliemann, Stamatakes was a nuisance from the very beginning. He treated the ephor with utter contempt. In his book on Mycenaean excavations, Stamatakes is barely mentioned and then only alluded to as an ignorant bureaucratic boor, a "government clerk," whose only concern was to impede the progress of Dr. Schliemann's pioneering researches undertaken for the greater glory of Greece. This was far from the truth. Stamatakes was a gifted archaeologist in his own right who made valuable contributions and is now ranked as one of the founding fathers of Mycenaean studies.[17]

As the record shows, Schliemann had no intention of abiding by the strict rules of the Archaeological Society and used all his cunning to have his way. When this failed, he would resort to tempestuous outbursts, threats to pick up and leave for America, and constant appeals over Stamatakes' head to the Athens authorities. There ensued a continuous, acrimonious confrontation between the two men of such different temperaments which took on almost comical proportions. Letters and telegrams between Athens and Mycenae (or, rather, the Nauplia post office) were exchanged at a dizzying pace and quantity. Mrs. Schliemann acted as a helpmate to her husband and went as a special emissary to Athens to plead against Stamatakes, but she also tried to soothe her husband's Jovian fury.

Stamatakes described the state of affairs at the site in a communication to his superiors:

> . . . A few days ago, he [Schliemann] found a wall superimposed on another wall, and wanted to pull down the upper one; I forbade it, and he stopped. Next morning, when I was not there, he had the wall pulled down and the lower one exposed. Then he left his wife there to supervise the excavation, and went himself to the acropolis, in order to avoid meeting me. When I later asked Mrs. Schliemann for information, she told me I had no right to reproach her husband. He was a learned man, this wall was Roman and was interfering with the progress of the work; I, on the other hand, was not a learned man and would be well advised to make no remarks, as Mr. Schliemann was very easily excited and would terminate the excavations if he got angry. . . . I met him on the acropolis, but I did not say anything to him. You must know that he eagerly demolishes everything Roman and Greek, in order to lay bare the Pelasgian walls.[18] If we find Greek or Roman vases, he looks at them in disgust, and if such fragments come into his hands, he lets them fall. . . . He treats me as if I was a barbarian. . . . If the ministry is not satisfied with me, I beg that I be recalled; I remain here at the expense of my health.[19] . . .

But in the end what muted poor Stamatakes and the Greek authorities was Schliemann's fantastic success. With an increasing number of men he had started at three different places inside and outside the Cyclopean walls.

Sophia was in charge of the large buried *tholos* ("treasury") near the Lion Gate. Within the citadel work concentrated on the gate itself, the nearby "Cyclopean houses," and the adjacent circular platform. Though two sculptured stelae, possibly gravestones, turned up in the first few weeks, Schliemann, strangely enough, continued to scatter his energies. He seems to have expected treasure above all from Sophia's dig because substantial finds from similar beehive structures had been reported (some by a local Muslim notable, Veli Pasha, as early as 1808), and this one was apparently buried and untouched.

Impressive objects were taken from the Cyclopean houses by the gate, among them fragments of the celebrated Warrior Vase (in the building now named for it), which shows in lively style and detail late Bronze Age soldiers on the way to battle.[20]

Even so, returns there were disappointing, and Schliemann was about ready to abandon the site, if not break off the campaign, when, as in his third year at Troy, his fortunes changed dramatically overnight. What followed is quite simply one of the star-studded episodes in archaeological history. Assisted by Sophia, who on her knees handled most of the sensitive work of extracting fragile objects with a penknife, Schliemann found another treasure. Once again his prediction, at odds with the informed opinions of contemporary scholarship, had come true.

What the Schliemanns took out of the earth was so stunning an amount of glittering and unique antiquities that the mind still boggles when reading—"I also found," "here were further found," "next to it we found," etc., etc.—that endless, almost tedious, catalogue of golden diadems, golden drinking cups, golden belts, golden seal rings, golden breastplates, golden face masks, finely cut gems, and on and on. The gold alone weighed some 33 pounds. But there was much more in the five grave shafts Schliemann explored: exquisite ceramics, bronze and copper implements, weapons (foremost inlaid niello dagger blades which, uncleaned, escaped Schliemann's attention), and the remains of at least fifteen bodies.[21] Obviously these were royal, or at least noble, burials. Schliemann was ever more certain they were the bodies of the unfortunate Atreids and corresponded precisely to the Homeric tradition and the account given by Pausanias. After beholding the relatively well-preserved face in the first grave—the last that he emptied—he declared, in a telegram to the Greek minister of education, that it resembled the features of Agamemnon as it had previously *appeared* to him. In all seriousness, he considered his own imagination conclusive proof. In ecstasy he lifted the golden face mask of the buried prince and kissed it.

Once again Schliemann hastened to advertise his discoveries, and

Cut through a Mycenaean treasury

persuaded his good friend the British Prime Minister Gladstone, now temporarily out of office, to write a preface to *Mycenae*, his about-to-be published book on Mycenaean antiquities.[22] Gladstone reluctantly undertook the task but warmed up to Schliemann's enthusiasm and agreed that the tombs of Agamemnon and Cassandra had been located. The English edition of the volume was dedicated to another powerful man, Dom Pedro II, Emperor of Brazil, whom Schliemann, upon the invitation of Turkey, had accompanied to the Troad. Later, during the actual campaign, he showed the emperor around the Mycenaean ruins and, rising to the occasion, entertained the imperial party by torchlight in "Agamemnon's Tomb."[23]

Mycenae is based on Schliemann's six dispatches to *The Times* (published in eight issues). Originally written in English, it was released in little over a year in German and English editions. A French edition followed soon after.

Like his previous work on Hissarlik, *Mycenae* is basically a day-to-day journal and has similar shortcomings. Unfortunately there is far too little information to indicate precisely where individual objects were found. Again the author's views are likely to change in the course of the work. Even though in editing his notes he freely incorporated expert opinions he gathered from learned friends, little attempt is made to integrate them and to give a synthesis.

Although Schliemann offered in his unpublished diaries the remarkable insight that the tombs could not possibly be the same that Pausanias saw and described as those of the Atreids, he was later so blinded by his discoveries that in his published report all critical thought was thrown to the wind and he convinced himself that he had indeed set eyes upon the mortal form of the Mycenaean king of kings. As at Troy, he jumped, even against his own better judgment, to sensational conclusions. As such, his last version, rather than being the best-reasoned, is often the most uncritical. The reverse of a scholar, Schliemann would not allow doubt to undermine his naïve faith. Similarly he came to disregard the brilliant observation by his friend Charles T. Newton, the director (keeper) of the British Museum and an excavator of renown, that vases from Rhodes of the same "Mycenaean" style could be dated through an Egyptian gem to about 1400 B.C.—a date at variance by two hundred years with the traditional one of the Trojan War (c. 1180 B.C.).

Many of Schliemann's dogmatically stated opinions have not stood the test of time. Some appeared patently wrong not only to antagonists but to sympathetic contemporaries. Carl Schuchhardt, an associate who with Schliemann's endorsement wrote a comprehensive book on the master's excavations in 1889, rightly challenged the thesis propounded by Pausanias that the *tholoi* were storehouses and treasure houses and not tombs, as they had been generally thought since antiquity. The lords of Mycenae were not likely to put away their riches in vaults outside the well-guarded walls. Besides, the smaller room in the Treasury of Atreus was obviously a burial chamber. And in Schliemann's lifetime an intact *tholos* at Menidi, not far from Athens, was opened containing the dead with their funerary equipment.

Schliemann's insistence that all the shaft graves were contemporaneous (and simultaneous), and hastily executed at that, a theory that was tailored to fit the account of Agamemnon's slaughter, was bizarre and implausible. The rich furnishings spoke against it, as did multiple burials successively deposited in the same roofed shaft, a fact Dörpfeld recognized by merely reexamining Schliemann's testimony. Other archaeologists, foremost among them Stamatakes who discovered a sixth grave in 1877, soon learned to assign different ages to the shaft graves.

Schliemann was also far too hasty in declaring the bodies to have been cremated, just because Homeric rites called for dead heroes being committed to funeral pyres. Had they been burned, so much bony matter could not have been preserved for three and a half millennia. Signs of fire and ashes probably point to some sacrifices during the burial ceremonies. But if anything, there are indications of mummification or embalming, perhaps due to Egyptian contacts, a notion that touches on the intriguing, though highly debatable, hypothesis that the much sought-for source of Mycenaean gold was none other than Egypt, which was assisted by Mycenaean mercenaries (kinsmen of the Philistines who settled along the Canaanite coast?) in expelling the Asiatic Hyksos.

As to the circular wall of parallel stone slabs around the shaft graves, Schliemann started by taking its vertically standing plates for grave stelae but in the course of excavation recognized that together they formed a contiguous fence covered by horizontal stone pieces. The wall then became in his view a bench and the entire platform an agora, rendered sacred by the royal tombs underneath. But this elaborate theory, buttressed by citations from classical literature, has likewise found few adherents. Nor, one must admit, has the Pausanias thesis itself or, rather, Schliemann's interpretation of it. At best it is an anachronism since, as Schliemann's colleague, the architect-archaeologist Friedrich Adler, soon after pointed out, the Lion Gate and adjoining walls were of more recent date (some one hundred and fifty to two hundred years later) than the shaft graves, which originally lay outside the fortress ramparts. Only a later extension of the Cyclopean circuit wall included the burial ground.[24] In fact, part of this graveyard was left remaining outside. Its graves have been traced after Schliemann. The low circular wall surrounding the burial platform was a later addition, too.

Speaking of age, one should also rectify Schliemann's belief (shared by Charles T. Newton and Arthur Evans) that the "treasuries" were older than the shaft graves. The reverse is true, though like the shaft graves the nine such structures so far located in and near Mycenae vary among themselves by several centuries and clearly show an evolution in design and construction.[25] Where the Atreids, if they are not entirely mythical, were actually buried, no one has yet been able to establish conclusively, though the tradition linking them with the "treasuries" may well be sound and in chronological terms would fit better.

Yet Schliemann's Homeric faith, even if wrongheaded, remained the fountainhead of his discoveries. And what discoveries they were! His finds in the royal tombs of Mycenae made Priam's Treasure pale. It was in every respect as sensational and unexpected as the discovery of Tut-ankh-amon's gold-laden tomb half a century later. Above and apart from the material value of the dazzling articles stands the superb artistry of the funerary objects that helped to reveal a virtually new chapter in ancient art and culture. Here, on a bleak, rocky promontory, the German-American amateur dug up within four months a pre-Dorian chapter of the Hellenic past of which next to nothing had been known, and the little that was known had not yet been assimilated by scholarship.

Like those at Troy, though on a far more advanced level, the treasures of Mycenae mirrored a cosmopolitan art. Glassware, an ostrich egg, and alabaster vessels were most likely Egyptian. Ivories, though probably of

Mycenaean make, suggested Near Eastern subjects. And there was amber from Schliemann's native Baltic. Mycenaean ceramics themselves belonged to a style that was widespread not only in Greece but has since been traced to Southern Italy, Egypt (where Flinders Petrie first described it as "Aegean"), the Syrian coast, the Aegean islands, and Asia Minor, including Troy. Even before Schliemann, similar ware had been excavated on Thera, Rhodes, and Cyprus. The close affinities of Mycenaean culture to Minoan Crete had barely been suspected in 1876.

Though Schliemann thought that he had come up with further proof for the factual basis of the Homeric poems—always his main endeavor—he instead gave the world nothing less than a lost civilization that preceded the events of the epics by some three hundred to four hundred years. Thanks to his impulse, historians speak today of a Mycenaean Age (c. 1600–1150 B.C.)—the first full-fledged civilization to flourish on the European mainland.[26] Now there was light behind the dark age from which classical Greece seemed to have sprung phoenixlike.

Schliemann's discoveries were to be the foundation of a whole branch of archaeological and historical studies which continue to make major contributions. They led directly to other peaks in archaeology: the still more ancient civilization of Crete; the finding and eventual decipherment of the ancient Mycenaean-Minoan script Linear B (its language turned out to be an archaic Greek dialect);[27] and the revolutionizing of all our views of Mediterranean and European prehistory.

Mycenae even more than Troy made the world listen to the unprepossessing ex-merchant. The news of his latest triumphs held several continents in awe. Some scholars may have still doubted his interpretations and criticized his methods, but grudgingly they had to acknowledge his marvelous results. Others became enthusiastic partisans. With the fame grew the Schliemann legend.

THE SEARCH FOR AGAMEMNON

from *Mycenae*

Mycenae, August 19, 1876.

I arrived here on the 7th inst. by the same road which Pausanias describes. The distance from Argos is only 50 *stadia*, or 5.8 English miles. . . . The situation of Mycenae is beautifully described by Homer, "In the depth of the horse-feeding Argos," because it lies in the north corner of the plain of Argos, in a recess between the two majestic peaks of Mount Euboea, whence it commanded the upper part of the great plain and the important narrow pass, by which the roads lead to Phlius, Cleonae, and Corinth. The acropolis occupied a strong rocky height, which projects from the foot of the mountain behind it in the form of an irregular triangle sloping to the west. This cliff overhangs a deep gorge, which protects the whole south flank of the citadel. Through the abyss below winds the bed of a torrent usually almost dry, because it has no other water than that of the copious fountain Perseia, which is about half a mile to the northeast of the fortress. . . . The cliff of the citadel is also more or less steep on the east and west side, where it forms six natural or artificial terraces.

The acropolis is surrounded by Cyclopean walls, from 13 to 35 feet high, and on an average 16 feet thick. Their entire circuit still exists, but they have evidently been much higher. They are of beautiful hard breccia, with which the neighbouring mountains abound. They follow the sinuosities of the rock, and show three different kinds of architecture. By far the greater portion of them is built exactly like the walls of Tiryns, although not so massively; and this kind of architecture is generally thought to be the most ancient. . . .

Notwithstanding the remote antiquity of Mycenae, its ruins are in a far better state of preservation than those of any of the Greek cities which Pausanias saw in a flourishing condition . . . and, owing to its distant and secluded position, and to the rudeness, magnitude, and solidity of the ruins, it is hardly possible to think that any change can have taken place in the general aspect of Mycenae since it was seen by Pausanias.

In the northwestern corner of the circuit-wall is the great Lions' Gate, of beautiful hard breccia. . . . The great gate stands at right angles to the adjoining wall of the citadel, and is approached by a passage, 50 feet long and 30 feet wide, formed by that wall and by another exterior wall, which runs nearly parallel to it, and which forms part of a large quadrangular tower erected for the defense of the entrance. Within these walls the enemy could advance only with a small front of perhaps seven men, exposed on three sides to the arrows and stones of the defenders. A zigzag road on immense Cyclopean substructions, now covered with large blocks which have fallen from the wall, led up to the entrance of the gateway. . . .

Over the space of about a square mile to the west-southwest and south of this acropolis, and exactly between the aforesaid deep ravines, extended the lower city, the site of which is distinctly marked by the remnants of numerous Cyclopean substructions of houses, by a Cyclopean bridge, by five Treasuries, and finally by the fragments of beautifully painted archaic pottery with which the ground is strewn. . . .

Much more interesting than all the other buildings in the suburb are the "Treasuries," which, owing to their great resemblance to ovens, are now called φοῦρνοι [phournoi] by the country people. One of them is just without [outside] the line of the town wall, on the slope of the hill near the Gate of the Lions. The doorway is visible, but it is nearly buried; the entrance is roofed with three large thick slabs; and the length of the passage is 18 feet, its width 7 ft. 9 in. Only a small part of the lower circular wall of the dome-shaped building can now be seen, the upper part having fallen in, probably ages ago. . . .

On the site of the enclosed city are the two largest Treasuries. One of these is the famous Treasury which tradition attributes to Atreus. The other, which is close to the Lions' Gate, appears to have been entirely under ground, and was therefore unknown in historical times; the upper part of its dome has fallen in, but I have not been able to ascertain whether, as some of the inhabitants of the Argolid affirm, this has occurred accidentally, or whether, as others maintain, it is the sacrilegious work of Veli Pasha, the son of the notorious Ali Pasha, who towards the end of 1820 attempted to force an entrance this way, but was prevented by the outbreak of the Greek revolution from proceeding much further.

The "Treasury of Atreus," which is about 400 yards further south, was entirely subterranean, being constructed under the eastern slope of the ridge which traverses the city, and towards the ravine of the same torrent which passes the south side of the cliff of the citadel. . . .

The site of Mycenae presented in the time of Pausanias just the same bare wilderness of rugged pasture land, interspersed with slopes and precipitous cliffs, as at the present day. No change can have taken place there, and the remnants of the lower city wall were undoubtedly in his time as trifling as they are now. Nay, such is their insignificance, that only the traces of the wall on the ridge seem to have been remarked by travellers, and nobody before me appears to have ever noticed the traces of the wall on the opposite side, which runs along the bank of the ravine torrent. . . .

I began the great work on the 7th August, 1876, with sixty-three workmen, whom I divided into three parties. I put twelve men at the Lions' Gate, to open the passage into the acropolis; I set forty-three to dig, at a distance of 40 feet from that gate, a trench 113 feet long and 113 feet broad; and the remaining eight men I ordered to dig a trench on the south side of the Treasury in the lower city, near the Lions' Gate, in search of the entrance. But the soil at the Treasury was as hard as stone, and so full of large blocks, that it took me two weeks to dig only as far down as the upper part of the open triangular space above the door, from which I could calculate that the threshold would be 33 feet lower.

I had also very hard work at the Lions' Gate, owing to the huge blocks by which the passage was obstructed, and which seem to have been hurled from the adjoining walls at the assailants, when the acropolis was captured by the Argives in 468 B.C. The obstruction of the entrance must date from that time, for the *débris* in which the boulders are imbedded has not been formed by a series of successive habitations, but it has evidently been gradually washed down by the rain water from the upper terraces.

Immediately to the left, on entering the gate, I brought to light a small chamber, undoubtedly the ancient doorkeeper's habitation, the ceiling of which is formed by one huge slab. The chamber is only 4½ feet high, and it would not be to the taste of our present doorkeepers; but in the heroic age comfort was unknown, particularly to slaves, and being unknown it was unmissed. . . .

At the north end of my trench [in the citadel] I have brought to light part of a Cyclopean water-conduit. . . . Close to it are twelve recesses, consisting of large slabs of calcareous stone and covered by smaller ones; in my opinion they cannot possibly be anything else than small cisterns. A few yards south of these reservoirs I have brought to light two tombstones, which stand in a direct line from north to south, and are ornamented with bas-reliefs of the highest interest. Unfortunately the tombstone to the north consists of a soft calcareous stone, in consequence of which it is broken in several places, and its upper part has not been preserved. . . . It shows one undivided picture, encompassed below as well as on both sides by a broad border, which is formed in the simplest way into rows, and it represents a hunting scene. On a chariot, drawn by one horse, stands the hunter, who holds in his left hand the reins, in his right a long broad sword. Owing to fractures in the stone the upper part of the chariot is not distinctly visible, but the wheel can be well seen, with its four spokes forming a cross. The outstretched fore and hind legs of the horse appear to indicate his great speed. . . .

At a distance of one foot from this sepulchral *stélé* and in the same line with it is the other, which is of much harder calcareous stone, and has been therefore much better preserved. . . . The lower part of the sculpture represents a warrior in a chariot, rather in a sitting than in a standing posture, for the lower part of his body is not visible. . . . The chariot is drawn by a stallion, whose outstretched legs seem to indicate that he is running at great speed. The tail of the animal stands upright, and its end only forms a curve. . . . Just before the horse is standing a warrior, apparently naked, who grasps the animal's head with his right hand, and holds in his uplifted left hand a double-edged sword; he seems to be full of anguish; his head is represented in profile, while the rest of his body is shown without the slightest perspective reduction. . . .

Mycenae, Sept. 9, 1876.

Since the 19th of August I have continued the excavations with an average number of 125 workmen and 4 horse-carts, and have made good progress. . . . The labourers here work much better and are much more honest than those in the Troad.

In the trench close to the Lions' Gate I have been obliged to stop the work for a time, the Archaeological Society of Athens having promised to send an engineer to repair the Cyclopean wall above and beside the gate, and to fasten the sculpture of the two lions with cramp-irons, so as to secure it against the shock of an earthquake.

In the large second trench I have brought to light a second wall of smaller stones, 12 feet high, which runs parallel with the great circuit wall, and thus forms a curve of about the third part of a circle. . . . On this wall are two parallel rows of large, closely-joined slabs of a calcareous stone, which show the same inclination as the wall, and appear to form, with the part in the adjoining field, a full circle. . . .

The space between the two slanting parallel rows of slabs was filled with *débris*, mixed with innumerable fragments of beautiful archaic pottery, and a great many Hera-idols, but no bones were found there. Within the curve, and very near to the two parallel rows of slabs, I brought to light two more sculptured tombstones of a hard calcareous stone, one of which is in the same line with the two sculptured slabs which I have already described, and only 1 ft. 5 in. south of them. . . . This newly discovered third tombstone shows, like the two others, on its western side, a sculpture in bas-relief, which

Detail of a stele from the Mycenaean Grave Circle

is divided by a horizontal fillet into two compartments, and is encompassed on all sides by two parallel fillets. . . .

The four sculptured and five unsculptured sepulchral slabs [found altogether] undoubtedly mark the sites of tombs cut deep in the rock, the exploration of which, however, I must needs delay until I have terminated all my excavations in the northern part of the acropolis.

The presence of these numerous sepulchres near the Lions' Gate, and thus in the most prominent part of the citadel, in a place where one would have expected to find the king's palace, is very significant; the more so, as the slabs of the two parallel rows perfectly resemble the five unsculptured tombstones and the slabs of the twelve small reservoirs, and all these monuments appear to have been erected simultaneously. . . .[1]

I do not for a moment hesitate to proclaim that I have found here the sepulchres which Pausanias, following the tradition, attributes to Atreus, to the "king of men" Agamemnon, to his charioteer Eurymedon, to Cassandra, and to their companions. But it is utterly impossible that Pausanias should have seen these tombstones, because, when he visited Mycenae, about 170 A.D., all the sepulchral monuments had for ages been covered by a layer of prehistoric *débris*, from 8 to 10 ft. thick, on which an Hellenic city had been built and had again been abandoned about four centuries before his time, after having added a layer of Hellenic ruins, 3 ft. thick, to the deep stratum of prehistoric remains. Thus he could only have known of the existence of these sepulchres by tradition. . . .

Mrs. Schliemann and I superintend the excavations from morning till dusk, and we suffer severely from the scorching sun and incessant tempest, which blows the dust into the eyes and inflames them; but in spite of these annoyances, nothing more interesting can be imagined than the excavation of a prehistoric city of immortal glory, where nearly every object, even to the fragments of pottery, reveals a new page of history. . . .

My supposition that the double parallel row of large slabs [on the terrace south of the Lion Gate] would be found to form a complete circle has been proved correct. One-half of it rests on the wall which was intended to support it in the lower part of the acropolis, the other half is founded on the higher flat rock, and touches the foot of the Cyclopean wall before mentioned; the entrance to it is from the north side.

At first I thought that the space between the two rows might have served for libations or for offerings of flowers in honour of the illustrious dead. But I now find this to be impossible, because the double row of slabs was originally covered with cross-slabs, of which six are still *in situ*; they are firmly fitted in and consolidated by means of notches. . . .

Mycenae, October 30, 1876.

. . . To my very greatest annoyance and displeasure, but by the most urgent demand of the Greek Archaeological Society in Athens, I have been forced to leave in the acropolis, on either side of the Lions' Gate, a large block of *débris* untouched *in situ*, because this institution has not yet sent, as it intended to do, an engineer to consolidate the sculpture of the two lions with cramp-irons, and to repair the Cyclopean walls to the right and left of it. But they still intend to do this work sooner or later, and they believe that the two masses of *débris* will facilitate the raising of the blocks and their insertion in the walls. . . . I call particular attention to this, because every visitor will naturally attribute the leaving behind of these two blocks of *débris* to my negligence.

Yesterday and to-day my excavations have had the honour of being visited by his Majesty Dom Pedro II, Emperor of Brazil. Coming from Corinth, his Majesty rode direct up to the acropolis, and remained for two hours in my excavations, which he attentively examined and re-examined. . . .

Mycenae, December 6, 1876.

The four sculptured tombstones having been removed to the village of Charvati, in order to be sent to Athens, I excavated on the site of the three with the bas-reliefs representing the warriors and the hunting scene, and found a quadrangular tomb, 21 ft. 5 in. long and 10 ft. 4 in. broad, cut out in the slope of the rock. . . .

In digging lower down I found from time to time a very small quantity of black ashes, and in this very frequently some curious objects; such as a bone button covered with a golden plate, with a beautiful intaglio ornamentation, or an imitation of a ram's horn cut out of ivory, having one flat side with two holes, by which the object must have been attached to something else, or other ornaments of bone or small plates of gold. I collected in this way twelve gold buttons covered with gold plates ornamented with intaglio work, one of which is as large as a five-franc piece. . . . Having dug down to a depth of 10½ ft., I was stopped by heavy rain, which turned the soft earth in the tomb to mud and I therefore took out the two unsculptured tombstones of the second line, which stood due east of the three sculptured ones, and at a distance of 20 ft. from them. In excavating around them I found another tomb cut in the rock. . . .

At a depth of 15 ft. below the level of the rock, or of 25 ft. below the former surface of the ground, as I found it when I began the excavations, I reached a layer of pebbles, below which I found, at a distance of three feet from each other, the remains of three human bodies, all with the head

Cow's head of silver with horns of gold

turned to the east and the feet to the west. They were only separated from
the surface of the levelled rock by another layer of small stones on which
they were lying, and they had evidently been burned simultaneously in
the very same place where they lay. The masses of ashes of the clothes
which had covered them, and of the wood which had partially or entirely
consumed their flesh, as well as the colour of the lower layer of stones and
the marks of the fire and the smoke on the stone wall, which at the bottom
of the sepulchre lined all the four sides—can leave no doubt whatever on
this point; nay more, there were the most unmistakable marks of three
distinct funeral piles. The wall, which at the bottom of the tomb lined
its four sides, consisted of pretty large stones joined without any binding material. . . . The small stones with which the bottom of the
sepulchre was strewn can, in my opinion, have had no other object than to
procure ventilation to the funeral pyres. These could not have been large,
and had evidently been intended to consume merely the clothes and partly
or entirely the flesh of the deceased; but *no more*, because the bones and
even the skulls had been preserved; but these latter had suffered so much
from the moisture, that none of them could be taken out entire.

On every one of the three bodies I found five diadems of thin gold-
plate, like those to be presently described, each 19½ in. long, and 4 in.
broad in the middle, from which it gradually diminishes to a point at both
ends. The pointed ends have been broken off, but, as several of the other
diadems have such points, there can be no doubt that all had been fashioned
in the same way. All the diadems were piped with copper wires in order
to give them more solidity, and a great many fragments of those copper
wires were found. All the fifteen diadems show the very same ornamentation of *repoussé* work, consisting of a border of two lines on either side,
between which we see a row of treble concentric circles, which increase or
diminish in size according to the breadth of the diadem, the largest circle
being in the middle. . . .

. I also found with the bodies many curious objects; for example, small
cylinders with a small tube throughout their length . . . a number of small
knives of obsidian, many fragments of a large silver vase with a mouth of
copper, which is thickly plated with gold and splendidly ornamented with
intaglio work; unfortunately it has suffered too much from the funeral fire to
be photographed. It appears that the Mycenean goldsmiths found it much
easier to plate on copper than on silver; hence they made the mouth of this
silver vase of copper. . . .

The four walls of the tomb [third shaft grave] which now occupies
us were lined with pieces of schist of irregular size, which were joined with
clay, and formed a slanting wall 5 ft. high and 2 ft. 3 in. broad.

I found in this sepulchre the mortal remains of three persons who, to judge by the smallness of the bones and particularly of the teeth, and by the masses of female ornaments found here, must have been women. As the teeth of one of these bodies, though all preserved, were evidently much used and were very irregular, they appear to belong to a very old woman. All had the head turned to the east and the feet to the west. As in the former tomb, the bodies lay at a distance of 3 ft. from each other; they were covered with a layer of pebbles and reposed on another layer of similar stones, on which the funeral piles had been raised. . . . The bodies were literally laden with jewels, all of which bore evident signs of the fire and smoke to which they had been exposed on the funeral piles.

The ornaments of which the greatest number was found were the large, thick, round plates of gold, with a very pretty decoration of *repoussé* work, of which I collected 701. I found them as well below as above and around the bodies, and there can consequently be no doubt that part of them were strewn all over the bottom of the sepulchre before the funeral pyres were dressed, and that the rest were laid on the bodies before the fire was kindled. . . .

On the head of one of the three bodies was found the splendid crown of gold which is one of the most interesting and most precious objects that I collected at Mycenae. It is 2 ft. 1 in. long, and profusely covered with shield-like ornaments. The work being *repoussé*, all the ornaments protrude and appear in low relief, giving to the crown an indescribably magnificent aspect, which is still further augmented by the thirty-six large leaves, ornamented in a like manner, which are attached to it. It deserves particular attention that the crown was bound round the head so that its broadest part was just in the middle of the forehead, and of course the leaves were standing upright around the upper part of the head, for had it been otherwise it would have shaded the eyes and the greater part of the face. Near each extremity can be seen two small holes, through which the crown was fastened by means of a thin golden wire. . . .

Mycenae, December 6, 1876.

Encouraged by my success, I resolved upon excavating the whole remaining space within the great parallel circle of slabs by which the agora is enclosed, and my attention was particularly directed to the spot immediately west of the sepulchre last excavated, although the site was marked by no tombstone. But, at marked variance with the colour of the soil elsewhere, I found here only black earth, which at a depth of 15 ft., was already intermixed with nothing else than hand-made and most ancient wheel-made pottery, show-

ing that the site had not been disturbed since a remote antiquity; and this
increased my hopes of making an interesting discovery.

At a depth of 20 ft. below the former surface of the mount I struck
an almost circular mass of Cyclopean masonry, with a large round opening
in the form of a well. . . . I at once recognized in this curious monument
a primitive altar for funeral rites, and was strengthened in this belief by
two slabs, in the form of tombstones . . . and a short column, which lay
in a horizontal position below the altar, and which, in my opinion, must
have once been erected on the spot to mark the site of a sepulchre. Fragments of beautiful hand-made or very archaic wheel-made pottery and
knives of obsidian continued to be the only objects of human industry I
met with.

At last, at a depth of 26½ ft., and . . . [close to] the tomb last described, I found a sepulchre, 24 ft. long, and 18½ ft. broad, which had been
cut into the rock to the depth of 6 ft. on its west side . . . its bottom being
33 ft. below the former surface of the mount.

It deserves particular notice that the funeral altar marked precisely
the centre of this tomb, and thus there can be no doubt that it had been
erected in honour of those whose mortal remains reposed therein. . . . As
in all the other tombs, the bottom was covered with a layer of pebbles, on
which, at about equal distances from each other, lay the bodies of five men;
three of them were lying with the head to the east, and the feet to the
west; the other two were lying with the head to the north and the feet to
the south. The bodies had evidently been burned on the very spot on which
each lay; this was shown, as well by the abundance of ashes on and around
each corpse, as by the marks of the fire on the pebbles and on the wall of
schist. . . .

The five bodies of this fourth tomb were literally smothered in jewels,
all of which—as in the other tombs—show unequivocal marks of the
funeral fires. . . .

Beginning the excavation of the lower strata of this tomb from the
south side, I at once struck on five large copper vessels, in one of which
were exactly one hundred very large and smaller buttons of wood, covered
with plates of gold, with a splendid intaglio work of spirals and other
ornamentation. . . .

We find copper vessels (λέβητες [lébētes]) continually referred to in the
Iliad, together with tripods, as prizes in the games or as presents. . . .

Close to the copper vessel with the gold buttons, I found a cow's
head of silver, with two long golden horns. . . . It has a splendidly ornamented golden sun, of 2⅕ in. in diameter, on its forehead; in the middle

of the head is a round hole, which may have served for flowers. I here remind the reader that the Egyptian Apis is represented with a sun between its horns. . . . There can be no doubt that this cow-head was intended to represent the goddess Hera, the patron deity of Mycenae. . . .

In further excavating from east to west I struck a heap of more than twenty bronze swords and many lances. Most of the former had had wooden sheaths and handles inlaid with wood, of which numerous remnants could be seen. Lying all along and in a heap of swords I found a large quantity of round plates of gold with beautiful intaglio work, and remnants of flat round pieces of wood, which had once, in unbroken series, adorned both sides of the sword-sheaths. The largest plate was at the broad end of the sheath, the smallest at the opposite extremity. The wooden handles of the swords had likewise been ornamented with large round plates, covered with rich intaglio work. The remaining space has been studded with gold pins, and gold nails can be seen in the large alabaster or wooden hilt-knobs of the swords. On and around the swords and the remnants of the sheaths could be seen a great quantity of fine gold-dust, which can leave no doubt that the handles and sheaths had also been gilded.

Some of the lance-shafts seemed to be well preserved, but they crumbled away when exposed to the air. Unfortunately the skulls of the five bodies were in such a state of decomposition that none of them could be saved; the two bodies with the head to the north had the face covered with large masks of gold-plate in rude *repoussé* work, one of which, unfortunately, has been so much injured in the funeral fire and by the heavy weight of the stones and *débris*, and, besides, the ashes stick so firmly to it, that it was impossible to get a good photograph of it. However, by looking at it for some minutes, one gets a tolerable idea of the features. It represents a large oval youthful face with a high forehead, a long Grecian nose, and a small mouth with thin lips; the eyes are shut, and the hairs of both eyelashes and eyebrows are well marked.

Quite a different physiognomy is represented by the second mask, which shews a round face, with full cheeks and a small forehead, with which the nose does not range in a straight line, as on the other mask; the mouth is but small, and has thick lips; the eyes are shut, and the eyelashes, as well as the eyebrows, which are joined, are tolerably represented.

A third mask of much thicker gold-plate was found covering the face of one of the three bodies which lay with the head to the east.

This mask . . . exhibits again a totally different physiognomy: the wrinkles to the right and left above the mouth, and the expression of the very large mouth with thin lips, can leave no doubt that we have here the portrait of a man of more advanced age. The forehead is very large and so are the eyes, which are open and have neither lashes nor brows marked: the nose has been much pressed by the stones and is out of shape. In this mask is preserved part of the skull of the man whose face it covered.

The physiognomies represented by these three masks are so widely different from each other, and so altogether different from the ideal types of the statues of gods and heroes, that there cannot be the slightest doubt that every one of them represents the likeness of the deceased whose face it covered. Had it not been so, all the masks would have represented the same ideal type.

A fourth heavy golden mask was found at the head of another of the three bodies which had their heads turned to the east. This object was bent double, and looked so little like a mask that I took it for a helmet . . . but, having unbent it, I see that it has nothing of the shape of a cap and can only have been intended for a mask to cover the face of the body: it had probably been accidentally removed in the process of cremation. . . . On closer examination, we find that it represents a lion's head, whose ears and eyes are distinctly seen. Being of the purest gold, it is so soft that several pieces have been broken away. . . .

Work in progress at Mycenae, showing the Schliemanns at left and right

I further found, with the three bodies whose heads were laid towards the east, two large golden signet rings and a large golden bracelet. The surfaces of both signets are slightly convex; the one represents in very archaic intaglio a hunter with his charioteer in a chariot drawn by two stallions, whose eight feet are in the air and in a line parallel with the ground, to indicate the great speed with which they are dashing forward. Their bushy tails are uplifted, and are very natural, as are also their bodies, except the heads, which are more like camels' than horses' heads. . . . The two men are naked, and wear merely a belt round the loins; their uncovered heads show thick but not long hair; both wear earrings. . . .

Still more interesting is the battle-scene on the other signet-ring; where we see four warriors, of whom the one has evidently vanquished the other three. One of the latter, who is wounded, sits on the ground to the right of the victor, supporting himself with his hands. He has only a short helmet on his head, and is otherwise completely naked. His beard is well shown, and the Mycenaean engraver has taken great pains to represent the anatomy of the body; though he is sitting and with his feet stretched sideways to the spectator, yet we see the full upper part of his body in front without any perspective diminution. . . .

When I brought to light these wonderful signets, I involuntarily exclaimed: "The author of the *Iliad* and the *Odyssey* cannot but have been born and educated amidst a civilisation which was able to produce such works as these. Only a poet who had objects of art like these continually before his eyes could compose those divine poems." . . .

There were further found with the five bodies of this sepulchre nine vessels of gold. . . . But the most remarkable of the vessels deposited in this sepulchre is an enormous massive golden goblet with two handles—δέπας ἀμφικύπελλον—weighing four pounds troy. It is one of the most splendid jewels of the Mycenean treasure; but, unfortunately, it has been crumpled up by the ponderous weight of the stones and *débris*, and its body has been compressed upon the foot, so that the spectator cannot fully realise from the engraving the magnificence of this royal cup. . . .

The body of this costly goblet is encircled by a row of fourteen splendid rosettes, between an upper band of three lines, and a lower one of two; the foot, by a band of large protruding globular points. Not only the flat sides of the handles, but even their edges, are ornamented. Here also may be seen the heads of the golden pins with which the handles are attached to the rim and body. . . .

Another splendid massive golden goblet is also defaced, having been pressed over to the left side of the spectator. It has two horizontal handles, each formed by thick plates, which are joined by a small cylinder. . . . On each upper plate of the two handles is soldered a beautiful little golden pigeon, apparently of cast-work, with the beak turned towards the goblet, so that the two pigeons are looking at each other. This goblet vividly reminds us of Nestor's cup.

Homer's description of this Nestorian goblet fully answers to the vase before us, except that the former is much larger and has four handles, each with two pigeons, instead of only two handles, each with but one pigeon. . . .

The whole immense sepulchre was strewn with small gold leaves, of which I collected about 200 grammes, or more than half a pound troy. I found them in masses even below the bodies, and I have, therefore, no doubt that they were spread in the tomb before the funeral piles were dressed there. . . .

Perhaps the most curious objects of all are three small edifices of gold in *repoussé* work. . . . They are too small for dwelling-houses, and I suppose, therefore, that they were intended to represent small temples or sanctuaries. In this belief I am strengthened, alike by the four horns on the top, by the pigeons with uplifted wings which are sitting at either side, and by the column with a capital, which is represented in every one of the three door-like niches. I call the reader's particular attention to the similarity of these columns to the column represented between the two lions above the Lions' Gate. . . .

Of the bones of the five bodies of this tomb, as well as of those of the bodies in the other sepulchres, I collected all which were not too much decayed, and they will be exhibited in the National Museum at Athens together with the treasures. Of course the contents of each sepulchre are to be kept separate. . . .

Mycenae, 6th December, 1876

For the first time since its capture by the Argives in 468 B.C., and so for the first time during 2,344 years, the acropolis of Mycenae has a garrison, whose watchfires seen by night throughout the whole Plain of Argos carry back the mind to the watch kept for Agamemnon's return to Troy, and the signal which warned Clytemnestra and her paramour of his approach. But this time the object of the occupation by soldiery is of a more peaceful character, for it is merely intended to inspire awe among the country-people, and to prevent them from making clandestine excavations in the tombs, or approaching them while we are working in them.

Already while engaged in the excavation of the large fourth tomb, the results of which I have described, I explored the fifth and last sepulchre, which is immediately to the northwest of it, and which had been marked by the large *stélé* with the bas-relief of frets or key-patterns resembling two serpents, and by an unsculptured tombstone, both of which were 11 ft. 8 in. below the surface of the mount, as it was when I began the excavation. . . . Unlike the other tombs, the four inner sides of this sepulchre were not lined with walls, but merely with large pieces of schist, which were placed in a slanting position against the low border of the tomb, and had not been joined with clay.

As usual, the bottom of the tomb was strewn with a layer of pebbles, on which I found the mortal remains of only one person, with the head turned towards the east, which, like all the other bodies, had been burned on the precise spot where it lay. . . .

The mud in the first sepulchre, whose site had been marked by the three *stélae* with low reliefs, having dried up in the fine weather, I continued the excavation there, and struck at last the bottom of the tomb. . . . The three bodies which the sepulchre contained lay at a distance of about 3 ft. from each other, and had been burnt in the very same place where I found them. . . . Only with the body which lay in the midst the case was different. The ashes had evidently been disturbed; the clay with which the two other bodies and their ornaments were covered, and the layer of pebbles which covered the clay, had been removed from this body. As, besides, it was found almost without any gold ornaments, it is evident that it had been rifled. . . .

The three bodies of this tomb lay with their heads to the east and their feet to the west; all three were of large proportions. . . . The bones of the legs, which are almost uninjured, are unusually large. Although the head of the first man, from the south side, was covered with a massive golden mask, his skull crumbled away on being exposed to the air, and only a few bones could be saved besides those of the legs. The same was the case with the second body, which had been plundered in antiquity.

But of the third body, which lay at the north end of the tomb, the round face, with all its flesh, had been wonderfully preserved under its ponderous golden mask; there was no vestige of hair, but both eyes were perfectly visible, also the mouth, which, owing to the enormous weight that had pressed upon it, was wide open, and showed thirty-two beautiful teeth. From these, all the physicians who came to see the body were led to believe that the man must have died at the early age of thirty-five. The nose was entirely gone. The body having been too long for the space between the two inner walls of the tomb, the head had been pressed in such a way on the breast, that the upper part of the shoulders was nearly in a horizontal line with the vertex of the head. Notwithstanding the large golden breast-plate, so little had been preserved of the breast, that the inner side of the spine was visible in many places. . . .

The colour of the body resembled very much that of an Egyptian mummy. The forehead was ornamented with a plain round leaf of gold, and a still larger one was lying on the right eye; I further observed a large and a small gold leaf on the breast below the large golden breast-cover, and a large one just above the right thigh.

The news that the tolerably well preserved body of a man of the mythic heroic age had been found, covered with golden ornaments, spread like wildfire through the Argolid, and people came by thousands from Argos, Nauplia, and the villages to see the wonder. But, nobody being able to give advice how to preserve the body, I sent for a painter to get at least an oil-painting made, for I was afraid that the body would crumble to pieces. Thus I am enabled to give a faithful likeness of the body, as it looked after all the golden ornaments had been removed. But to my great joy, it held out for two days, when a druggist from Argos, Spiridon Nicolaou by name, rendered it hard and solid by pouring on it alcohol, in which he had dissolved gum-sandarac. As there appeared to be no pebbles below it it was thought that it would be possible to lift it on an iron plate; but this was a mistake, because it was soon discovered that here was the usual layer of pebbles below the body, and all of these having been more or less pressed into the soft rock by the enormous weight which had been lying for ages upon them, all attempts made to squeeze in the iron plate below the pebble-stones, so as to be able to lift them together with the body, utterly failed. There remained, therefore, no other alternative than to cut a small trench into the rock all round the body, and make thence a horizontal incision, so as to cut out a slab, two inches thick, to lift it with the pebble-stones and the body, to put it upon a strong plank, to make around the latter a strong box, and to send this to the village of Charvati, whence it will be forwarded to Athens as soon as the Archaeological Society shall have got a suitable locality for the Mycenaean antiquities. With the miserable instruments alone available here it was no easy task to detach the large slab horizontally from the rock, but it was still much more difficult to bring it in the wooden box from the deep sepulchre to the surface, and to transport it on men's shoulders for more than a mile to Charvati. But the capital interest which this body of the remote heroic age has for science, and the buoyant hope of preserving it, made all the labour appear light.

The now nearly mummified body was decorated with a golden shoulder-belt, 4 ft. long and 1¾ in. broad, which, for some cause or other, was not in its place, for it now lay across the loins of the body, and extended in a straight line far to the right of it. In its midst is suspended, and firmly attached, the fragment of a double-edged bronze sword, and to this latter was accidentally attached a beautifully-polished perforated object of rock crystal, in form of a jar (*pithos*), with two silver handles. It is pierced in its entire length by a silver pin. . . .

A glance at this shoulder-belt will convince every one that it is by far too thin and fragile to have been worn by living men. Besides, I feel certain that no living warrior has ever gone to battle with swords in sheaths of wood ornamented on either side with rows of gold plates, which are merely glued on the wood. Thus, we may consider it beyond all doubt that a great part of all the golden ornaments have been expressly prepared for funeral use. There was also found an alabaster stand for a vase. . . .

In a perfect state of preservation, on the other hand, is the massive golden mask of the body at the south end of the tomb. Its features are altogether Hellenic and I call particular attention to the long thin nose, running in a direct line with the forehead, which is but small. The eyes, which are shut, are large, and well represented by the eyelids; very characteristic is also the large mouth with its well-proportioned lips. The beard also is well represented, and particularly the moustaches, whose extremities are turned upwards to a point, in the form of crescents. This circumstance seems to leave no doubt that the ancient Myceneans used oil or a sort of pomatum in dressing their hair. Both masks are of *repoussé* work, and certainly nobody will for a moment doubt that they were intended to represent the portraits of the deceased, whose faces they have covered for ages.

The question now naturally arises: have they been made in the lifetime, or after the death, of the persons? Probably after their death; but then we wonder again how the masks can have been made so quickly; because here, as in all hot climates, the dead are buried within twenty-four hours after their decease; and this must have been the custom here at all times. . . .

But this skill of the early Mycenaean goldsmiths shows a great practice in similar work, and it can leave no doubt that they were preceded by a school of artists which had flourished for ages before such work could be produced. . . .

Having in the preceding pages described the five great sepulchres and the treasures contained in them, I now proceed to discuss the question, whether it is possible to identify these sepulchres with the tombs which Pausanias, following the tradition, attributes to Agamemnon, to Cassandra, to Eurymedon, and to their companions. . . . For my part, I have always firmly believed in the Trojan War; my full faith in Homer and in the tradition has never been shaken by modern criticism, and to this faith of mine I am indebted for the discovery of Troy and its Treasure. . . .

My firm faith in the traditions made me undertake my late excavations in the acropolis [of Mycenae], and led to the discovery of the five tombs, with their immense treasures. Although I found in these tombs a very high civilisation, from a technical point of view, yet, as in Ilium, I found there only hand-made or most ancient wheel-made pottery, and no iron. . . .

I have not the slightest objection to admit that the tradition which assigns the tombs in the acropolis to Agamemnon and his companions, who on their return from Ilium were treacherously murdered by Clytemnestra or her paramour Aegisthus, may be perfectly correct and faithful. I am bound to admit this so much the more, as we have the certainty that, to say the least, all the bodies in each tomb had been buried simultaneously. The calcined pebbles below each of them, the marks of the fire to the right and left on the internal walls of the tombs, the undisturbed state of the ashes and the charred wood on and around the bodies, give us the most unmistakable proofs of this fact. Owing to the enormous depths of these sepulchres, and the close proximity of the bodies to each other, it is quite impossible that three or even five funeral piles could have been dressed at different intervals of time in the same tomb. . . .

The identity of the mode of burial, the perfect similarity of all the tombs, their very close proximity, the impossibility of admitting that three or even five royal personages of immeasurable wealth, who had died a natural death at long intervals of time, should have been huddled together in the same tomb, and, finally, the great resemblance of all the ornaments, which show exacty the same style of art and the same epoch—all these facts are so many proofs that all the twelve men, three women, and perhaps two or three children, had been murdered simultaneously and burned at the same time. . . .

What reader can follow this vivid picture, in the light furnished by my discovery of the agora at Mycenae, without feeling that the poet had often witnessed such a scene, perhaps on this very spot? . . .

But though buried deep below the new city, the precise site of each tomb was perfectly remembered by the inhabitants of the Argolid. After an existence of about 200 years, the new city was, for some cause or other, again and finally abandoned. But still the tradition remained so fresh, that nearly 400 years after the destruction of the new town the exact place of each tomb was shown to Pausanias. . . .

The five tombs of Mycenae, or at least three of them, contained such enormous treasures, that they cannot but have belonged to members of the royal family. But the period of the kings of Mycenae belongs to a very remote antiquity. Royalty ceased there at the Dorian invasion, the date of which has always been fixed at 1104 B.C. . . .

Athens, March 1, 1877.

My engineer, the Lieutenant Vasilios Drosinos, of Nauplia, having proceeded on the 20th of January to Mycenae, in company with the painter D. Tountopoulos, who had to make for me an ichnography [ground plan] of the five large sepulchres and the circular agora by which they are surrounded, in verifying the plans he had made for me, recognised, due south of the agora the form of a tomb.[2] . . .

But as the tomb is immediately east of the large Cyclopean house, of which I had excavated many rooms down to the rock without finding anything particular, I had considered the sepulchre as a dependency of the house, and had not cared to excavate the little *débris* which still covered its site.

But my most excellent engineer was more keen-sighted. Being struck by the appearance of the walls built in a much ruder way than those of the

Cyclopean house, he at once recognised the identity of the masonry with that of the masonry in the large tombs, and as he saw the northern wall partly and the eastern entirely leaning against the rock, he had the firm conviction that it was a sepulchre. Therefore on his return to Nauplia he communicated his important discovery to a government clerk of the name of Stamatakes, who had been sent that very day by the Director-general, Mr. P. Eustratiades, to Nauplia, in order to choose a place in the acropolis of Mycenae on which to build a wooden hut for the watchmen. Mr. Drosinos indicated to him on my plans the precise site of the tomb, and gave him the most minute information in relation to it, so that the clerk found the place at once, and engaged a workman, at whose first or second blow of the pickaxe a golden vessel came to light, and in less than half an hour the following objects were gathered. First, four large golden goblets with two handles. . . . All the four goblets have exactly the same form and are nearly of the same size. . . .

In this tomb was further found a gold seal-ring of the same form, but more than twice as large, as those which I discovered in the fourth sepulchre. It is entirely covered with intaglio work. . . .

In conclusion, let me call attention to the fact that in consequence of the discovery of a sixth tomb in the agora of Mycenae, after my departure, there has been an attempt to deny the identity of these tombs with those which the tradition reported by Pausanias points out as the burial-places of Agamemnon, Cassandra, Eurymedon, and their companions.[3] But one need only re-read the famous passage of Pausanias to see that it does not clearly give the number of the tombs. It speaks distinctly of six; but one may admit that there were even more than six, and yet do no violence to Pausanias's text. . . .

Schliemann lecturing on his Mycenaean discoveries
before the Society of Antiquarians at Burlington House
in London in 1877. From the *Illustrated London News*.

Mycenae was the high-water mark in Schliemann's archaeological career. Though he was to be fully active for the remaining decade and a half left to him and made creditable contributions, everything after Mycenae was anti-climactic. Perhaps it was a growing sense of archaeological responsibility, commanding slower pace and a more cautious technique, that henceforth somewhat tamed his boldness. From now on, when he increasingly deferred to experts at his campaigns, his activities were relatively subdued, though he would still train his sights on spectacular objectives. His discoveries, too, lacked the excitement of archaeological Klondikes. Yet he rarely faltered in his allegiance to Homer—or Pallas Athene for that matter. That was why an offer to dig in Yucatán or even his brief probing in Italy, in Sicily, and along the Sea of Marmara never caught fire with him. When he wrote to Gladstone his *e pur si muove*— "Homer does not describe myths, but historical events and tangible realities"—it was clear that in his mind Homer remained both poet and historian.[1] Never mind confused and contradictory evidence, somehow, somewhere, all had to fit into preestablished Homeric harmonies.

To Schliemann, Mycenae was an irrefutable confirmation of his Homeric inspiration. After writing his book on the excavation in just eight weeks, it seemed a good time to pause and take account. Flattering tributes poured down on him from such good friends as Charles T. Newton of the British Museum, Émile Burnouf, and even Max Müller. The last, while expressing doubt "whether any of your treasures has ever been handled by Helen," admitted: "I look forward to much information which they ought to afford on the local civilisations of that interesting part of the world which you have previously and successfully explored."[2]

Germans also began to take pride in their Mecklenburg countryman. In 1877 the German Anthropological Society, undoubtedly through the initiative of Virchow, its founder, named him an honorary member. The curlicued Latin document recommended him for "having brought to light from centuries of limbo the royal residences of Priam and Agamemnon."[3]

Yet, once again, Schliemann's romantic attributions at Mycenae were not readily accepted by all scholars. One or the other German professor declared the golden accoutrements to be Celtic, Hellenistic, or even medieval, while a Russian (of German origin) maintained that both the Mycenaean and Trojan treasures by rights belonged to the Czar since they had been deposited by Gothic (or Celtic) invaders from the Russian steppes. Schliemann may have been a fantast, but his academic opponents could be as reckless as the starry-eyed dilettante.

Unlike his previous writings, *Mycenae* (1878) was a publishing success and something close to an archaeological best seller. Messrs. Scribner, Armstrong & Co. of New York City, who brought out the American edition, reported to the author: "Your *Mycenae* has met with the most flattering reception by the press and the public, and it is, and bids fair to remain, the leading publication of the year."[4]

In spring 1877, Schliemann was back in London. Here he met with his friends and advisers, consulted with his publisher John Murray, and had dinner with Gladstone, who was so captivated by a photograph of Sophia and Andromache Schliemann had proudly shown him that he purloined it. This time Schliemann was even more feted in England than the previous year. "The Londoners overwhelm me with courtesies. Ten societies have asked for lectures. I have only taken on three. . . . I continue to be the lion of the season. I receive invitations from lords and dukes every day," he wrote to his wife, who was sick in Athens.[5] When he was advised that the Royal Archaeological Society was going to bestow its medal on both him and Sophia, he persuaded her to come posthaste to London. During the acceptance ceremony, she delivered to resounding applause a speech in English recounting her labors in the mud-filled shaft graves of Mycenae's golden circle. At the time she was pregnant with their son. His name to be: Agamemnon. At his baptism, some six months later, the solicitous father, to the consternation of the officiating Greek Orthodox priest, plunged a thermometer into the baptismal font to take the water's temperature. Prior to the Christian baptism he placed a copy of the *Iliad* on the infant's head to invest him with the spirit of Homer. Alas, the boy took after his father the financier, not the Philhellene archaeologist.

Schliemann had no desire to return to Mycenae. Troy was again uppermost in his mind. Had he not run into an unpleasant confrontation with the Dardanelles governor and his henchmen at Hissarlik, he would have dug there again in 1876. Meanwhile he had to negotiate a new *firman*, which meant a return to the usual high-powered Byzantine backroom politics. Schliemann luckily could thenceforth count on a whole battery of foreign ambassadors at Constantinople. As usual, American and Russian envoys were his natural protectors. He also had a claim on German diplomats, and his contacts with Virchow, the Hereditary Prince of Meiningen, and later with Bismarck, were duly brought into play. Occasionally he would also enlist French, Austrian, Italian, and even Spanish dignitaries. And there were, as always, the Calvert brothers to act as intermediaries and, for local transactions, the various consuls of foreign powers at the Dardanelles.[6] At this point, the affection of the English proved most productive. When needed, Gladstone could be induced to drop a hint through diplomatic channels. Luck would have it that at the time the ambassador of Her Britannic Majesty to the Sublime Porte was Sir Austen Layard, who had himself undertaken celebrated excavations at Nimrud and Nineveh in Mesopotamia around the middle of the century. But despite all this support, Turkish mills still ground slowly.

The waiting period, so trying for the impetuous Schliemann, was taken up in July 1878 by an exploration of Ithaca, the first since his 1868 pilgrimage. It, too, was inspired by his continuing quest for Homeric heroes. His original views on the archaeology of Troy and Mycenae, as laid down in his early book, *Ithaca*, had borne marvelous fruit, but the castle of Odysseus was still missing. He spent close to three weeks on the island, and to his chagrin, found no sizable accretion of prehistoric debris anywhere. On steep Mount Aëtos, which, as before, he considered the most propitious site, erosion had long ago washed its archaeological promise away. However, he located, on a slope, traces of some 190 Cyclopean houses which contained quite ancient shards. While Odysseus' Palace failed to emerge, the evidence for Eumaeus' stables near the coast seemed to him still convincing. But probes in the island's modern centers like Vathi and Polis (Polys) yielded nothing of consequence, and even the fabled Grotto of the Nymphs, where Odysseus hid his treasures, now had lost its luster. Its southern "entrance of the immortal gods" simply resulted from a breakthrough to let sacrificial (or camp?) fires escape. In drawing a balance sheet of his Ithaca expedition he bluntly stated: "I regret to say that systematic excavations for archaeological purposes are altogether out of the question here."[7]

In September 1878 the Trojan coast was finally clear and Schliemann set out for Hissarlik immediately, this time without his wife. Sophia declined to come along on this trip; Agamemnon II needed maternal care. The fairly short two-month stint from the end of September to the end of November 1878 is usually counted as Schliemann's fourth (regular) season and the first year of his second major (two-year) campaign in the Troad. His work schedule of about fourteen hours a day demanded as much from his low-paid laborers as from himself. The results were modest and added little that was new. At the onset he had defined his goal as primarily clearing the large building northwest of the "Scaean Gate" and tracing the circuit wall as far as possible from both its sides. His designs on the former were most likely linked with the hope of finding further precious articles. In this respect he was not to be disappointed, though after a while digging up treasure became almost a routine. In the entire 1878/1879 campaign he extricated an additional nine or ten caches in and about the "palace," most of them packed in metal or terra-cotta jars.[8] Though not as varied and opulent as "Priam's Treasure," they were sizable and included gold, silver, and electrum objects: earrings, bracelets, necklaces, rings, pins, beads in great profusion, and even lumps of unworked gold. The abundance of such precious loads and their concentration in one area confirmed Schliemann's belief that the "find place" must have been a royal residence. By the same token, he remained certain that they were dropped in a hurry when the people had to flee the burning city. Ergo, this could have been nothing but the last quarters of the Trojan King. Schliemann could insist on that now "with more assurance than ever."[9]

Despite such apodictic airs, a new hesitancy was noticeable. For one, Schliemann thenceforth made it a point to avoid such loaded terms as "Priam's Palace," "Scaean Gate," and "Priam's Treasure." Instead he would use neutral labels for these features—"the city chieftain's house" or "royal residence," "the gate," and so on. This prosaic terminology was forced on him by the ridicule of his critics. Yet Schliemann continued to be convinced that the palace was indeed Priam's who had inhabited the very same city that was burned in the Trojan War, and that Homer's account was authentic.

However, intimations of a new attitude toward material evidence became far more pronounced in the second year of the campaign, which was to last from the end of February to the beginning of July 1879. It was mainly due to the presence of two men of outstanding caliber—his friend of long standing, Émile Burnouf, and the newly gained intimate, Professor Virchow. In his egocentric fashion Schliemann credited them with having "both assisted me in my researches to the utmost of their ability."[10] The patronizing tone notwithstanding, they were teachers rather than "assistants" and peers.

Émile Louis Burnouf (1821–1907), whom Schliemann had counted on from almost the beginning of his archaeological career, was an established archaeologist as well as a trained engineer, a geologist, an expert surveyor and map maker, a skillful artist, an author, and a scholar of Oriental religions and Sanskrit. He had on previous occasions pressed on Schliemann sound principles of excavation besides making drawings of his digs (as did his daughter). He also acted at times as Schliemann's unofficial liaison with French academe. Only recently he had written a glowing account of the Mycenaean discoveries for a French journal.

Burnouf arrived at Hissarlik early in spring of 1879. One of his main contributions was making maps of Troy for the publication of *Ilios*. Several of the picturesque views of the mound in that volume were his, as were sketches of artifacts. During excavations he showed particular keenness in tracking down missing portions of the circuit wall. He can also be credited with establishing the sequence of seven layers of Troy—later to be replaced by Dörpfeld's nine—which from then on gave a valid framework to Schliemann's studies.

Rudolf Virchow (1821–1902) was no less a figure. The Berlin pathologist of international reputation had impressive archaeological credentials. A physical anthropologist of note who, however, obdurately refused to accept any fossil evidence for modern man's hominoid or primate ancestry, he was also a founding father of cultural anthropology in Germany. His wide-ranging interests included all the natural sciences, and he was master in most. Schliemann, of the same age as Virchow (and Burnouf), was probably attracted to him not just as an influential celebrity, but because of their closely similar origins. Virchow, too, was largely self-made. He had risen high in the academic world, met the powerful and well-born on equal terms, but as a member of the German Reichstag was a fighting liberal and critic of Bismarck. He was perhaps the one close friend Schliemann had in his last years, though because of Schliemann's intransigence and misplaced *amour-propre* they fell out on occasion.

A man of literary gifts far superior to Schliemann's, Virchow brought to the Trojan researches a trained, lucid, analytical, and cool mind. A pillar of strength and sanity, unlike Schliemann he was uncompromisingly honest with himself, free from vanity, and secure enough to be indifferent to success. Fortunately Schliemann respected him and listened. He even published in *Ilios* extracts from a speech Virchow made in Berlin, praising his efforts and enthusiasm, but mildly criticizing the methods used in his earlier Hissarlik excavations.

Virchow's beneficial influence is noticeable at every step in the new excavations. He strengthened Schliemann's awareness of the overall terrain, in which his interest until that time had been largely sentimental. Virchow demonstrated the validity of such pursuits by empirical studies on the fauna, flora, and topography of the entire Troad, later crystallized in his still highly regarded *Beiträge zur Landeskunde der Troad* ("Contributions to the Geography of the Troad"). Though the busy universalist stayed only a few weeks, his output in so short a time was impressive, the more so since he was constantly engaged in caring for the native sick (an attractive account of Virchow's medical practice in the Troad is appended to *Ilios*).

Like Burnouf, Virchow helped to bring order into Schliemann's self-created labyrinth. Their geological investigations once and for all demolished a hypothesis going back to antiquity that the plain between the Hissarlik hill and the sea represented post-Trojan War alluvial deposits and, therefore, in Homeric terms, Hissarlik could not be Troy since the wide stretch of land necessary for the Achaean encampment did not yet exist. Borings showed that the lowland was anything but recent. Probably it was older than the Dardanelles themselves.

Virchow and Burnouf also took part in exploration of the major tumuli (man-made mounds) in the Scamander Valley, as did Frank Calvert, who directed at Schliemann's expense the digging of the Hanai Tepe (Hanaï Tepeh). Though Calvert found signs of burials in that earthwork, Schliemann was convinced that this was an aberrant instance belonging to an alien culture. In general, he held that Troad tumuli were commemorative monuments. Rather than tombs, he classified them as cenotaphs.

In the company of Virchow, Schliemann undertook a five-day trip through the Troad, visiting various ruined, mostly Hellenistic or Roman sites, including the Ballidagh, and climbed up the Ida massif. However, bad weather kept them from scaling the highest peak. It was a fine setting for a warm friendship to grow. Virchow made good use of it by trying to reconcile Schliemann with Germany. He knew very well that Schliemann had purged himself of German patriotism ever since, as a youth of twenty-two, he left his native land, which, he thought, had treated him so shabbily. The derisive treatment he had received from German scholars further embittered him. But he had never forsworn his native Mecklenburg. And it was that chord Virchow knew how to touch. When the two men rested in a mountain meadow, he picked a flowering twig of blackthorn and handed it to his friend with the words: "A nosegay from Ankershagen."[11]

. The patriotic evocation hit its mark. It seemed to open floodgates of repressed *Vaterlandsliebe* (love of fatherland) in Schliemann. A few days later, before Virchow left Troy, he had elicited from Schliemann the pledge that he would leave the Trojan treasure to Germany. At the time it was on exhibit in the South Kensington museum, where Schliemann had sent it on loan in 1877 as a token of gratitude to England. The pledge was vague and probably, as far as Schliemann was concerned, not final. In *Ilios* he dropped the Delphic comment that the treasure would eventually go to "the nation I love and esteem most."[12] In light of Schliemann's shifting national loyalties, it sounded like the words of an aging Oriental potentate who wished to keep his sons guessing who his favorite was and who ultimately would inherit his kingdom—maybe he had not yet made up his mind.

To his collaborators at Troy in 1879 Schliemann was also indebted for major contributions to his summing-up volume, *Ilios*, whose English edition (the original) was dedicated to Sir Austen Layard, the American to Gladstone, and German to Virchow. His German friend wrote a generous preface, which he concluded: "And now the treasure-digger has become a scholar, who, with long and earnest study, has compared the facts of his experience, as well as the statements of the historians and geographers, with the legendary traditions of poets and mythologers."[13]

Ilios, indeed, marked a turning point for Schliemann. The formidable tome of close to 900 pages made a dogged attempt to compensate for the loose, haphazard diary notes of his previous books. Gone were, with rare exceptions, the chapter-to-chapter contradictions and changes of mind. Materials of similar type and origin were grouped together. However, a strong personal note was retained in the opening autobiographical excursus, from whose inclusion Virchow tried in vain to dissuade him. Otherwise, the plan was sound and systematic, just as the tone was low key. Physical evidence was thoroughly weighed, examined, and compared. Schliemann obviously worked hard to come up with a scientifically respectable publication. Given bookmaking standards of the day, the typography and quality of the illustrations (some one thousand six hundred) and maps were excellent.

Hellenistic temple ruins near New Ilium

After a general chapter discussing the ancient and modern topography of the Troad, Schliemann described the ethnology of the land and then reviewed the history of the site and the long debate over the "true" location of Homeric Ilium. There followed separate chapters dealing with excavation results from the seven consecutive strata, of which he had gained some clarity during the 1878/1879 campaign. The formidable index alone ran to some fifty pages. Valuable appendixes included individual essays by his learned friends. Virchow, in two such supplements, reported on the natural setting, skeletal finds, and his medical practice. The Dublin classicist J. P. Mahaffy expounded on the relation of Novum Ilium (or Ilium Novum) to the Ilios of Homer. The Oxford Orientalist A. H. Sayce opened a Pandora's box with his inquiry into preclassical "inscriptions" found at Hissarlik.[14] Frank Calvert summarized his study of the Hanai Tepe tumulus. Henry Brugsch-Bey (Heinrich Brugsch), the German-born Egyptologist, investigated both the Hera bo-ōpis thesis and possible relations between Troy and Egypt. Shorter reports on the flora of the Troad were signed by five experts, including Virchow. In addition there was a brief discussion on copper metallurgy by A. J. Duffield, while a special dissertation by Max Müller on the right- and left-turning swastika appeared in the main body of the text.

Schliemann conscripted several of his friends and associates, notably Burnouf, Virchow, and Sayce, to check sources and data, make suggestions for improvement, and read the printer's galleys. Several of his helpers were amply remunerated. Schliemann later complained, however, that Burnouf was of no help when it came to making constructive changes, while Sayce was first-rate.

In this manner, *Ilios*, for which, of course, Schliemann took full credit, was in reality a joint effort, a kind of symposium on Troy. It is therefore impossible to say how much in content, not to speak of writing or editorial polish, it owed to others. Yet it must be admitted that for all its learned apparatus and detailed presentation, it threw relatively little new light on the Trojan problem. The multiple contributions blow up the book without getting to the key questions. Unity and clarity are sacrificed to a learned polyphony. At times the book seems to affect a solemn reburial of the ransacked hill. After a while one suspects that Schliemann had mobilized the academic machinery with a vengeance.

In fact he labored on his magnum opus for a year and a half, and declared that it contained all there was to be known and all that could be known about Ilian Troy. He had excavated seven eighths of the Homeric city, and Troy was now forever enshrined in his book. To his prospective American publisher, Ed. Harper of New York, he wrote in January 1880 without due modesty: "There is no other Troy to excavate. In the Hissarlik-Troy I have brought to light the whole ancient city, the third from the virgin soil, with all its walls. Therefore, this my present work will remain in demand as long as there are admirers of Homer in the world, nay as long as this globe will be inhabited by men."[15]

Here we hear the old Schliemann again, untarnished by scientific sobriety. His air of jubilance, however, did not veil his persistent doubts. Already in the campaign of 1878/1879, the proud Great Tower had turned out to be nothing but a section of the double-walled battlement. Much else had fallen besides. Could he continue to believe in "Priam's Palace"? Had the Hissarlik mound really given up all its secrets? What about the first city, with its strange herringbone masonry which Müller and Virchow urged him to investigate more thoroughly? And the Hellenistic and Roman remains that he had largely disdained? How was it that the Troy of Priam and the Mycenae of Agamemnon, though supposedly contemporary, were worlds apart?

In Ilios, disregarding its general tenor of finality, Schliemann vented his uneasiness when admitting: "I wish I could have proved Homer to have been an eyewitness of the Trojan War! Alas I cannot do it."[16] Even more revealing is what he wrote to Brockhaus late in November 1879: "Now the only question is whether Troy has only existed in the poet's imagination or in reality. If the latter is accepted, Hissarlik must and will be universally acknowledged to mark its site."[17] In truth, the mound of Troy was still a maze of mysteries.

THE SECOND TROJAN CAMPAIGN

from *Ilios*

I recommenced my excavations at Troy towards the end of September 1878, with a large number of workmen and several horse-carts, having previously built felt-covered wooden barracks, with nine chambers for my own accommodation and that of my overseers, servants, and visitors. I also built a wooden barrack, which served both as a storehouse for antiquities and as a small dining-hall, together with a wooden magazine, in which the antiquities were preserved, which were to be divided between the Imperial Museum [in Constantinople] and myself, and of which the Turkish delegate had the key; also a wooden magazine for my implements, wheelbarrows, hand-carts, and other machinery for excavating; besides a small stone house for the kitchen, a wooden house for my ten gendarmes, and a stable for the horses. All these buildings were erected on the northwest slope of Hissarlik, which here descends at an angle of 75° to the plain. . . .

The ten gendarmes . . . were all refugees from Rumelia,[1] and were of great use to me, for they not only served as a guard against the brigands by whom the Troad was infested, but they also carefully watched my labourers whilst they were excavating, and thus forced them to be honest.

How necessary the ten gendarmes were to me could not have been better proved than by the fight which took place a short time after my departure in the village of Kalifatli, only twenty minutes' walk from Hissarlik, between the peasants and a large number of armed Circassians, who in the night attacked the house of a villager reputed to possess 10,000 frs. The villager ascended the terrace of his house and cried for assistance, whereupon his neighbours hurried out with their rifles and killed two of the assailants, but unfortunately lost two of their own number—the brother-in-law and son-in-law of the demarch of Kalifatli. . . .

My endeavours were now principally directed to the excavation of the large building to the west and northwest of the gate, and of the northeastern prolongation of the gateway. I had always identified the large building with the residence of the last chief or king of Troy, because in it, or close to it, had been found not only the large treasure I myself discovered, but also the treasure which had been concealed from me by my labourers and seized by the Turkish authorities, besides a vast quantity of Trojan pottery; but I now maintain that identity with more assurance than ever, having again discovered in it, or close to it, three small treasures and a large one of gold jewels. Of these the first was found and excavated on the 21st of October . . . in a chamber in the northeast part of the building, at a depth of 26 ft. 5 in. below the surface of the mound. It was contained in a broken hand-made terra-cotta vessel, which lay in an oblique position about 3 ft. above the floor, and must have fallen from an upper storey. . . .

The longest wall of the town-chief's house runs parallel with the great external wall of the city, and is 53 ft. 4 in. long and 4 ft. 4 in. high; it consists of smaller and larger stones joined together with clay. Near the northwestern extremity of this wall, and just 3 ft. above the ground, I found, in a layer of grey wood-ashes, two more small treasures, both contained in broken hand-made terra-cotta vases, of which the one lay in an oblique, the other in a horizontal position, from which circumstance I conclude that both had fallen from an upper part of the house; the orifices of the vases nearly touched each other. Only 3 ft. from this discovery, but on the house-wall itself, and at a depth of 26 ft. below the surface of the ground, a larger treasure of bronze weapons and gold jewels was found. . . .

I also continued excavating on the site of my former platform, on the north side of the hill, but, on account of the winter rains, was obliged to stop the works on the 26th of November. According to the stipulations of my firman, I had to give up two-thirds of all the objects I found to the Imperial Museum, and carried off only one-third myself.

I went to Europe, and returned to the Dardanelles towards the end of February 1879. Having again procured the services of ten gendarmes or *zaptiehs* and 150 workmen, I recommenced the excavations on the 1st of March. Up to the middle of March I suffered cruelly from the north wind, which was so icy cold that it was impossible to read or write in my wooden barracks, and it was only possible to keep oneself warm by active exercise in the trenches. To avoid taking cold, I went, as I had always done, very early every morning on horseback to the Hellespont to take my sea-bath, but I always returned to Hissarlik before sunrise and before the work commenced. These rides in the dark were not without accidents. Travellers to the Troad will see a large block missing from the northern edge of the bridge of Kum Kioi. This stone was broken out when once in the dark I rode too near the edge, and I was precipitated with my horse into the bushes below. The horse having fallen upon me, I could not extricate myself from beneath it; and my gendarmes having gone ahead, could not hear my cries. A whole hour I was in this desperate position, till at last my gendarmes, not seeing me coming to my usual bathing-place at Karanlik, returned and extricated me. Since that accident I always alight before passing a Turkish bridge, and lead my horse over by the bridle. Two of my gendarmes always served me as a guard in the bathing excursions, or whenever I absented myself from Hissarlik. But the cold weather did not last longer than a fortnight, and after that we had a succession of fine weather. The storks appeared in the beginning of March.

At the end of March I was joined at Hissarlik by my honoured friends Professor Rudolf Virchow of Berlin, and M. Émile Burnouf of Paris, Honorary Director of the French School at Athens. . . .

My endeavours were this time principally directed towards bringing to light the entire circuit of the walls, and I therefore excavated to the east and southwest of the gate . . . and to the northwest and north of the house of the chief, as well as to the east of my great northern trench. It being especially important to preserve the houses of the burnt city, I gradually excavated the ruins of the three upper cities horizontally, layer by layer, until I reached the easily-recognizable calcined *débris* of the third or burnt city. Having brought down to one level the whole space I intended to explore, I began at the extremity of the area, excavating house by house, and gradually proceeding with this work in the direction of the northern slope, where the *débris* had to be shot. In this manner I was able to excavate all the houses of

A *pithos* from Troy

the third city without injuring their walls. But of course all that I could bring to light of them were the substructions, or first storeys, 3 to 10 ft. high, built of bricks or of stones cemented with earth. The great number of jars they contain can hardly leave any doubt that these served as cellars; though at first sight it is difficult to explain the scarcity of doorways, of which visitors will see but few. . . .

Professor Virchow calls attention to the fact that, in an architectural point of view, the condition of this third city is the exact prototype of the kind of building which still characterizes the villages of the Troad. It was only when his medical practice had introduced him into the interior of the present houses that he was able to understand the architectural details of those of the ancient state. The characteristic of the architecture is, that in most cases the lower part of the houses has no entrance, and is surrounded by a stone wall. The upper storey, which is built of quadrangular sun-dried bricks, serves as the habitation for the family; the lower one, which is entered by stairs or ladders from above, serves as a storehouse. Whenever the ground-floor has a door, it is also very frequently used as a stable for the cattle. When, as often happens also at the present day, modern houses of this kind fall into ruin, the ruins present precisely the same aspect as those of the third or burnt city of Hissarlik. . . . The rooms enclosed by these Trojan house-walls contain those gigantic terra-cotta jars which often stand in whole rows, representing a considerable fortune by their huge size, which is so great that a man can stand upright in each of them. . . .

I further excavated to the east and southeast of the "Great Tower," where I was forced to destroy a number of house-walls close to the magazine containing the nine great jars discovered in 1873, in order to unearth the city wall and its connection with the two gigantic stone walls called by me "the Great Tower." All this has been accomplished. My excavations to the south, southwest, west, northwest, and north of the gates, have also enabled me to uncover the city wall in these directions; so that it is now disclosed in its entire circuit, except where it has been cut through by my great trench. In the course of these researches I found, in the presence of Professor Virchow and M. Burnouf, on the slope of the northwestern part of the wall another treasure, consisting of gold ornaments. . . .

I give here an extract from the speech which Professor Virchow made on his return to Berlin from his expedition to the Troad, before the Berlin Society for Anthropology, Ethnology, and Pre-historic Archaeology, on the 20th of June, 1879: .

"That part of the citadel-hill of Hissarlik in which the calcined ruins of the 'burnt city' were found had at the time of my departure from the Troad been cleared away, in a considerable number of places, down to the virgin soil. At one place we reached the rock itself, on which the most ancient city had been built. In the midst of the great trench Schliemann had left standing a mighty block, which, as long as it holds together, will indicate to visitors the original level of the surface. . . .

"How long the aforesaid block can resist the influences of the weather, I dare not say. At all events, it will for a long time to come give testimony, not only to the gigantic height of these masses of ruins, but also, as I believe, to the incredible energy of the man, who has with his own private means succeeded in removing such enormous masses of earth. If you could see what mounds of earth (in the full sense of the word) had to be dug away and removed, in order to have a view of the lower layers, you would indeed scarcely believe that a single man in the course of a few years could have accomplished so great an undertaking. On this occasion I would stand up for Schliemann against a reproach which, though plausible in itself, falls to the ground on closer consideration—the reproach that he has not excavated from the surface, layer by layer, so as to obtain a complete plan for each successive period.

"There is no doubt that the manner in which he has excavated, by making at once a large trench through the whole hill, has had, in the highest degree, a destructive effect on the upper layers. In those near the surface were portions of temples of the Hellenic period, columns, triglyphs, and all kinds of marble fragments, thrown together *pêle-mêle*. Nevertheless, with great care and attention, such as that with which the excavations at Olympia are carried on, it might perhaps have been possible to have reconstructed a temple, at least in part. But Schliemann felt no interest in a temple belonging to a period far too late for him. I may also say that, after having seen a considerable proportion of the fragments, I doubt whether, if all had been brought together, an essential gain would have been contributed to the history of art or to science. I allow that it has been a kind of sacrilege. Schliemann has cut the temple (of Athené) right in two; the building material has been thrown aside and partly again buried; it will not be easy for any one, even with the largest expenditure, to collect it again. But, undoubtedly, if Schliemann had proceeded in such a way as to remove the ruins stratum by stratum from the surface, he would, owing to the vastness of the task, not even to-day have reached the layers in which the principal objects were found. He only reached them by at once extracting the nucleus of the great hill. . . ."[2]

In closing this account of the result of my researches on the site of "sacred Ilios" and in the country of the Trojans, I would express the fervent hope that historical research with the pickaxe and the spade, which in our time engages the attention of scholars with more curiosity and more diversity of opinion than any other form of study, may be more and more developed, and that it may ultimately bring forth into broad daylight the dark pre-historic ages of the great Hellenic race. May this *research with the pickaxe and the spade* prove more and more that the events described in the divine Homeric poems are not mythic tales, but that they are based on real facts; and, in proving this, may it augment the universal love for the noble study of the beautiful Greek classics, and particularly of Homer, that brilliant sun of all literature!

In humbly laying this account of my disinterested labours before the judgment-seat of the civilized world, I should feel the profoundest satisfaction, and should esteem it as the greatest reward my ambition could aspire to, if it were generally acknowledged that I have been instrumental towards the attainment of that great aim of my life.

As on my last journey to England and Germany I have heard it repeatedly stated that, carried away by ambition, I am ruining myself in my archaeological explorations, to the prejudice of my children, who will be penniless after my death, I find it necessary to assure the reader that, although

Excavations at Troy

on account of my present scientific pursuits I am bound to keep aloof from all sorts of speculation and am compelled to content myself with a small interest on my capital, I still have a yearly income of £4,000 as the net proceeds of the rents of my four houses in Paris, and £6,000 interest on my funded property, making in all £10,000; whilst, inclusive of the large cost of my excavations, I do not spend more than £5,000 a year, and am thus able to add £5,000 annually to my capital. I trust, therefore, that on my death I shall leave to each of my children a fortune large enough to enable them to continue their father's scientific explorations without ever touching their capital.

I avail myself of this opportunity to assure the reader that, as I love and worship science for its own sake, I shall never make a traffic of it. My large collections of Trojan antiquities have a value which cannot be calculated, but they shall never be sold. If I do not present them in my lifetime, they shall at all events pass, in virtue of my last will, to the Museum of the nation I love and esteem most.

A tumulus on the plain of Troy, called by tradition
the Tomb of Ajax.

BETWEEN THE EXERTIONS of the spade and of the pen, the nearly sixty-year-old Schliemann rarely allowed himself to bask in his glory. Though the composition of the formidable *Ilios* tied him for long stretches to his desk—as in his days as a commodity clerk, he usually stood while writing—he observed his peripatetic regimen even then. When in Athens, he would ride to Phaleron, the nearby Aegean port, at four or five in the morning, at times accompanied by his wife or daughter, and go for a vigorous swim. Somewhat of a health faddist, he never abandoned his belief that saltwater bathing was the very foundation of good health and long life. Schliemann once remarked that he could do a day's work, without any signs of fatigue, only if he had been on horseback for two hours.

It is nearly impossible, and unprofitable, to trace Schliemann's giddy pace from one end of Europe to the other: his frequent trips to London, where he could always count on finding surcease and learned communion (but how he disliked English Sundays!), the repeated calls on the administrator of his Paris real estate properties, the visits to prehistoric collecions, and the countless stays at spas and health resorts—Bad Kissingen, Carlsbad, Boulogne-sur-Mer, Thun, Biarritz (those just in the months after the second Hissarlik campaign), where his neurasthenic young wife sought the "cure" and he, as well, might imbibe more or less noxious kinds of mineral waters.

Berlin, too, was to be a magnet from now on. There, on August 5, 1880, his lecture on the 1871–1879 Troy excavations before the 11th Congress of the German Anthropological Society, which had made him an honorary member in 1877, was a highlight that earned him academic accolades. The Crown Prince and other notables joined in the applause. Membership in the society provided Schliemann with an intellectual haven. Now he was a peer among peers in German academe.

The second season at Troy in 1879 had barely wound up when the Schliemanns turned up in Bad Kissingen in Western Germany, which

Virchow, in his indulgent role as family medical adviser, had prescribed. There the couple were asked one day in July to lunch with Otto von Bismarck. Schliemann had formerly taken a dim view of the Iron Chancellor's aggressive militarism, but the man of humble birth melted before the man of power and he was favorably impressed by the statesman's grasp of archaeology. Bismarck was, of course, a man to cultivate. He could prove useful in Constantinople. In fact, he was soon to figure in the tortuous transactions connected with the donation of the Trojan treasure.

Later the following year, Schliemann stayed for three months in Leipzig to be in close contact with his publisher Brockhaus. All that time he worked industriously on *Ilios*, sought the advice of erudite friends everywhere, enlisted collaborators for the English and German editions, and was in touch with prehistorians from Denmark to Hungary for information on pottery that could be compared to the Hissarlik ware. In addition, he made thorough inquiries about Ankershagen, which he had briefly visited with Sophia after Kissingen, and the people he had known there since his boyhood. In particular, he refreshed his memory of the ghost tales and storied sites that had so deeply impressed him as a child.[1] The Mecklenburg material was to be used in the autobiographical introduction to *Ilios*, to prove that his later career in archaeology was deeply rooted in his childhood.

In the same spirit he built up the love story with Minna. To Virchow, who took exception to it, the romance lacked psychological plausibility. Nor was the actual Minna, now a portly provincial widow, altogether happy with the role written for her. To soothe her, he could hold out the promise that through his great book her name would become a household word, not only in Germany, but in France, the French colonies, and wherever *Ilios* was bound to be read. "All I have written can only redound to your credit. What other German women have been immortalized in similar fashion?"[2] Inviting Minna on this occasion to visit him at his home in Athens, he invoked in all seriousness the parallel of Cleopatra calling on Julius Caesar in Rome.

Schliemann's research on Mecklenburg revived old memories and kindled in him a stronger attachment than he had ever had for his native land. Genuine as these sentiments were, they undoubtedly had overtones of the small-town-boy-makes-good variety. But be this as it may, he now recalled people he thought he had long forgotten and searched them out, taking up correspondence with boyhood chums and inquiring about their marital status, offspring, brothers, and sisters. He advised a retired friend to take up a hobby. He located the ne'er-do-well miller's son whose recitation of Homer had captivated him in the Fürstenberg grocery and who, miraculously, had survived his alcoholic binges to become a respectable citizen. To him Schliemann wrote a charming note: "Dear Herr Nieder-höffer, I still remember clearly how on the morning after that evening on which you entranced me by reciting Homer, you came to the shop again, wearing a beautiful bright blue coat with shining buttons, at which we marveled no less than at your handsome face."[3] He liberally supported several needy cases, including his aged former teacher Carl Andres, who had gone to seed. The symbolic blossom picked at Mount Ida had come to full bloom.

Virchow's cunningly laid scheme met with still more tangible success. Yet its instigator learned that, for him at least, the blackthorn had a sting, and he may well have occasionally regretted his initiative in extracting a promise from Schliemann to will his treasure to the German nation. During his lifetime Schliemann seems to have first intended to retain ownership. He probably planned to house it in his new villa, now under construction in Athens. But, as always, he was considering other alternatives.

It so happened that just then his dissatisfaction with the South Kensington museum came to a head. The treasure had been on exhibit there for the past two years. But, to Schliemann's irritation, the curators had failed to label and catalogue the individual objects properly. Schliemann complained that he had never even been issued a formal receipt. At a loss over what to do with the precious collection but adamant on removing it, he considered offers to display it in Edinburgh or Paris, and inquired of Virchow if facilities were available in Berlin. Arrangements had already been initiated to make over other Trojan materials stored at the Dardanelles to the Berlin museums. Among these were artifacts and skeletal remains—in which Virchow took a special interest—from Frank Calvert's dig at the Hanai Tepe tumulus. Now it appeared that Germany might have it all. Whether Schliemann had by then decided to donate everything outright is difficult to tell. One gets the idea that he was overtaken by the recent German response to his work. Virchow, in turn, knew that he had to keep prodding while the iron was hot.

A crisis intervened in March 1880, threatening to scuttle all Virchow's efforts. Schliemann had accidentally learned that Virchow was about to release a scientific paper on prehistoric skeletons found in the Troad. To Schliemann this was treason—a flagrant breach of their agreement. He had paid for Virchow's trip, and Virchow had been his guest at Troy. Thus, Schliemann alone had a title to the finds, and the prerogative to report on the costly campaign was his. No one should anticipate *Ilios*. Schliemann had, indeed, hinted when inviting Virchow—who by no means was overeager to come—that his new work on Ilium should have precedence over other publications that might result.[4]

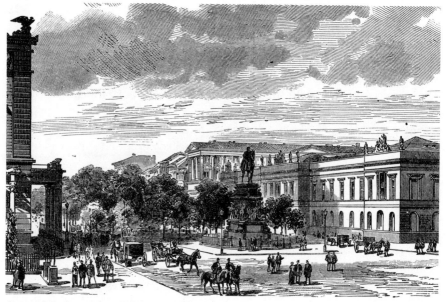

Imperial Berlin in the 1880s

Virchow, however, had put together an esoteric article that in no way could distract from the forthcoming general volume or even anticipate it. Of specialized interest, it would be read only by a few specialists, while *Ilios* was designed to appeal to a wider audience. Furthermore, Virchow's notes were meant to elucidate the anatomic materials now in Berlin, which otherwise would be meaningless. Such arguments were advanced by Virchow in letter after letter, but Schliemann did not bother considering them. Instead he sent his friend an abrupt telegram in the form of an ultimatum: "Publish nothing about Hanai Tepe. Else friendship and love for Germany both perish."[5] The intent was clear. Schliemann's love for Germany waxed and waned with the respect paid to his ego. Unless Virchow withdrew the paper (which had already been sent off to an academic society), it was a case of no love, no jewels. Virchow, left with no choice but to comply, promised to postpone publication. And Schliemann, with a sigh of relief, answered, "Now we remain friends."[6]

The unpleasant incident over, Virchow resumed negotiations on behalf of the treasure. Sooner or later, the director of the Berlin museums (Richard Schöne), the Prussian minister of education (Herr Puttkamer), middling German princes, and Bismarck himself were brought in. Though a political enemy of the chancellor, Virchow humbled himself to ask the great man's assistance in the matter. He even put up with waiting for an audience outside Bismarck's office for two hours. The affair was made difficult, if not grotesque at times, not only by the conflicting authorities of the Reichstag and the government, of museum officials, and of Prussian versus all-German magistrates, but also by Schliemann's ever-growing list of demands. Above all, he requested that his trophies had to be displayed in adequate museum quarters, specially set aside and marked for all time with the name SCHLIEMANN. He never tired of telling Virchow the sacrifices he was making with such a bequest, a bequest that was bound to turn the countries who had shown him the greatest regard and affection, England and the United States, into his bitter enemies. He did not speak of Greece, but Sophia was up in arms, and her husband's planned slight to her people, direct descendants of Priam and Agamemnon who should have first claim on the Trojan heirlooms, almost threatened their marriage. Only the intervention of their loyal friend, the Hereditary Prince of Saxe-Meiningen, won her over. In the end she even wanted to be a party to her husband's reconciliation with Germany. Besides, she came to realize what German honors and the support of the mighty empire would mean to his future work.

Virchow used infinite tact and quiet diplomacy to reach a settlement. But he was often at loss to comply with yet another Herculean labor Schliemann foisted on him. Yes, the treasure would be donated to none but the German nation, though placed under Prussian administration. Yes, he would get his own museum wing as soon as the new Museum für Völkerkunde (Ethnological Museum) was completed. Yes, Schliemann would have the right to arrange the articles himself. But he had also requested that the city of Berlin make him an honorary citizen, a rare honor indeed considering that only Bismarck and Field Marshal Helmuth von Moltke, the architects of victory in the Franco-Prussian War, had received it.[7] Wrote Virchow: "Your idea about the honorary citizenship is excellent. Only the matter cannot be put through so rapidly. . . . Also, do not forget that city councils are unwieldy bodies, with whom such weighty business requires time. One does not make honorary citizens every day, and I should like a little time to warm them up and make all the necessary preparations. . . . But I will gladly do all in my power and I feel very hopeful."[8]

That was not the end of Schliemann's demands. He also wanted the high Prussian order Pour le Mérite, which Virchow could not promise ("It is a kind of lottery"[9]), since membership was limited and eligibility depended on a vacancy in the particular field of endeavor rewarded by that medal. Schliemann also hoped for a medal for his "longtime assistant," Mrs. Schliemann. As if that were not enough, he was casting an eye on the Prussian Academy of the Sciences in Berlin, a highly exclusive institution that was nearly impossible for an outsider to breach. For once Virchow could not veil his impatience and wrote: "You did not give your collections to Berlin for the sake of receiving decorations."[10]

Finally all was settled and in the winter of 1880 Schliemann went to London and supervised the packing of the treasure in forty boxes, which soon after arrived in Berlin. The donation was acknowledged in February 1881 in the official government bulletin (Reichsanzeiger) as "a present in perpetuity, to be kept inalienably in the Imperial capital."[11] A personal letter from Emperor Wilhelm I confirmed the conditions the benefactor had stipulated for the preservation of the treasure and expressed the nation's thanks for his "patriotic gift—a testimony to his attachment to the fatherland, and a collection of the greatest importance to science."[12]

Early in 1881, Schliemann, with Sophia, was busily engaged in laying out the exhibit, which was to be housed provisionally at the Berlin Kunstgewerbemuseum (Museum of Decorative Arts). At last, the great moment arrived on July 7, when the little man from Mecklenburg, the expatriate who had found wealth and fame far from the Teutonic land of his birth, was given honorary citizenship of Berlin, the Reichshauptstadt (Imperial capital). The ceremony took place in the town hall. The great princes of the realm were present. Sophia was escorted by the future emperor, Prince Wilhelm. The new Berliner was hailed in a moving address by none other than Virchow.

Before the long-drawn-out treasure episode had been brought to so festive a conclusion, Schliemann had returned to archaeological fieldwork. With the Greek government's permission, he undertook a campaign at Orchomenos, a ruined site in Boeotia northwest of Thebes, positioned like Mycenae on a desolate cliff ringed by high mountains. The place had both Homeric and Pausanian credentials. According to Homer it must have once been a mighty city.[13] In fact, the bard ranked it with Mycenae and Troy as "rich in gold." They were the only three cities given that distinctive epithet, and for that reason alone it was inevitable that Schliemann would sooner or later turn his attention to it—unless forestalled by others. He was furthermore impressed by Pausanias' reference to the "Treasury of Minyas," which the Hellenistic Karl Baedeker declared to be among the greatest archaeological wonders of Greece. Minyas was the legendary king of a remote age.[14] His so-called treasury closely resembled the tholos structures of other Mycenaean centers, in particular that of Atreus in Mycenae (in fact, the two were so much alike that Dörpfeld, on a visit to Schliemann's excavations in 1881, remarked that both must have been built by the same architect). Alas, the tholos was in a dismal state of collapse, and its entrance (dromos) was blocked by stones. In vain had Lord Elgin tried to gain access on one of his freebooting operations early in the nine-teenth century.

Schliemann brought his wife to Orchomenos. He seems to have con-sidered her presence a good omen for unusual archaeological rewards. Whether he expected another bonanza *à la* Mycenae and Troy, he would not say. Later he disclaimed it, though there is little doubt that the Homeric description had long instilled in him the wish to take soundings at Orchomenos. Apart from his wife, he was accompanied by his British Orientalist friend A. H. Sayce (who stayed twelve days) and by Professor Ernst Ziller of Athens, the Austrian-born architect who designed his palazzo now taking shape in Athens, and later his mausoleum, and who had par-ticipated himself in some minor excavations in Asia Minor and Greece. A high official from the Greek Archaeological Society was also present, prob-ably for the anticipated contingency that precious objects were to emerge. The party stayed for one month, from the beginning of November to early December of 1880.

As was his habit, Schliemann put to work a large shock troop of laborers—including women, who received a lower rate of pay—and had them dig shafts and formidable trenches in and about the ancient citadel with its Cyclopean walls. But no royal graves showed up. Sophia again concentrated on the treasury. While no spectacular material finds were made, it was the treasury that scored. There, in the main, the campaign

Detail of the carved ceiling at Orchomenos

was continued from the end of March to mid-April 1881 (Schliemann returned briefly with Dörpfeld in 1886). In its small side chamber, called *thalamos* by Schliemann, Sophia was apparently the first to sight beautiful fragments of carved green slate plates that turned out to have covered the ceiling, whose roof had collapsed only a few years earlier. The geometric bas-relief decoration consisted of splendid interwoven arrangements of spirals, leaves, and rosettes. The intriguing pattern reminded Sayce of ornaments on sculptured Assyrian monuments, while Ziller associated them with Oriental carpets. However, the decidedly Mycenaean style, with close parallels among the friezes and stucco works at Mycenae and Tiryns, was later recognized. As such, the ceiling is a jewel of Mycenaean craftsmanship. The Schliemanns labored long in piecing it together so that drawings and photographs could be made, and a copy later went to Berlin. As at Mycenae, Schliemann persisted in declaring the Minyas *tholos* a true treasury.

Archaeologically at least as valuable was Schliemann's excavation of monochromatic, mostly gray, glazed pottery, made on a potter's wheel, that appeared to him at first unique and which he called "gray Minyan ware." This turned out to be a misnomer, however, for similar ceramics have since been traced all over Greece, the Aegean islands, and western and central Asia Minor. It is also met with in Troy VI. Modern scholars, who have tracked down its dissemination and fixed it chronologically, have learned to associate it with the Indo-European invaders into Greece around 1900 B.C. As such, it is of supreme importance in the stratigraphic record of Hellenic sites in the eastern Mediterranean. Wherever it is found, a cultural and ethnic break seems to have taken place. It thus may mark the very coming of the Greek and, possibly, the advent of the horse and war chariot.[15]

Shortly before returning to Orchomenos for a second season, the Schliemanns again called on Olympia. With his growing respect for systematic procedures in excavation, Schliemann was bound to be impressed by the achievements ("truly masterful"[16]) of the German team of experts. Virchow and Burnouf had taught him the overriding need for technically trained assistants, but here he was face to face with a neat demonstration of what specialists working together could accomplish. The Schliemanns were shown around by the expedition's bright young architect, twenty-seven-year-old Dr. Wilhelm Dörpfeld. The meeting was to be historic.

After Schliemann closed the Orchomenos campaign in 1881, on which, by the way, he did not issue a full-length book, he allowed himself but a brief respite. Just then his new home in Athens on University (today also called Venizelos) Street, a palatial multistoried villa in massive quasi-Tuscan Renaissance style, was nearing completion. It was a project on which he had lavished money and attention for years. Reminiscent of an American millionaire planting a Palladian mansion on a Florida key, Schliemann expended vast sums, constantly added eccentric details, and hoarded exquisite objects and materials for the villa on his trips throughout Europe. Ostentatiously austere in the grand manner, the pleasure dome was big enough to later accommodate a high court.[17] He called it Ilíou Mélathron, the "hut" of Ilium (though *mélathron* in Greek also means palace), in memory of the humble wooden shack he had shared on the Hissarlik hill with Sophia. Its name was carved on the center of the façade in large Greek majuscules.

Schliemann had conceived the villa to mirror his eclectic tastes, besides being a monument to his affluence and stature, rather than to cater to his or his family's comfort. He imported craftsmen from Italy, England, and Germany to install fixtures and decorations. The mansion was replete with fresco paintings, marble walls and statues, inscriptions, and the like, giving it a Pompeian touch. Loggias opened to a full view of the Acropolis. A gallery of twenty-four statues of Greek gods and goddesses, mostly undraped, fringed the flat roof. (Later, after Schliemann's death, they had to be removed as hazards to passers-by.) Everywhere there were iconographic allusions to the landlord's own epic life: murals showed views of Indianapolis and New York, mosaics sparkled with copies of his Mycenaean and Trojan finds, putti with likenesses of himself (wearing glasses!) and his children, graven excerpts from Homer and other classic authors, and a scattering of the swastika (on the iron gate outside) to honor his Aryan forefathers. The ground floor was occupied, aside from servants' quarters, by large halls where he kept most of his archaeological exhibits, while the second floor provided the actual living and sleeping accommodations for the family, as well as his study and library. Since he held with the ancient Greeks (and Japanese) that only a minimum of furniture was needed, the palace had an air of stark emptiness. Sophia may have felt little more comfortable than the consort Louis XIV installed in the drafty halls of Versailles. Cold and grandiose, but unappealing, the building blends quite well with the sterile nineteenth century Bavarian classicism still so much in evidence in present-day Athens.

Schliemann's home was to be a magnet for a steady stream of foreign visitors, who, ushered in by "Bellerophon" and "Telamon," the renamed footmen, would call on the great man and view his private collection of antiquities. Unless addressing his guests in their own language, Schliemann would hold forth in ancient Greek or, rather, his own brand of the sacred idiom, which he had evolved and perfected throughout the years.

In May 1881, Schliemann was back in Turkey, landing in Çanakkale, his customary entrepôt for Hissarlik. This time the entire Troad was his objective, including, and beyond, the ground he had covered with Virchow on their five-day ramblings in 1879.[18]

Except for local guides, Schliemann went alone, crisscrossing the historic region on horseback for fifteen days. As well known to him, the Troad was strewn with ruins and abandoned towns, many of unknown or disputed identity. His ambition was to reexamine the sites, place them culturally and historically, and take issue with some of the ascriptions made by other antiquarians. Not devoid of a geographic sense for the environs (a notable example of what the British call "field archaeology"), and strengthened by schooling from Virchow, he kept his eyes open for geological phenomena, vegetation, and ethnological and cultural byways. Always in the back of his mind was the hope that he would discover archaeological objects that might add to the Trojan evidence. He seems to have held out for another ancient settlement in the area to excavate. But his main concern was to reveal the Homeric stamp on the entire region.

Predictably, he felt he had made singular contributions. Thus, he stated quite explicitly in the opening sentence of his fifty-page account of the trip that "it supplements many points of Homeric geography which have until now seemed obscure, and it tends to explode theories, which have existed for thousands of years, and which have as yet never been contested."[19] Little in the original text bears out such a boast. But Schliemann was unable to touch any ancient site without being compelled to "revolutionize" the existing knowledge about it. On these wanderings he actually failed to come up with anything nearly as heterodox as his reading of Pausanias' reference to the Atreid graves, nor did he locate another Troy.

Wherever he investigated an area, Schliemann relied on his blind axiom that the only reliable guides to ancient buried ruins were substantial accretions of debris and potsherds. As in Italy and Sicily, on this trip he found virtually all sites lacking in that, to him, essential criterion. To cheer himself, he asserted that such a (negative) fact could but "further enhance the general interest attached to Hissarlik."[20] He excepted only two tumuli, the Hanai Tepe and Besika Tepe, which he had previously investigated for their prehistoric materials. At the end of his report he reached the disconcerting conclusion that, "with the exception of Assos, which is being explored by distinguished American investigators [from Boston], no excavations, with a view to find interesting antiquities of classical times, are possible anywhere in the Troad, except perhaps on some spot in Alexandria Troas, but even there I certainly cannot advise any archaeologist to lose his time in digging."[21] But this dogmatic counsel of despair he could have only half believed himself, since he planned a return with Virchow just a few months later and repeatedly talked of further explorations and trial digs in the Troad, which he actually launched in 1882 during his third major campaign at Hissarlik. In fact, twentieth century archaeologists have found in the area, which has by no means been thoroughly combed, sites as old and almost as rich as Troy II and some considerably older like Kum Kale (Koum Kale) near the northwest tip of the Troad.[22]

The tour culminated in a complete ascent of the Mount Ida massif, the legendary seat of Zeus, which previously had eluded Schliemann and Virchow. With customary gusto Schliemann believed he had found a slab from the god's altar at the Jovian aerie, approximately where Homer led him to expect to find it.

In Schliemann's incessant and passionate archaeological journey in Greece and the Troad, his third Hissarlik campaign, from March to July 1882, was a giant step forward. True enough, his friend Virchow had already announced Schliemann's conversion to scientific professionalism complete, but few critics were overly impressed with the interpretations of his Trojan finds given in the ponderous *Ilios*. Barely had the book been published, settling, according to its author's by now obbligato pronouncement, the Homeric Question for good, than Schliemann himself had second thoughts. He was never one to readily accept any disagreement with his judgments, but some of the basic objections raised against his *Ilios* conclusions happened to be in tune with his own. They furnished him, however, not with a reason to change his mind but with a welcome excuse to exorcise the heresies he reluctantly had embraced at the expense of his "sun" Homer.

It did not escape Schliemann—just as the critics would not let him forget—that the Troy he had found was a far cry from the glorious princely citadel described in the *Iliad*. Yet he could not seriously entertain the impious thought that the place he had dusted off may not have been the historic city after all. Thus he found himself in a nearly insoluble dilemma. If one were to blame the glaring discrepancy between tradition and fact on Homer's poetic fantasy, as Schliemann had tended to suggest to his own heartache, then there remained but a tiny step to open the sluices of destructive disbelief and reduce all of the *Iliad* to fiction. The Homeric fortress was liable to collapse, and Schliemann's own high purpose was bound to be leveled with it.

It was, as usual, in Schliemann's nature to agonize, but he would not stay in the vale of despair for long. Somehow he always bounced back. Come what may, Homer remained for him ultimate reality. And now, in a moment of crisis, he was as confident as ever that Homer spoke the truth, except, like the mathematician Gauss, he was not quite certain how he could prove it. Somewhere in his researches he had gone wrong. But what the spade had upset, more spadework may put right again. Perhaps, though categorically rejected in *Ilios*, his Troy was a "priamus" (citadel) after all, and the common people lived outside the walls in the lowland—as he had thought all along before stubborn facts got in his way. Typically enough, barely had that thesis been reembraced than it turned into a foregone conclusion and physical data invariably bore it out.

Schliemann, it must be admitted, remained an alien to the cool and detached scientific attitude to the end of his career, even though he had come to realize definite technical shortcomings in his former explorations. In the latter respect, his new campaign of 1882 spelled a turning point. He now accepted the tools and methods of systematic research in the hope that they could be utilized to restore the reality of Homer. And, with the aid of his skilled assistants, this is precisely what happened. They conjured up for him a virtually new Troy, which, though it upset many of his former tenets, allowed him to uphold with still greater conviction the historic validity of Homer.

Schliemann's return to Hissarlik on March 1, 1882, had been preceded by the customary wranglings with Turkish authorities. Only this time he was to make full use of his recently cemented connections with the mighty Reich. He would never let anyone forget that, because of his generous bequest to the fatherland, the German establishment owed him strong support. He appealed to or, rather, conscripted Virchow, the Prince of Meiningen, Bismarck, Richard Schöne, and the German diplomatic envoys. If they did not sufficiently, and promptly, deliver, they became the butt of his ire and were presented with an exhaustive catalogue of his services and accomplishments. Letters and telegrams issued endlessly from Athens, Constantinople, Biarritz, or wherever he was. If everything else failed, he would urge them to have the Emperor or Crown Prince intervene directly at the Sublime Porte. All the time he never ceased rubbing in how he had slaved in a "pestilential climate" under total abrogation of his own comfort—and at 400 francs' daily expense to his pocket—to make the age's most momentous discovery, a discovery which had escaped other men for two thousand years.[23] The fruits of his genius accrued to the glory of Germany. His treasures, he loved to remind his fellow Berliners, added to the magnetic attraction of the capital, which would now become a mecca for people from all over the world who were eager to gaze at King Priam's crown jewels.

At one time or another, Bismarck was unceremoniously told that Gladstone or Lord Dufferin would have gotten him his *firman* by now.[24] Virchow and Schöne were treated to similar tactless needling. Had he, Schliemann, not consented to conciliation with Germany, the leaders of other nations whom he had turned into deadly enemies (one of his favorite strictures) by his patriotic deeds, would have gladly and expeditiously settled his score with Turkey. "Since the fatherland now once again recognizes me," he wrote to Bismarck in January 1882, "and I have given it the most precious thing in my possession . . . I can henceforth only turn to the German Legation in Constantinople."[25] Likewise, he played up to German national pride when intimating that the all-powerful German empire was weak-kneed in its relations with a secondary power like Turkey. How was it that Britain could obtain carte blanche for excavations in all of Mesopotamia, while he, an honored representative of mighty Germany, was still waiting? When at the end of his patience, he would drop a hint that if he were finally forced to turn to his former friends, be it Britain, or even Italy, it might have dire consequences for the fatherland and dry up his largess. He estranged his devoted friend, the Prince of Meiningen, by sending him on a mission to his Imperial relatives, while boasting in public that Bismarck was settling the matter directly in Constantinople.

In the course of these transactions he developed a taste for politics and soon chose to dabble in it. By making no bones about his displeasure with the German diplomats in Constantinople, he called for their replacement.[26] He even pushed his own candidate, Count J. M. von Radowitz, who had been of assistance to him in Athens and was actually soon after—probably by coincidence—named to the post. The effectiveness of the German "foreign office" (he termed it that even in his German letters) was constantly called in question. To Virchow he proposed an absurd deal for the return of Alsace-Lorraine to France. In another political gambit, he asked Richard Schöne to have the empire put pressure on Turkey to cede to Germany, for display outside a Berlin museum, the famous Spartan votive bronze statue of three serpents given to the Oracle of Delphi and taken some one thousand six hundred years ago to Constantinople. Its removal to Berlin, he assured Schöne, "would cause joy all over the world."[27]

With the fervor of a neonationalist, Schliemann declared all of a sudden that his hero was Bismarck, and he lost no time in stating that he was thoroughly disgusted with Gladstone's politics. So much did he now identify with German "national destiny" that when Bismarck began to toy with imperialistic adventures to acquire colonies for Germany, Schliemann plainly instructed the liberal Virchow to cease resisting the Iron Chancellor's policies. To buttress the colonial arguments, he would even use the claptrap about the millions of Germans who lost their German identity while building the United States. This sounded strange indeed coming from a quasi-American expatriate who at one point became Russified and raised a Russian family, only to marry in later years a Greek woman and bring up an Agamemnon and an Andromache.

The *firman* had actually been granted in October 1881 but was delivered in January 1882. To Schliemann it turned out to be a bitter disillusionment, because it was narrowly confined to the Hissarlik hill, while he had set his eyes also on the plain below and the Troad at large. Again there followed outcries, finally resolved in March, a few days after he had resumed his campaign.

Chastened by his critics and after exchanging views with friends and associates, Schliemann started with a fairly concise program. On the Hissarlik hill, foremost in the as yet little-tapped eastern section, he intended to proceed "layer by layer," studying and registering each successive settlement until he reached the lowest stratum. Likewise he would pay attention in this area to Hellenic, Hellenistic, and Roman edifices and look for sculptures. For this purpose, later in the campaign, he would reexamine the debris he had mercilessly discarded in his first years. He would even search for looted statuary down in the plain in Turkish cemeteries. To gauge the limit of the prehistoric city yet to be detected in the eastern "suburb," he proposed to dig a trench eighty meters long. Some activity was also to be devoted to the Roman theater, for whose neglect he had often been reproached. The most important work was, however, carried out in the central area of Troy II, leading to the discovery of a major compound of buildings.

As Müller and Virchow had previously urged, Schliemann would now take a closer look at Troy I, the earliest settlement on the Hissarlik rock. Another project was the sinking of shafts (he planned drilling two hundred and fifty) in the plain, where, once more, he hoped to find the city proper of the Trojan people. A pressing item on his agenda was the search for the necropolis of prehistoric Troy.[28] Analogies to sites elsewhere led him to believe that digging along the ancient roads radiating from Hissarlik might put him on the trail for the burial site. In addition, he was resolved to make all the Troad a domain for his spade. Places like Ballidagh, Kurshunluh, and Chali Dagh he wanted to scrutinize again, in addition to the remaining tumuli that had not yet been excavated.

Schliemann's intention then was clear. By training his sights on the larger environment of Hissarlik, he hoped to come up with a greater Troy, one that approximated the Homeric concept of it. Further explorations in the Troad, and in the case of the tumulus of Protesilaos across the Hellespont on European soil in Thrace, were to extend the Trojan context and add to the knowledge of the whole area's remote prehistory.

The Hissarlik scene of 1882 was as varied in participants as in its objectives. Schliemann drew in *Troja* a colorful picture of the ethnically varied workers; of his new household help from Greece (inevitably renamed after ancient Greek figures); his enterprising and faithful major-domo Nikolaos (for whom he had such respect that he was permitted to retain his original name); water carriers, bodyguards, foremen, and Turkish overseers. The last were, as always, a personal affront to him, though certainly no worse than the overseer assigned to his previous Hissarlik campaign, the "crude, ignorant Kadri Bey, whose only concern was to create obstacles in my work."[29] Actually, when asking for a new *firman*, he declared he was willing to settle on anybody but Kadri Bey.

And then, of course, there were—besides a Polish engineer and a Greek photographer—Dr. Wilhelm Dörpfeld and Joseph Höfler, both with flawless academic records and highly recommended by the leading archaeologists of Berlin and Vienna. To Dörpfeld, who had just been named to the German Archaeological Institute in Athens (he became its director a few years later), Schliemann had warmed up during his visit to Olympia and further meetings at Berlin and Orchomenos. In Olympia, where the four-year German campaign had come to an end in 1881, the young architect had proven his uncanny skill when unearthing the Hera temple. If an architect could throw so much light on a fairly simple, relatively little-stratified place like Olympia, how much more did the multilayered labyrinth of Hissarlik cry for his expertise. Schliemann needed little further persuasion from his friends to realize that from now on architectural help was essential in major excavations.[30]

Schliemann soon made up his mind to recruit Dörpfeld for Troy. But negotiations broke down, since the young man, about to be married, wanted a guarantee for three years and what may have seemed to Schliemann an excessive compensation. Meanwhile, he hired Höfler instead, a capable architect from Vienna, also trained in archaeology. However, Dörpfeld, once assured of the Athens appointment, reconsidered and was immediately added to the staff. He arrived in Troy in the middle of March.

Schliemann never regretted his choice. Neither did other archaeologists, who, perhaps a bit maliciously, were to declare Dörpfeld "Schliemann's greatest discovery."[31] In any case, there developed between the two men, though separated by more than thirty years, a most fruitful and, it seems, on the whole cordial partnership that lasted until Schliemann's death. At all the large-scale excavations from now on, Dörpfeld was no doubt a decisive force. Schliemann, though grudgingly on occasion, more and more deferred to Dörpfeld's unobtrusive skill. But in his publications he showed no hurry to give the younger man full credit for his contributions. Ultimately, it was he, Schliemann, who discovered the *megara* of Troy II and the palace of Tiryns. On the other hand, he has Burnouf share the blame for choosing Troy III over Troy II in 1879.

However, in a letter to Gladstone early in the campaign on May 3, 1882, he more openly surveyed the dramatic changes in the picture of Homeric Troy brought about by his keen architects:

> For this year's explorations of Troy I had engaged the two very best German architects I could get hold of. . . . They have found out, and proved to me, that the *first* city, whose ruins are 23 feet deep, has been succeeded by a *large* city, which used Hissarlik merely as its acropolis and sacred precinct of its temples, as well as for the residence of its kings and family.[32] They have laid bare the ruins of two very large buildings in this city, each of which was about 33 ft. broad and 100 ft. long. . . . Blocks of bricks which in my *Ilios* we had mistaken for remnants of the city wall, are parts of the buildings. . . . The ten treasures I found belonged, except one, to this 2nd city. . . . There are besides distinct marks that the walls extended to the plateau on which must have stood the lower city. The Pergamus, and no doubt also the lower city, was destroyed by a fearful conflagration. . . . I regret not having had such architects with me from the beginning, but even now it is not too late.[33] . . .

At the same time, Schliemann wrote even more emphatically to Schöne in Greek (because it would be sacrilege to write in any other language from holy Troy): "The large second city, which had a lower town and a castle with two splendid temples and two or four other proper edifices we now ascribe without any reservation to the celebrated Ilion, since it is completely identical with Homer's Troy."[34] It goes without saying that the unqualified conviction that Troy II was identical and in total agreement with Homer's city, and that it definitely had a suburb, is Schliemann's own dogmatic—and wishful—way of registering the new discoveries.

Schliemann, to be sure, was overenthusiastic. Of the lower town nothing of consequence ever showed up, unless it be considerable deposits of ancient pottery shards. Equally negative was the search for the prehistoric necropolis. Yet the achievements were undeniable. His architects in little time had managed to clear up much of the hopeless jigsaw puzzle of intertwined walls, jumbled blocks of stone, warrens of ditches, and amorphous masses of debris. By patiently separating strata and joining walls and masonry that appeared to belong together, they could relate buildings in time and space and to each other. When not interfered with by the Turkish authorities, they carefully measured building fundaments and subsequently entered them on ground plans. In due course there emerged, as from a developed film, a meaningful, fairly detailed picture—and even a succession of pictures. One of their principal finds, proudly mentioned in the above-quoted letter to Gladstone, was a complex of three adjoining buildings in the center of Troy II (partly, alas, previously destroyed by Schliemann's north-south trench), whose elongated *megaron* designs, with an entrance porch (*pronaos*) and single-aisled rec-

tangular main hall or sanctuary (*cella* or *naos*) closely resembled the prototype of the classical Greek temple. Later it was shown to have been the basic
structure of Mycenaean palaces.[35] As Dörpfeld first noted, it also fitted the
description of Paris' palace in the *Iliad*. Schliemann, under the influence of
his young architects, tended to think the buildings represented temple com-
pounds, preferably of Pallas Athene. But finds made later elsewhere were
soon to change his and Dörpfeld's opinion.

Out of chaos the architects now clearly sorted out successive layers, necessitating the return to Troy II for the burned "Homeric" city. What
Schliemann had labeled the third turned out to be, at least in part, a late sub-
stratum of the second. The former "house of the town chief" was once again
reduced to well-deserved insignificance. It actually covered in part, and in-
truded into, an older and larger building that was coeval with the longhouses in the center and which Schliemann now chose to refer to as the
royal palace. The majority of the treasures found in previous seasons had been
deposited in or near its precincts. (This time no treasure was encountered
except for caches of nonprecious metal articles.)

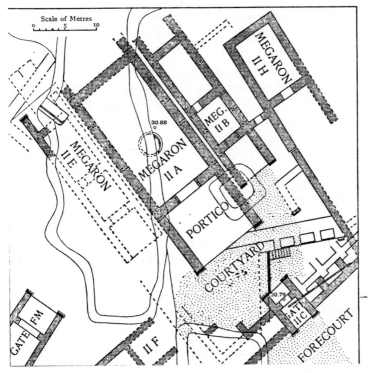

The central buildings of *megaron* design from Troy II

Of equal importance was the tracing of the circuit wall far beyond its former limits; even various stages of its development during the existence of Troy II could be discerned.[36] Along its course two additional gates were unearthed. For the first time Schliemann, thanks to his architects, was able to gain a clear and vivid picture of a prehistoric palace-fortress with its spacious buildings and formidable ramparts occupying the second stratum of the ancient hill. As for the rest of Hissarlik, Dörpfeld eventually was to establish a sequence of nine major strata, a system that has held up since, even though American excavators in the 1930's would distinguish no less than forty-six sublayers.

Schliemann's target in the Troad at large were the mounds or tumuli that are scattered all over this corner of Asia Minor and which tradition had linked with the burial places of Homeric heroes. But, as before, he found such mythological connections spurious. He reiterated his conviction that the majority did not contain real burials. Surprisingly, he met with the most interesting results outside the Troad proper at the so-called tumulus of Protesilaos. Only here did he dig up artifacts of the same age and style as the oldest Trojan settlement, a fact that made some people (such as the journalist Karl Blind) rashly conclude that the roots of Trojan culture, or at least of the Trojan people, were to be sought in Europe rather than Asia.[37] However, the Turkish commander of a nearby fort issued strict orders for Schliemann to stop digging after barely two days. An offer by Schliemann to finance a completion of the dig by the Turks themselves was rejected.

The Turks, at times, were haunted by a pathological fear of being spied upon. They took every archaeologist for a cleverly disguised foreign agent. An observer at Troy alerted a high-placed officer of the Turkish army and convinced him that Schliemann and his staff were in reality engaged at Troy in tracing the Turkish coastal fortifications. The authorities duly banned all measuring, drawing, and note taking. Under such circumstances, the architects were severely limited in carrying out their duties and were unable to produce the maps that were needed. In fact, the notorious Beder Eddin Effendi threatened upon the least transgression to have the architects taken in chains to the Turkish capital. Despite Schliemann's outraged protests and frantic appeals to his political mentors, the ban was not lifted. Only after the excavations had been closed did the new German ambassador, von Radowitz, obtain personally from the Sultan a clearance. Late in November 1882, with the onset of winter rains and storms, Dörpfeld, assisted by another young architect, Otto Puchstein, speedily executed a ground and floor plan.[38] Additional map work had to be postponed to April 1883.

The third campaign at Hissarlik was, as usual, a stormy one, and by the time it had been brought to a satisfactory conclusion, Schliemann himself had fallen victim to a severe attack of malaria that he tried to fight in vain with strong doses of coffee and quinine. It continued to torment him months after, even while he attempted to recover in company of his wife at Marienbad.

As was his habit, he was then already busy with gathering together his new publication to be named *Troja: Results of the latest researches and discoveries on the site of Homeric Troy . . . 1882*. Written in English, he translated it into German himself. Brockhaus brought it out in 1884. The English and American editions (John Murray in London; Harper's in New York) followed the same year. The entire publication was worked into the French edition of *Ilios* of 1885, which was to occupy Schliemann for a long time.[39]

In outline *Troja* closely resembles the pattern established in *Ilios*. A general chapter, giving an overall narrative of the 1882 explorations, is followed by successive treatments of the now accepted six prehistoric settlements at Hissarlik. Further chapters discuss investigations of the tumuli and the Troad in general. Assiduous "Notes" range over such varied ground as "The advance of the sea upon the shores of the Hellespont," "Demetrios of Skepsis," "Testimony of Plato for the site of Troy," and much more. Seven appendixes include Schliemann's own lengthy "Journey in the Troad in May 1881" as well as his meteorological observations at Hissarlik and essays by Virchow, Mahaffy, and Karl Blind (an Anglo-German publicist who had actively, and probably remuneratively, been promoting Schliemann in England) on "The Teutonic kinship of Trojans and Thracians." A. H. Sayce furnished a graceful preface. Schliemann dedicated the German and English editions to the Crown Princess Victoria of Germany. The American edition was inscribed "to all who love the poetry of Homer, and to all who are searching for the light thrown on history by the science of archaeology." It was a fitting description of his own passionate, unabated quest.

TROY, TROAD, AND TUMULI

from *Troja*

By my excavations on the hill of Hissarlik in 1879, in company with Professor Rudolf Virchow of Berlin and M. Emile Burnouf of Paris, I suppose that I had settled the Trojan question for ever. I thought I had proved that the small town, the third in succession from the virgin soil . . . must necessarily be the Ilium of the legend immortalized by Homer; and I maintained this theory in my work *Ilios,* which I published at the end of 1880. But after its publication I became sceptical . . . and my doubts increased as time wore on. I soon found it no longer possible to believe that the divine poet . . . could have represented Ilium as a great, elegant, flourishing, and well-inhabited, well-built city, with large streets, if it had been in reality only a very little town. . . . Nay, had Troy been merely a small fortified borough, such as the ruins of the third city denote, a few hundred men might have easily taken it in a few days, and the whole Trojan War, with its ten years' siege, would either have been a total fiction, or it would have had but a slender foundation. I could accept neither hypothesis, for I found it impossible to think that, whilst there were so many large cities on the coast of Asia, the catastrophe of a little borough could at once have been taken up by the bards. . . .

I therefore resolved upon continuing the excavations at Hissarlik, for five months more, to clear up the mystery, and to settle finally the important Trojan question. . . .

Fortunately, in June 1879, I had left a Turkish watchman at Hissarlik, to guard my wooden barracks and the magazine, in which were stored all my machinery and implements for excavating. Thus [in March 1882] I now found everything in the best order, and had only to cover my houses with new waterproof felt. As all of them were built in one continuous line, the danger of fire was great. I therefore separated them and put them up in different places, so that, in case one of the barracks caught fire, none of the others could be reached by the flames, even with the heaviest storm blowing. The barrack in which I and my servants lived had five rooms, two of which I occupied; another had two, a third had three, and a fourth had four bedrooms. We had, therefore, ample room, and could also conveniently lodge seven visitors. One barrack, of only one room, served as a dining-hall, and was called by that proud name, though it consisted of rude planks, through whose crevices the wind blew incessantly, so that frequently it was impossible to burn a lamp or light a candle. Another large barrack served as a store for the antiquities, which were to be divided between the Imperial Museum at Constantinople and myself.

My honoured friends, Messrs. J. Henry Schröder & Co., of London, had kindly sent me a large supply of tins of Chicago corned beef, peaches, the best English cheese, and ox-tongues, as well as 240 bottles of the best English pale ale. I was the sole consumer of these 240 bottles of pale ale, which lasted me for five months, and which I used as a medicine to cure constipation, from which I had been suffering for more than thirty years, and which had been aggravated by all other medicines, and particularly by the mineral waters of Carlsbad. This pale-ale-cure proved perfectly effectual.

I heard that the country was infested by marauders and highway robbers; besides that, the continual acts of brigandage in Macedonia, where a number of opulent men had been carried off by the robbers to the mountains and ransomed for heavy amounts, made me afraid of a like fate at Hissarlik. I therefore required at least 11 gendarmes for my safeguard. . . . They were picked out . . . 'from among the strongest and most trustworthy Turks of the Dardanelles. . . .

The workmen were for the most part Greeks from the neighbouring villages of Kalifatli, Yeni Shehr, and Ren Kioi; a few of them were from the islands of Imbros or Tenedos, or from the Thracian Chersonese. Of Turkish workmen I had on an average only twenty-five; I would gladly have increased their number had it been possible, for they work much better than the Asiatic Greeks, are more honest, and I had in them the great advantage that they worked on Sundays and on the numerous saints' days, when no Greek would have worked at any price. Besides, as I could always be sure that they would work on with unremitting zeal, and never need to be urged, I could let them sink all the shafts and assign to them other work, in which no superintendence on my part was possible. For all these reasons I always allotted to the Turkish workmen proportionally higher wages than to the Greeks. I had also now and then some Jewish labourers, who likewise worked much better than the Greeks.

I may take this occasion to mention that all the Jews of the Levant are descendants of the Spanish Jews who, to the ruin of Spain, were expelled from that country in March 1492, under Ferdinand and Isabella. Strange to say, in spite of their long wanderings and the vicissitudes of their fortunes, they have not forgotten the Spanish language, in which they still converse among themselves, and which even the Jewish labourer speaks more fluently than Turkish. If one of these Jews now returned to Spain, his vocabulary would of course excite much amusement, for it abounds with antiquated Spanish words, such as we find in *Don Quixote*, and it also contains many Turkish words. . . .

I had two Turkish delegates, one of whom, called Moharrem Effendi, was supplied to me by the local authorities; I had to provide him with lodgings and to pay him £7 10s. monthly. The other delegate, Beder Eddin Effendi, was sent to me by the Minister of Public Instruction at Constantinople, by whom he was paid; I had merely to provide him with a bedchamber. I have carried on archaeological excavations in Turkey for a number of years, but it had never yet been my ill fortune to have such a monster of a delegate as Beder Eddin, whose arrogance and self-conceit were only equalled by his complete ignorance, and who considered it his sole office to throw all possible obstacles in my way. As he was in the em-

ploy of government, he had the telegraph to the Dardanelles at his disposal,
and he used it in the most shameless way to denounce me and my architects to the local authorities. At first the civil governor listened to him,
and sent trustworthy men to investigate the charges; but having repeatedly
convinced himself that the man had basely calumniated us, he took no
further notice of him. A Turk will always hate a Christian, however well he
may be paid by him, and thus it was not difficult for Beder Eddin Effendi
to bring all my eleven gendarmes over to his side, and to make so many
spies of them. . . .

We had a south wind for only the first three days in March; afterwards
until the end of April, and therefore for fifty-eight days uninterruptedly, we
had a strong north wind, increasing at least four times a week to a severe
storm, which blew the blinding dust into our eyes, and interfered seriously
with the excavations. Only a few of my labourers had dust-spectacles; those
who had none were obliged to cover up their faces with shawls, and thus
the host of my veiled workmen looked very like the muffled attendants at
Italian funerals. At the same time the weather was very cold. . . . Mount
Saoce, on Samothrace, remained covered with snow till about the end of
March. The chain of Ida was entirely covered with snow till about the
20th of March. Afterwards only the higher peaks remained snow-clad; but
the snow gradually diminished, and by the end of May snow could only be
seen on and near their summits. . . .

The Plain of Troy used to be covered in April and May with red and
yellow flowers, as well as with deep grass; but this year, for want of moisture,
there were no flowers and barely any grass at all, so that the poor people had
hardly anything for their flocks to feed upon. We had not, therefore, to
complain this year of being annoyed, as in former years, by the monotonous
croaking of millions of frogs, for the swamps being dried up in the lower
Simois valley, there were no frogs at all, except a few in the bed of the
Kalifatli Asmak. The locusts appeared this year later than usual, namely,
towards the end of June, when nearly all the grain had been harvested; they
therefore did not do much damage.

The first flocks of cranes passed over the Plain of Troy on the 14th of
March; the first storks arrived on the 17th of March. The cranes do not
make their nests here; they merely stop a few hours for food, and fly on to
more northerly regions.

A slight shock of earthquake occurred on the 1st of April. . . .

One of my first works was to bring to light all the foundations of the
Hellenic or Roman edifices in the part of Hissarlik still unexcavated, and
to collect the sculptured blocks belonging to them as well as to other build-

ings of which the foundations could no longer be traced. . . .

One of my greater works was a trench, 80 mètres long and 7 mètres broad, which I dug in March and April across the eastern part of the acropolis, which was then still unexcavated, in order to ascertain how far the citadel of the earliest prehistoric cities extended in this direction. This work was exceedingly difficult, on account of the immense masses of small stones and huge boulders which we had to remove, as well as on account of the depth (no less than 12 mètres) to which we had to dig to reach the rock. The trench was excavated simultaneously throughout its whole length, the *débris* being carried off by wheelbarrows as well as by man-carts and horse-carts; but the deeper we penetrated the more difficult and fatiguing did the labour become, for we were obliged to carry up the *débris* in baskets on narrow zigzag paths, which became steeper and steeper with the increasing depth. When we had reached a depth of from 10 to 12 mètres the side paths had to be cut away, and all the *débris* had to be removed by man-carts, and shot out on the slope. But this fatiguing work has been rewarded by interesting results for the topography of the ancient acropolis; since it has enabled us to ascertain that this whole eastern part of the citadel-hill originated after the destruction of the fourth city, and that it was heaped up to extend the original Pergamos. . . .

It is very remarkable that below the Hellenic layer of ruins we found . . . only Lydian terra-cotta[1] . . . of the fifth and fourth settlements, but none at all of the three lowest cities. . . .

I further dug a trench 40 mètres long close to the acropolis on the north-west side, where I hoped to find the prolongation of the great wall of the second city. In fact, I found there, at the exact place where it must be supposed to have existed, the rock artificially levelled, so that there can be no doubt that the wall once stood here; but not a stone of it remained *in situ.* . . .

My architects have proved to me that, together with M. Burnouf, my collaborator in 1879, I had not rightly distinguished and separated the ruins of the two following settlements, namely, the Second and Third; that we had rightly considered as foundations belonging to the second city the walls of large blocks 2.50 m. deep; but that we had been mistaken in not connecting with it the layer of calcined ruins which lies immediately upon these walls, and belongs to the second city, and in attributing this burnt stratum to the third settlement, with which it has nothing to do. We had been led into this error by the colossal masses of *débris* of baked, or, more rightly, of burnt bricks of the second city, which in a very great many places had not been removed by the third settlers, and were lying on a level with their house-foundations, and often even much higher. These *débris* of burnt bricks are partly derived from houses destroyed in a terrible fire, partly they are the remains of brick walls, which, after having been completely built up of crude bricks, have for solidity's sake been artificially baked by large masses of wood piled up on both sides of them and set on fire simultaneously. The burnt city proper is, therefore, not the third, but the second, all of whose buildings have been completely destroyed; but, the third city having been built immediately upon it, the layer of *débris* of the second city is often but insignificant, and in some places even only 20 cm. deep. The house-foundations of the third settlers having been sunk into the calcined *débris* of the second city, we erroneously attributed these latter to the third settlement, with which they have nothing to do. . . .

I may mention here that the wall of the Homeric Troy was likewise provided with numerous towers. With one exception, we found all these substruction walls still crowned with brick walls, more or less preserved, and we may assume with certainty that all of these belonged to the second city, and that they had merely been repaired by the third settlers. This appears the more certain, as on the east side the brick wall of the second city is for the most part in an admirable state of preservation. . . . The third settlers, consequently, needed only to repair the upper part of the destroyed acropolis-wall in some places, in order to be able to use the wall again. For this reason we may consider it also certain, that the great treasure found by me at the . . . end of May 1873 was contained in the brick-*débris* of the second city; the more so as, by excavating the substruction wall to its foundations, we have brought to light, precisely in this place, a tower of the second city. It is even possible that the brick-*débris*, in which the great treasure was found, was the real brick wall. . . .

But a still more weighty proof that all the treasures belong, not to the third, but to the second, the burnt city, is found in the condition of the more than 10,000 objects of which they are composed, for every one of them, even to the smallest gold drop, bears the most evident marks of the fearful incandescence to which it has been exposed. But these marks of heat are still more striking on the bronze weapons than on the gold ornaments. . . .

When the whole wall of the acropolis was still entire, and when the gigantic substruction-wall was still surmounted by the brick-wall crowned with numerous towers, it must have had a very imposing aspect, particularly on the high north side which faces the Hellespont; and this may have induced the Trojans to ascribe its construction to Poseidon, or to Poseidon and Apollo.

But the legend that the walls of Troy were built by Poseidon may have a much deeper meaning, for, as Mr. Gladstone has ingeniously proved, a connection with Poseidon frequently denotes Phoenician associations; and further . . . Herakles is the representative of the Phoenicians, and the tradition of his expedition to Ilium may point to an early conquest and destruction of the city by the Phoenicians, just as the building of Troy's walls by Poseidon may denote that they were built by the Phoenicians.

But this second settlement on the hill of Hissarlik constituted only the acropolis, to which a lower city was attached on the east, south, and south-west sides. . . .

Among the double-handled goblets found in my Trojan campaign of 1882 there are some of very large size. The largest of them . . . contains [in volume] not less than ten bottles of Bordeaux wine; filled with wine it would therefore be sufficient for a company of forty persons, if each of them were supposed to drink as much as a quarter of a bottle. . . .

With but few exceptions, these double-handled cups are always wheel-made. All the unpolished plates are also wheel-made. But otherwise wheel-made terra-cottas are exceedingly rare, nearly all the pottery being hand-made.

One of my most interesting discoveries in 1882 was a small treasure of objects of copper and bronze, which was found in the layer of *débris* of the second settlement, . . . where I had found a gold treasure on the 21st of October, 1878. It consisted of two quadrangular nails . . . but without disks; of six well-preserved but very plain bracelets, two of which are treble; and of three small battle-axes. . . . I may here mention that the British Museum contains six battle-axes of copper or bronze of a similar shape, which were found in the island of Thermia in the Greek Archipelago, and of which three are perforated in like manner.

There were also a large battle-axe, 23 cm. long . . . and the lower part of another. Also a curious object of copper in the form of a seal, on which however no engraved sign is visible. . . .

But by far the most interesting object of the little treasure was a copper or bronze idol of the most primitive form. . . . It has an owl's head, and round protruding eyes, between which the beak is conspicuous. There is a hole in each ear, which, however, does not go through, and therefore cannot have served for suspension. The neck is disproportionately long, indeed, fully twice as long as a human figure of this size would have; no breasts are indicated; the right arm is represented by a shapeless projection, which is bent round so as to make the end, where the hand ought to be, rest on the place where the right breast ought to be; and this circumstance can hardly leave a doubt that a female figure was intended. The left arm is broken off; but the stump which remains of it extends too far horizontally to admit the supposition that this arm could have had an attitude similar to that of the right arm; we rather think it stood out in a straight line, and this is also probably the reason that it was broken when the idol fell. No delta or vulva is indicated. The legs are separated: probably merely to consolidate them, a shapeless piece of copper has been soldered to them from behind, which protrudes below the feet, and ought not to be mistaken for a stay or prop, because it can never have served as such, for the simple reason that it is longer than the feet, and is fastened almost parallel with them. . . .

The figure is 15.5 cm. long, and weighs 440 grammes (nearly 1 lb.). I think it probable that it is a copy or imitation of the famous Palladium, which was fabled to have fallen from heaven, the original of which was probably much larger, and of wood. Fortunately . . . it had broken into three fragments; I am indebted to this lucky circumstance for having obtained it in the division with the Turkish Government; for the three pieces were covered with carbonate of copper and dirt, and altogether undiscernible to an inexperienced eye. . . .

The "Tomb of Achilles" along the shores of the Hellespont

Another object of special interest was my exploration of eight more of the conical mounds, the so-called Trojan Heroic Tumuli. I began with the excavation of the two tumuli situated at the foot of Cape Sigeum, the larger of which the tradition of all antiquity attributed to Achilles, the smaller one perhaps to his friend Patroclus. . . . I discovered that one of the large massive windmills to the southeast of Sigeum is actually built on the top of an ancient conical tumulus, which makes up the number three, as stated by Strabo. With regard to the large conical hill on the projecting headland, there can be no question that it is the very tumulus to which tradition unanimously pointed as the sepulchre of Achilles; but we have nothing to guide us as to which of the two remaining tumuli was attributed by the ancients to Antilochus, and which to Patroclus, for the name "tomb of Patroclus," which the smaller unencumbered tumulus now bears, seems to have been given to it less than a century ago by Lechevalier or Choiseul-Gouffier,[2] and the other tumulus, which is crowned by the windmill, has not come under the notice of any modern traveller, and is therefore marked on no map. . . .

That the large tumulus on the jutting headland was considered in the historical times of antiquity as the sepulchre of Achilles, is evident from Strabo, Arrian, Pliny, Lucian, Quintus Smyrnaeus, Dion Cassius, and others. It was situated within the fortified town of Achilleum, which seems to have extended to and enclosed the site of the present little Turkish town of Koum Kaleh; for fragments of marble columns and other architectural blocks, which are found near the surface, denote the existence of an ancient city on that site. The existence of an ancient settlement to the south and east of the tumulus is attested by the masses of ancient pottery with which the ground is covered.

The tumulus of Patroclus is about 350 yards to the southeast of the sepulchre of Achilles, and the third tumulus, on which the windmill stands, is about a thousand yards still farther to the south.

The tomb of Achilles . . . is situated immediately to the northeast of Cape Sigeum, at a lesser height, on the very border of the high table-land which falls off abruptly, and is about 250 yards from the Hellespont. On account of its high situation it can be seen from a great distance out at sea, and it answers therefore very well to the indications of Homer. "Then we the holy host of Argive warriors piled over them (thy bones) a great and goodly tomb on a jutting headland upon the wide Hellespont, that it might be visible far off from the sea, to men who now are, and to those that shall hereafter be born."

In the spring of 1879 the proprietors of these tumuli asked me £100 for permission to explore the tomb of Achilles, and as much for that of Patroclus, but now they had considerably modified their pretensions and asked only £20 for each, whilst I offered only £1. Happily the civil governor of the Dardanelles, Hamid Pasha, came out in April to see my works, and I profited by this opportunity to explain the matter to him, and to convince him that the demand of the proprietors was exorbitant and ridiculous. He thereupon decided that I should at once commence the exploration of the two tumuli, with or without the consent of the proprietors; and that, in case they were not satisfied with £2, or at the utmost £3, he would, after the exploration had been finished, send out an expert to get the damage estimated and ascertain the indemnity the two proprietors were entitled to. Being afraid to come off second best by waiting, the two men now eagerly accepted £3 in full settlement of their claim. But as by the Turkish law they were entitled to one-third of any treasure-trove that might be discovered, they watched the progress of the excavation most vigilantly, and never left it for a moment. But they were greatly disappointed, not I; for, having found no gold or silver in the six tumuli which I had explored before, I had not the slightest hope of discovering any now. All I expected to find was pottery, and this I found in abundance. I assigned to each tumulus a gendarme and four of my very best Turkish workmen, of whom I was sure that they would work just as assiduously without an overseer as with one. The duty of the gendarme was to look sharp that all, even the smallest potsherds, were carefully collected, and nothing thrown away. . . .

[The tumulus of Achilles] had been explored in 1786 by a Jew, by order and on account of Count Choiseul-Gouffier, who was at that time the French ambassador at Constantinople. . . . He pretended to have found in the cavity a large quantity of charcoal, ashes impregnated with fat, several bones, among which were the upper part of a tibia and the fragment of a skull; also the fragments of an iron sword, and a bronze figure seated in a chariot with horses, as well as a large quantity of fragments of pottery, exactly similar to the Etruscan, some of which was much burnt and vitrified, whereas all the painted terra-cotta vessels were unhurt. But as no man of experience or worthy of confidence was present at the exploration, scholars appear to have distrusted the account from the first, and to have thought that the Jew, in order to obtain a large reward, had procured and prepared beforehand all the objects he pretended to have found at the bottom of the tumulus. . . .

As in all the tumuli of the Troad explored by me in 1873 and 1879, I found in the tumulus of Achilles no trace of bones, ashes, or charcoal—in fact no trace of a burial. . . . Of fragments of pottery large quantities were turned up, among which there are two or three pieces of the lustrous black hand-made pottery which is peculiar to the first and most ancient city of

Hissarlik. But these potsherds must have lain on the ground when the tumulus was erected. . . .

The tumulus described in the *Odyssey* as the tomb of Achilles, situated on the jutting headland on the shore of the Hellespont, can be no other than this mound; and there can be no doubt that the poet had this one also in view, when he makes Achilles order the tumulus of Patroclus to be erected: "I do not, however, advise you to make the tomb too high, but as is becoming; at a future time you may pile it up broad and high, you Achaeans who survive me and remain in the ships with many oars."

The passage just cited seems to prove that in Homer's mind there was only one tumulus raised for Patroclus and Achilles. But it is highly probable that the two neighbouring tumuli also existed in the Homeric age, or at least the one which is now attributed to Patroclus. This latter had been excavated in 1855 by Mr. Frank Calvert, of the Dardanelles, in company with some officers of the British fleet. They sank an open shaft in it and dug down to the rock, without finding anything worth their notice. But at that time archaeologists had not yet given any attention to the fragments of ancient pottery. . . .

I was very anxious to excavate the tumulus of Patroclus again, in order to gather the potsherds, which I felt sure of finding. . . .

I found in this tumulus exactly the same archaic pottery as in the tumulus of Achilles, though in a much less considerable quantity; further, a long fragment of a flute of potstone, the *lapis ollaris* of Pliny, of which also the flutes are made which I found in my excavation in Ithaca and Mycenae. I found here likewise neither human bones, nor ashes, nor charcoal, nor any other traces of a burial. We have, therefore, to add the conical mounds of Achilles and Patroclus to the six other tumuli, which my previous exploration had proved to be mere *cenotaphia* or memorials. . . .

Far more interesting than any of the tumuli explored by me in the Troad, is the mound attributed by the tradition of all antiquity to the hero Protesilaus, who led the warriors of Phylacé in Thessaly against Troy, and not only, on the arrival of the fleet, was the first Greek who jumped on shore, but also the first who was killed. . . .

The tumulus of Protesilaus lies near the further end of the small but beautiful valley of exuberant fertility, which extends between Seddul Bahr and Elaeus. This sepulchre . . . is now only 10 m. high, but as it is under cultivation, and has probably been tilled for thousands of years, it must originally have been much higher. In order to facilitate its cultivation, its west, south, and east sides have been transformed into three terraces, sustained by masonry, and planted with vines, almond-trees, and pomegranate-trees.

The top and the northern slope are sown with barley, and also planted with vines, olive-trees, pomegranate-trees, and some beautiful elms, which last vividly called to my recollection the dialogue in Philostratus between a vinedresser and a Phoenician captain, in which the former speaks of the elm trees planted round the tomb of Protesilaus by the Nymphs, of which he says that the branches turned towards Troy blossomed earlier, but that they also shed their leaves quickly and withered before the time. It was also said that if the elms grew so high that they could see Troy, they withered away, but put forth fresh shoots from below. . . . This tumulus is now called "Kara Agatch Tepeh," which means, "hill planted with black trees."

On my visit to the place, I went in company with my Turkish delegate Moharrem Effendi, a servant, two gendarmes, and four strong workmen, on horseback down to Koum Kaleh, whence we crossed the Hellespont in a boat to Seddul Bahr, and proceeded thence on foot. I was amazed to find not only the tumulus, but also the gardens around it, strewn with fragments of thick lustrous black pottery; of bowls with long horizontal tubes for suspension on two sides of the rim . . . or of vases with double vertical tubular holes for suspension on the sides; also with fragments of shining black bowls, with an incised ornamentation filled with chalk to strike the eye. . . . This pottery only occurs at Troy in the first city, and it is by far the most ancient I have ever seen. It is therefore quite inconceivable how, after having been exposed here for perhaps four thousand years to frost and heat, rain and sunshine, it could still look quite fresh; but it bewilders the mind still more to think how the chalk, with which the ornamentation was filled in, could have withstood for long ages the inclemencies of the seasons. I also picked up there many feet of terra-cotta tripods; saddle-querns of trachyte; small knives or saws of chalcedony or flint; some rude hammers of black diorite, together with a very fine specimen of a perforated hammer and axe of diorite, and a fine axe and hammer of grey diorite with grooves on both sides, showing that the perforation had been commenced but abandoned. . . .

Having heard that the proprietor of the tumulus, a Turk in Seddul Bahr, was in prison for the theft of a horse, and feeling sure that I could easily settle the indemnity later on by the intervention of the kind civil governor of the Dardanelles, Hamid Pasha; being moreover afraid that the ever suspicious and envious military governor of the Dardanelles, Djemal Pasha, might throw obstacles in my way; I did not lose a moment of my precious time, and, having brought with me pickaxes, shovels, baskets, etc., I at once ordered the four workmen to sink, just in the middle of the summit, a shaft three mètres in length and breadth. . . . [Two days later, when the work was stopped by the suspicious Turks] my four workmen had dug down to a depth of 2.50 m., and had found large quantities of most ancient pottery, similar to that of the first and second cities of Hissarlik; some perforated balls of serpentine; a number of excellent axes of diorite; large masses of rude stone hammers, corn-bruisers, saddle-querns, and other interesting things, among which was a pretty bronze knife. . . .

The pottery with which the tumulus and the gardens around it are strewn, and which also predominates among the terra-cottas in the hill, is most decidedly identical with that of the first city of Troy, and proves with certainty that here, on the Thracian Chersonese, there lived in a remote prehistoric age a people of the same race, habits, and culture, as the first settlers on the hill of Hissarlik. With the *débris* of this ancient settlement, and probably long after it had ceased to exist, was erected the tumulus of Protesilaus, to the probable date of which we have a key in the latest pottery contained in the tomb. Now as I find among the pottery a great quantity of a similar type and of a like fabric to the pottery of the second, the burnt city of Troy, and nothing later, we may attribute the tumulus with the very greatest probability to the time of the catastrophe, which gave rise to the legend of the Trojan War. . . .

As the latest pottery contained in Kara Agatch Tepeh is identical with that of the second settlement of Troy, there is nothing to contradict the tradition, that this tumulus belongs to the actual time of the Trojan War; and who then shall gainsay the legend that it marked the tomb of the first Greek who leaped down on the Trojan shore on the arrival of the fleet? . . .

Now to recapitulate the results of my five months' Trojan campaign of 1882: I have proved that in a remote antiquity there was in the plain of Troy a large city, destroyed of old by a fearful catastrophe, which had on the hill of Hissarlik only its acropolis, with its temples and a few other large edifices, whilst its lower city extended in an easterly, southerly, and westerly direction, on the site of the later Ilium; and that, consequently, this city answers perfectly to the Homeric description of the site of *sacred Ilios*. . . .

My work at Troy is now ended for ever, after extending over more than the period of *ten years*, which has a fated connection with the legend of the city. How many tens of years a new controversy may rage around it, I leave to the critics: *that* is their work; *mine* is done. . . . How it has been performed I now leave finally to the judgment of candid readers and honest students. . . .

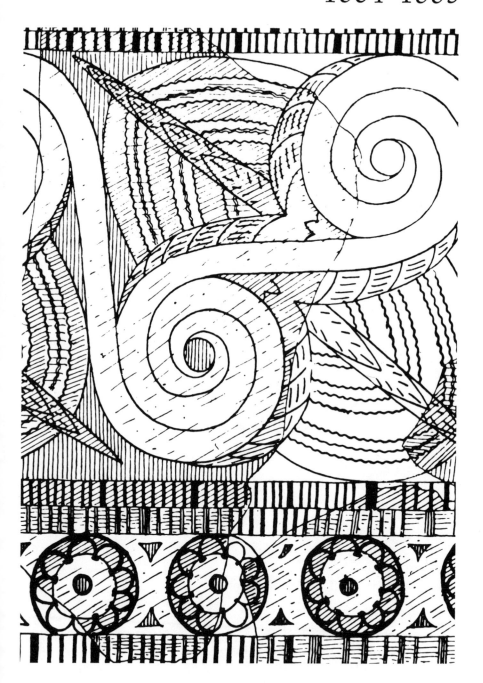

WITH HIS TROJAN LABORS terminated "forever" after the 1882 campaign, many projects buzzed in Schliemann's head. In his letters he would drop a string of names: Samos, Delphi, Asine (Argolis), Lamadeia (Boeotia), Marathon, Pylos, Sparta, Tiryns, and more. He asked Virchow's opinion on Goshen in Egypt. Sayce suggested Sardis, the old Lydian capital, while another British colleague recommended Boghazkoi (Hattusas), the Hittite center in central Anatolia. Professor Max Müller called for exploring India. Later Schliemann seriously considered Kadesh on the Orontes (Syria), but he was kept away from it by an outbreak of the plague. The subject of the Oriental roots of and contacts with the Homeric world, so evident in the objects he had found, increasingly drew his interest and turned him toward the East. More and more there began to loom Crete. It seems to have been first brought to his attention by classicist friends, foremost Arthur Milchöfer, a historian of Greek art and architecture associated with the German Archaeological Institute at Athens, and Dr. Ernst Fabricius, who had been with Federico Halbherr in Gortyn[1] and who had reported on the dig by a Cretan amateur, fittingly named Minos Kalokairinos, at a hill near Herakleion, the alleged site of King Minos' palace at Knossos. Always the optimist, Schliemann was already proclaiming that he was going to start there in the summer of 1883. To that end, he now mobilized the German ambassador in Constantinople, von Radowitz, and contacted the governor of the Ottoman-ruled island, J. Photiades Pasha—the same man who as Turkish ambassador in Athens had reached a final settlement with him over the Trojan treasure affair and had since become a friend.

Meanwhile Schliemann was occupied in the years 1882 and 1883 with his usual postcampaign chores. His letters of that period are a veritable jeremiad on his backbreaking literary labors. Even while he traveled—to Frankfurt in August 1882 to attend the annual meeting of the German

Anthropological Society (there he delivered a lecture on his latest discoveries at Troy), to Marienbad for his health, then to Paris and Boulogne-sur-Mer —he was constantly at work. Packages from printers and editors trailed him everywhere. Because of these duties Schliemann was forced to confine himself to archaeological sideshows. In Athens in the winter of 1882, he received permission (to be implemented by agreements with individual property owners) to dig along the ancient road to the Academy, outside the Dipylon (gate) where, according to Pausanias, some illustrious Athenians such as Pericles were buried. Sophia joined him in the venture. But since most of the area was covered by houses and gardens whose owners refused him access, Schliemann had to throw in the spade. Soon after, in January 1883, he made his way to Thermopylae, looking for the burial ground (Polyandreion) of Leonidas' 300 Spartans felled by the Persians in 480 B.C. But, as during his previous visit in 1874, he was unable to locate the graveyard. To Virchow, who had been promised half the skeletons to be found, he had to telegraph *"unauffindbar"* (untraceable).

Work on the Trojan tumuli pointed to corresponding mounds on the Greek mainland. The brief abortive foray at Thermopylae was a start. A few months later, ostensibly to get away from his desk and work outdoors for a while, Schliemann focused on the famous Soros at Marathon, northeast of Athens, near which Greek warriors (among them 192 Athenians) were killed in battle against the Persians and where they were supposed to have been laid to rest in 490 B.C. Sophia again joined him. Schliemann cut deep trenches into the mound and, with an unusual air of cold skepticism, reached in a few days the conclusion that it was without any trace whatever of ancient dead. In this instance, later excavation by the Greek archaeologist P. Stamatakes was to prove Schliemann wrong.[2] In archaeology, as Schliemann's own successes dramatize, faith may not only move mountains but uncannily will help to snuff out their hidden secrets. Yet the reverse is equally true. Given his preconceived idea that ancient tumuli were, as a rule, cenotaphs, his Olympian gods were not going to bless him with counterevidence.

For the year 1883, Schliemann had planned a long rest period. But the Erinyes, in the guise of manuscripts and galley proofs for three books, pursued him. The drudgery somewhat soured for him the five-week stay with Sophia and the children at Ankershagen, where he had rented his father's former parsonage from its present occupant. Old friends, including Minna, kept calling, and his work made little progress. Immediately before the return to Mecklenburg, he had gone to Oxford to receive there on June 13, 1883, together with the King of the Netherlands, an honorary doctorate. At the same time he was named honorary fellow at that university's venerable Queen's College. After leaving Ankershagen, he took the cure at Bad Wildungen, a small German spa in Hesse. Then it was Paris again to confer with his highly trusted real estate manager.

When *Troja* was about to be sent to the printers, Schliemann became increasingly alarmed by new criticism of his work at Troy and Mycenae. It was then that he took first notice of the noisy nonsense propagated by a retired German officer, Hauptmann A.D. (ex-captain) Ernst Bötticher [Boetticher]. In Bötticher's opinion, the hill of Hissarlik, which he had not bothered to visit, had never been settled but was a so-called fire necropolis, a kind of crematorium-cum-columbarium probably stemming from Assyrians or Persians.

However, at that point Schliemann was more concerned with the aspersions cast on his Trojan findings by the eminent Scottish scholar R. C. Jebb of Glasgow (later of Oxford). Jebb had ventured to disagree with Schliemann on the various strata at Troy and raised doubts about the "Lydian ware" of the sixth city.

In Schliemann's opinion Jebb had proposed "lunatic theories." When writing to Virchow, he tried to account for them by the fact that the "donation of the Trojan treasures to the German people has turned several English scholars into my enemies."[3] Forgetting his recent honors at Oxford and the persistent German attacks on him, Schliemann made an ugly nationalist issue of Jebb's criticism, a stand the more absurd because he had formerly felt himself most vilified by the Germans. He now declared his own views were "those of any German archaeologist," which has shades of the Nazis' "German physics."[4] He then appealed to Virchow to come to his defense against the "raging English slanderer Jebb" and to contribute speedily a clarifying essay to the *Troja* appendix. Virchow obliged with a balanced retort, as he had done earlier in the case of the Russian crackpot L. Stephani, who declared the Mycenaean and Trojan treasures looted Celtic objects, and as he was asked to do again and again by an overwrought Schliemann crying on his shoulder ("Come to my defense!") and was about to do against Bötticher. He followed Schliemann's injunction not to honor Jebb by mentioning his name. Instead, Schliemann took it upon himself to attack Jebb violently in the text of *Troja*. When Harper and Brothers of New York accepted the book for American publication, they inserted in the contract a clause that the author should refrain from all insults. They now insisted on having Schliemann tone down his ill-tempered statements. Murray in London followed suit, and even the German editors extracted some concessions to good manners from the author.

Schliemann's immediate hopes for Knossos dimmed in early 1884, but just as the Troad led to Thermopylae and Marathon, so Troy was

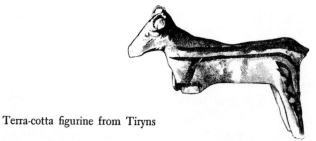

Terra-cotta figurine from Tiryns

a link to his next choice, Tiryns. Dörpfeld was again to be his right hand. This time the Greek Archaeological Society complied at once with his request, and the minister of education manifested at every turn his friendly cooperation. At last, Schliemann was held in high esteem in Greece.

All along he had been convinced of the importance of the formidable citadel that he had inspected as early as 1868 on his way to Troy. Tiryns, some nine miles south-southeast of its sister fortress and erstwhile rival Mycenae and only one mile from the sea, was built on a low rocky promontory above the Argive littoral. Reputedly the domain of Hercules, it was most likely older than Mycenae (definite Neolithic traces and a large circular early Bronze Age structure have been traced after Schliemann), though it may well have fallen under the latter's control, as suggested by legends and traditions. Its imposing, roughly elliptical walls, reflecting at least three main phases of enlargement, enclose, stepwise, three plateaus, with the highest one forming the citadel proper. To Pausanias its Cyclopean galleried circuit walls, all that he reported had been left of the mighty stronghold, were the most majestic monuments in Greece. Tiryns, like other Mycenaean centers, had come to an abrupt and catastrophic end by conflagration. However, smaller resettlements were planted in classical times, and as Schliemann had noticed on his second visit in 1876, there were on the acropolis ruins of a Byzantine church. Even then he suspected underground remains from the Turkish occupation.

The few days of surveying Tiryns in early August 1876 had raised Schliemann's expectations. But at that time he was about to launch his large-scale operations at Mycenae and had to content himself with digging trial shafts and, at the highest point of the citadel, one "long, broad, and deep trench" (as usual vandalizing almost everything that was in his way). He then brought to light some "Cyclopean" house walls, besides extracting numerous terra-cotta ("Hera") idols, vases, spindle whorls, loom weights, and the like. Unfortunately, he did not reveal the location and depth where the individual objects had been found, a shortcoming that would persist into his 1884 campaign and thereby render most of the materials useless for dating purposes.[5]

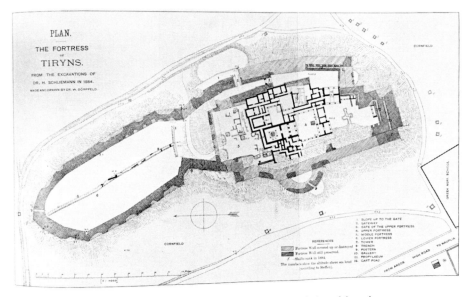

Wilhelm Dörpfeld's map of the fortress of Tiryns, showing the ground plan of the palace complex excavated by Schliemann.

A modern aerial view of Tiryns and the present state of the excavations.

The northwest ramp leading to the upper level of Tiryns, bordered by roughly hewn boulders of the Cyclopean walls.

A view of the corbelled gallery that forms a part of the imposing Tiryns battlements.

Reconstructed wall paintings from the
palace at Tiryns, showing a horse-drawn
chariot with two female figures (left); and a
hunting scene with a wild boar pursued by
dogs (below).

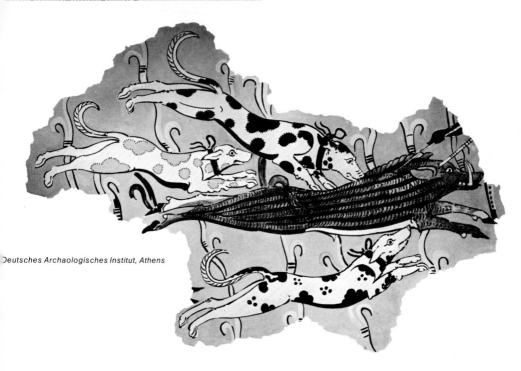

A northwestern view of the heavily eroded and deeply excavated hill of Troy at the time of Schliemann's last campaign in 1889-1890.

HISSARLIK
WIE ES IST.

Fünftes Sendschreiben
über
Schliemann's
Troja
von
ERNST BOETTICHER.

Auf Grund der Untersuchungen
vom 1. bis 6. December 1889
und
im Frühjahr und Sommer 1890.
(Nebst Protokoll der Zeugen.)

Mit 14 Plänen und 21 Abbildungen.

Berlin.
Als Handschrift gedruckt im Selbstverlage
des Verfassers.
1890.

The title page of one of the many pamphlets written by Captain Ernst Bötticher, a persistent and malicious critic, who claimed that Schliemann's major excavations at Troy were nothing more than cremation and burial sites.

Schliemann invited several prominent scholars to a conference at Troy in 1889 to settle his dispute with Bötticher, who is standing at the left next to the native guard. Schliemann is sitting in the center of the group, with Dörpfeld standing behind him at the right.

Schliemann and Major Bernhard Steffen, a German military man and expert map maker, examine a cut in the Trojan hillside during the 1889 conference.

Excavation of the eastern fortifications of Troy, begun by Schliemann and continued by Dörpfeld, which laid bare walls associated with the Homeric age.

The walls of the second city of Troy, with a view of a rail line constructed to remove the debris.

The northeastern tower of the sixth level of Troy, a monumental construction which Dörpfeld, who continued excavations here after Schliemann's death, thought to be part of the Homeric citadel.

Schliemann in Paris a few days before his
death in 1890.

The stately mausoleum in Athens, inscribed
"TO THE HERO SCHLIEMANN," dominated by
a portrait bust, and encircled by a frieze
showing the Schliemanns and workmen
digging at Troy.

Schliemann had gone to Tiryns in 1876 with his wife and three archaeology professors from the University of Athens. Fifty-one workers had
been engaged. But estimating that debris of an average depth of some
eleven feet (or thirty-six thousand cubic meters) had to be removed in
order to clear the upper, middle, and lower citadel, he regretfully admitted
that this was too large an undertaking for the time being. He, of course,
was convinced that nothing but near-total carting away of the accumulated
matter above the rock bottom would do. "I hope to accomplish that work
some day," he wrote, "but first of all I must finish the more important
excavation in the acropolis of Mycenae, and of the treasury close to the
Lion Gate, which I intend to commence forthwith."[6] Schliemann's three
Greek friends then returned to Athens, while he and his wife kept their
appointment with Agamemnon's shadow.

Whether Schliemann or even Dörpfeld had a concept of what lay in
store for them at Tiryns is difficult to tell. Schliemann's own account
hints that he knew and planned accordingly, while Dörpfeld when writing
after his arrival at Tiryns to his father-in-law and mentor, Professor Friedrich Adler (who had directed the German Olympia excavations with Ernst
Curtius), mentioned only the clearing of the fortress walls as an objective.
However, the uncovering and mapping of the newly discovered temple or
palace buildings of Troy II called for a comparison with the structures of
a Mycenaean citadel, then believed to be contemporaneous. In 1876,
Schliemann had failed to form an idea of the Tiryns interior layout. Conceivably, the insights gained at Troy in 1882 made him think of possible
parallels on the Greek mainland, and a full-scale investigation of a Mycenaean "acropolis" in Mycenae, Tiryns, or elsewhere became a logical step.
Ironically, the very fact that some building remains in Tiryns were still
visible on the ground and that others were relatively close to the surface
made Schliemann ignore them in 1876. According to his archaeological
canon, remains so close to the surface could not be that ancient. He seems
to have thought of them as Frankish. It is doubtful, given his rigid principles, whether without Dörpfeld he would have concentrated at all on the
highest platform, unless, of course, he had decided to demolish most of it
in order to reach the rock face. However, once the outlines of a vast and
intricate building complex emerged under Dörpfeld's sure hand, Schliemann brought his newly acquired know-how to bear on it, even though the
principal work was done by the young architect.

At Tiryns then, Schliemann was to approach a measure of archaeological
maturity, the wisest of all being that he gave Dörpfeld pretty much free rein.
His hope of finding treasure, which lurked behind his previous undertakings,
exerted very little influence on the actual work, except for his pressing the

search for graves on the lower terraces. He shared with Dörpfeld the main purpose of elucidating the building history of the ancient citadel. Thus his method became both more modest and more certain. For once, next to nothing was made of Homeric connections. The task of freeing the fundaments of the intricate palace complex was delegated to Dörpfeld. Schliemann himself was to supervise the workers, decide on further areas of excavation, and deal with such objects as pottery, effigies, spear and arrow points, obsidian knives, bronze statuettes, ivories, glassware, spindle whorls, and weaponry. By the way, no gold, except for a minute "ornament," was encountered.

In *Tiryns*, the report on the expedition which was significantly subtitled *The prehistoric palace of the kings of Tiryns*, the chapters on the buildings were written by Wilhelm Dörpfeld. For once, Schliemann's assistant was not relegated to the back of the book. Such generosity was perhaps a token of his balance and detachment. However, it was a difficult concession for him to make, and he arrived at it only after his publisher had convinced him not to consign so central a discussion to an appendix. So much had Schliemann learned to rely on the younger man that in the 1884 season, which lasted from mid-March to the beginning of June, he absented himself for several weeks to entertain a high-born guest in his Athenian palace. In the 1885 season, from mid-April to mid-June, Dörpfeld was left in full charge and Schliemann paid only brief visits.[7] In between, in the summer of 1885, he was in London to receive from the Queen the Royal Gold Medal of the British Institute of Architects.

The preface to *Tiryns* was a searching essay by Professor Friedrich Adler which has become a minor classic on the subject of prehistoric architecture. Therein Adler also cast doubt on the thesis, firmly asserted by Schliemann and Dörpfeld, that the Phoenicians were the founders and builders of the Mycenaean citadels. Adler also suggested that the *tholos* structures were tombs rather than treasuries. But his view that the shaft graves of Mycenae represent a gradually built necropolis of successive burials Schliemann brusquely rejected in a note following Adler's preface.[8]

Oddly, Schliemann's brief account of the excavations hardly conveyed the importance of the Tiryns finds. Nothing less than the hitherto unknown palace architecture of Mycenaean civilization emerged full-fledged. Just as the graves near Mycenae's Lion Gate had revealed the dead of that lost age in their full regalia, the buildings on Tiryns' citadel evoked with equal force and detail the abode of Mycenaean royalties when they were alive. There was a long ramp climbing through a portal toward a once heavily guarded massive main gate at the eastern battlement. From there one gained entrance via a propylaeum (columned vestibule) to a large courtyard, lined by halls and storerooms. Another propylaeum led into a magnificent colonnaded inner court with an altar[9] facing the large palace—a *megaron*, columned too, and consisting of a porch, an anteroom, and a main hall.[10] The hall, with a large circular hearth in its center, was undoubtedly the central building of the royal residence, resembling closely in basic design the large oblong edifices discovered in 1882 at Troy II. It was adjoined in turn by a multiplicity of chambers and smaller buildings, including other *megara*.[11] Nearby, to be entered from the left through the porch, was a bathroom with remains of a terra-cotta tub resting on an enormous monolithic slab of limestone weighing an estimated 65,000 pounds.

The entire palace was richly decorated, reflecting a prehistoric architectural splendor never before beheld on Greek soil. It added a whole chapter to the history of pre-Hellenic art and architecture. A few fragments of decorations from houses in Mycenae and the low relief ceiling from Orchomenos had been only a foretaste. Yet their motifs and patterns were repeated in the friezes and carvings of Tiryns. The palace walls, covered with alabaster plates, were inlaid with blue glass paste. There were well-preserved mosaics and painted floors. Most of the frescoes consisted of colorful geometric designs. Even more striking were tantalizing fragments depicting legendary animals, battle and hunting scenes, and, above all, a scene with a slim-waisted youth leaping on a sinewy bull. Such magnificence and vivacity reminded the excavators invariably of the Orient, and now more than ever they were certain they saw the handiwork of Egyptians and Phoenicians. The even closer affinity to the older (than Mycenae) civilization of Minoan Crete

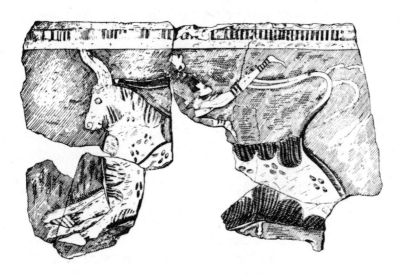

Wall painting from the palace at Tiryns: boy leaping on a bull

was still largely unsuspected. Dörpfeld's trained eye came to see the spacious *megaron* of Tiryns as part of an unbroken chain of Greek architecture whose early stage he and Schliemann had glimpsed at Troy and whose further development was mirrored in the Doric Hera temple he had excavated at Olympia. It reached its apogee in the Ionian temple of the Parthenon of Periclean Athens.

It is indeed surprising that in *Tiryns* Schliemann refrained from invoking the very close and real parallels to Homer's descriptions of heroic palaces. Up to the blue glass decorations the poet furnished counterparts. The layout of the royal palace with its halls, vestibules, and porticoes invariably reminds one of the castle of the king of the Phaeacians visited by Odysseus. Odysseus' own mansion has a circular hearth in its center just like that of the king of Tiryns. Homeric heroes—for example, Telemachos when calling on King Nestor in Pylos—are bathed before appearing in the palace hall of their royal host.

While Schliemann practiced unusual restraint in *Tiryns* and left the field to his more prosaic, clear-eyed assistant, he was more volatile in his correspondence. On reading his letters, telegrams, and notes, it almost seems that he had decided to dedicate his energies to publicizing the Tiryns discoveries rather than taking an active part in them. Within barely four weeks of the start of the campaign, he advised Schöne, Virchow, Brockhaus, and others of the amazing windfall. Contrary to the position he adopted in the book, Schliemann took full center stage. "Long live Pallas Athena," he wrote to Virchow on April 12 from Tiryns, "due to whose protection I have uncovered here a prehistoric palace decorated with innumerable Doric columns, which occupies the entire fortress. All its walls, constructed from large cemented stones, are preserved up to a height of 50 cm. to one meter; the top part of it consists as in Troy of tiles. . . . Most strange are the multicolored wall paintings, among them the pattern of the *thalamos* ceiling of Orchomenos. . . . I am writing this in greatest haste."[12] A few days earlier he sent a triumphant telegram to a magazine editor in Athens, reminiscent of the one he expedited to the King of Greece on Mycenae, thereby releasing the great news to the world at large. In May, writing to a prominent Russian, he did not hesitate to call his recent discovery of a giant prehistoric palace "one of the most astonishing of this century."[13] To Gladstone he rushed a similar terse news bulletin. His honored friend Vulpiotis (Boulpiotes), the Greek minister of education, was treated to an epistle in Schliemann's own flamboyant brand of ancient Greek. Therein he expressed his thanks for the minister's invaluable help: "In my book on Tiryns you will be mentioned as benefactor of this enterprise. I realize with prideful joy that once again the gods granted me an opportunity to enrich Greece with one of the most important archae-

Staircase within the fortress at Tiryns

ological discoveries ever made. Until now, the ground plan of the ancient Greek house was unknown. I, however, thanks to good fortune have brought to light not a common habitation but the great palace of the legendary kings of Tiryns so that from now till the end of time (till the Last Judgment) it will be impossible to ever publish a book on ancient art that does not contain my plan of the Palace of Tiryns. . . ."[14]

Despite the era of good feeling he had now entered with the Greek authorities, during the campaign Schliemann had his customary spats with the Greek official dispatched as inspector of operations. It was the Stamatakes story all over again. The archaeology delegate protested Schliemann's high-handedness, reported to the *ephoria* (Archaeology Society) in Athens, and got nowhere. True to pattern, the delegate repeatedly asked to be relieved of his awesome duties. But Schliemann had become persona grata, and the official was advised to put up with the eccentric German's whims.

Schliemann and Dörpfeld's momentous achievements were never quite greeted with the same fanfare as the Trojan and Mycenaean bonanzas. For that one can hardly blame Schliemann. He did his utmost to keep Tiryns in the public eye and would see that articles (some probably commissioned and paid for by him) appeared in the press. In the summers of 1884 and 1885 he traveled to the annual meetings of the German Anthropological Society in order to apprise his fellow members of his spectacular Tiryns discoveries. The lectures were accompanied by the showing of special maps and sketches Dörpfeld had been pressed to prepare in a hurry.

At Breslau in 1884, Schliemann and Virchow were lionized by the entire city, and their names were written in flames from oil lamps against the sky. The fact that his name vanished first put Schliemann, however, into a gloomy mood and prompted one of his now more frequent premonitions of death and oblivion. The next year, at the Karlsruhe congress, he quarreled with Virchow for some unknown reason, and the friendship was, in Schliemann's terms, forever dissolved. However, within a year and a half Sophia availed herself of an ancient Greek privilege to bring the two men together again.

Like Schliemann's previous contributions, Tiryns occasioned as much debate as applause. Once again doubts were raised in England. W. J. Stillman, an American ex-diplomat now a correspondent for The Times of London, revived the old view that the Tiryns buildings were Byzantine and not prehistoric. This then by no means out-of-the-way opinion was backed by the highly respected F. C. Penrose, a scholar noted for his measuring of classical Greek buildings and his description of planned asymmetry and of the phenomenon of entasis (swelling of Greek columns). The long-standing dispute was finally brought before the Society for Hellenic Studies in London in 1886. Schliemann and Dörpfeld were present and successfully pleaded their case. Penrose, himself, after visiting Tiryns, completely rejected the Byzantine hypothesis. Stillman, however, had in the meantime been transferred to America, where he found a new target in Luigi P. Cesnola, the director of the Metropolitan Museum and erstwhile excavator in Cyprus.

Tiryns did credit to the author, coauthor, and publishers. Its writing was more succinct than that of all the previous works. Fine illustrations included Dörpfeld's meticulous maps, sensitive drawings of galleries and walls by the second architect during the 1885 season, Georg Kawerau of Berlin, and excellent colored reproductions of wall paintings and other ornamental fragments.[15]

This time Schliemann had called on Professor John P. Mahaffy to help with the English edition, particularly with the translation of Dörpfeld's text. Mahaffy, who was presumably compensated by Schliemann, was treated to constant nagging by the author. Dörpfeld's frequent revisions caused the translator considerable headaches and delays. Mahaffy, rather piqued, told Schliemann to inscribe Shakespeare's "Too swift arrives as tardy as too slow" on the walls of his palace. Under such pressure, and fully mindful of Schliemann's rude avowal that he was not to share in any credit or glory, Mahaffy had to confess that the labor had turned sour for him.[16]

When the book was about ready for distribution in October 1886, Schliemann sent Brockhaus a list of people to whom copies should go on his account. However, he informed his publisher that he would not pay for those review copies which "will enormously facilitate sales for you," since he himself had already paid for the reviews. Among such recipients was Dr. Karl Blind of London, "whom I cannot pay less than £50 for his dissertations."[17]

Tiryns had the same publishers as before in England (Murray) and Germany (Brockhaus), but for the American edition Schliemann reverted to Scribner's.

Upon receipt of the new opus, Schliemann received a cheering letter of congratulation from Sayce, who called the work "the fitting capstone of all your wonderful discoveries. . . . No one can have any hesitation in saying that it is the most important contribution to archaeological science that has been published this century. The mouths of all your enemies are now stopped forever. . . ."[18]

EXCAVATING HERCULES' FORTRESS

from *Tiryns*

It was not till March 1884 that I was able to realise my long-deferred hope of exploring Tiryns. The necessary permission was readily granted me by M. Boulpiotes, the learned Minister of Education, who was constant in helping me to overcome the many obstacles arising during the operations. . . .

In order to ensure that none of the information likely to be obtained from architectural fragments should be lost, I again obtained the assistance of the eminent architect of the German Archaeological Institute at Athens, Dr. Wilhelm Dörpfeld, who had conducted for four years the architectural department of the German excavations at Olympia, and who had helped me for five months at Troy in 1882. . . .

The necessary apparatus I brought from Athens, viz. 40 English wheelbarrows with iron wheels; 20 large iron crowbars; one large and two small windlasses; 50 large iron shovels; 50 pickaxes; 25 large hoes, known all through the East by the name of *tschapa,* and used in vineyards; these were again of the greatest use in filling the baskets with *débris.* The baskets necessary, known even in Greece by the Turkish name *senbil,* I bought in Nauplia. For the storage of these tools, for the stabling of my horse, and for the lodging of my overseers, I hired room in the buildings of the model farm started by Capo d'Istria, close to the south wall of Tiryns.[1] It has now decayed into a tumbledown farmhouse.

Dr. Dörpfeld and I found this house too dirty; and as there was near Tiryns only one suitable residence, for which they asked 2,000 frs. for three months, we preferred to live in the Hôtel des Étrangers in Nauplia, where we got for 6 frs. per day a couple of clean rooms, as well as a room for Oedipus [Schliemann's personal servant], and where the worthy host, Georgios Moschas, did all he could to make us comfortable.

My habit was to rise at 3:45 A.M., swallow four grains of quinine as a preservative against fever, and then take a sea bath; a boatman, for 1 frs. daily, awaited me punctually at 4 o'clock, and took me from the quay to the open sea, where I swam for five or ten minutes. I was obliged to climb into the boat again by the oar, but long practice had made this somewhat difficult operation easy and safe. After bathing, I drank in the coffee-house *Agamemnon,* which was always open at that hour, a cup of black coffee without sugar, still to be had for the old sum of 10 lepta (a penny) though everything had risen

Vase fragment: two warriors, a horse and a dog

enormously in price. A good cob (at 6 frs. daily) stood ready, and took me easily in twenty-five minutes to Tiryns, where I always arrived before sunrise, and at once sent back the horse for Dr. Dörpfeld. Our breakfast was taken regularly at 8 A.M., during the first rest of the workmen, on the floor of the old palace at Tiryns. It consisted of Chicago corned beef, of which a plentiful supply was sent me by my honoured friends Messrs. J. H. Schröder & Co., from London, bread, fresh sheep-cheese, oranges, and white resined wine (*rezinato* [retsina]), which, on account of its bitter [taste] agrees with quinine, and is more wholesome during heat and hard work than the stronger red wines. During the workmen's second rest, beginning at 12 and lasting at first an hour, in greater heat one hour and three-quarters, we also rested, and two stones of the threshing-floor at the south end of the acropolis, where we afterwards found the Byzantine church, served us for pillows. One never rests so well as when thoroughly tired with hard work, and I can assure the reader, that we never enjoyed more refreshing sleep than during this midday hour in the acropolis of Tiryns, in spite of the hard bed, and the scorching sun, against which we had no other protection than our Indian hats laid flat upon our faces.

Our third and last meal was at our return home in the evening, in the restaurant of the hotel. As my London friends had also supplied me with Liebig's Extract of Meat, we had always excellent soup; this, with fish or mutton, fried in olive-oil, cheese, oranges, and resined wine, completed our menu. Fish and many kinds of vegetables, as potatoes, broad beans, French beans, peas and artichokes, are excellent here, but are so ill-cooked with quantities of olive-oil, that to our taste they are almost useless.

Although wine mixed with resin is not mentioned by any ancient Greek author except Dioscorides, and even Athenaios makes no allusion to it, yet we may assume with high probability that it was in common use in the ancient Greek world, for the fir-cone was sacred to Dionysos, and the *thyrsos*, a light staff wound with ivy and vine branches, which was carried in processions by the priests of Bacchus, was ornamented at the upper end with a fir-cone.[2] Pliny also, among the various fruits useful for making wine, enumerates the fir-cone, and says that it is dipped and pressed in the must. . . .

The plain of Argos was apparently in early prehistoric times a bay running far inland; this was gradually filled up by the deposit of the numerous streams descending from the sounding hills, which, though now bare and barren, were then covered with forests. These mountains are highest and wildest on the west. . . .

In the southeastern corner of the plain of Argos, on the west and lowest and flattest of those rocky heights which here form a group, and rise like

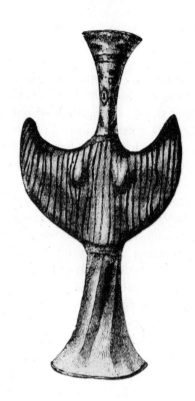

Terra-cotta idols

islands from the marshy plain, at a distance of 8 stadia, or about 1,500 m. from the Gulf of Argos, lay the prehistoric citadel of Tiryns, now called Palae-ocastron.³ . . .

It was held in the highest veneration as the birthplace of Herakles, and was famed for its Cyclopean walls, which in ancient days were regarded as a miracle.⁴ Pausanias indeed places them side by side with the Pyramids of Egypt, saying, "Now the Hellenes have a mania for admiring that which is foreign much more than that which is in their own land, and thus the most eminent writers have agreed to describe the Pyramids with the greatest minuteness, whilst they bestow not a word on the treasure-house of Minyas [at Orchomenos] or the walls of Tiryns, which nevertheless are fully as deserving of admiration." Even Homer expresses his admiration by the epithet τειχιόεσσα [teichióessa, "walled"] which he [also] bestows on Thebes:

"For those that held Argos and the walled Tirynth."

Pausanias says further of the walls of Tiryns, "The surrounding wall, which is all that remains (of Tiryns) was built by the Cyclopes. It is formed of unhewn stones, each of which is so large, that a yoke of two mules could not move the smallest from its place; the interstices are filled with little stones, in order to fix the great stones more firmly in their beds."

The stones of the surrounding wall are on an average about 2 m. in length and 90 cm. broad, and to judge from the existing remains the entire height must have been about 15 m. Had the blocks been hewn, they would certainly have disappeared centuries since; they would have been used in building the neighbouring towns of Argos and Nauplia, but the gigantic size of the blocks and their roughness protected the walls; for later builders found it easier and more convenient to hew out their own materials from the foot of the rock, than to disturb the walls and break up the colossal stones.

The quarry from which the blocks of the wall of Tiryns were hewn can be easily recognised at the foot of a rock on the high road between Tiryns and Nauplia, upon the summit of which stands a chapel dedicated to Elias the prophet. . . .

The great towers of Tiryns, of which one still stands on the east side, may have occasioned the fame of the Tirynthians as the inventors of tower building.[5] . . .

We may . . . assume, with great probability, that the gigantic walls of Tiryns were built by Phoenician colonists, and the same is probably the case with the great prehistoric walls in many other parts of Greece.[6] . . .

The myth of the birth of Herakles in Tiryns, and of the twelve labours laid upon him by Eurystheus, the king of the neighbouring Mycenae, is, I believe, to be explained by his double nature, as Phoenician Sun-god, and as Hero. It is but natural that fable should place the birth of this mightiest of all heroes within the strongest walls in the world, which were regarded as the work of supernatural giants, and as Sun-god he must have had many temples in the plain of Argos, and a famous cult in Tiryns, for the marshy lowlands by which the fortress was surrounded are even at this day in some places barren on account of their moisture, and in ancient days, as at present, produced pestilential fever, and could only be improved by incessant toil and the beneficent influence of the sunshine.

Thus the fable appears quite natural that Herakles as Sun-god had to perform the twelve labours for Eurystheus, king of Mycenae, to whom the whole plain belonged; these twelve labours being none other than the twelve signs of the Zodiac, through which the sun appears to pass in the annual rotation of the earth.

The panorama which stretches on all sides from the top of the citadel of Tiryns is peculiarly splendid. As I gaze northward, southward, eastward, or westward, I ask myself involuntarily whether I have elsewhere seen aught so beautiful, and mentally recall the ascending peaks of the Himalayas, the luxuriance of the tropical world on the Islands of Sunda, and the Antilles; or, again, I turn to the view from the great Chinese wall, to the glorious

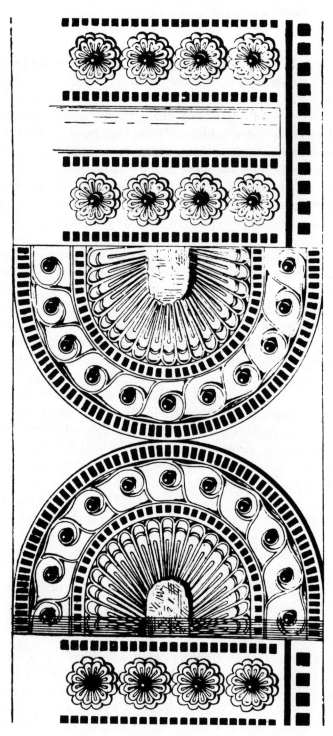

Restored alabaster frieze from the palace at Tiryns

valleys of Japan, to the far-famed Yo-Semite Valley in California, or the high peaks of the great Cordilleras, and I confess that the prospect from the citadel of Tiryns far exceeds all of natural beauty which I have elsewhere seen. Indeed the magic of the scene becomes quite overpowering, when in spirit one recalls the mighty deeds of which the theatre was this plain of Argos with its encircling hills. . . .

I commenced the excavation on the 17th of March, with sixty workmen, who were shortly increased to seventy, and this remained the average number of my labourers during the two and a half months' campaign at Tiryns in 1884.

The daily wages of my workmen were at first 3 francs: this, however, increased as the season advanced, and before Easter rose to 3½ francs. I also employed women, finding them quite as handy at filling baskets as men; their wages at first were one and one-half francs, and later were increased to two francs. At sunrise all the workers came with the tools and wheelbarrows from the depot to the citadel, where as soon as I had called over the roll, work began, and lasted till sundown, when all tools and wheelbarrows were again returned to the depot. In spite of these precautions, many tools and a wheelbarrow were stolen from me.

For work with the pickaxe I chose the strongest men, as it is the heaviest; the others suited for the wheelbarrows, for filling the rubbish into the baskets, and for clearing them again. As I desired to provide my people with good drinking-water, I set aside a labourer for the purpose, that he might fetch it in barrels upon a wheelbarrow from the nearest spring.

Another workman, with some knowledge of carpentry, I set aside for the repairs of wheelbarrows and tools; a third served me as groom. Unfortunately, I was debarred the pleasure of employing my old servant Nikolaos Zaphyros Giannakis, who since the beginning of 1870 had served me in all my archaeological campaigns as comptroller of the household and cashier, for, unhappily, he was drowned in August 1883, in the Skamander, on the east of Yeni Shehr [in the Troad], so I had to manage without him.

The labourers were mostly Albanians from the neighbouring villages of Kophinion, Kutsion, Laluka, and Aria. I had only about fifteen Greeks from the village of Charvati, who had worked with me eight years ago in Mycenae, and who distinguished themselves by their industry above the Albanians. . . .

Our first great work was to dig away the rubbish down to the floor made in the manner of mosaic, of lime and small stones, which stretches over the whole higher plateau of the acropolis, and was covered one to one and one-half metres deep with *débris* consisting of fragments of brick, tumbled-

Mycenaean stirrup vase

down masonry of stones bonded with clay and mostly calcined, and of black earth. It then appeared that the walls found by my excavations of 1876, consisting of large stones without mortar, were only the foundation-structure of an immense palace, occupying the whole of the upper citadel. Of its walls, the lower portion, built of smaller stones and clay about ½–1 mètre high, had been remarkably preserved by the close covering of *débris* over all the building, which came down from the higher walls of the edifice made of unburnt bricks, and from the flat roofs, which consisted probably of clay. This preservation is also due to the conflagration by which the palace was destroyed; for its heat was such, whenever beams of timber fed the flames, that the stones were calcined, the binding clay turned into real brick, and the whole reduced to so hard a mass, that our strongest men had the greatest difficulty in breaking it with pickaxes. Many of these walls thus burnt were visible on the surface, and had misled the best archaeologists,[7] as they were assumed to be mediaeval, and it had never been imagined that they could be perhaps 2,000 years older, and belong to the palace of the mythical Kings of Tiryns. In all guide-books for Greece, therefore, the opinion is expressed that nothing of interest is to be found at Tiryns. . . .

Owing to these many remains of walls as hard as stone, reaching to the surface, which the peasants could not break, the upper plateau could never be tilled—a circumstance which may have contributed not a little to the preservation of the remains of the palace. But the lower terrace, as well as the lower acropolis, and the narrow tract of land around the citadel, and enclosed by the roads, were let to a peasant in Kophinion, who had sowed it with caraway, and sued me at law for the damage done by my excavations. By the friendly intervention of M. J. Mavrikos, in Nauplia, the Director of the Excise, the damage was carefully estimated by experts, and fixed at 275 frs., with which the farmer had to be content. . . .

Our second great work was the clearing of the mid-terrace, where Dr. Dörpfeld thinks badly-built dwelling-houses must have once stood, which required frequent renewing, for we there found at various successive levels thin walls of broken stones and clay, with no plan now recoverable. The accumulation is there about six metres.

Our third work was the opening in the lower citadel of two trenches— a wide one along and a smaller across it—reaching down to the rock, by which it was shown that there also buildings, or at least foundations of buildings, exist. The accumulation of *débris* here reaches a height of three metres, though occasionally the rocks penetrate to the surface.

As our fourth work, I may mention the excavation and clearing of the ascent to the palace on the east side of the citadel. This gave us immense trouble, on account of the enormous quantity of huge blocks which had fallen on to it from the walls, and which had to be cleared away or broken up. Further, we cleared a part of the great gallery to the southeast, of which the upper part forms a pointed arch, and it should be remarked that we found therein a floor formed of concrete.[8] We also cleared one of the niches or window openings of this gallery, and partly excavated three other similar galleries.

The trenches which we opened in all directions under the acropolis, in which we found the same pottery as in the citadel, and much *débris* of burnt bricks, leave no doubt that the lower town extended round the citadel.

Dr. Dörpfeld and I have carefully cleared, before our departure, all parts of the walls of Tiryns which had been covered up during the excavations, and I can assure the reader that not two stones of the old masonry remain hidden by the *débris* shot by me. This can for the rest be easily proved by Hauptmann Steffen's excellent map, on which all remnants of the walls of Tiryns are carefully indicated. I have left the *débris* only in those places where the slopes of the acropolis consist of native rock or of earth covered with sporadic stones, and where, consequently, the clearing away of the newly-shot *débris* was to no purpose.

XIII
TROJAN FINALE
1889–1890

The plain of Troy, a drawing from Lechevalier's early
nineteenth-century travel book on the Homeric lands.

"THE STRENUOUS WORK has worn me out so much that I must definitely take a long rest, otherwise it will soon be the end of me."[1] So wrote Schliemann in a Greek letter to a friend in November 1885, announcing his book *Tiryns*, which had just been released in Leipzig, Paris, London, and New York. To see his latest opus, "probably my last," simultaneously through the presses in three languages and four editions, he wailed in the same letter, was "toil beyond description."[2] Schliemann had always groaned under the load of his publications, irritated by his compulsion to rush them through after the spade and pickax had barely been put aside, with no time allowed for reflection. But from now on hints of his failing health and allusions to his not-too-distant demise occur with ever greater frequency. Dörpfeld began to notice at the time signs of nervousness and exhaustion in the visibly aging man. Increasingly he was tormented by ear- and headaches, and there were signs of deafness. Maybe that is why he absented himself from the second-year campaign at Tiryns, even though his pace was undiminished, as was the number of projects he hatched. He was still racing all over Europe. Athens, his home, could never hold him for long. In the magic triangle of Paris, London, and Berlin he would as before stop at spas, attend congresses, see his publishers and search through museum collections. Nevertheless, he was contemplating longer respites.

Early in 1886 he once more, and by himself, crossed the Atlantic to spend a few blissful weeks in Cuba, St. Thomas, Santo Domingo, and Puerto Rico. He vowed that since his 1859 travels in Egypt he had never enjoyed a voyage so thoroughly. Though he looked into his Cuban railroad investments (he was not overly impressed with one of the railroads) and, as on former occasions, reported to the firm of Schröder on economic conditions on the island, he considered it a pleasure trip and later credited it with restoring him to health and vigor after he already had "one foot in the grave."[3] The trip did have economic consequences, however. When a year later Schliemann learned that the director of the Havana Railroad had left the company, he immediately sold out all his bonds and plowed them into real estate, mainly in Berlin and Athens. The purchase and administration of his new properties added to his work load. In his last years he even built and supervised new houses, some on behalf of the German embassy and German Archaeological Institute in Athens.

Back in Greece in April 1886, he was ready to plunge into new archaeological ventures. First he turned to Boeotia and with Dörpfeld reconnoitered in vain for an ancient shrine (Trophoneion) at Lebadeia. Afterward the two men took another look at Orchomenos and its famous treasury. However, the hoped-for royal graves, additional beehive "treasuries," and the ancient palace of the Minyan kings eluded them. By then Schliemann had again set his sights on what he thought would be the crowning of his archaeological career—Crete.

The island of Minos had first entered Schliemann's orbit in 1883, but when difficulties arose, he opted for Tiryns instead. Now, with his and Dörpfeld's discovery of a splendid Mycenaean palace, which bespoke of unexpected luxury and artistry, his attention turned with still greater urgency to possible links outside the Greek mainland. That the Mycenaean sites could not have emerged in isolation was suggested not just by Homeric traditions but by the profusion of Egyptian and Asian elements. Schliemann only on rare occasions doubted these Oriental connections. *Ex Oriente lux* ("The light comes from the Orient") was then a ruling concept of European prehistory. In any case, the fact that Mycenaean-type wares were being reported from all over the Eastern Mediterranean countries of three continents vouched for extensive contacts, which called for further exploration. Even though he believed in original Phoenician colonization, Schliemann, like many of his peers, was convinced that the island of Crete, poised between Egypt, Syria, and mainland Greece, would turn out to yield a vital clue. A few intriguing finds announced from time to time only helped to strengthen the likelihood for astonishing discoveries to be made in Crete.

Crete, in particular the hill of Kephalia Tselempe (outside Herakleion), where one had good reason to expect the buried palace of King Minos of Knossos, thus became another obsession with Schliemann. To Gladstone he called it "still virgin soil to archaeology."[4] Crete, he noted, would be just right for him because there was enough there to occupy him for the rest of his days. Since he had specialized in Greek prehistory, Knossos—like Troy and all of ancient Greece—was to him preordained territory.

"My days are numbered," he had written as early as December 1883 to Virchow, "and I would love to explore Crete before I am gone."[5] His friends, hearing of his choice, welcomed it wholeheartedly. Virchow answered, "Your plan for Crete has my full applause. Had you previously asked me for a suggestion, I would have made the very same. No other place is apt to yield a way-station between Mycenae and the East."[6] And Max Müller recommended the island neatly as "a perfect rookery of nations," adding what is surely one of the acutest prophetic remarks in the annals of archaeology: "There, if anywhere, you ought to find the first attempts at writing, as adapted to Western wants."[7]

But dogged attempts to get a *firman*, despite the assistance of the Turkish governor of Crete and the German ambassador in Constantinople, failed again and again. Worse, Schliemann's friend the governor was dismissed. Crete turned out to be a hornets' nest of political intrigue and partisanship. The governor was usually at odds with the local parliament. Besides, as in Athens, an important voice in these matters was wielded by the Cretan Archaeological Society or Syllogos in Herakleion. However, Schliemann, perhaps remembering Indiana, was inclined to think that "one can obtain anything there, one only has to choose the right means."[8]

At last, he decided to see for himself. On May 15, 1886, right after leaving Orchomenos, he went with Dörpfeld to Crete. In the main, the two men examined Gortyn, where the celebrated Greek (Doric) law code had been found carved on stone, and Knossos near Herakleion, the island's principal modern city. It was evident that Knossos represented an artificial stratified hill like Hissarlik. To judge from its sizable walls that Kalokairinos had laid free in 1877, Knossos no doubt contained a vast corridored prehistoric mansion. As at Troy, large *pithoi* were in evidence, which, as Schliemann noted in a sarcastic aside to Captain Ernst Bötticher, the ingenious apostle of fire necropolises, unfortunately contained nothing but lentils or beans.[9] He was struck, as he reported to Virchow (as well as to Brockhaus and Schöne) on his return to Athens in June 1886, by the strange fact that "otherwise one found in the edifice only pottery of Tirynthian and Mycenaean shapes and decorations."[10] That observation prompted him to pose "the interesting question, what one will find in the lower levels of this hill, if such very ancient terra-cottas are already scattered on the surface."[11]

During his stay, Schliemann met Dr. Joseph Chatzidakis, a physician and local political figure who was the founder of the Herakleion museum and presided over the Syllogos.[12] He promised his assistance in purchasing the Knossos hill and getting permission to dig. Again Schliemann's hopes were buoyed. He expected to start with Dörpfeld in October. However, he was less than sanguine about the Cretan stipulation that he would have to hand over all the articles he found to the Herakleion museum. Against Dörpfeld's advice, he tried instead to hold out for at least a modest share—

by now it had become his self-appointed mission to "enrich" the Berlin museums. Dörpfeld was certain that Schliemann would eventually receive duplicates and objects that the Cretan antiquarians deemed worthless, just as the Germans had at Olympia, though by law everything belonged to the Greeks.

In the meantime, Chatzidakis located the elusive owner, who demanded the exorbitant sum of 100,000 francs. In the purchase price was included, besides the hill, a supposedly large plantation of olive trees. To reduce costs, Schliemann now urged Chatzidakis to find a buyer for the plantation. He was prepared to wait.

For once Schliemann thoroughly enjoyed being without any immediate commitments. No books had to be written or proofs corrected. His alternate plan to excavate with Dörpfeld the "acropolis" (or palace) of Mycenae had been turned down by the Greek government in favor of Greek archaeologists. Schliemann was sure that his Greek confrères would botch it and sooner or later Mycenae would fall into his lap.[13] Finding himself with nothing to do and elated over his freedom, he planned to go on a long trip beginning in December 1886 and lasting into March 1887 with his wife up the Nile to the Second Cataract at Wadi Halfa.

Schliemann did it in style. He rented a luxurious multichambered *dahabiyeh* (houseboat with sails) from Thomas Cook & Son. A crew of ten would look after his needs. At the last moment, however, Sophia, afraid of seasickness and hesitant to leave her two children, backed out. So Schliemann, boarding his bark in Cairo, went it alone, taking along only a consumptive servant ("Pelops"), whom he hoped the Egyptian climate would cure. Alas, the dying man soon had to be put ashore. Before leaving Cairo, Schliemann visited the Bulaq museum.[14] The mummies of the New Kingdom pharaohs such as Ramses II and Sethi I made the greatest impression on him, but he lamented that little was done to keep them in a good state of preservation.

His third visit to Egypt (he had been there last on his trip around the world) afforded Schliemann balm as well as excitement. Floating on the great river at a leisurely pace, he would occasionally dock and visit the succession of overpowering sites of ancient civilization that lined the shores. Egypt was old when Rome and Athens and Jerusalem were young— old even when the lords of Mycenae and Troy warred against each other. He went into ecstasy over the gigantic reliefs at the Ramesside temples of Abu Simbel, "the world's most powerful works of art."[15] On disembarking he would look after the medical needs of the natives and recite to them from the Koran. Though he had formed a low opinion of his Egyptian servants, he fell in love with the black-skinned Nubians and could not admire enough their cleanliness, physical bearing, and natural nobility. He thought the women, though mutilated by jewelry implanted in their faces, among the most beautiful anywhere. On his shore visits he was also on the lookout for Egyptian antiquities but frankly felt uncertain about their age and value. In the main, he collected ancient stone tools and Nubian and Egyptian pottery which he thought were virtually unknown in Europe and needed to be represented in the "Schliemann Museum" of Berlin. Most of the time, however, was spent in exhilarating isolation walking on the deck, reading (mainly Homer and the Greek classics), and writing his 257-page diary, in which he entered motley numerical data (daily temperatures, river depths, etc.) and copied Greek inscriptions and hieroglyphic signs.

He had hardly returned to Athens when he made plans for another Nile voyage. This time he hoped to entice Virchow, who was intrigued by the hope for skulls of the most ancient Egyptians. A date was set for October but later postponed until February 1888.

During Schliemann's trip to Egypt, the Cretan business made little progress. Chatzidakis managed to reduce the asking price for the Knossos estate to some 70,000 francs, but Schliemann was not inclined to buy all the land, particularly since he learned that it consisted of separate plots, including worthless marshland and decrepit buildings. He quoted the Apostle Paul, "The Cretans are all liars" and remarked that he had "lost all enthusiasm to start the great work."[16] Instead, he applied to the Greek minister of education to be allowed to excavate the Apollo Oracle at Delphi with Dörpfeld but was refused. The site went to French archaeologists. He briefly seems to have considered returning to Troy but was discouraged by the fact that his faithful factotum Nikolaos had died.

Schliemann's second Nile trip within a year was to be, at least in part, a busman's holiday. Before Virchow's arrival in February 1888, Schliemann had made plans to excavate for one week in Alexandria. Naturally he had set for himself a high target—nothing less than the lost mausoleum (Soma) of Alexander the Great. The Egyptian prime minister, Nubar Pasha, who had previously been approached by the German ambassador in London, was most cooperative in letting the celebrated archaeologist demonstrate his infallible instinct. But when Schliemann was ready to arrange for the excavation, Alexandrine religious authorities, who owned the land where he suspected Ptolemaic palaces and graves, put their foot down. Schliemann had reached the conclusion that the mausoleum was—at least in part— underneath the mosque of the Prophet Daniel and that was holy ground not to be desecrated by a nosy infidel digging for a long-dead pagan conqueror. However, as a consolation prize, the prime minister let him try his luck at the city outskirts, which probably included parts of the Ptolemaic palace compound. Thus, in order to pass time until the friend's arrival, Schliemann dug near a railroad station. At the bottom of a shaft, twelve meters deep, he came upon a Hellenistic marble bust that he strongly suspected to be the portrait of Queen Cleopatra VII herself. To Schöne he wrote that he was bewitched by the head and would like to keep it in his studio. However, he soon after advised Bismarck of his donation of the splendid "masterpiece" to the German nation and was tickled by the Chancellor's personal note of thanks.

On the trip Virchow stuck to his plan to study the cranial peculiarities of ancient and modern inhabitants of the Nile Valley and made a start right at the Bulaq museum with the royal mummies whose fate Schliemann had bemoaned the previous year. He also extended his researches to statues to establish predominant anthropological types. (In those days and long after, the distinction between brachy- [round] and dolichocephalic [longheaded] races was the alpha and omega of physical anthropology and of incipient racist interpretations of human history.)

In order to gain time, the two friends took an Egyptian mailboat from Cairo to Aswan. Soon after passing the First Cataract on another vessel, their party was treated to attacks from the Mahdi's remaining hordes of frenetic Muslim dervishes. But thanks to border posts and Anglo-Egyptian troops stationed there, they fought clear. One entire week was spent in contemplation of Abu Simbel. There Schliemann and Virchow conceived of excavating Kadesh on the Orontes, where Abu Simbel's builder fought the Hittites, as vividly depicted in the reliefs.[17] While in Upper Egypt, they learned of the death of the old Emperor Wilhelm I.

On the way back, they stopped for another week at Luxor. All the time Virchow collected skulls, while Schliemann, on behalf of the Berlin Ethnological Museum, kept on the lookout for painted ceramics, bronze weapons, and glassware.[18] In company of the ethnographer Georg Schweinfurth, they undertook an excursion into the Fayum and nearby Hawara, where Flinders Petrie was digging into a pyramid and had opened the adjacent Labyrinth. They delighted in the painted mummy masks and Ptolemaic-Roman funerary portraits Petrie had excavated. Petrie's charnel house also yielded them skulls.

Before parting, the two men traveled together back to Athens and jointly paid a brief visit to Mycenae and Tiryns. Schliemann was then compelled to stay in Athens for the next few months, supervising the construction of new buildings. Thus he was even unable to accompany his family during their summer vacation in the Engadin and was condemned to spend lonely hours in his empty palace. The new premises of the German Archaeological Institute, designed, like Schliemann's home, by Ernst Ziller, were

Effigy vase from Troy

about to be completed. Schliemann took great joy in the façade, decorated as it was with pictures of the Muses, and in the statuary on the terraces. He had seen to it that the interior was also done in the "Pompeian" fashion and had himself selected passages from the Greek classics to be inscribed on the walls of each room. Echoing Nietzsche's *Bildungsphilister* (educated Philistine), he solemnly observed of these cultural displays: "They strike an especially festive note and will fill many future generations of scholars with awe."[19] In another letter he remarked of the new archaeological quarters: "It is a splendiferous building, worthy of the Institute of the greatest nation on earth."[20]

In early fall Schliemann undertook an overdue Western European tour. Then he set out, under the aegis of the Greek government, on one of his whirlwind field trips through Greece. On his first leg—from the end of November to early December 1888—he headed for the southern Peloponnese. On Kythera (Cythera), Aphrodite's (and Watteau's) purple isle off the southernmost tip of the peninsula, he thought he had located the goddess' temple under a Byzantine chapel and sent off a telegram to *The Times* of London announcing it as a discovery of the first order, as important as his Mycenaean and Trojan coups. Then he looked futilely for Pylos and its royal graves and King Nestor's palace, which Blegen began to excavate with such success in the spring of 1939.[21] Sparta Schliemann judged to be totally barren of ancient remains. During a brief reconnaissance on the island of Sphacteria, where a Spartan army had been trapped (425 B.C.) in the Peloponnesian War, he located ancient polygonal masonry. Actually, he couldn't make much of it, but "because of its historical associations" he chose to label it—superlatively so to speak—as "one of the strangest monuments of all of Greece."[22]

The following year—mid-March to mid-April 1889—he continued in the same manner in the northern Peloponnese, pausing at Mantinea, Megalopolis (the birthplace of Polybius), and Lykosura, and then went

island hopping in the Ionian Sea. A special survey was devoted to the setting of the naval battle of Actium (31 B.C.), in which Mark Antony was
defeated by Octavian. Afterward Schliemann ambled through Roman ruins
along the coast before celebrating a homecoming to the Homeric world on
a revisit to his beloved Ithaca. On these two excursions he composed
lengthy letters to Virchow. Studded with an impressive apparatus of literary
references and learned comments, they were obviously meant to be passed
on for publication.

The Cretan business was still very much on Schliemann's mind. He
had not given up on an eventual agreement. All the time he stayed in correspondence with Chatzidakis. To Virchow he wrote, using almost the
same words as five years earlier: "I would like to conclude my life's work
with a great undertaking in the to me familiar field of Homeric geography,
that is to say, with the excavation of the prehistoric palace of Knossos."[23]
But the more he learned of the conditions in Crete, the more involved and
frustrating the project seemed. As to their antiquities, the Cretans were
basically split into two factions. One favored archaeological research and
was ready to remove obstacles at once. The other, more political, feared
that any excavated valuable objects were in danger of either being taken to
Constantinople or being destroyed in a coming revolution and hence
preferred waiting until the island passed to Greek sovereignty, as they were
confident it would in the near future; in the meantime, the buried cities
should lie undisturbed.

In January 1889, Schliemann learned that the Knossos estate had only
888, not 2,500, olive trees. Thus, Chatzidakis advised him, the owner (or
owners?) was prepared to lower the price to some 40,000 francs. The
Cretan urged him to close the deal by sending a substantial advance.
But the proposal disturbed the cunning ex-merchant, whose suspicions were
further aroused by the number of olive trees. Shortly after, he appeared on
the scene, bringing his gardener ("Priamos") along as an expert—on olive
trees, one assumes. When Schliemann confronted the owner, the price was
suddenly back to 100,000 francs, an amount that did not even include the
olive trees. There was a good deal of hemming and hawing, and no deal
was reached.[24]

At the time, Schliemann was also in consultation with the new governor, who simultaneously presided over parliament. Though Schliemann got
no binding endorsement, he went away with the prospect that the
Cretan legislature would give him a clearance during the coming ses-
sion, permitting him to dig anywhere in Crete as long as the Syllogos ap-
proved and he promised to turn over everything to the Herakleion museum.
To Virchow he confessed after his return that he had a miserable time in

Crete and repeated St. Paul's low opinion of the people. There is no indication, as usually asserted, that Schliemann ever gave up for good his Cretan project. Nor can it, in fairness, be maintained that the project foundered on his penny-pinching. "The truth is that I will not abandon hope," he declared at the time, "to excavate in Knossos or somewhere else in Crete."[25] However, it so happened that other events intervened. As anticipated, political unrest broke out in Crete and transactions were stalled. Schliemann himself was diverted by pressing matters elsewhere that for the time being eclipsed his pursuit of King Minos.

Once again he felt himself severely tested by controversies. True enough, the Yankee journalist was stalking a new victim back in America, Jebb was silent, Penrose had officially declared that he had been mistaken on all grounds, Ernst Curtius, now a friend, had long ago acknowledged Schliemann's great contributions, the German academic establishment had virtually made him one of their own, honors and medals were heaped on him, and kings and princes sought out his company. But there was one source of attack that never dried up—the former German artillery officer, Captain Ernst Bötticher. He was able to totally unnerve Schliemann, who, insecure, self-righteous, and hypersensitive as ever, was never able to rise above his persecutor.

Bötticher and his crackpot accusations had first come to Schliemann's knowledge in 1883, just as he was beginning to train his eye on Crete. Oddly though, it was not Crete, but Bötticher, that occupied and haunted Schliemann's final years. Perhaps he was the more appalled by the monomaniacal amateur wedded to an unrealistic phantom because he heard echoes of his own obsessive tenets. Besides, Schliemann's overreaction was based in part on his being something of an accomplice to, if not the inspiration of, the deranged captain's hypothesis.

In the main, Bötticher claimed that Schliemann had excavated, at Hissarlik and elsewhere, not human habitations but burial grounds, a claim that may have stemmed from Schliemann's early readiness to see in every vase he excavated a funerary urn, and to turn cinders and even burned pulverized tiles into human ashes. Schliemann no longer made such flagrant errors, and all the other evidence from his excavations—the circuit walls, ramps, houses, palaces—totally contradicted Bötticher's claims. Although Schliemann and his associates had frantically searched for burials, they had not found any. Yet nothing would convince the captain. When the facts spoke clearly and loudly against his speculations, he quite bluntly stated that Schliemann and Dörpfeld had fraudulently tampered with them. In time he also implicated Virchow and anyone else who was associated with Schliemann's campaigns. Those who endorsed Schliemann publicly, he insinuated—perhaps not entirely without justification—were in Schliemann's pay. Furthermore, Bötticher asserted, to make Hissarlik (which naturally was not the site of the real Troy; Bötticher tended to place it in the lowland along the Scamander) or Tiryns look like the habitations of human beings, the archaeologists had torn down walls in one place and joined fundaments in another to create the semblance of houses. By the same token they had produced fake maps. Obviously not just malicious but also unbalanced, Bötticher put out pamphlet after pamphlet, sent off articles to newspapers and magazines, and blessed academic gatherings with his appearance and yet another paper on his deadly necropolis theme. Strangely enough, Bötticher was given a hearing wherever he turned. To Schliemann's infinite anger, Bötticher got himself into print in reputable publications whose editors Schliemann considered his allies.

Over the years, Schliemann tried various strategies to silence his enemy. He coaxed his friends to reply, write articles, take up the matter in meetings, and launch a war of words. At times, his own obsession with the debate easily matched that of his wrongheaded antagonist. Dörpfeld, though busy enough, was made to produce posthaste an exposé for *The Times*. Patient and obliging as ever, though not necessarily in agreement with Schliemann's combative strategy, Virchow rarely had any peace from this time forward: he had to speak out against Bötticher at the congresses and local meetings of the German Anthropological Society and produce reams of copy for the press. In January 1884, Schliemann told Virchow in no uncertain terms that if Bötticher achieved recognition in Germany, he would stop sending the fatherland any more of his Trojan antiquities. "Otherwise, however, I would be pleased to fill the Schliemann Hall [at the Berlin Ethnological Museum], since I have an entire floor in my house stuffed with things." Voicing his pain and self-pity he goes on to admit that Bötticher's "vicious articles have made me ill. I have to spell this out for you, because it helps

Terra-cotta whorl

to calm me down. . . ."²⁶ Thus, a few days later Virchow, always ready to cater to the friend's tender nerves, dutifully reported that "in last Saturday's meeting of the Anthropological Society I dealt with Herr Bötticher, I dare hope to your satisfaction. You have had once again your way and I pray it will soothe your tyrannical temperament."²⁷

Several of Schliemann's scholarly friends—among them Sayce, Ernst Fabricius, Schuchhardt, Johannes Ranke—politely declined to waste their time with retorts which would only help popularize Bötticher's cause and play into his hands. Anyhow, Bötticher was not open to rational argument. They strongly urged Schliemann to ignore such a quack and conserve his energies for better things. But Schliemann could be just as stubborn as Bötticher— and as irrational. When stung he had to fight back. He happened to be in Paris at the International Anthropological Archaeological Congress in August 1889 when Bötticher presented his latest brainchild, the pamphlet *Le Troie de Schliemann, une nécropole à incinération.* Schliemann was beside himself when his foe got a sympathetic hearing from the respected young French scholar Salomon Reinach. Yet he was cheered by the cordial reception he received from his French colleagues. At the congress he responded to Bötticher with his favorite argument, which had been first suggested to him by a natural scientist cousin: Where would the place of the living be if the dead were laid to rest high on the hill? In short, how was it possible that their cities had not been found? Was it likely that the Hissarlik people would settle in the malarial lowland, as Bötticher maintained, and deposit their dead on the salubrious ridge above? Of course, Bötticher could not be convinced. Schliemann, in turn, was as irritated as ever. Nothing but silencing Bötticher completely would do.

To appease the master, Dörpfeld then hit upon the idea of challenging Bötticher to accompany him to Hissarlik. Schliemann agreed to shoulder all expenses. Bötticher was evasive. Then Schliemann announced—in a letter to Virchow—that, thanks to Pallas Athene, suddenly at 3:30 in the morning of September 13, 1889, he had an inspiration on how to deal with the charlatan once and for all. (His plan was actually a modification of Dörp- feld's.) He was going to reopen excavations at Troy. Preparations were to start immediately "by installing tramways for the quick disposal of debris; constructing cottages at the foot of the hill; surrounding myself with a general staff of natural scientists, architects, and archaeologists, and asking Bötticher to participate."²⁸

Schliemann already had the work laid out for the new campaign. He was to follow the roads radiating from the three gates of the Pergamus into the "lower town." Then he was to clear more of the first settlement's wall, which had been first sighted in 1872. In addition, he would remove all that remained of the "acropolis" (in particular the western slope) stratum by stratum. Virchow's presence was both "desirable and necessary." The letter was sent from Paris, where the Anthropological-Archaeological Congress was still in full swing and Schliemann was due to talk on the civilizations of Troy, Mycenae, and Tiryns. It was the year of the fourth Paris World's Fair and the opening of the Eiffel Tower. To Schliemann, a starry-eyed admirer of modern technology, it was, indeed, the greatest show on earth. To enjoy it to the fullest, he decided to prolong his stay by several weeks. Virchow later joined him and was equally captivated by the spectacle.

While eagerly taking in the fair, Schliemann laid the groundwork for the Trojan meeting. Brockhaus was informed, "with greatest regret," that because of Bötticher Schliemann was forced to resume "at enormous expense and trouble" to himself the Hissarlik excavations in the company of a commission of scholars.[29] The German ambassador at Constantinople quickly procured a *firman*. Eventually two men were selected as neutral arbiters. One was Major Bernhard Steffen, an active German military officer who outranked Bötticher and who had made a name for himself through his maps of Mycenae and the Argolis in general. The other was Professor Georg Niemann, of the Academy of Fine Arts of Vienna University, who had distinguished himself as the architect at the Samothrace excavations. Bötticher had little choice but to come, especially as Schliemann paid for all his guests.

The conference started on December 1 and lasted for five days. Bötticher was shown around by Dörpfeld under the watchful eye of the two observers. The captain appeared to acknowledge the overwhelming evidence and conceded that his views might have been unjust, but in his own defense he claimed that his libelous accusations had only been made to stimulate discussion. He stood by his not altogether unreasonable opinion that there was no "lower town." He also refused to make a public apology for his personal insults, as Schliemann and Dörpfeld demanded. Schliemann then decided to break off any further relations. Bötticher was told that horses had been saddled to take him away. No sooner did he arrive in Constantinople than he renewed his attacks with an article in the *Levant Herald*. Needless to say, the two witnesses, Steffen and Niemann, disagreed with Bötticher on all points and signed a protocol to that effect. When winter storms set in on December 10, Schliemann closed the work for the season, only to reconvene a new conference at Troy for the end of March 1890.

This time it was to be truly international: attended by eight delegates —among them Virchow and Calvert, the Turkish director of the Imperial Museum in Constantinople, O. Hamdy Bey, and, as representative of the Smithsonian Institution of Washington, D.C., Dr. Charles Waldstein

(Walston), the director of the American School of Classical Studies in Athens. Schliemann must have relished the idea of being surrounded by an international elite of scholars who, no doubt, would acclaim his expertise over the sick figments of Bötticher's imagination—hardly a fair or worthwhile match. Somehow, the whole overblown affair smacked of a lavish party given by a parvenu magnate to gain social acceptance from the impoverished denizens of the old nobility. As such, the outcome was as much a foregone conclusion as the previous conference. No truly constructive debate of Schliemann's methods or interpretations was on the agenda. The protocol of March 30, 1890, only dealt with the rebuff of a strawman's absurdities and confirmed the Niemann-Steffen document. And it did not silence Bötticher.

If these conferences were expensive and needless puppet shows catering to their host's wounded ego, the excavations launched by Schliemann and Dörpfeld—mainly in the second year, from March 1 to August 1, 1890 —were among the most important in the long siege of the Hissarlik hill. Virchow put them in proper perspective when he remarked that Bötticher deserved thanks for having provoked Schliemann into launching yet another campaign at Hissarlik.

At the outset the second city had been the main objective. But Schliemann had all along cast a hungry eye on what he called the "lower city," and commissioned by him, Calvert had in 1889 found a Roman graveyard in the plain below. Would more ancient burials emerge?

Work could now proceed rapidly at various points thanks to the newly installed railroads, which hauled the debris away in no time. Dörpfeld's concern was to disentangle the three phases of the second settlement he had begun to suspect in the 1882 campaign. This time he was able to clearly discern the three different rows of walls belonging to Troy II which marked an expansion of the city in successive periods. While occupied with the walls, he came across additional gates, one positioned at the end of a ramp like the formidable entrances of Mycenae and Tiryns. The inner buildings, too, reflected various stages. However, these valuable contributions paled beside unexpected results from digging outside the walls of Troy II.

Because of Schliemann's initiative, major excavations were also initiated in the "lower city." Relatively little progress was made on the south side, where great masses, fifty feet deep, had accumulated, and time was too short to deal with them in a systematic and careful manner. However, substantial results were reported from another artificial hillside just outside the southeastern gate of the second city, where Schliemann wanted to stage an all-out effort to locate the necropolis of the ancient kings of Troy. Working on the assumption that it may have been built like the Mycenaean grave circle close

to—though outside—the main gate, he deliberately picked that so far untouched block. To come up with the burial ground of the prehistoric princes
would be the most effective argument against Bötticher, he reasoned. His
ambitions nevertheless went beyond a somewhat futile point of debate. He
was convinced he had a good chance to open the royal graves and hit upon
riches. Such expectations he repeatedly voiced in his letters. Writing to
Dörpfeld before the beginning of this, their last season, he talked openly
of the anticipated treasure. He had already made up his mind that it should
not serve to enrich the Turks but "would be needed to embellish our capital
[Berlin]."[30]

Alas, no shining gold was forthcoming, even though the prize turned
out to be greater and longer lasting. From his letters and reports one senses
Schliemann's impatience with Dörpfeld's disciplined procedures. Vast deposits had to be removed. To the younger man this was a first-rate opportunity to reexamine, within a smaller context, all the strata above the second
one, together with their remains of buildings and artifacts. His patron thought,
however, that they were losing precious time, because Dörpfeld would not
allow any of the structures which followed the second burned Troy to be
dismantled before they had been carefully cleared and photographed.[31]
Luckily Schliemann deferred to his young assistant and came to appreciate
the soundness of this approach. Later, in his own report he gave a clear
description of the "layer by layer" operations. (In this account Schliemann
at last produced a model of a well-balanced, unexcited progress report. But
fittingly his final archaeological summary closed with an invocation of
Homer.)

The startling discovery came about when the workers laid free two large
buildings. They had reached roughly the middle of the height, the fourth
layer from the top and the sixth from the bottom. This stratum immediately
stood out from the rest. Its ruins revealed parts of two archetypical *megara*,
recalling more strongly even than Troy II the palace complex of Tiryns. The
ceramics scattered about were of basically two kinds—monochromatic pots
that Schliemann had previously called "Lydian" and other quite different
shards that were of an unmistakably Mycenaean cast, with their graceful
shapes, painted surface, and distinct decorations (spirals, circles, stripes,
plants, etc.). Most telling, the ceramics included stirrup cups, jars, or cans,
which archaeologists have come to consider the very *Leitgestein* of Mycenaean
culture layers.[32] None of that specific Mycenaean ware had thus far shown up
in any other Hissarlik settlement.

At the time neither Schliemann nor Dörpfeld would commit himself
on the implications of this astonishing windfall. In their preliminary reports
both left open the question of whether the presence of Mycenaean-type

artifacts necessarily meant that they were contemporaneous with the flowering of these centers on the Greek mainland. Before all the ceramics had been analyzed and more excavations carried out, no rash judgment should be passed.[33] It is opportune to quote Dörpfeld's careful evaluation:

> This circumstance . . . allows us to draw the further conclusion that the second stratum . . . must be older than this stratum with the Mycenaean vases. How much older it is impossible to say, but the interval cannot have been a short one, as between the two lie three other strata of poor settlements. We cannot go any further than these relative dates. . . . It is certain that the jugs with stirrup handles appear as early as the 14th century B.C., but whether precisely similar ones were not used much later, e.g., in the 9th and 8th centuries, and eventually imported to Troy, must remain uncertain for the present.[34]

Both archaeologists agreed that at least two more seasons' work was needed at Troy. Schliemann already announced continuing the campaign in early spring 1891. Admittedly, the testimony from Schliemann's own writings is by no means clear as to how far he was aware of the importance of these finds or if he was prepared to face them head on. Probably he was more concerned with locating the necropolis of the princes of Troy II. All that can be said is that, like some sort of Moses, Schliemann in the 1890 season came to the very brink of his lifelong ambition—to behold Homeric Ilion and to perhaps solve the Trojan riddle.[35]

However, we have it from Dörpfeld that the surprises from Troy VI suggested ominous questions. The distinct possibility then arose that they had come across buildings belonging to a later and mightier "city" with circuit walls far beyond the limits of the second settlement. Could some of the impressive walls, previously held to be "Greek," actually have belonged to Troy VI? If so, one may have to consider that Troy II was considerably older than Troy VI with its Mycenaean affinities. But was it also much older than the Trojan War?[36]

Fate decreed that it was left to Dörpfeld to uncover, in 1893 and 1894, Troy VI, which was ultimately shown to be akin in age and civilization to the Mycenaean citadels of Greece. Whether it was also the Troy of Homer, as Dörpfeld firmly believed until the end of his long life in 1940, or whether that title should go to its less impressive successor, Troy VIIa, as Carl Blegen and his fellow excavators in the 1930's maintained, has never been definitively answered, even though Blegen has the edge at present. Acceptance of either stratum creates difficulties. But it is not without a sense of bemusement that one realizes that Schliemann seems to have hit the Mycenaean walls during his first campaign at Hissarlik, when he took them for Hellenistic structures raised by Lysimachus. Fair-minded Dörpfeld was the first to argue that had it not been for the Romans' leveling the top center of the Hissarlik hill to build the "acropolis" of Novum Ilium, chances are that Schliemann would not have missed Mycenaean or Homeric Troy, instead of fixing on a small, more primitive prehistoric settlement older by roughly one millennium. But Schliemann's dogged drive down to the naked soil speaks against his halting at Troy VI, since he then took literally Homer's allegation that the Trojans of his epic were the first settlers on the promontory. One should also remember that Mycenaean analogies were at the time virtually unknown.

During his last season at Troy, Schliemann found greatest satisfaction and joy in a discovery that is not even mentioned in his report—and for good reason. Toward the end of the campaign, near the eastern margin of Troy II and in the presence of Dörpfeld and only one worker, he had come across another treasure. It contained a number of small gold "needles" and other minor metal objects, but the prize pieces were four flawlessly carved and polished stone axes 33 centimeters long—three of green nephrite and one of violet lapis lazuli. Material and craftsmanship are now believed to point to Bessarabia in the Balkans as the place of origin, though an occasional claim has been made for a Central Asian source of the lapis lazuli.[37]

In his eagerness to top all his previous accomplishments and compensate for Knossos, Schliemann did not hesitate to call the pieces the most precious find he ever made. Some months later he wrote, on December 9, 1890, in all seriousness (in classical Greek, of course) about the cache to his colleague Alexander Conze: ". . . Thus it happened that when toward the end of June[38] I saw Pallas Athena in front of me holding in her hands those treasures which are more valuable than all those I uncovered in Mycenae, I was shaken by intense emotions. Unintentionally I fell to the ground before her. I cried for joy, fondled and kissed her feet. I thanked her from the bottom of my heart and begged her fervently that henceforth she should watch over me and continue to bestow her blessings on me."[39] Whom the gods wish to destroy . . .

Two weeks later Schliemann was dead.

The mystery Schliemann spun around his last Trojan treasure meant that he just plainly did not want to hand it over to the Turks.[40] Like the Bourbons he had learned nothing; he was still ready to break the law at his own convenience, while constantly ranting at the injustice done to him. In the light of such well-nigh incurable propensities, it must seem a miracle that government officials were prepared to trust his pledges at all and on the whole were not more suspicious. This last delinquency may well have been the reason that the German ambassador to the Sublime Porte, J. M. von Radowitz, who for many years had unfailingly stood up for Schliemann, noticeably cooled.

Schliemann's intention was clear. He wanted the cache for Berlin, and though nothing is known about how he proceeded—indeed, biographers making much of "Priam's Treasure" and his "just" behavior then, have usually ignored the incident—he smuggled them to Greece and there, in order to fool both the Greeks and Turks, declared them at customs as Egyptian antiquities so they could be reexported.

He would not have been Heinrich Schliemann had he kept his latest blessing to himself. Under the mantle of secrecy he informed Virchow, still from Troy, on July 15, 1890: ". . . I thought I was no longer Fortuna's special favorite . . . , when, on the 8th of this month, I found a treasure of immeasurable worth between the fundaments of a building. . . . It contains relatively little gold. Its enormous value is due to four colossal axes. There are also seven large scepter pommels of rock crystal and 50 'hemispheres' of the same material. . . . Greatest secrecy has to be observed. Even my wife will hear nothing of it. . . . Should I find the royal graves, then I'll stay until the end of the year."[41] Once in Athens "secret" communications went out to Schöne, the Prussian minister of education, and others. All these were warned that, should the Turks hear of it, Schliemann would be barred from returning to Troy next year, a trip which was necessary "to get rid of my libelist Bötticher."[42] In short, Schliemann had hitched his wagon to the royal graves of Troy.

Sad to say, Fortuna failed to watch over the Trojan treasures that she so generously helped to gain for their lucky finder and let him snatch away from "Turkish greed." Practically all the precious articles kept at the Berlin Ethnological Museum, including the stone axes, vanished during the fall of Berlin at the end of World War II (1945). Supposedly they were taken away by the Russians, but their whereabouts are unknown. (Some of the pottery reportedly was wantonly smashed in a Prussian castle where it was stored.)

Schliemann's ear troubles took a turn for the worse during the 1890 campaign at Troy. For longer periods now he was nearly deaf. He had to seek the help of a German otolaryngologist in Constantinople. On a short trip with Virchow to Mount Ida in April, the doctor became alarmed about his friend's deteriorating health. He examined his ears and noticed bony obstructions. He urged Schliemann to consult a surgeon who specialized in operations of this kind in Halle but told him to avoid surgery unless absolutely necessary. When during the course of the year his pain and deafness got worse, Schliemann decided to travel to Germany and insisted on going alone. While he was browsing through his extensive wardrobe before leaving, Sophia overheard him mumbling: "I wonder who will wear these clothes after I am gone." On the other hand, Schliemann seemed cheerful and promised to be back in Athens in six weeks. In Halle he underwent on November 12 a serious operation on both ears which lasted one and three-quarters hours. His condition soon improved. In the hospital he read, in Arabic, the *Arabian Nights* and worked on the proofs of his last publication, a report on the 1890 campaign at Troy that Brockhaus was bringing out with Dörpfeld's account and the protocol of the international conference.[43]

Bent on spending Christmas with his family in Athens, Schliemann left Halle prematurely on December 12. Despite the surgeon's warnings of a possible infection, he went on to Leipzig to see Brockhaus, then met in Berlin with the manager of his property, inspected the Schliemann Collection with Virchow and breakfasted with him, continuing the same day to Paris in a drafty train. In Paris he had to see a doctor, but seemingly on the mend, he wrote to Virchow: "Long live Pallas Athena! At last I can hear again with my right ear, and the left will get better."[44]

The next call was to be at Naples, where Schliemann wanted to visit the new exhibits at the museum and the recent excavations at Pompeii. Violent pains forced him again to consult a doctor, who, ill-advisedly, joined the famous man on a one-day tour to Pompeii. From then on Schliemann took a turn for the worse. Twice he cabled his family that he was delayed but would be home shortly after Christmas. On Christmas Day, maybe on the way to the doctor or to the post office, he collapsed while crossing a Naples square. Semiparalyzed and unable to speak, he was taken to a hospital. Carrying no identification, he was refused admission and carted off instead to a police station. Nobody knew who he was until the Neapolitan doctor whose prescription he was carrying was summoned. Conveyed to his hotel, a doctor opened his left ear, but it became evident that the inflammation had reached the brain.

The next day, on December 26, while a group of eight doctors conferring in the next room decided to operate, Schliemann died. Telegraph messages of his death went out to Athens and Berlin and from there by wire services to all corners of the globe. Wilhelm Dörpfeld and Sophia's oldest brother rushed from Athens to take the body home to Greece. Nine days later the coffin was placed under a bust of Homer in Schliemann's Athenian villa. Copies of the *Iliad* and *Odyssey* were placed in the coffin. The Hellenic King and Crown Prince held vigil. Eminent scholars and Greek and foreign dignitaries filed past the dead hero. The ambassador of the United States, Archibald Loudon Snowden, eulogized his compatriot as a true representative of the American spirit. Dörpfeld spoke for all when he took leave from his mentor and colleague: "Rest in peace, you have done enough!"

SCHLIEMANN REMEMBERED

In the early years living with this explosive, dedicated and tireless man of genius was a stern trial. . . . Throughout my own girlhood he would often get me up at five o'clock in the morning in winter to ride horseback five miles down to Phaleron to swim in the sea, as he himself did every day. He built us a veritable palace to live in, but it contained not one stick of comfortable furniture. He worked and studied standing at a high bookkeeper's desk. As a gentle hint Mother made him a present of an armchair, but he banished it to the garden.

His concern with health was fanatical. When my younger brother was baptized, with many guests solemnly assembled in the church, my father suddenly whisked out a thermometer and took the temperature of the holy water. There was a great commotion; the priest was outraged. It took my mother's gentle intervention to reinvest the water with holiness.

Beneath these imperious traits Father was warmhearted and generous to a fault. He was humble, too, in his own way. . . .

—Andromache Schliemann Mélas

Whittaker, the editor and proprietor of the *Levant Herald*, happened to be at Dardanelles when we arrived, and gave us an account of his first introduction to Dr. Schliemann. One morning when he was in his office, a knock came at the door and a visitor entered in the shape of a little man with a round bullet-like head, very little hair and a reddish face. "You are Mr. Whittaker, I think," he asked. "Yes," said Whittaker. "I understand," said his visitor, "that you are better acquainted with Turkish than most of the other foreigners here: how many words are there in the Turkish dictionary?" This was, said Whittaker, rather a poser, but he replied, "Well, I should not like to commit myself definitely to an answer, but I should say about so many thousand." "Thank you, Mr. Whittaker," said the little man; "in that case if I learn so many words a day, at the end of six weeks I shall know all the words of the language"; and he departed. At the end of six weeks a knock came again at the door and the same little man entered the office. "I am very much obliged to you, Mr. Whittaker," he said; "you were quite right in your calculation, and I now know all the words contained in the Turkish dictionary. Here is my card." It was Schliemann.

—A. H. SAYCE

Gobineau to the Countess Mathilde-Marie de La Tour

In view of Troy, Oct. 16, 1876

... We are at present on a steamboat chartered by the Emperor [Dom Pedro II of Brazil]. It is five in the morning. We shall disembark again and, traveling on horseback, look at another place [Bunarbashi] where Troy may have been, after having seen yesterday the site of the excavation of the great Schliemann, who is nothing but an impudent charlatan, a liar, and an imbecile. All this spoils the Troad a bit for me....

[Gobineau continued the letter after his return from Bunarbashi and Tenedos.] ... I am sending you a few myrtle leaves taken from the tumulus of Hecuba and a nice little white flower from the wall of Troy. As for the rest of the voyage, we made it under a cloud of pedantry, with Dr. Schliemann on the right and another German professor [Dr. Carl Henning] on the left. Fortunately, they took a dislike to each other.... Yesterday morning the Emperor made me swear not to contradict them. I have kept my word and agreed with them completely, making them say such inane things that the Emperor laughed himself sick. But what ingratitude! He bitterly reproached me, professing his innate dislike of mockery. This did not keep me from telling him today that everybody was on my side, including himself....

[On October 27, Gobineau wrote from Athens.] I was delighted to see

Mycenae again. The detestable Schliemann is digging there. He has found bas-reliefs which, if authentic (I consider him capable of any falsehood), are of major interest and may well change our opinions on the origin of art. We had a charming meal in the Tomb of Agamemnon on a floor strewn with laurel branches. . . .

—ARTHUR DE GOBINEAU

A special chance allowed me to be one of the few eye-witnesses of the last excavations at Hissarlik [1879], and to see the "Burnt" City emerge, in its whole extent, from the rubbish-heaps of former ages. . . .

It is now an idle question, whether Schliemann, at the beginning of his researches, proceeded from right or wrong presuppositions. Not only has the result decided in his favour, but also the method of his investigation has proved to be excellent. It may be that his hypotheses were too bold, nay arbitrary; that the enchanting picture of Homer's immortal poetry proved somewhat of a snare to his fancy; but this fault of imagination, if I may so call it, nevertheless involved the secret of his success. Who would have under-taken such great works, continued through so many years,—have spent such large means out of his own fortune,—have dug through layers of *débris* heaped one on the other in a series that seemed almost endless, down to the deep-lying virgin soil,—except a man who was penetrated with an assured, nay an enthusiastic conviction? The Burnt City would still have lain to this day hidden in the earth, had not imagination guided the spade.

—RUDOLF VIRCHOW

Dr. Schliemann generally spent the intervals of rest at Athens. His palatial house in the rue de l'Université reminds us at every point of the world in which its owner lived and moved. In the mosaic floors the chief specimens of the Trojan vases and urns are represented. Along the wall run friezes with classical landscapes and pictures from the Greek epic, with appropriate Homeric quotations. The visitor was admitted by the porter Bellerophon and conducted by the footman Telamon to the master, who was generally found reading one of the Greek classics and stopping at intervals to complain of the number of Stock Exchange lists brought by the morning post from Paris, London, and Berlin. These used to lie piled up on a chair by his side and had an incongruous appearance among the other surroundings. Dr. Schliemann was no longer engaged in business, but the management of his great fortune and the ownership of the several houses which he let in Paris, Berlin, and Athens obliged him to keep up his relations with the world of commerce.

Even the flying visits which tourists always made a point of paying him gave a glimpse of his family life. Dr. Schliemann was not like Goethe, who only now and then made a momentary appearance at the grating of his hall door. With unwearying courtesy he ushered visitors several times a day into his drawing room. There they found Mrs. Schliemann (*née* Kastroménos of Athens), a kind and gentle hostess, with her daughter Andromache, who has just reached womanhood, and her son Agamemnon, a boy of twelve. It was only within this circle that the warmth and tenderness of Dr. Schliemann's character came out. These traits explained not only his eager adherence and trustful loyalty to mythical tradition, but also the charity of his judgment toward opponents, which became every year more remarkable. He thus formed an exception to the general rule, that, with advancing age, men become more obstinate in their opinions.

—CARL SCHUCHHARDT

One of the most unique houses in Athens was then the sumptuous marble palace which Schliemann had erected for the display of his Trojan antiquities and as domicile for himself and his family. Murals and Greek inscriptions covered the walls, all tied in with Homer, Schliemann's actual household god. We [the German diplomats] maintained at the time active personal contacts with that strange man, since he had donated to the German nation the remarkable gold objects found in Troy, as well as large quantities of terra-cottas and several beautiful pieces of marble. It had been my duty to transmit to him a gracious note of thanks from the Kaiser for this valuable gift, which was on exhibit at the Berlin Museum. This put him into ecstasy. I therefore had to suffer through a detailed inspection of more than a thousand old Trojan pots which, lacking any artistic merit, commanded only paleontological interest.

However, I should mention a particular festivity that took place in the Schliemann house in the first week of March [1881]. To officially consecrate his new residence, he gave a dinner for all foreign ambassadors known to him, in addition to a number of Greek politicians. Culinarily speaking, the meal appeared to be more suitable to the palates of the ancient Trojans than to the requirements of modern digestions. During it Schliemann got up and held a speech in which he took each of the diplomats to task. He discussed the various countries they represented in an odd kind of French, spiced with even odder comments, which frequently, though most likely unintentionally, verged on insults and which produced varying degrees of embarrassment on the stunned faces of my colleagues. Schliemann, nevertheless, sat down fully satisfied with his performance and signaled to his wife. Thereupon she rose and read from a paper what was nothing less than a proclamation to her diplomatic guests. Directed at Europe as a whole, it was in reality a summons to assist the noble Hellenes, descendants of Pericles and Alexander, in their rightful claims to extensive lands at the expense of the barbaric Turks. Mrs. Schliemann, a native Athenian, was a person of great beauty, a pleasant, well-educated woman, who was joined with Schliemann in their common interests in antiquity. The rhetorical assault could not be left unanswered, and that task fell upon me as doyen of the diplomatic corps. I disposed of it at once by improvising as spirited a speech as I could muster on the superiority of Hellenic women so splendidly exemplified in our hostess—a theme on which all of us were pretty much in agreement and for which we could enlist far more enthusiasm than for any disagreeable political topic. Thus the whole show concluded with unanimous applause, though it had threatened to take a nasty turn because some of the people present lacked the necessary humor to cope with the situation. Afterward the incident was reported in the press, but fortunately in a mild version which helped to calm down my colleagues.

—JOSEPH MARIA VON RADOWITZ

In January [1888] Dr. H. Schliemann, the distinguished archaeologist and excavator, visited Aswân in one of the old dhahabîyahs, which were so roomy and comfortable. As soon as he arrived his secretary, or companion, landed and sent some of the crew to announce to the native officials that his great master had arrived, but with what object he did this no one understood. The British military authorities had not been instructed from Cairo to give Dr. Schliemann a public reception, and they did nothing. Mr. Henry Wallis, the artist, who very kindly made for me many drawings of the Aswân tombs, was very anxious that some one should show civility to Dr. Schliemann, and offer to act as guide for him over the tombs. Therefore he, Major Plunkett, and I were rowed over to the dhahabîyah, and announced ourselves. The butler received us civilly, and led us into the large reception room in the stern of the vessel, and after the usual salutations and coffee and cigarettes, Major Plunkett acted as spokesman, and said that we had called to offer him our boat and crew if he wished to go over to the tombs, and that we were ready to accompany him at any time, and show him what we had done. Dr. Schliemann replied very stiffly, "It is very kind of you to be so amiable. I should like to place my archaeological science at your disposal by showing and explaining to you the tombs, but I have not the time as I am going up to Halfah." He then reached out one hand, and lifted up a paper-bound copy of the Greek text of Homer's "Iliad," in the Teubner Series, which he was holding in his hand when we entered (it was then lying face downwards on the cushion), and went on with his reading. Major Plunkett, lighting another cigarette, asked in a sweetly soft voice if we had his permission to withdraw, and we did so with as much dignity as was possible under the circumstances.

—E. A. WALLIS BUDGE

On a visit by Schliemann and Virchow to Petrie's Fayum excavations:

. . . Schliemann, short, round-headed, round-faced, round-hatted, great round-goggled eyes, spectacled, cheeriest of beings, dogmatic, but always ready for facts.

—W. M. FLINDERS PETRIE

His enthusiasm called back into being the ancient spirit of chivalry. . . . He had to encounter in the early stages of his work both frowns and indifference, yet the one and the other alike had to give way, as the force and value of his discoveries became clear, like mists upon the sun. The history of his boyhood and youth were not less remarkable than that of his later life. Indeed they cannot be separated, for one aim and purpose moved them from first to last. Either his generosity without his energy, or his energy without his generosity might well have gained celebrity; in their union they were no less than wonderful.

—W. E. GLADSTONE

In a speech to honor the memory of Heinrich Schliemann on March 1, 1891, in the Berlin town hall:

. . . . There was a time when learning was confined to cloistered rooms, particularly with regard to the study of ancient history. But it was the great merit of our Schliemann that he contributed to a decisive breakthrough. How often are we told today that the lively interest in classical antiquity, which inspired the age of Lessing, Winckelmann, Herder, and Goethe, has died out. Yet with what excitement did educated people on both sides of the Atlantic follow every step of Schliemann! Did we not witness that, when doubt was cast on a result of his discoveries in *The Times*, a meeting was immediately summoned in London to debate before a large assembly the disputed points as if a burning issue of contemporary politics was at stake? It is irrelevant how many centuries may separate us from a bygone age. What matters is the importance of the past to our intellectual and spiritual existence. In the life of the mind, the most remote may become to us the closest and the most vital. . . .

—ERNST CURTIUS

I am old enough to recall the first authentic accounts that Schliemann sent to *The Times* of his discoveries at Mycenae, and the intense interest they aroused. I had the happiness later to make his personal acquaintance on the fields of his glory, and I still remember the echoes of his visits to England, which were his greatest scenes of triumph. . . . Something of the romance of his earlier years still seemed to cling to his personality, and I had myself an almost uncanny memory of the spare, slightly built man of sallow complexion and somewhat darkly clad, wearing spectacles of foreign make, and through which—so the fancy took me—he had looked deep into the ground.

—ARTHUR EVANS

As a child, before I had even learned to read, I shook hands with him at my father's table. Ten years later, I stood before the long glass cases in the Berlin Museum and gazed on the gold of Troy. Thus my earliest ideas of greatness and glory, of legend, poetry and scholarship, were linked with his name. Everything about him was romantic—the kings whose treasures he unearthed, those others who bestowed treasures upon him—and yet, what sticks in my memory is his kind brown eyes.

—EMIL LUDWIG

Among English and French *savants* smooth, polished and sceptical, among German *Gelehrten*, each in his own field omniscient and indifferent to all outside it, Schliemann moved as a being intensely real, full of imaginations and prejudices, of love and hatred. This strong colour of personal feeling he infused into all his work; his discoveries were his children, and he was ready to fight for them as a lioness fights for her young. He regarded all criticisms of his views as libels and calumnies, and attacked them in the spirit of a theologian who has to combat an insidious heresy.

—PERCY GARDNER

. . . As I sat [in the lobby of the hotel on the Piazza Umberto in Naples] that evening, a dying man was brought into the hotel. His head bowed down to his chest, eyes closed, arms hanging limp, and his face ashen, he was carried in by four people. This morbid group moved directly past the chair in which I sat, and after a while the manager of the hotel approached me and asked, "Do you know, Sir, who that sick man is?" "No." "That is the great Schliemann!" Poor "great Schliemann!" He had excavated Troy and Mycenae, earned immortality for himself, and—was dying. . . .

—HENRYK SIENKIEWICZ

No student of Hellenism can think without deep regret that . . . there is no fresh discovery to be hoped for from the unwearying devotion and unstinted generosity of the famous merchant enthusiast. But the work which he has done is in no way dependent on his individual life; it has been no less than the creation of prehistoric Greek archaeology. Dr. Schliemann was essentially "epoch-making" in this branch of study, and it is not for epoch-making men to see the rounding off and completion of their task. That must be the labour of a generation at least. A man who can state to the world a completely new problem may be content to let the final solution of it wait for those that come after him.

—WALTER LEAF

AFTERWORD AND
ACKNOWLEDGMENTS

A WORD ON THE EXCERPTS from Schliemann's writings that have been quoted in these pages. Since the selected pieces were written over a period of nearly half a century, Schliemann's spellings of proper names, be it of German townships or classical figures, varied constantly. Thus, the German umlaut was used interchangeably with the diphthong (e.g., *ä* or *ae*); the Latin ending *-us* frequently replaced *-os* in Greek names; Roman deities were substituted for their Greek counterparts; some spellings appeared with the French *ou* rather than the English *u*; Anglicization was haphazard, and so on. To strive for consistency would have been next to impossible, and would have distorted the character of the writing. After all, our own habits in such matters are quite irregular. We tend to prefer Hercules to Heracles, Priam or Priamus to Priamos, Lysimachus to Lysamachos, but Knossos to Knossus, Orchomenos to Orchomenus. Where discrepancies were so slight that they would barely have been noticed, or where they represented immediately recognizable variants, I have let well enough alone. In cases of more obscure and exotic renderings I have added, at least at their first occurrence, the more common equivalents in brackets or, on occasion, have replaced them directly in the text, particularly when they were misspelled or were a strictly foreign usage. Where alternate names were used interchangeably—for example, ancient and modern designations for the same place—either one or the other has been given in brackets and/or appears in the Index. Hissarlik has been used for the Anatolian site in general, whereas Troy or Ilion (Ilium) has been used as a rule to reflect Homeric associations. As a matter of course, I have tried to check names of persons or places to make sure of accepted spellings. However, in the case of Turkish, Far Eastern, and even some Greek names, three or more variants exist (i.e., Ithaca, Ithake, Thaki), which made it sometimes impossible or futile to list them all. Names for Oriental towns have been repeatedly and bewilderingly changed over the years, and even current reference books are in disagreement on which is preferred for general purposes. A few

355

of the names used by Schliemann are not even listed in encyclopedic works and are difficult to identify.

As to overall spelling practices, I have tried to establish a measure of uniformity but again exerted moderation when it came to antiquated or British renditions, obsolete accents, Schliemann's own idiosyncrasies, and the like which I felt belonged to the time and milieu of the writing and hence should stand. For quotations in foreign tongues, I have given translations; however, with those in Greek I have dropped the original in most cases, since it was not likely to be meaningful to the general reader.

Since most of the text has been culled from lengthy books, it frequently represents drastic abridgments. The cuts I have indicated, according to common practice, by ellipses. But in no instance have I tampered with the original or added anything apart from bracketed statements. Several of the chapters and the majority of the letters originally written in French and German I have translated myself, endeavoring to retain Schliemann's style and integrating them with those selections that were available in English. Schliemann's own published English writings were clearly edited by others before they appeared in print. Not so the letters and journals which he composed in English and which are by no means flawless. Blatant misspellings or evidently wrong renderings in the collections of his correspondence published in Germany (and probably the fault of latter-day editors and printers) had to be emended, though here, too, I have kept changes to a minimum and corrected only the most glaring errors that might have caused the reader difficulties. Now and then in the text I have taken it upon myself to break up long paragraphs or, for continuity's sake, join shorter ones. The chapter titles are as a rule my own.

Even more confusing than the variant spellings in Schliemann's writings was the veritable hodgepodge of measures, weights, temperature, and currencies. Schliemann used both metric and popular units and a bewildering number of monetary denominations. He had a kind of mania for figures and petty details of all kinds. It so happens that few of his numerical data are reliable, and little purpose would have been served by conversions from one system to the other. Most of the measures, as well as the main currencies used by Schliemann, will be known to the average reader, however, and required no elaboration. But I have furnished approximate equivalents for such "exotic" measures as Russian *versts* and *puds*.

In the following pages I have given the sources of Schliemann's writings that have been quoted in the text. The sources of his letters and the miscellaneous quotations which appear in the text have been listed in the Notes section, where I have also introduced additional materials, both by Schliemann and other authors, to rectify or amplify the text. On occasion, I have found it worthwhile to indicate archaeological developments after Schliemann. However, no attempt has been made to give full coverage of Mycenaean and Aegean archaeology or enter the battlefield of modern controversies that have come to take on the semblance of another Trojan War.

While the Schliemann writings that have been quoted in these pages consist in the main of excerpts from his published works, in order to lend greater balance and enrich the autobiographical fabric I have endeavored to include in my commentaries profuse quotations from Schliemann's letters, whose unguarded vividness, frankness, and informativeness add another authentic voice. Regrettably, a great many of his private papers deposited at the Gennadeion Library in Athens have not yet been published and are of difficult access even to those able to use that fine collection.

In the years of searching, selecting, coordinating, translating, and editing these diverse writings, as well as probing into nineteenth-century backgrounds, archaeological history, and Aegean-Mycenaean scholarship, I have drawn on sources from many lands, and many institutions and libraries—far too many, in fact, to acknowledge my indebtedness. I am grateful to them all. I am also under obligation to a few personal friends for their unflinching support, especially in light of the strains put on them (and the author) by a protracted crisis-prone project. As on previous occasions, Charles Blackwell offered valuable editorial advice throughout all stages. Professor Lotte Kohler of the City University of New York, and Mrs. Gertrud Deuel and Richard Passanah of Zürich were particularly helpful in locating vital but not readily available pamphlets, books, and illustrations. Repeated sojourns at the South African home of my sister Hedda and her husband Gunter Philipp afforded the congenial atmosphere and carefree tranquillity for making substantial strides in my labors.

Finally, on a nearly impossible assignment at the request of the publishers, long after the manuscript had been completed and scheduled to be released, Burton Beals deserves my respect for the sensitive and judicious way in which he applied his editorial skill.

LEO DEUEL

New York
1976

SOURCES OF THE
SCHLIEMANN NARRATIVES

For full descriptions of titles listed, see Selected Bibliography. Aside from Part I, references to letters are given in the Notes.

I HOMERIC VOICES 1822–1841

CHILDHOOD IN MECKLENBURG

Ilios, pp. 1–7; Shirley H. Weber, ed., *Schliemann's First Visit to America, 1850–1851,* p. 4.

II SELF-MADE MAN 1841–1850

HAMBURG—AMSTERDAM—ST. PETERSBURG

Ernst Meyer, ed., *Heinrich Schliemann Briefwechsel,* Vol. I, pp. 9–32 *passim* (letter from Amsterdam to Wilhelmine and Doris Schliemann, Feb. 20, 1842, translated by Leo Deuel); *Ilios,* pp. 9–12.

III AMERICAN INTERLUDE 1850–1852

JOURNEY TO CALIFORNIA

Weber, pp. 21–29, 52–54 *passim.*

GOLD RUSH DAYS

Weber, pp. 54–58, 63–70, 72–75, 77–89, 98–100 *passim.*

IV MIDAS TOUCH 1852–1864

WEALTH AND ITS DISCONTENTS

Ilios, pp. 12–18.

V TWO YEARS AROUND THE WORLD 1864–1866

La Chine et le Japon au temps présent, pp. 3, 9–17, 30–31, 39, 41–47, 50, 52–57, 81–83, 87–89, 101–102, 106–108, 110–113, 125–129, 132–133, 136–139, 151, 154–156, 163, 165, 169 *passim* (translated by Leo Deuel).

VI HELLENIC PILGRIMAGE 1868

ODYSSEUS' ISLAND—ITHACA

Ithaka, der Peloponnes und Troja, pp. v–vi (translated by Leo Deuel); *Ilios,* p. 18; *Ithaka,* pp. xiv, 1, 7–10, 14–32, 34–37, 39–41, 54–59, 78 *passim* (translated by Leo Deuel).

AEGEAN CITADELS—ARGOS TO ILIUM
    Ithaka, pp. 80–82, 85–91, 94–97, 101–109, 124–128, 134, 137–141, 143, 147, 149–152, 160–161, 163–166, 189–190, 201–202, 213 *passim* (translated by Leo Deuel).

VII ASSAULT ON HISSARLIK 1870–1872

THE CAMPAIGN BEGINS
    Troy and Its Remains, pp. 58–62, 64, 66, 75–82, 85, 89, 96–97, 98–100, 107–108, 112–114, 116–117, 121, 130–133, 144–147, 184–185, 188–189, 194, 198, 201–204, 211–212, 216 *passim.*

VIII "PRIAM'S TREASURE" 1873

A MOMENTOUS DISCOVERY
    Troy and Its Remains, pp. 224–230, 248–249, 251, 253, 257–258, 265, 275–278, 287–288, 300–306, 318–319, 322–328, 331–335, 340–349, 556 *passim; Ilios,* pp. 43, 485, 43 *passim; Troy and Its Remains,* pp. 22–23, 52–54 *passim.*

IX THE GOLD OF MYCENAE 1874–1876

THE SEARCH FOR AGAMEMNON
    Mycenae, pp. 24–29, 32, 35, 39, 41–43, 61–62, 64–66, 80, 82–84, 87–89, 100–102, 117, 123–124, 144, 151–152, 154–159, 161, 164–165, 184, 186, 212–215, 218–225, 227, 231, 235–237, 266–267, 284, 290–291, 293–300, 311–313, 334–337, 339, 343–344, 351–352, 354, 376 *passim.*

X THE SIEGE CONTINUES 1878–1879

THE SECOND TROJAN CAMPAIGN
    Ilios, pp. 45, 50–54, 60, 62–63, 672, 65–66 *passim.*

XI RETURN TO ASIA MINOR 1882

TROY, TROAD, AND TUMULI
    Troja, pp. 1–2, 5–7, 11–12, 15, 17–20, 26, 52–53, 57–58, 61–62, 164–169, 242–245, 247–248, 250–252, 254, 256–260, 277 *passim.*

XII TIRYNS 1884–1885

EXCAVATING HERCULES' FORTRESS
    Tiryns, pp. 2–5, 11, 15–19, 28–30, 52, 6–10 *passim.*

XIII TROJAN FINALE 1889–1890

SCHLIEMANN REMEMBERED
    Andromache Schliemann Mélas. "The Most Unforgettable Character I've Met," *The Reader's Digest* (June 1950), p. 76.
    A. H. Sayce. *Reminiscences* (London: Macmillan, 1923), pp. 166–167.
    Arthur de Gobineau, in Janine Buenzod. "Arthur de Gobineau, Lettres d'un voyage en Russie, en Asie Mineure et en Grèce, 1876," *Études de Lettres* (Lausanne), serie II, tome 4, no. 4 (Oct.–Dec. 1961), pp. 185–188 (translated by Leo Deuel).
    Rudolf Virchow, *Ilios,* Preface, p. ix.
    Carl Schuchhardt. "Life of Dr. Schliemann," in *Schliemann's Excavations,* pp. 15–16.
    Joseph Maria von Radowitz. *Aufzeichnungen und Erinnerungen aus dem Leben des Botschafters J.M.v.R.,* ed. by Hajo Holborn (Stuttgart: Deutsche Verlags-Anstalt, 1925), vol. 2, pp. 168–169 (translated by Leo Deuel).

E. A. Wallis Budge. *By Nile and Tigris* (London: John Murray, 1920), vol. 1, pp. 108–109.

W. M. Flinders Petrie. *Seventy Years in Archaeology*, p. 83.

W. E. Gladstone, letter of condolence to Schliemann's widow, in Ludwig. *Schliemann*, p. xii.

Ernst Curtius, speech in honor of the memory of Heinrich Schliemann, March 1, 1891, *Zeitschrift für Ethnologie*, vol. 23 (1891), pp. 59–60 (translated by Leo Deuel).

Arthur Evans. Preface to Ludwig. *Schliemann* (London ed.); also quoted by Joan Evans. *Time and Chance*, p. 387.

Emil Ludwig. *Schliemann*. Preface, p. v.

Percy Gardner. "Heinrich Schliemann," *Macmillan's Magazine*, no. 378 (April 1891), p. 479.

Henryk Sienkiewicz. *Letters from Africa* (Polish ed., 1901), Engl. transl. of excerpt in *Archaeology*, vol. 11, no. 3 (Sept. 1958), p. 218.

Walter Leaf, in Schuchhardt, *Schliemann's Excavations*, Introduction, p. xxi.

NOTES AND REFERENCES

ABBREVIATIONS

B	Meyer, Ernst, ed. *Briefe von Heinrich Schliemann.*
BW I, BW II	*Heinrich Schliemann Briefwechsel. Vol. I, 1842–1875; Vol. II, 1876–1890.*
Brueckner	Brueckner, Alfred. "Schliemann, H.," *Allgemeine Deutsche Biographie*
EL	Ludwig, Emil. *Schliemann: The story of a gold-seeker.*
EM	Meyer, Ernst. *Heinrich Schliemann: Kaufmann und Forscher.*
Ilios	Schliemann, H. *Ilios: The city and country of the Trojans.*
Ithaka	Schliemann, H. *Ithaka, der Peloponnes und Troja.*
Lilly	Lilly, Eli, ed. *Schliemann in Indianapolis.*
Mycenae	Schliemann, H. *Mycenae: A narrative of researches. . . .*
Schuchh.	Schuchhardt, Carl. *Schliemann's Excavations.*
Tiryns	Schliemann, H. *Tiryns: The prehistoric palace of the kings of Tiryns.*
Troja	Schliemann, H. *Troja: Results of the latest researches. . . .*
T&R	Schliemann, H. *Troy and Its Remains.*
Weber	Weber, Shirley H., ed. *Schliemann's First Visit to America, 1850–51.*

EPIGRAPHS

1. To half-brother Ernest, April 9, 1863 (*BW I*, p. 121).
2. To half-brother Ernest, January 19, 1868 (*BW II*, p. 30).
3. To C. T. Newton, July 26, 1873 (*BW I*, p. 235).

INTRODUCTION

1. Thus, Jacquetta Hawkes in the introduction to her two-volume anthology of archaeology, *The World of the Past*: "Yet in reality no man was less dominated by success and self-won grandeur. Many of us have known young men who determined to make money in order to be able to carry out some cherished ambition. But how very few have kept their plan. . . . Schliemann was inflexibly true to his childhood's dream" ([New York: Alfred A. Knopf, 1963], p. 56).

2. A gifted German writer, Ludwig (born Cohn) (1881–1948) wrote successful popular biographies that were often a favorite target of "professional" historians, possibly one reason why he felt a natural empathy for the amateur Schliemann.

3. In his later years, Schliemann frequently referred to himself as a treasure-seeker (*Schatzgräber*). He was always on the lookout for "royal" tombs. In his final campaign at Hissarlik in 1890 he was still itching for treasure-laden graves of the prehistoric rulers of Troy. Similar hopes were kindled by Knossos. Indeed, it was toward the end of his excavation career that he developed a passion for filling the Schliemann halls at the Berlin Ethnological Museum with artifacts, thus reverting to old-style archaeology which was oriented toward the collection of prize pieces for showcases. However, Wilhelm Dörpfeld, who assisted him in his last campaigns, has insisted: "As excavator, he was not a gold-seeker" (introduction to Ernst Meyer, ed., *Briefe von Heinrich Schliemann*, p. 8).

4. An estimated sixty thousand letters of his correspondence and eighteen diaries of his travels and explorations, in addition to some 150 notebooks, business records, and collections of various motley trivia, survive. They are being stored at the Gennadeion Library in Athens, where Schliemann's heirs deposited them in the 1930's.

5. *BW I*, pp. 172–73. Schliemann addressed his older son variously as Sergei, Sergej, Sergius, and Serge; Sergej is the form he used most commonly.

6. *BW I*, p. 82; *BW II*, p. 14.

7. *EL*, pp. 63–64.

8. *BW I*, p. 138.

9. *BW I*, p. 243.

10. Friedrich Schlie, "Das Leben Schliemanns," *Neues Reich*, 34 (1876), 281.

11. *BW I*, p. 82.

12. *BW II*, p. 67.

13. *EL*, p. 50.

14. Schliemann met all three: Layard while he was serving for some time (1877–1880) as British ambassador in Constantinople, and Burton in 1887, when he lived in semi-retirement as British consul-general in Trieste. According to Victor von Hagen's *Maya Explorer* (Norman: University of Oklahoma Press, 1947, pp. 295–296), he encountered Stephens in Panama during his first American trip. Stephens then was active on behalf of the Panama Railroad Company. Schliemann himself did not mention such a meeting.

15. Robert Payne, *The Gold of Troy*, p. 176. (I was unable to locate this reference in Arnold.)

16. Müller once wrote to Schliemann: "I know but one Ilium, and that is the Ilium sung by Homer. It is unlikely that that Ilium will be located in the trenches of Hissarlik, but much rather will it be found among the Muses who reside on Mount Olympus" (*BW I*, p. 274).

17. Such a place—Wilios, Wilusiya, or Wilusas—is actually mentioned in the Hittite records from Boğazköy but apparently was not placed in the Troad. The name Tarusiya (Troia?) also appears on a geographical list. Other, though inconclusive, references in these ancient archives give names of foreign princes such as Atarisiyas (Atreus?), Alaksandrus (Alexander-Paris?), and even a kingdom of Akhiyawa (Achaia?), which some scholars tend to place on Rhodes.

18. Biblical archaeology, too, has long been addicted to literal-mindedness and the obsession to prove the Bible right. The overworked thesis that it *is* history, which has spawned many popular books for the past hundred years, has been thoroughly discredited, particularly by modern archaeologists. It disregards the true nature of religious writing to which factual data are incidental. Belief in the Bible can neither be strengthened nor weakened by historical veracity. It should be stressed, however, that while not history itself, the Bible—like the Homeric epics—may still throw light on institutions, customs, and material objects of the pre-Classical ages. But here again scholars remain in disagreement over which age is illuminated by Homeric references. Some men, foremost today Denys L. Page in his brilliant *History and the Homeric Iliad* (1959), are convinced that the epics essentially mirror late Mycenaean culture and may have originated in that age. Others, like M. I. Finley, though not denying a few minor Mycenaean associations, argue as

persuasively for the rougher "Dark Age" or early Greek Iron Age. Page and Finley also take opposite views with regard to the historical value of the Hissarlik excavations since 1870 and whether archaeology helped confirm Homeric tradition. Schliemann, needless to say, recognized Homeric parallels in most of the artifacts he brought to light, particularly those from the shaft graves of Mycenae, which, as we now know, are easily three hundred years earlier than the time of the Trojan War, while Troy II preceded it by a full millennium.

19. *EL*, p. xi.

20. Michaelis, *A Century of Archaeological Discovery*, p. 217.

21. Daniel, *A Hundred Years of Archaeology*, p. 165.

22. *BW II*, p. 81.

23. F. Duhn, in *Heidelberger Jahrbücher I* (1894), p. 154.

24. Arthur Milchhöfer, "Erinnerungen an H.S.," *Deutsche Rundschau* (May 1891), p. 280.

25. Thus, for instance, Wieland Schmied, whose Schliemann book *Kein Troja ohne Homer* (Munich: Goldmann Taschenbücher, n.d.) refers in the subtitle to Schliemann as the "founder of archaeology." Similarly Paul MacKendrick in *The Greek Stones Speak—* "the founder of the new science of archaeology" (p. 21); Alan E. Samuel in *The Mycenaeans in History* (p. 8); and many more.

HOMERIC VOICES 1822–1841

1. The full title of the autobiographical chapter is "Introduction. Autobiography of the author, and narrative of his work at Troy" (pp. 1–66).

2. The omission was insisted upon by his English publisher and was also adopted in the American, German, and French editions.

3. *Ilios*, p. 1.

4. *Ilios*, p. 1.

5. Dr. Alfred Brueckner (Brückner), who helped with the analysis of ceramics during the last season at Troy (1890) and served again under Dörpfeld in 1893, was chosen to complete the work. In the Schliemann tradition, he was not given proper credit for having written the bulk of this expanded "autobiography."

6. It has never been made available in English, though it has been translated in recent years into French and Italian.

7. *BW II*, 114 (December 1880). "The description of this early love bears probably the most obvious stamp of later embellishment" (*B*, p. 35).

8. In order to stress his amazing determination—and achievement—Schliemann, even before the publication of *Ilios*, would on occasion describe himself without any education whatever when he left home. In a letter to a Greek friend of June 11, 1856, he stated that he "could barely read and write my mother tongue" (*BW I*, p. 82). Likewise, in the autobiographical sketch preceding his American journal of 1850–1851, which apparently he had composed (or rather edited) with a Russian audience in mind, he "took lessons in the German language [in Holland], which I learned to speak correctly" (*Weber*, p. 10).

CHILDHOOD IN MECKLENBURG

1. German, Ernst. Full name, Ernst Johann Adolf, b. 1780; d. 1870. Mother's name: Luise Therese Sophie (Bürger), b. 1793; d. 1831.

2. The well-known German translator of Homer, Johann Heinrich Voss (1751–1826), also a Mecklenburger, served in the same castle as private tutor. His verse versions of the *Iliad* and *Odyssey* were tremendously popular and had great influence on

German classicism, noted for its "tyranny of Greece." Schliemann's father used to read to his children from this translation.

3. *Braden* is Low German for "roast"; *Kirl* is "fellow."

4. Schliemann added in a footnote: "According to the tradition, one of those legs had been buried just before the altar. Strange to say, when some years ago the church of Ankershagen was being repaired, a single legbone was found at a small depth before the altar, as my cousin the Rev. Hans Becker, the present clergyman of Ankershagen, assures me" (*Ilios*, p. 2).

5. There exists a record of his father's university examination that appraises his thorough understanding of the New Testament "in the original tongue," which must have been Greek. It is also on record that his elder brother Friedrich instructed him in Greek (*EL*, p. 71). In addition, he was adept in Hebrew, probably as a requirement for a theology degree, and once translated "God Save the King" into Hebrew. Knowledge of Latin was routine at the time for any high school student and certainly for a university graduate.

6. After his Uncle Friedrich's death in 1861, Schliemann remained in contact with his widow Magdalene. He was especially close to his five-year-older cousin Adolf.

7. High school stressing "useful studies"—business courses, mathematics, and modern languages.

8. Hückstaedt took over shortly after Schliemann had entered as apprentice. In a legal document of the transfer, young Schliemann is listed as part of the "inventory" the new owner acquired from his predecessor. Schliemann, nonetheless, held no grudge against his former employer. When famous, he renewed relations with Hückstaedt's widow and became godfather to one of her grandchildren, Nausikaa.

9. The incident happened in 1837. The miller was then twenty-four years old. Him, too, Schliemann was to seek out later in life. At the age of sixty-six Niederhöffer still recited Virgil and Homer "with the same warm enthusiasm." He had achieved respectability as a collector on a turnpike road.

10. Schliemann biographers have asserted that the young miller, like Schliemann himself, did not understand what he was reciting. But this is unlikely. As a former *Gymnasiast* he undoubtedly studied Greek and did not just commit a text to memory without the least understanding of it. Learning Homeric verses by heart was part of Greek-language instruction.

II   SELF-MADE MAN   1841–1850

1. Schliemann's daughter Andromache (Mélas) believed that this long letter represented a mere exercise in composition. But its very form and address—as well as addenda—militate against such a thesis.

2. *BW I*, p. 33.

3. *B*, p. 32, *fn.*

4. *BW I*, p. 32.

HAMBURG—AMSTERDAM—ST. PETERSBURG

1. His father was then living with his second wife, Sophia (Behnke), at Gehlsdorf outside Rostock. He did not marry the maid (Fiekchen Schwarz) he had taken up with in Ankershagen.

2. An older brother who died ten weeks after Schliemann's birth and from whom, according to a common custom, he assumed the first name Heinrich, though he had been baptized Julius (Johann Ludwig Heinrich Julius). Schliemann was the fifth of nine children. His father had two more sons by his second wife.

3. A distant cousin the same age as Schliemann, she seems to have been the "other" great love of his youth. Later he considered proposing to her but was dissuaded by one of his sisters. When she died unmarried twenty-nine years later, Schliemann was stricken with grief and self-reproach.

4. A friend of Schliemann's parents who kept an eye on him during his Hamburg stay.

5. A brother-in-law of Schliemann's mother.

6. A Hamburg shipper and school friend of Schliemann's mother who also seems to have been a pupil of his father's (a teacher before he turned to theology), J. F. Wendt was another mentor during Schliemann's Hamburg days and even helped him after his shipwreck. In other autobiographical sources he is usually credited with having procured him the job in La Guaira and passage as "cabin boy" (see *Ilios*, p. 8).

7. A German mile equals about four and a half miles, hence about fifty miles.

8. The word "dolefully" is here added from another version.

9. In *Ilios* Schliemann narrated that a "little box, containing a few shirts and stockings, as well as my pocketbook . . . was picked up" (p. 8). Because of this, he says, his shipmates gave him the nickname Jonah.

10. Spellings of proper names vary considerably in Schliemann's various autobiographical writings. In *Ilios*, he refers to the consuls Sonderdorp and Ram (p. 8).

11. He wrote in *Ilios*: "But I declined to return to Germany, where I had been so overwhelmingly unfortunate, telling them that I regarded it as my destiny to remain in Holland . . ." (p. 8).

12. In November 1847 Minna married a farmer nearly twenty years her senior, Friedrich Richers of Friedland in Mecklenburg.

III AMERICAN INTERLUDE 1850–1852

1. *EL*, p. 44.
2. *BW I*, pp. 34–35.
3. *BW I*, pp. 35–37.
4. *EL*, p. 38.
5. *BW I*, p. 38.
6. Paul later turned to agriculture and committed suicide in 1852.
7. *BW I*, pp. 39, 41.
8. *BW I*, p. 45.
9. *Ilios*, p. 12.
10. Once in the United States, Schliemann supposedly learned that his brother had left some $30,000, but Louis' partner had made away with the money. Schliemann thought it useless to prosecute. Whether the alleged embezzler is identical with the man named Behrens, whom Schliemann dined with in New York, is not known.
11. Shirley H. Weber, ed., *Schliemann's First Visit to America, 1850–51.*

GOLD RUSH DAYS

1. New Granada was roughly present-day Venezuela, Colombia, and Ecuador.

2. As in the introduction to his American journal—and later in the prefaces to the travel book on Greece and the narrative on the first Troy campaign—Schliemann proclaimed Ankershagen his birthplace. It seems that his strong attachment and sentimental associations persuaded him to adopt Ankershagen as a more fitting place for the beginning of his romantic life.

IV MIDAS TOUCH 1852–1864

1. *BW I*, p. 20.
2. *BW I*, p. 58 (letter to father, April 1, 1854).
3. *BW I*, p. 80.
4. *EL*, p. 47.
5. *EL*, p. 48.
6. His first daughter, Natalia (Natalya, Natasha), was born in 1858. His second daughter, Nadezhda (Nadeshda, Nadja), followed three years later, in 1861.
7. *BW I*, p. 67.
8. *BW I*, p. 60.
9. *BW I*, p. 101.
10. *B*, p. 39, fn. 3, in a letter to his cousin Adolf, March 14, 1871.
11. *BW I*, p. 88.
12. *EM*, p. 133.

WEALTH AND ITS DISCONTENTS

1. A classical scholar from Lausanne.
2. This remark in the London and New York editions of *Ilios* is directed to English-speaking readers. In a footnote Schliemann maintains that since Russians pronounce Greek precisely in the same manner as their contemporaries in Greece, the pronunciation of the ancient tongue could not have changed for *at least* one thousand years since Russia adopted the Greek Orthodox faith.
3. In the preface to *Ithaka*, dated December 31, 1868, Schliemann speaks more generally of "studies," though he refers later to archaeology as "the science that has the greatest attraction for me."

V TWO YEARS AROUND THE WORLD 1864–1866

1. *BW I*, p. 124.
2. Even his friend Virchow had to admit that Schliemann lacked any true feeling for nature.
3. In one instance at least, Schliemann appears to have pretended that he visited a "standard" site—Mecca. Though his Greek family, as well as Virchow and Ludwig, believed that he entered it, his claim was most likely mere fabrication. Even Ernst Meyer discounted it in his biography. In any case, it cannot chronologically be fitted into any of Schliemann's trips to the Near East. Perhaps he thought that such a feat, carried out by several nineteenth-century European adventurers, would add to his stature as a fluent Arabist and resourceful explorer. Schliemann let it transpire that he kept his visit a secret because he was afraid of the revenge of Muslim fanatics. But since he was never one to keep a secret, particularly if it cast him in a romantic light, such explanation lacks conviction. Besides, the men who had reached Mecca, in disguise, were never threatened after their return. Nor were they cagey about their exploits—or afraid to divulge them.
4. At an auction in Shanghai he bought tea for the Schröders. Later in Havana he would purchase large blocks of securities.
5. *The Gold of Troy*, p. 61.
6. *EM*, p. 224.
7. *EM*, p. 226.

THE GREAT WALL OF CHINA

1. Schliemann means Central America (Nicaragua, Panama). He never visited South America proper.

JAPAN

1. Presumably a selection of Buddhist and Shintoist writings.

VI   HELLENIC PILGRIMAGE   1868

1. *B*, p. 110 (February 10, 1866).
2. *BW I*, p. 99.
3. Since Schliemann later presented letters from his wife as court evidence when suing for divorce in Indianapolis, it may well be argued that he set a trap with his "invitation" that she and the children move with him to America—an absurd proposition considering that she had refused previously to leave Russia for Dresden and Paris.
4. *BW I*, p. 129.
5. *BW I*, p. 131.
6. *BW I*, p. 137.
7. *BW I*, p. 131.
8. *BW I*, p. 131.
9. *BW I*, p. 131.
10. *EL*, p. 92.
11. *BW I*, p. 133.
12. *BW I*, p. 130.
13. *EL*, pp. 94–95.
14. Apparently *not* Malayans, as Malacca seems to imply. Schliemann probably meant the Malabar coast, since he contemplated going to Bombay, and Hindus rather than Malayans were brought into the Caribbean area and the Guyanas. He also proposed to the Schröders to "ship" northern Chinese to Cuba.
15. *BW I*, p. 320.
16. A close parallel to Schliemann's pursuits is offered by his German contemporary, the theologian Constantin von Tischendorf (1815–1874), who, in his quest to prove the authenticity of biblical texts, was driven to search for ancient manuscripts in the Near East. In the manner of Schliemann, he set out to counter the destructive criticism of philologists of the F. A. Wolf school, who claimed that the New and Old Testaments, like the works of Homer, were a spurious medley of relatively late composition with little relevance to actual events. Like Schliemann he made phenomenal discoveries which, if they did not fully persuade his peers, strengthened his own faith, besides being a major contribution to scholarship. See my *Testaments of Time* (New York: Alfred A. Knopf, 1965; London: Secker & Warburg, 1966), pp. 257–303.
17. *BW I*, p. 140. In a similar vein he "blamed" his cousin Adolf for making him take the road to Troy. "It is all your fault, because without having heard you recite the beautiful Homeric hexameters in 1832, which still resound in my ear, I would have never thought of learning Greek . . ." (*B*, p. 115). On another occasion, he paid tribute to his teacher Carl Andres (Andress) and, above all, to the young miller who recited from the *Iliad* at the Fürstenberg grocery.
18. *Ithaka*, p. xiv. The German version is cited throughout.
19. The German translation was by his old Kalkhorst teacher Andres, though his name was not mentioned. Schliemann, who was unhappy with it, probably revised it himself.

20. The rash and unwarranted conclusion that he had found ashes—to which he also jumped at Hissarlik—was to cause Schliemann much annoyance later on.

21. *EM*, p. 238.

22. *BW I*, pp. 139–140.

ODYSSEUS' ISLAND—ITHACA

1. In *Ilios*, Schliemann added to the nearly identical statement "and the country of the heroes whose adventures had delighted and comforted my childhood" (p. 18).

2. Opinion on the identity of Ithaca is by no means unanimous. In fact, Schliemann's "assistant" at Troy and Tiryns, Wilhelm Dörpfeld, later was to opt for the neighboring island of Leukás (Levkas) rather than modern Itháke (Thaki).

3. The term "Cyclopean" is usually meant to refer to prehistoric structures raised from large unhewn stones, with pebbles or clay intervening. According to Greek tradition, the Cyclopeans, a race of master builders from Lycia in Asia Minor, were responsible for some of the formidable fortresses such as Mycenae and Tiryns, which, though in ruins, seemed to have been contructed by giants.

4. Curiously reminiscent of the Maya ceremonies at their cenotes.

5. Here, as elsewhere, Schliemann erroneously accepts any description given by Homer as reflecting the period of the Trojan War. In fact cremation was uncommon in the late Mycenaean or Helladic age when the events depicted in the *Iliad* presumably took place.

AEGEAN CITADELS—ARGOS TO ILIUM

1. Actually the Fountain House of the Peirene.

2. Despite formidable counterevidence, Schliemann from here on remained more or less convinced that the *tholos*, or "beehive," Tomb of Agamemnon and all similar Mycenaean structures were storerooms or treasuries rather than mausoleums.

3. Referred to by Schliemann in his later writings as *thalamos* (Greek for "chamber"). Again, he stubbornly resisted the view that it was a burial crypt.

4. One hundred leptas equal one drachma.

5. Schliemann here echoes an opinion of Pausanias. However, Dörpfeld later observed that the claim did not hold true with all Cyclopean boulders (*Tiryns*, p. 178).

6. Schliemann dates from the "Hedshra."

7. At the time American vice-consul at the Dardanelles. An Englishman and a long-time resident of Turkey, Frank Calvert and his brothers owned large estates in the Troad. The eastern part of the Hissarlik hill belonged to him, and he had carried out some excavations there. His hospitable house at the Dardanelles was a meeting ground for visiting savants, who would also inspect his fine collection of local antiquities.

VII ASSAULT ON HISSARLIK 1870–1872

1. There is, however, little acknowledgment of Calvert's crucial help in the book. Schliemann never said outright that the American consular agent directed him first to Hissarlik. The flattering tone of his letter—"You will find that the name of the great scholar Frank Calvert to whom the science of archaeology is indebted for so many important discoveries, has frequently been mentioned in the book" (*BW I*, p. 141)— possibly served to make up for not giving Calvert sufficient credit.

2. *BW I*, p. 141. A month earlier Calvert had promised to give Schliemann "all the assistance I can in carrying on your excavations. . . . All my lands are at your disposal to examine as you may think best" (*BW I, p.* 140).

3. *BW*, pp. 141–142.

4. Before Schliemann's coming, Calvert is reported to have tried to persuade the British Museum to excavate the Hissarlik hill.

5. *BW I*, p. 147.

6. The cousin, Adolf Schliemann (1817–1872), then *Justizrat* of Schwerin, Schliemann called "brother"; it was with his family that he had stayed as a boy in Kalkhorst in 1832. Adolf had a distinguished legal career and rose to be a judge on the Reichsgericht, the highest German court, in Leipzig in 1870. He was also a *Privatdozent* (lecturer) at the University of Rostock. Schliemann helped him, as he did Theokletos Vimpos, with his gambling debts.

7. The "autobiography" mentions only his second, archaeological work (*Ithaka*), but according to his correspondence with his cousin, both early works were submitted. A Rostock professor reporting on *Ithaka* commented favorably on the author's erudition, though he suspended judgment on his conclusions.

8. Cousin Adolf also advised Schliemann on his divorce. However, the decision to initiate the proceedings in Indianapolis rather than New York seems to have been made *after* his arrival in New York.

9. Schliemann immediately left Indianapolis after selling his share in the starch factory, which apparently he had acquired only to impress the court with his firm intention to settle in the city for good. The house he sold later, but purchased another in 1879 with the purpose of backing up his retention of American citizenship. That house was inherited by his surviving Russian daughter, who later took up residence there. Eventually she went to work in Paris for a branch of an Indianapolis bank.

10. *BW I*, p. 146. In another letter the figure is twenty-five instead of fifteen.

11. *BW I*, p. 146.

12. *BW I*, p. 148.

13. *BW I*, p. 149. Good tidings for the Schröders, who held substantial parcels of Cuban railroad securities (some floated by their London house) and, of course, for Schliemann himself.

14. *BW I*, p. 153.

15. *EL*, p. 112.

16. The original surname Kastromenos was later readopted by all members of the family.

17. "Give me my son," he beseeched Ekaterina right after obtaining his divorce. His Russian children, however, tended to side with their mother and considered their father's American divorce invalid and his second marriage a case of bigamy.

18. *Lilly*, p. 31.

19. *Lilly*, p. 33.

20. *Lilly*, p. 33.

21. *Lilly*, p. 48.

22. *Lilly*, p. 37.

23. *Lilly*, p. 48.

24. *EL*, p. 117.

25. The day before his remarriage, September 23, 1869, Schliemann wrote to his family in Germany: "If, therefore, Sophia has ever cause to shed a single tear, you will be justified in saying that I am a villain and deserved all the unhappiness of my first marriage" (*EL*, p. 117). Sophia's crying spells in Paris were probably not, however, the only time the egotistical Schliemann brought his young wife to tears. There were his frequent absences and the divided loyalties between her family and an aging husband. At one time, when she was pregnant with their son, Schliemann left her all alone in Paris without even sufficient funds for her upkeep.

26. *BW II*, p. 382.

27. *BW I*, p. 161.

28. Interesting excavations, anticipating Schliemann's and Evans' discovery of the Minoan and Mycenaean civilizations, were undertaken at Thera in 1862 by Ferdinand André Fouqué, a volcanologist, who dug up frescoed walls under more than twenty feet of lava. He dated the eruption at about 2000 B.C., when Thera was severed from what is today Therasia.

29. BW I, p. 173.

30. BW I, p. 181.

31. BW I, p. 181.

32. T&R, p. 76.

33. EM, p. 262.

34. The Aryan ideology was then a rising myth that turned into a mania. It had been stimulated by comparative linguistics. Schliemann's friends Émile Burnouf, former honorary director of the French Archaeological Institute in Athens, and Professor Max Müller, the Anglo-German Sanskrit scholar, subscribed to it. The swastika—whether turning right or left—is, of course, a universal (sun?) symbol to be found in virtually all cultures, including pre-Columbian Indians, Africans, and Semites. Yet despite his Aryan loyalties, Schliemann was at least as much impressed by the impact of the Near East on Aegean culture.

35. T&R, p. 102.

36. Lynn and Gray Poole, One Passion, Two Loves, p. 97.

37. T&R, p. 80.

38. Ilios, p. 22.

39. BW I, p. 202.

40. BW I, p. 209.

41. BW I, p. 336.

42. Jean Baptiste Lechevalier or Le Chevallier (1752–1836) propagated the hypothesis—in Voyage de la Troade (Paris, 1794)—that Bunarbashi, because of its commanding strategic location, better fit the Homeric picture of ancient Troy.

43. T&R, p. 12.

THE CAMPAIGN BEGINS

1. A Macedonian general (c. 360–281 B.C.) under Alexander the Great. After the latter's death he ruled for a while as king over Macedonia, Thrace, and a large part of Asia Minor, and is credited with rebuilding Troy. The well-preserved ramparts Schliemann ascribed to him were probably much older and may have belonged to Troy VI.

2. This principle, basic to an ancient stratified settlement, Schliemann observed and described years earlier at Jerusalem in April 1859. He then wrote to his father and sisters: "The roads which our Saviour walked here in Jerusalem are some 40 to 50 feet below those of today, because following each of the 17 destructions of the city the new fundaments were every time put up on the ruins of the ancient houses" (B, p. 107).

3. Even though Schliemann occasionally commented on Zaphyros' acquisitiveness and dubious skill as an excavator, the latter became a most trusted all-around helper at Hissarlik until his much lamented death by drowning in the Scamander. His full name was Nikolaos Zaphyros Jannakis.

4. Both Schliemann's diary and letters indicate that Sophia was not present at the beginning and joined him only later in the season.

5. Schliemann owned shares in this prosperous road.

6. According to Schliemann, classical scholars mistranslated the term glau-kōpis, which Homer bestowed on the goddess Athene, as "grey-eyed," while he insisted it meant "owl-eyed," the owl being, of course, Athene's very own bird. On such flimsy

philological and archaeological grounds, he then conjured up a whole inconography of the goddess from the facial urns, figure vases, and other anthro- and zoomorphic pottery at Hissarlik. One of his main motivations was to establish kinship between the Athene-worshiping Athenians and Trojans.

VIII "PRIAM'S TREASURE" 1873

1. The likelihood of making finds similar to the Apollo relief, Curtius thought, might persuade the German government to undertake excavations. That "feeler" reveals the conventional fine art- and museum-oriented archaeology of the German academic establishment, rather than an interest in prehistory per se. Yet as leader of the Olympia excavations (1875–1880), Curtius ranks as pioneer of scientific archaeology.

2. BW I, p. 235.

3. BW I, p. 234, and elsewhere.

4. The director at that time was Dr. P. A. Déthier, who happened to be German.

5. Naturally, the pilgrimage to Troy and the Troad had preceded Schliemann's coming to Hissarlik; it had been going on for more than two millennia. In a way, Schliemann was just one in an endless procession.

6. BW I, p. 231.

7. B, p. 129.

8. Dörpfeld, however, from talks with Schliemann, asserted that the great treasure was found in the shape of a compact cube inmured in a niche of the circuit wall of air-dried bricks and enveloped by a layer of reddish ash and calcinated debris (Troja und Ilion, p. 8).

9. In the light of more recent research, Troy II may be looked upon as not so much a unique prehistoric center but a "type site" which just happens to be the most thoroughly studied. To quote Carl W. Blegen: "As indicated by sporadic finds and graves, further explorations will probably show that the culture we call Trojan was widely spread over a relatively broad area in this part of Anatolia . . ." (Troy and the Trojans, pp. 57–58).

10. Against the overanxious apologists of Schliemann, one should consider that the idea of keeping antiquities in the country where they were found and, better still, at or near their original sites, was by no means alien to Schliemann's age. Hence, the strict legislation for the retention of artifacts in Greece and elsewhere. The founding of the Bulaq (later moved to Cairo) museum in Egypt before Schliemann appeared on the scene and the indomitable Mariette's struggle on its behalf are ample proof. Attempts to preserve Pompeii with all its excavated remains—and not just museum pieces—go back to the early nineteenth century.

11. B, p. 132.

12. EM, p. 274.

13. BW I, p. 240.

A MOMENTOUS DISCOVERY

1. The data given were, however, of little use to other researchers. Blegen remarked on the difficulty of attributing objects excavated by Schliemann to specific settlements, "for exact records from the early campaigns, when most of the digging was done, are scanty and incomplete. The pottery and other objects of Troy I [because of their unmistakable character] could for the most part be recognized; but in his Catalogue of the Schliemann Collection, Herbert Schmidt was unable to "differentiate with certainty the pottery and most of the other material from the layers of Troy II, III, IV, and V, all of

which had to be lumped together as an enormously large group representing a long era" (*Troy and the Trojans*, p. 36).

2. According to Ernst Meyer, a biographer of Schliemann and editor of his letters, this report was actually written (and hence antedated) in Athens after Schliemann had left Hissarlik.

3. Probably a copper bowl rather than a shield.

4. This type of vessel, familiar in clay and gold from the mid-third-millennium Aegean islands and Greek mainland, is usually referred to in the literature as a "sauce boat (*saucière*)." Its purpose is unknown; possibly it was used for religious libations. Schliemann's equation with Homer's *dépas amphikýpellon*, or double-handled vessel, is arbitrary. He added further confusion by calling a quite different double-handled elongated goblet by the same Homeric name. The latter, however, not at all rare at prehistoric Anatolian sites, has been known under that name ever since.

5. Believed by Dörpfeld and others to be a copper chisel not connected with the treasure.

6. These were the elaborate ornaments Sophia put on to pose for a famous photograph. Possibly they were worn by a prince.

7. Schliemann was baffled throughout over the possible presence of writing in the pre-Hellenic settlements of Hissarlik and played it hot and cold. For a long time he fervently searched for an inscription verifying Homeric Troy's identity but eventually despaired. However, scribblings on pottery and the like were at one time or another thought by various savants to be Phoenician, Assyrian, Chinese, and a number of other languages. But all the evidence remains inconclusive. The verdict must be that prehistoric Trojans were most likely illiterate.

8. MacVeagh was actually the U.S. ambassador.

9. Probably revoked in 1873. Schliemann reported in a letter of March 4, 1873, to the Austrian ambassador in Constantinople that he was being threatened with the annulment of his *firman* (*BW I*, pp. 223–224).

IX THE GOLD OF MYCENAE 1874–1876

1. *B*, p. 133.

2. *BW I*, pp. 236–237. A parallel to Schliemann's intervention on behalf of a wrongly accused official happened during the Mycenae campaign in 1876 as an aftermath of the visit of the Emperor of Brazil, Dom Pedro. A police captain who had guarded the latter was given a measly sum by the emperor to distribute among his men. He was accused of having withheld a much larger amount from his subalterns and was disgraced. Schliemann, firmly believing in the man's innocence, cabled the emperor, who by then was in Cairo, and thus had the wronged captain reinstated.

3. *BW I*, p. 237.

4. Schliemann declared he had "made peace with the Turks" (*B*, p. 145).

5. Earlier, Schliemann himself had estimated the treasure to be worth one million francs.

6. *B*, p. 138.

7. Fiorelli was a former superintendent of the Pompeian excavations and Italy's director-general of antiquities; Schliemann had met him in Pompeii in 1868.

8. *B*, p. 141.

9. Years later Dörpfeld tried, with uneven success, to convert Schliemann to such a balanced attitude: "Scientific questions cannot be decided by abuse, but only by objective proof" (*EL*, p. 220).

10. *EL*, p. 156.

11. *BW I*, p. 223.

12. *Ilios*, p. 43.

13. *BW II*, p. 44.

14. *EL*, p. 181.

15. He wrote to Queen Sophie on March 2, 1876, announcing that he had selected "the best ten Tanagra figurines . . . from my own [!] collection. . . . Unfortunately I cannot send them by direct steamer, the exportation of antiquities being strictly prohibited in Greece. If I do not find an earlier opportunity, then I shall send the box from Troy in the Hellespont . . . (*BW II*, pp. 36–37).

16. *BW I*, p. 302.

17. Stamatakes later rose to become director-general of antiquities in Greece and directed excavations on the Acropolis in Athens. By that time Schliemann paid him due respect and seems to have enjoyed amiable relations with him. In *Tiryns* (1885), Schliemann explicitly praised Stamatakes and deplored his recent death (p. 368).

18. Pelasgian was a term used by the ancient Greeks themselves for early non-Greek inhabitants of their country and its islands. Homer mentions Pelasgian allies of Troy. Some pockets of Pelasgian-speaking people were reputed to exist in antiquity.

19. *EL*, pp. 167–168.

20. Unlike the objects which Schliemann found later, which were much older, the vase is approximately contemporaneous with the traditional date of the Trojan War (c. 1200 B.C.).

21. According to some sources there were eighteen bodies, including two children (evoking Cassandra's two murdered children). A sixth shaft grave discovered by Stamatakes contained two additional male corpses.

22. Schliemann dedicated the American edition to Gladstone.

23. This visit interrupted work at Mycenae for two weeks.

24. Graves have even been suspected under the Lion Gate.

25. The Grave Circle Schliemann discovered, referred to in the literature as "A," has by now also lost its uniqueness, since Greek archaeologists in the 1950's have been able to pin down another such circle, "B," with more than twenty shaft graves and almost as rich in objects. "B" is located in the lower city, within its less formidable walls, and appears to be even older, sharing the closest relation to Stamatakes' grave 6, probably the oldest of Grave Circle A. In recent years, Mycenaean grave circles have also been discovered in the southwestern Peloponnese (Peristeria) and, possibly, on Leukas.

26. Named Mycenaean by accident of discovery rather than by the fact that its civilization was centered or confined to this Peloponnesian Bronze Age fortress which, nevertheless, may have played a prominent role. The Mycenaean Age is more or less coeval with the Late Helladic (c. 1600–1200 B.C.), which is divided into several subperiods.

27. Michael Ventris and John Chadwick dedicated their fundamental *Documents in Mycenaean Greek* (Cambridge, Eng.: Cambridge University Press, 1956) "To the memory of Heinrich Schliemann 1822–90, Father of Mycenaean Archaeology."

THE SEARCH FOR AGAMEMNON

1. The citadel proper, on the highest terrace farther east, was later shown by Greek archaeologists to include the palace buildings. Why one should expect the royal residence at a lower point near the gate Schliemann fails to clarify. Did he think of an analogy to *his* image of Priam's Troy? The Mycenaean palace, by the way, is, like the Lion Gate, several centuries younger than the Grave Circle.

2. Perhaps not a tomb at all, but a reburial of (looted?) grave treasure by the wall of a Cyclopean house. Not to be confused with grave 6, found later in the year by Stamatakes, which contained bodies, a mask, and funerary furniture.

3. It is unclear whether Schliemann refers here to Drosinos' cache or to Stamatakes' discovery of an actual sixth shaft grave; it is probably the former.

X   THE SIEGE CONTINUES   1878–1879

1. *BW II*, p.68.
2. *BW II*, p. 67.
3. *BW II*, p. 71.
4. *BW II*, p. 72.
5. *EL*, p. 182.
6. These men also helped in the procurement of workers, the transport of equipment, and the shipment of archaeological objects. To show his gratitude, Schliemann forever urged his German contacts to secure medals for them.
7. *Ilios*, p. 45.
8. Altogether some nineteen treasures were reportedly taken from Troy.
9. *Ilios*, p. 51.
10. *Ilios*, p. 53.
11. The incident is described in Virchow's recollections of Schliemann in the German magazine *Gartenlaube* of 1891.
12. *Ilios*, p. 66.
13. *Ilios*, p. xvi.
14. Few have followed Sayce along these abstruse and speculative avenues. Carl Schuchhardt had to admit, in reference to the multifold "inscribed" Hissarlik objects: "On none of them . . . can anything beyond mere decoration be made out" (*Schliemann's Excavations*, p. 72).
15. *BW II*, p. 86. Schliemann must have been intrigued by this hyperbole since, as with other of his bombastic statements, he used it repeatedly—for example, when submitting *Troja* to the New York publisher Scribner's a few years later.
16. *Ilios*, p. 517.
17. *B*, p. 164.

THE SECOND TROJAN CAMPAIGN

1. A former administrative division of the Ottoman Empire in the central and eastern Balkans, with Sofia as its center. During the time it was still under Turkish control and torn by political strife.
2. Major ruins of a Hellenistic settlement in the southwestern Troad. A former seaport, it was twice visited by St. Paul.

XI   RETURN TO ASIA MINOR   1882

1. For example, M. A. Niederhöffer's *Mecklenburgs Volkssagen*, 4 vols. (1864). The author, a Mecklenburg pastor, was the father of the "legendary" young miller of the *Ilios* "autobiography." Carl Andres called Schliemann's attention to this and related works.
2. *BW II*, p. 114.
3. *EL*, p. 244.
4. "Your presence at Troy is a necessity to science and of the greatest interest to me. It is understood that I shall pay the expenses of the round trip. I only ask you that everything you wish to publish on Troy will benefit my new, strictly scientific work on Ilium" (*B*, p. 155).
5. *EL*, p. 214.
6. *B*, p. 166 fn.; *EL*, p. 215.
7. Moltke, a notable topographer, also happened to be a staunch defender of the Bunarbashi thesis, on which he had published a book.
8. *EL*, p. 241.
9. *EL*, p. 242.

10. *EL*, p. 243.
11. *Brueckner*, p. 180.
12. *Brueckner*, p. 180.
13. Probably it once even controlled Thebes.
14. Intensive archaeological work after Schliemann established Orchomenos, like nearby Gla, as a very ancient settlement going back to Neolithic and early Bronze Age times.
15. Its occurrence may possibly throw light on the invasion route of the early Indo-European-speaking "Greeks," though it should be added that more recent researches tend to date their arrival as early as 2200 to 2100 B.C. Also, the abrupt break in style with ceramics and other artifacts from preceding strata—particularly those at Anatolian sites—is now disputed, as is, on occasion, the whole Minyan hypothesis.
16. *B*, p. 187.
17. It was sold by the Schliemann family in 1926.
18. Later in the year, when Virchow was attending an ethnological congress in the Caucasus and digging in the Kuban, Schliemann and he planned to cover jointly much the same ground. However, Virchow's Black Sea steamer was delayed, and further explorations in the Troad had to be postponed.
19. *Troja*, p. 303.
20. *Troja*, p. 303.
21. *Troja*, p. 347.
22. It has been suggested that Kum Kale was settled in Neolithic times by a Near Eastern people who landed at the coast. The same people may have then colonized the virgin Hissarlik ridge in the early Bronze Age.
23. Yet he could also wax lyrical over the Troad, revel in its beauties, and call it "the most fascinating landscape in the world" (*B*, p. 183). He once remarked that he preferred excavating in Asia Minor to any other place.
24. Frederick Blackwood, Lord Dufferin, British ambassador at Constantinople (1881–1882).
25. *B*, p. 192.
26. Just as he had agitated against the governor of the Dardanelles, Ibrahim Pasha, in 1876.
27. *B*, p. 185.
28. Which so far has eluded all archaeologists, including Dörpfeld and Blegen. (But Blegen found a burial ground associated with Troy VI.)
29. *B*, p. 181.
30. The need for archaeologically trained architects to serve on excavations had been espoused for some time by German scholars, in particular by Alexander Conze, the excavator, since 1873, of Samothrace.
31. This remark is attributed to various people, among them Sir Arthur Evans. But Dörpfeld's biographer, Peter Goessler, thinks it was first made by a Serbian diplomat and wit. It is somewhat analogous to Minna's generous remark about Schliemann's second wife, Sophia.
32. This is, of course, what Schliemann beforehand had made up his mind to find in the 1882 campaign, rather than what his "excellent architects" happened to establish.
33. *BW II*, pp. 142–143.
34. *B*, p. 203.
35. Modern prehistorians have found the *megaron* already adopted by primitive Neolithic settlements in Anatolia. It is likewise present in Troy I and, by around the late Middle Helladic (c. 1900–1800 B.C.), on the Greek mainland. All indications speak against the once cherished belief of its European origin.
36. Dörpfeld came to clearly distinguish three stages of Troy II, but Blegen was later to add four more.
37. Schliemann seems to have subscribed to this thesis for a while, but had it riddled

by Virchow. The debate over the origin of early and middle Bronze Age Trojan culture (ceramics, architecture, etc.) still rages today, though partisans of Asia certainly have the edge (*cf.* n. 35, above).

38. Puchstein later excavated at Baalbek.

39. *Ilios. Ville et pays des Troyennes* (Paris: Librairie Firmin Didot et Cie, 1885).

TROY, TROAD, AND TUMULI

1. Apparently at what Dörpfeld came to identify as the sixth and seventh levels from the bottom.

2. Marie Gabriel Florent Auguste, Comte de Choiseul-Gouffier (1752–1817), a French diplomat and traveler, wrote *Voyage pittoresque dans l'Empire Ottoman, en Grèce, dans la Troade, les îsles de l'archipel et sur les côtes de l'Asie*, 3 vols. (Paris, 1780–1826).

XII TIRYNS 1884–1885

1. Where a 500 B.C. Dorian law code carved in stone was found and near where Halbheer later dug up the Minoan palace complex of Phaestos.

2. Schliemann's much maligned former antagonist, Stamatakes, met with positive results at the battle site of Plataea (479 B.C.) in southeastern Boeotia.

3. *B*, 232. His English publisher John Murray later wrote him (May 1886): ". . . You must not consider that we English are jealous of you. It is in the fate of all discoverers to be carped at by small men . . ." (*BW II*, p. 245).

4. *B*, p. 232.

5. See Paul MacKendrick, *The Greek Stones Speak*, p. 85.

6. *Mycenae*, p. 19.

7. English friends persuaded Schliemann to continue operations at Tiryns in 1885, but he provided only limited funds.

8. He likewise put Adolf Furtwängler in his place when the latter published (with Georg Löschke) his epochal study on Mycenaean ceramics (*Mykenische Vasen*) in 1886.

9. Now believed to be of a later date than the Mycenaean structures.

10. The term *megaron* is Homeric. Originally, it may have referred only to the main hall, not the entire building with columned porch, anteroom, and occasional apsidal annex (storeroom?).

11. The one just to the right of the large *megaron* is often identified as women's hall or quarters—as distinguished from a supposed men's hall. However, this "sexist" division, despite certain Homeric references, remains unproved. Besides, the adjacent smaller *megaron* is now considered of different age, thus making the whole scheme irrelevant.

12. *BW II*, p. 187.

13. *BW II*, p. 189.

14. *BW II*, p. 192.

15. An expensive American facsimile reprint unfortunately renders these reproductions in black and white (New York: Benjamin Blom, 1967).

16. Credit was denied, though Schliemann excerpted in his text a long essay by John P. Mahaffy, "On the Destruction of Mycenae by the Argives" from the *Dublin University Journal*.

17. *B*, p. 249. As far as one can gather from the incomplete editions of his letters, Schliemann seems to have paid some, if not most, of his contributors, as well as the editorial and scientific helpers on his publications, who included renowned scholars. His biographers do not discuss the matter.

18. *BW II*, p. 224 (November 7, 1885).

EXCAVATING HERCULES' FORTRESS

1. Capo d'Istria was a hero of Greek Independence (1776–1831).
2. The reference is to Dioscorides Pedanius, a Greek physician of the first century A.D. who served in the Roman army and wrote a standard work on drugs. Athenaios (Athenaeus) is another first century Greek physician who practiced in Rome; he wrote on medicine and dietetics.
3. A quite common name in Greece for ruined citadels, meaning "ancient castle."
4. Though Hercules assumed the kingship of Tiryns, traditions vary as to his place of birth, with Mycenae being the favorite.
5. According to Aristotle and Theophrastus.
6. The Phoenician hypothesis of Greek cultural origins is today utterly discredited, but it was very popular in the nineteenth century and thus at least deserves the attention of the historian of ideas. However, many references in Homeric and mythological traditions, as well as etymological affinities in place names, the later introduction of the Phoenician alphabet, and the likelihood of Phoenician colonies in the Aegean area, hardly allow us to dismiss the thesis in its entirety. Phoenician contacts, though at a later age than that posited by Schliemann, were undoubtedly frequent and profound. Several Hellenic cities claimed Phoenician founding fathers; Phoenician-sounding names, as Schliemann tried to prove at length, existed in the nineteenth century and survive to the present day. Phoenician traders, seafarers, craftsmen, colonists, and the like may well have been preceded by proto-Phoenician (Canaanite) elements of the Syria-Palestine littoral. Yet some modern scholars talk of Schliemann's Phoenician thesis as an "aberration" and express an almost racist aversion for it, maintaining that it was forced on him by academicians against his own better judgment. (Archaeology, also, has its conspiracy myths!) Allegedly, he adopted it only in his later years. William A. McDonald in his magisterial survey of the rediscovery of Mycenaean and Minoan civilizations (*Progress Into the Past*, 1967), which seems to follow Joseph Alsop (*From the Silent Earth*, 1964) in this controversial issue, expresses, with noticeable relief, that "fortunately . . . [it] was firmly rejected by the leading scholars actually working in Greece" (p. 72). Nevertheless, Dörpfeld, a leading scholar working in Greece if ever there was one, continued to subscribe to the theory long after Evans' discoveries in Crete. He seems to have allowed for common Syrian ("Phoenician") roots of both Mycenaean and Minoan civilizations. The thesis may conceivably undergo a survival in some form if Cyrus Gordon's admittedly not widely accepted claim to have deciphered Linear A tablets from Crete (containing North Semitic texts?) should find acceptance. McDonald is right when stating that Schliemann wavered in his view. But that was indicative of his insecurity and frequent change of mind (simultaneously he also subscribed to the Aryan thesis) rather than a "capitulation." I can find no evidence that he "long and stoutly resisted" these theories. In fact, there are already hints of them in his first archaeological book, *Ithaka*. McDonald is demonstrably wrong when asserting that he "never adopted them in his official publications" (p. 70).
7. Including Schliemann himself during the brief 1876 season.
8. The arch is corbeled and not a true arch.

XIII TROJAN FINALE 1889–1890

1. *B*, p. 252.
2. *B*, p. 251. The French edition of *Ilios*, over which Schliemann labored for close to five years, also came out at about the same time.
3. *B*, p. 252. The often repeated anecdote that with his appearance in Cuba

Schliemann drove up the prices of railroad shares in order to dispose of them at an enormous profit right then and there does not seem to hold water.

4. *BW II*, p. 166.

5. *EM*, p. 354.

6. *BW, II*, p. 155.

7. *BW II*, p. 248.

8. *B*, p. 231.

9. Recently, however, archaeologists excavating historic cemeteries at Yortan and Bobaköy in northwestern Anatolia near the Troad, believed to be contemporary with Troy II, found the dead buried in large *pithoi*. At these two sites, by the way, only burial places, and not the settlements to which they must have belonged, have so far been encountered. The reverse is true of Troy I–V, where the graveyards remain to be located.

10. Apparently his first letter to Virchow since the break in August 1885.

11. *BW II*, p. 247.

12. Chatzidakis later helped Arthur Evans purchase the Knossos hill. Schliemann seems to have treated Chatzidakis with suspicion.

13. Actually, under the leadership of Tsountas, Greek excavators proved themselves extraordinarily competent. They indeed found the palace—*megara* and all—which now could stand with the Tyrinthian royal citadel as a prime example of a Mycenaean princely residence.

14. The Egyptian National Museum was later moved to Cairo.

15. *B*, p. 260.

16. *BW I*, p. 269

17. Schliemann's sure instinct (probably stimulated by A. H. Sayce) directed him to the Hittites, once masters over much of Asia Minor. Unknown to him, the Hittite documents from Bogazköy, discovered and deciphered since his time, may have contained an actual reference to "Ilios." They also contained an account of the battle of Kadesh, which makes it likely that Ramses II, despite his boasts, was bested by the Hittites.

18. Berlin museum officials took a rather dim view of Schliemann's Egyptian expertise and found most of the material he collected of indifferent value but did not have the heart to tell him so.

19. *B*, p. 281.

20. *BW II*, p. 290.

21. The location of King Nestor's palace city has long been a matter of debate, particularly since several sites in the southwestern and western Peloponnese bear that name. In 1939, Blegen found near the Bay of Navarino in Messenia a magnificent buried citadel which is now widely regarded as the Pylos of Homer. Blegen's Pylos gained additional stature from its large deposit of tablets inscribed in Linear B.

22. *EM*, p. 250.

23. *EM*, p. 355.

24. The account given here of the intricate transactions over several years is but a simplified digest of the more involved, and sometimes contradictory, data in Schliemann's correspondence.

25. *BW II*, p. 304.

26. *BW II*, p. 173.

27. *BW II*, p. 179.

28. *B*, p. 288.

29. *B*, p. 289.

30. *B*, p. 299.

31. *B*, p. 303, in a letter to the German Chancellor's son, Herbert von Bismarck: "Much precious time is lost on the houses of the five settlements successive to the

second burnt city, because we cannot dismantle those structures before cleaning and photographing them."

32. The cups, jars, and cans had stirrup-like handles. Incidentally, parallels occur in pre-Columbian vases. In *Tiryns*, Schliemann had referred to the ubiquity of this type of vessel not only in Mycenae and Tiryns, but on Salamis, Thera, and various sites in Crete, Cyprus, Rhodes, and even Egypt (pp. 138–139). Most of such "Mycenaean" ware was dug up before Schliemann's excavations.

33. The analysis was being done by Dr. A. Brueckner, who was also present at the campaign. Dörpfeld, in "History of Excavations of Troy," the introductory chapter to his *Troja und Ilion* (1902), implied that in 1890 he and Schliemann freely discussed the possibility that Troy VI rather than Troy II was the "Homeric" city. However, both his and Schliemann's own reports offer no such clue. By allowing for other reasons for Mycenaean ceramics' being found in a settlement more recent than Troy II (*e.g.*, conceivably they represented late imported survivals), Schliemann and Dörpfeld apparently had not yet fully conceded to so radical a revision. This seems to be borne out, too, by the second edition of Schuchhardt's comprehensive work on Schliemann's excavations, which shies away from Troy VI. In fact, Schuchhardt, usually far in advance of Schliemann's opinions, stuck to the view that the identity of Troy II was "incontestable." As with most scientific advances, the switch from Troy II to Troy VI, given the evidence we have now, seems ex post facto obvious and inevitable. But seen in the context of the time, the preconceptions and characters of the men involved, and the contemporary problems and dogmas, so logical a course is rarely ever followed immediately.

34. Schuchhardt, p. 349.

35. Schliemann may well have thought that there was no longer any mystery, that the results of the 1882 and 1889/1890 campaigns had established once and for all Troy II as Priam's city. I think it is pretty certain that Schliemann died believing just that, no matter what later writers have maintained.

36. *Troja und Ilion*, p. 17.

37. Similar objects have since been found in Bessarabia.

38. In his letter to Virchow, Schliemann says the trove was found on July 8. Again, as with the great treasure, there is a confusion of dates.

39. *BW II*, p. 390.

40. E. Meyer, Schliemann's fawning biographer, insisted that there was no need to hide the cache since the director of the Turkish Imperial Museum, Hamdy Bey, at the second Hissarlik conference, had let Schliemann keep "broken pottery and stone tools" (*BW II*, n. 399, p. 462). Obviously, Schliemann himself had good reasons not to think that this on-the-spot largess extended to his trove. Why else would he be afraid of not getting his *firman* renewed? Also, Meyer's point is meaningless since the treasure included gold and other metal objects.

41. *BW II*, p. 368.

42. *BW II*, p. 380.

43. When published early in 1891, it carried a brief introduction by Sophia Schliemann. The English edition, slightly abridged, was appended to Carl Schuchhardt's *Schliemann's Excavations*.

44. *B*, p. 316.

SELECTED BIBLIOGRAPHY

To my knowledge, there exists no Schliemann bibliography worthy of the name. Even the "standard" works on him are sparse and sketchy in their listings. Perhaps most helpful are the scattered references in Ernst Meyer's biography and his editions of Schliemann's letters, and in the card catalogue at the Gennadeion Library in Athens. Though the literature on Schliemann is vast and ever growing, little of substance has been produced. But this happens to be characteristic of the entire field of the history of archaeology, where the popularizers have the field and professionals popularize.

Unfairly maligned by the defenders of the Schliemann legend, Emil Ludwig's book is not only the first full-length "life" but still the best. Apart from being well written and immensely readable, it reflects a sympathetic understanding of the man based on original research and personal acquaintance with the Schliemann family. Robert Payne's book stands out as a brilliant profile by an eloquent Philhellene. Recent German biographies are marred by uncritical piety, a trait conspicuous in Ernst Meyer's conscientious, though cumbersome, study, the result of a lifelong absorption in the Schliemann papers. Meyer's research is neverthe-less invaluable, and everybody digging into the subject remains in his debt.

Foremost among Meyer's contributions are the three volumes of correspond-ence he edited. Despite their size, these volumes are, however, quite selective and, as the compiler concedes, owe their impulse to an "unqualified admiration" of the man. Meyer freely admits that he discarded what he thought was written by Schliemann in a state of temporary excitement and which allegedly runs counter to the "true nature" of the letter writer. He purposely avoids what he called the danger of divesting Schliemann of his greatness by incorporating "commonplace and all-too-human" matters. Hence, there are serious gaps, such as those pertaining to Schliemann's motley transactions, feuds, and personal relations—particularly his marriages. Meyer was also adamant in bringing out Schliemann's "idealism" and his "unbroken" ties to the German nation. (Typi-cally, he would accuse Ludwig of lacking, because of a "materialist" and un-patriotic—namely, alien—mentality, the organ for such finer sentiments.) Luckily, Ludwig's biography, quoting amply from unpublished journals and letters, just the same acts as a useful corrective. Other valuable material was incorporated in Eli Lilly's *Schliemann in Indianapolis*. Thus far unpublished letters in the possession of Schliemann's grandson, Alexander Mélas, were used by Lynn and

Gray Poole in their *One Passion, Two Loves,* which deals with Sophia and Heinrich's marriage and partnership. The same phase of Schliemann's life is also the subject of Irving Stone's recent (1975) novel, *The Greek Treasure,* which came out after I had completed my manuscript.

Since this is primarily a book on Schliemann, the vast literature on Aegean prehistory, Mycenaean archaeology, and the Homeric debate can be indicated only by a few entries, which, however, will guide the reader to other salient titles. These fascinating studies bear, of course, on Schliemann's own researches and, though dealing with remote cultural epochs, represent one of the exciting, if not explosive, frontiers of modern inquiry. I can think of few other fields in which the curious outsider will be able to immerse himself with as much intellectual profit and stimulation. Joseph Alsop's *From the Silent Earth,* a report on his journey into these realms of discovery and controversy, bears impressive witness to the pleasurable rewards of such pursuits. For the serious student, the opening volumes of the new (third edition) *Cambridge Ancient History,* with their ample bibliographies, are mandatory. A continuing bibliography on Mycenaean studies (revolutionized by Michael Ventris' decipherment of Linear B), under the title *Nestor,* is being periodically issued by the University of Wisconsin at Madison. A good start can be made with the concise volumes in the exemplary "Ancient Peoples and Places" series on Troy and Mycenae. Convenient popularizations at their best are the McDonald and Cottrell books listed below.

For lucid critical expositions of questions concerning the historicity of the Trojan War, the general reader should turn to two short essays, one by M. I. Finley, "Lost: The Trojan War," in *Aspects of Antiquity* (London: Chatto & Windus; New York: Viking Press, 1968; Penguin Books—Pelican [U.K.], 1972, pp. 31–42), and by Carl Nylander, "The Fall of Troy," in *The Deep Well* (London: George Allen & Unwin; New York: St. Martin's Press, 1969; Penguin Books—Pelican [U.K.], 1971, pp. 127–137). Sinclair Hood's *The Home of the Heroes* (London: Thames & Hudson; New York: McGraw-Hill, 1967) is particularly stimulating for its dissenting views on early Greece and Crete and the decipherment of Linear B.

An able popular summary of the archaeology of Troy in the light of modern knowledge and of the problematic connection between the Homeric poems and the material evidence is given by L. Sprague and Catherine C. de Camp in "Troy and the Nine Cities," Chapter IV of *Ancient Ruins and Archaeology* (New York: Doubleday, 1964), reissued in paper under the title *Citadels of Mystery* (New York: Ballantine, 1973, pp. 67–94). The de Camps, by the way, relate a startling episode on the fate of Trojan ceramics, stored during World War II in an East Prussian castle, where they were allegedly smashed during a frolic by the local people. The fate of the Schliemann collection at Berlin is also discussed in the Poole book.

In the following entries, I aimed at listing, to the best of my knowledge, both English and American publishing data, as well as paperback (PB) editions and reprints of older works. Overlengthy, mainly nineteenth century, titles are usually given only in part. Subtitles, unless they contain proper names or German nouns, can be distinguished by their lower-casing.

Alsop, Joseph. *From the Silent Earth: The Greek Bronze Age.* New York: Harper & Row, 1964; London: Secker & Warburg, 1965; PB, Penguin Books—Pelican (U.K.), 1970.

Blegan, Carl W. *Troy and the Trojans*. Ancient Peoples and Places, Vol. 33. London: Thames & Hudson; New York: Praeger, 1963.

Brueckner, Alfred. *Allgemeine Deutsche Biographie*, under "Schliemann, H." Vol. 55. Leipzig: Duncker & Humboldt, 1910, pp. 171–184.

Brustgi, Franz G. *Heinrich Schliemann*. München: Nymphenburger Verlagshandlung, 1971.

Chadwick, John. *The Decipherment of Linear B*. London–Cambridge and New York: Cambridge University Press, 1958. PB, Penguin (U.K.), 1961; Random House–Vintage Books, 1966.

Cottrell, Leonard. *The Lion Gate* (Amer. title: *Realms of Gold*): *A journey in search of the Mycenaeans*. London: Evans Brothers; Greenwich, Conn.: New York Graphic Society, 1963. PB, Pan Books (U.K.), 1967.

Daniel, Glyn E. *A Hundred Years of Archaeology*. London: Gerald Duckworth, 1950; repr., 1952.

Dörpfeld, Wilhelm. *Troja und Ilion. Ergebnisse der Ausgrabungen in den vorhistorischen und historischen Schichten von Ilion, 1870–94*. 2 vols. Athens: Beck & Barth, 1902.

Evans, Joan. *Time and Chance. The story of Arthur Evans and his forebears*. London: Longmans, Green & Co., 1943.

Finley, Moses I. *Early Greece, the Bronze and Archaic Ages*. London: Chatto & Windus; New York: W. W. Norton, 1970 (also PB).

———. *The World of Odysseus*. New York: Viking Press, 1954 (rev. ed., 1965); London: Chatto & Windus, 1956. PB, Viking Press–Compass Books, 1965; Penguin (U.K.), 1967.

Goessler, Peter. *Wilhelm Dörpfeld*. Stuttgart: W. Kohlhammer, 1951.

Gurney, O. R. *The Hittites*. Harmondsworth, Eng.: Penguin Books; rev. ed., 1952, 1961.

Lilly, Eli, ed. *Schliemann in Indianapolis*. Indianapolis: Indiana Historical Society, 1961.

Lloyd, Seton. *Early Anatolia*. Harmondsworth, Eng.: Penguin Books, 1956.

———. *Early Highland Peoples of Anatolia*. London: Thames & Hudson; New York: McGraw-Hill, 1967 (also PB).

Ludwig, Emil. *Schliemann: The story of a gold-seeker*. Translated by D. F. Tait. London: G. P. Putnam's Sons; Boston: Little, Brown & Company, 1931.

McDonald, William A. *Progress Into the Past: The rediscovery of Mycenaean civilization*. New York: Macmillan; London: Collier-Macmillan, 1967. PB, Indiana University Press, 1969.

MacKendrick, Paul. *The Greek Stones Speak: The story of archaeology in Greek lands*. London: Methuen; New York: St. Martin's Press, 1962. PB, New American Library, 1966.

Meyer, Ernst. *Heinrich Schliemann: Kaufmann und Forscher*. Göttingen: Musterschmidt Verlag, 1969.

———, ed. *Briefe von Heinrich Schliemann*. Berlin: Walter de Gruyter, 1936.

———. *Heinrich Schliemann Briefwechsel*. Vol. I, 1842–1875; vol. II, 1876–1890. Berlin: Gebr. Mann, 1953–1958.

———. "Schliemann's Letters to Max Müller in Oxford," *The Journal of Hellenic Studies*, vol. 82 (1962), pp. 75–105.

Page, Denys L. *History and the Homeric Iliad*. Berkeley and Los Angeles: University of California Press, 1959.

Payne, Robert. *The Gold of Troy: The story of Heinrich Schliemann and the buried cities of ancient Greece.* London: Robert Hale; New York: Funk and Wagnalls, 1959. PB, Paperback Library, 1961.

Petrie, W. M. Flinders. *Seventy Years in Archaeology.* London: Sampson, Low, Marston, 1931.

Poole, Lynn and Gray. *One Passion, Two Loves: The story of Heinrich and Sophia Schliemann, discoverers of Troy.* New York: Thomas Y. Crowell, 1966; London: Gollancz, 1967.

Samuel, Alan E. *The Mycenaeans in History.* Englewood Cliffs, N.J.: Prentice-Hall, 1966. (PB).

Schliemann, Heinrich (with W. Dörpfeld). *Bericht über die Ausgrabungen in Troja im Jahre 1890.* Leipzig: F. A. Brockhaus, 1891. An English translation is attached to Schuchhardt's *Schliemann's Excavations* (see below).

————. *La Chine et le Japon au temps présent.* Paris: Libraries Centrale, 1867.

————. *Ilios: The city and country of the Trojans.* London: John Murray, 1880; New York: Harper & Brothers, 1881. Reprint. New York: Benjamin Blom, 1968.

————. *Ithâque, le Péloponnèse, et Troie, recherches archéologiques.* Paris: C. Reinwald, 1869. German ed.: *Ithaka, der Peloponnes und Troja.* Leipzig: Giesecke & Devrient, 1869. Reprints. Ernst Meyer, ed. Darmstadt: Wissenschaftliche Buchgesellschaft, 1963, 1973.

————. *Mycenae: A narrative of researches and discoveries at Mycenae and Tiryns.* London: John Murray; New York: Scribner, Armstrong & Co., 1878. Reprint. New York: Benjamin Blom, 1967.

————. *Orchomenos: Bericht über meine Ausgrabungen.* Leipzig: F. A. Brockhaus, 1881. English version: "Exploration of the Boeotian Orchomenos," *The Journal of Hellenic Studies,* vol. 2 (1881), pp. 122–163.

————. *Reise in der Troas im Mai 1881.* Leipzig: F. A. Brockhaus, 1881. English version "Journey in the Troad, appendix to English edition of *Troja* (see below).

————. *Selbstbiographie, bis zu seinem Tode vervollständigt* [by A. Brueckner], 1st ed. (1892) by Sophie Schliemann. Wiesbaden: F. A. Brockhaus, 10th ed. by Ernst Meyer, 1968.

————. *Tiryns: The prehistoric palace of the kings of Tiryns.* New York: C. Scribner's Sons, 1885; London: John Murray, 1886. Reprint. New York: Benjamin Blom, 1967.

————. *Troja: Results of the latest researches and discoveries on the site of Homer's Troy* . . . London: John Murray; New York: Harper & Bros., 1884. Reprint. New York: Benjamin Blom, 1968.

————. *Troy and Its Remains.* Translated by L. Dora Schmitz; edited by Philip Smith. London: John Murray, 1875. Reprint. New York: Benjamin Blom, 1968.

Schmied, Wieland. *Kein Troja ohne Homer.* Zürich: Christiana Verlag, 1960. PB, München: Wilhelm Goldmann Verlag; Goldmann Taschenbücher (Germany), n.d.

Schuchhardt, Carl. *Schliemann's Excavations: An archaeological and historical study.* Translated by Eugénie Sellers. With an appendix on the recent discoveries by Dr. Schliemann and Dr. Dörpfeld. London: Macmillan, 1891. Reprints. New York: Benjamin Blom; Chicago: Ares, 1974.

Scott, John A. "Schliemann and Indianapolis," *The Classical Journal*, vol. 17 (1921–1922), pp. 404–406.

Stoll, Heinrich Alexander, ed. *Abenteuer meines Lebens: Heinrich Schliemann erzählt*. Leipzig: F. A. Brockhaus, 1960.

Taylour, Lord William. *The Mycenaeans*. Ancient Peoples and Places, vol. 39. London: Thames & Hudson; New York: Praeger, 1964.

Vermeule, Emily. *Greece in the Bronze Age*. Chicago and London: University of Chicago Press, 1964.

Wace, Alan J. B. *Mycenae: An archaeological and historical guide*. Princeton: Princeton University Press, 1949. Reprint. New York: Biblo & Tannen, 1964.

————, and Frank H. Stubbings. *A Companion to Homer*. London: Macmillan; New York: St. Martin's Press, 1962.

Weber, Shirley H., ed. *Schliemann's First Visit to America, 1850–51*. Gennadeion Monographs, no. 2. Cambridge, Mass.: Harvard University Press for the American School of Classical Studies at Athens, 1942.

INDEX

Schliemann, Heinrich (*cont'd*)
Ankershagen: childhood at, 23–8;
revisited, 85–6, 274, 308–9
appearance, 8, 9, 33, 90, 165, 348, 352–3
apprenticeship in Fürstenberg grocery,
29–30, 33–4, 366
archaeological and antiquarian interests in
youth, 1, 15, 16, 22, 25, 27, 60, 91,
100, 104, 279, 368
archaeological methods, 2, 13–16, 195–6,
261, 267–8, 284, 311–12, 342, 349;
see also Schliemann: excavator
archaeology as career, 100, 103, 128–9
Argos, 142–3, 146–7
Athens excavations, 308
Athens permanent home from 1870, 163
autobiographical sketches, 2, 21–3, 33–4,
92–3, 103, 367
"autobiography" in *Ilios*, 22–3, 62, 103,
222, 261, 365, 371
banker in Sacramento, 75
baptized Johann Ludwig Heinrich Julius,
366
biographers of, 1, 2, 13, 15, 23, 103, 345,
366, 368, 374, 378, 381, 383
birth in Neu Buckow, 23
birth of daughter Andromache, 163, 166
birth of son Agamemnon, 163, 166–7
birth of son Sergei, 91
boasts and exaggerations, 3, 5–8, 12, 34,
90, 161, 165, 282, 314–5, 376
bookkeeping course, 37–8
Bunarbashi-Ballidagh trial dig, 148–52
burial in Athens, 17, 346
business: career, 1, 8, 34–7, 51–4, 59–61,
64, 73, 75, 90–100, 349, 368; reverses,
60–1, 92, 96–7; *see also* Schliemann:
commodity dealer; real estate ventures;
wealth . . .
in California, 4, 35, 69–80, 108
character and personality, 2, 3, 5, 6, 8–9,
14, 17, 33, 221, 337, 353; *see also such
entries under* Schliemann *as* boasts and
exaggerations; kindness and generosity;
etc.
Chicago, 125–6
childhood and youth, 4, 21–30, 33, 37–8
China, 107–12
clerk in Hamburg and Amsterdam, 3, 34,
40–2, 51–5, 59
commodity dealer, 1, 36, 56, 59–61, 90,
92, 99–100, 105
Corinth, 141–3
correspondence, 2, 9, 23, 34–5, 61, 89,
161, 314, 364, 380, 383; *see also*
Schliemann: letters
courtship of Sophia Engastroménos,
160–2
Crete excavation projects, 307, 330–3,
336–7

Schliemann, Heinrich (*cont'd*)
critics and criticism of, 6, 7, 13–15, 17,
132, 168, 219–20, 256, 260, 285–6,
303, 309, 316, 353
Cuba, 64, 108, 125, 128, 329, 379–80
death, 344, 346–7, 353–4; premonitions
of, 191, 329, 330, 345–6
death of daughter Natalia, 163
death of mother, 27–8, 33
debt to others, 5–6, 8, 16, 158, 169–70,
228, 259–61, 274, 280, 287–8, 370
destructive excavations, 5, 13, 14, 15,
158, 169, 184, 210, 227, 268, 310–11,
380–1; *see also* Schliemann:
archaeological methods; excavator
deteriorating health, 329, 345
diaries, 2, 22, 38, 60, 63, 90, 94, 104–5,
108, 127–8, 167, 229, 261, 333, 364,
367; *see also Schliemann's First Visit to
America*
dilettantism, 3, 5–6, 12–13, 17, 130, 166
divorce from first wife, 21, 159–62, 369,
371
doctorate from Univ. of Rostock, 158–9,
371
dogmatism, 9, 16–17, 282, 308, 353
donation of Trojan treasure to Germany,
260, 277–8
doubts and despair, 5, 28, 29, 37, 46, 55,
60–1, 92, 103, 108, 167, 170, 263,
282–3
ear ailment, 105, 107, 345–7
early excavation at Ithaca and in Troad,
130–1, 136–8, 150–4
early love, 26–7, 28, 29
Egypt, 98, 103–5, 332–4
England, 60, 165, 224–5, 250, 256,
269
enthusiasm and energy, 14, 17, 29, 33–5,
126, 129–30, 352, 354
"epoch making" contributions, 7–8, 232,
354
errors and misinterpretations, 6, 8, 12,
16–17, 166, 178–9, 195, 204, 210,
230–2, 296–7, 308, 311–12, 343–4,
349; *see also* Schliemann: archaeological
methods; stratigraphic confusion and
ignorance
excavator, 5, 13–16, 129–30, 167, 184,
268, 311, 343–4; *see also preceding*
excitement caused by his discoveries, 3, 7,
17, 21, 192, 217, 248, 352–3
faith in Homer, 1, 3, 4, 9, 12, 16–17, 22,
27, 129, 131–2, 158, 166–7, 171–2,
188, 197, 231, 255, 269, 283, 288, 292,
303, 365, 369, 370
fame and reputation, 1, 2, 3, 5, 7, 8, 12,
13, 17, 18, 21, 192, 217, 232, 274,
352, 354, 365, 375
family ties, 4, 61

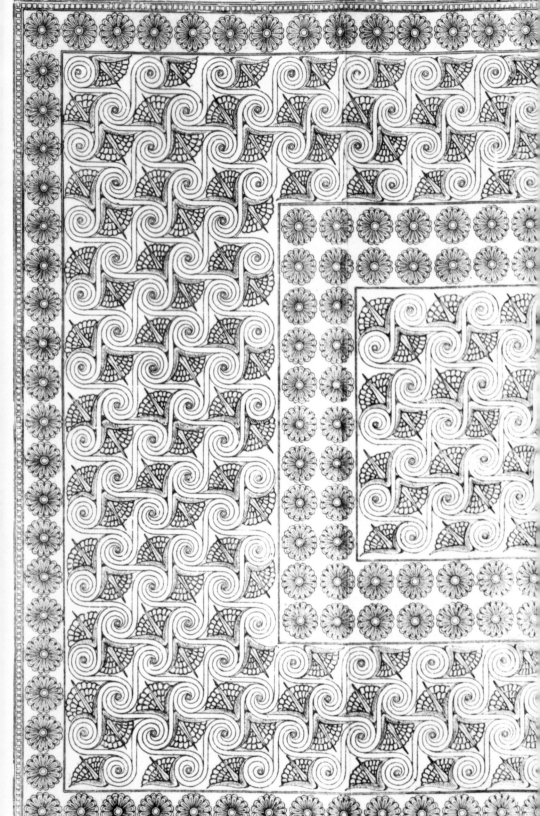